MOBILIZING BLACK GERMANY

BLACK INTERNATIONALISM

Edited by Keisha N. Blain and Quito Swan

This series grapples with the international dimensions of the Black freedom struggle and the diverse ways people of African descent articulated global visions of freedom and forged transnational collaborations.

A list of books in this series appears at the end of this book.

MOBILIZING BLACK GERMANY

AFRO-GERMAN WOMEN AND THE MAKING OF A TRANSNATIONAL MOVEMENT

TIFFANY N. FLORVIL

UNIVERSITY OF ILLINOIS PRESS
Urbana, Chicago, and Springfield

Library of Congress Cataloging-in-Publication Data
Names: Florvil, Tiffany Nicole, author.
Title: Mobilizing Black Germany: Afro-German women and the
    making of a transnational movement / Tiffany N. Florvil.
Description: Urbana: University of Illinois Press, [2020] | Series:
    Black internationalism | Includes bibliographical references
    and index. |
Identifiers: LCCN 2020027486 (print) | LCCN 2020027487
    (ebook) | ISBN 9780252043512 (cloth) | ISBN 9780252085413
    (paperback) | ISBN 9780252052392 (ebook)
Subjects: LCSH: Afrodeutsche Frauen. | Initiative Schwarze
    Menschen in Deutschland. | Women, Black—Political
    activity—Germany. | Women political activists—Germany. |
    Blacks—Political activity—Germany. | Feminism—Germany.
    | Social movements—Germany. | African diaspora. |
    Internationalism.
Classification: LCC DD78.B55 F55 2020 (print) | lcc dd78.b55
    (ebook) | DDC 305.48/896043—dc23
LC record available at https://lccn.loc.gov/2020027486
LC ebook record available at https://lccn.loc.gov/2020027487

For Glenda and Isaac
with so much love and gratitude

CONTENTS

ACKNOWLEDGMENTS

Whoa, it has been a long road to get to this point. But *Mobilizing Black Germany* has been worth it! Through the course of writing this book, I grew and learned so much about who I am as a researcher, thinker, scholar, activist, and friend. I also learned to balance familial obligations in new ways, though I still struggle a little on that front. But writing this book was not an easy task, and I would be lying if I didn't mention that there were many times that I despaired. I suffered bouts of depression and sadness, which only exacerbated my anxieties and insecurities. But I persisted! I persevered because many of family (biological and chosen), friends, and colleagues lifted me up and made me feel like it was possible to write this book. Here I offer my gratitude to those people who shaped, assisted, and loved me and this project throughout the years.

I need to take my appreciation all the way back to my undergraduate years at Florida State University. I want to thank my undergraduate professors, especially those in the Department of Modern Languages and Linguistics and the Department of History. In Modern Languages and Linguistics, Birgit Maier-Katkin's courses were my favorite because I developed my German voice and cultivated a critical literary eye. In History, Maxine Jones modeled what an African American historian could be and accomplish, and she was the only African American professor in the department. Dr. Jones pushed you to strive for excellence in her classes. Both of these professors shaped me and my academic pursuits.

Even though my graduate experience at the University of Wisconsin–Madison proved difficult on a number of levels, I remain grateful for the professors and friends I met there. Those professors include Rudy Koshar, James Sweet, Brenda Gayle Plummer, B. Venkat Mani, and Sabine Modersheim. While there I met many great graduate students, several of whom are now in the professoriate, and those include: Crystal Moten, Chris Fojtik, Erika Hughes, Kathy Kae, Solsi del Moral, Andreas Matias-Oritz, Gabby Kuenzli, and Stacy Milacek. At the University of South Carolina, there were many influences. First and foremost, I want to thank my amazing advisor, Ann Johnson. It was her faith in me as a scholar that truly enabled me to succeed. When others doubted my abilities in the department, she had no doubt whatsoever. In fact, under her supervision, I excelled, finishing my dissertation and landing a tenure-track job. Sadly, Ann died in 2016 and was unable to see the completion of this project. But I believe she would have been proud of what I accomplished in these pages. I also want to thank other professors at the other USC: Carol Harrison, Yvonne Ivory, Matt Childs, Dan Littlefield, Emil Kerenji, Anne Gulick, Kathryn Edwards, and Bobby Donaldson. Carol has continued to support me since I graduated in 2013. I had a nice cohort at USC, and those individuals include Candace Cunningham, Gabby Dudley, Christiane Steckenbiller, Sarah Scripps, Tara Strauch, Michael Woods, Laura Foxworth, Kathryn Silva, and Ramon Jackson. After USC I spent a short time in Bloomington, Indiana, and I want to thank the people I met inside and outside the History Department: Ellen Wu, Micol Seigel, Wendy Gamber, Jason McGraw, Christina Snyder, Felicity Turner, Claudia Drieling, and Susan "Suz" Eckelmann Berghel. In particular, Susan and I developed a great friendship, and I am grateful for her presence in my life.

Throughout the years, many people and institutions have supported me and made my research possible. I am grateful for these colleagues, professionals, friends, and otherwise. In Germany, there were many gracious people who spent time with me, opened their homes to me, and made my time enjoyable: Ria Cheatom, Marion Kraft, Katharina Oguntoye, Cassandra Ellerbe, Paulette Reed Anderson, Ricky Reiser, Ika Hügel-Marshall, Dagmar Schultz, Silke Hackenesch, Inez Templeton, Andreas Kurz, Rebecca Brückmann, Katrin Summa, and Helga and Andreas Mandt. I want to say a special thank you to one of my best friends, Inika "Inie" Otto. Our more than twenty-year-old friendship has been a balm in my life, and I am glad that we bonded in our English *Leistungskurs* so many years ago. I also want to thank Alicia Villarosa at Villarosa Press as well as the archivists at Spinnboden Lesbenarchiv und Bibliothek in Berlin; the Freie Universität Berlin's University Archive (especially Frank Lehmann and Birgit Rehse), the Frauenforschungs-,-bildungs- und -informationszentrum in Berlin, and the Zentrale Bibliothek Frauenforschung, Gender & Queer Studies in Hamburg. In the United States, I want to thank the archivists at Spelman Archives in Atlanta (especially the late Taronda Spencer, Holly Smith, and Kassandra Ware). I express my gratitude to the talented Diana Ejaita for granting me permission to use her beautiful artwork for the cover of my book.

In addition, I am grateful to have received the following fellowships: the American Council on Germany's Dr. Richard M. Hunt Fellowship for the Study of German Politics, Society, and Culture; the Feminist Research Institute's Faculty Research Grant at the University of New Mexico; the German Academic Exchange Service (DAAD); the Walker Institute of International and Areas Studies Ceny Walker Graduate Fellowship at the University of South Carolina; the Becht Family Endowment Fund Dissertation Preparation Fellowship at the University of South Carolina; the College of Arts and Sciences Dean's Dissertation Fellowship at South Carolina; and the Rhude M. Patterson Trustee Graduate Fellowship at the University of South Carolina. This support made it possible for me to conduct research trips in Europe and the United States.

I also especially want to thank the multiple generations of scholar-activists in Black German studies on both sides of the Atlantic. Their efforts inside and outside academia are appreciated: Joshua Kwesi Aikins, Robbie Aitken, Christine Alonzo, Maisha-Maureen Auma, May Ayim, Carol Blackshire-Belay, Jeff Bowersox, Eddie Bruce-Jones, Tina M. Campt, Ria Cheatom, Sonya Donaldson, Jasmin Eding, Fatima El-Tayeb, Nadine Golly, Judy Gummich, Silke Hackenesch, Leroy Hopkins, S. Marina Jones, Natasha Kelly, Katja Kinder, Kevina King, Philipp Khabo Koepsell, Marion Kraft, Priscilla Layne, Sara Lennox, Heidi Lewis, Azziza Malanda, Peter Martin, Nancy Nenno, Katharina Oguntoye, Sharon Dodua Otoo, Rosemarie Peña, Peggy Piesche, Vanessa Plumly, Paulette Reed Anderson, Ricky Reiser, Eve Rosenhaft, Marilyn Sephocle, Kim Singletary, Kira Thurman, Victoria Toney-Robinson, Jamele Watkins, Alexander Weheliye, Michelle Wright as well as others that I may have forgotten. I want to express my sincere gratitude to Vanessa and Jamele, for they read several chapters of the book and have been so reassuring and considerate. Vanessa, in particular, has become a dear friend, colleague, and collaborator I have grown to treasure. To her, thank you from the bottom of my heart. I want to thank Dagmar Schultz for permission to print some materials. I also want to thank other scholars and colleagues who willingly took time out of their busy schedules to read my work and offer feedback and/or support: Rebecca Brückmann, Susan Eckelmann Berghel, Mary Dudziak, Felix Germain, Jennifer Foray, Silke Hackenesch, Kennetta Hammond Perry, Jane Jones, S. Marina Jones, Nicholas Jones, Robin Mitchell, Crystal Moten, Nancy Nenno, Vanessa Plumly, Kimberly Singletary, Vanessa

Valdés, and Jamele Watkins. In fact the two Vanessas (Plumly and Valdés), along with S. Marina Jones and Silke Hackenesch, have read substantial parts of the book, and for that I am grateful. It is better because of them, and I am indebted to them. But if there are any faults in the book, they are mine alone.

I have presented portions of *Mobilizing Black Germany* across this country and in Europe, and I valued the many exchanges. For their kind invitations, thoughtful comments, and incisive questions, I thank graduate students Pamela Ohene-Nyako and Mélanie Evely Petremont at the University of Geneva in Switzerland; Nina Martin, Louna Sbou, and Nora Chirikure at Be'Kech Anti-Café in Berlin, Germany; Vance Byrd and Javier Samper Vendrell at Grinnell College; Jamele Watkins at Stanford University; Tanya Nusser, Sunnie Rucker-Chang, and Felix Chang at the University of Cincinnati; Martin Sheehan at Tennessee Technological University; Christoph Ribbat and Alexandra Hartmann at the University of Paderborn in Germany; Derek Hillard and Janice McGregor at Kansas State University; and S. Marina Jones at Oberlin College.

Since my arrival at the University of New Mexico in 2013, I have appreciated the support I have received. To those colleagues (past and present) in the History Department and the wider university, thank you for your care, support, and friendship. Many of them provided food, laughter, and drinks: Tamsen Song Anderson, Melissa Bokovoy, Judy Bieber, Cathleen Cahill, Sarah Davis-Secord, Jeffrey Erbig, Kimberly Gauderman, Fred Gibbs, Linda Hall, Luis Herrán Ávila, Elizabeth Hutchinson, Tamara Kay, Barbara Reyes, Mike "Rockstar" Ryan, Enrique Sanabria, Andrew Sandoval-Strausz, Virginia Scharff, Jane Slaughter, Myra Washington, and Shannon Withycombe. In the larger Albuquerque community, I want to thank Cynthia Schomel and Yoni Young for their kindness and care. Namaste! I even want to thank my haters. They know who they are, and I appreciate their disbelief in me because it only propelled me to accomplish more. Thanks!

I am so glad I developed this book with Dawn Durante at the University of Illinois Press, and I am honored to be a part of the Black Internationalism Series with Keisha N. Blain and Quito Swan at the helm as sharp series editors. Dawn has been enthusiastic, encouraging, and supportive every step of the way and believed in the project when others did not. I also want to thank the two reviewers of the manuscript, who really shaped the book in considerable ways.

Thank you to my family—Glenda, David, Bill, and Peg—for their love, care, and support. A special note of profound gratitude to my mother (Glenda) and partner (David) for always believing in me and this project. Mom has been my biggest cheerleader since forever, and she has been an important anchor in my life. But together, their cheerleading and unfailing love have sustained me more than they realize.

Finally, my love, Isaac: thank you for filling my heart with so much love and giving my life such rich purpose. Isaac arrived while I was still figuring out what to do with this project and turned my world completely around in all the best ways. Tehee! I am so glad you came into my life when you did, and I hope you will read this book one day.

*   *   *

Portions of chapters 1 and 4 were published in a shorter form as "Emotional Connections: Audre Lorde and Black German Women," in Stella Bolaki and Sabine Broeck, eds., *Audre Lorde's Transnational Legacies* (Amherst: University of Massachusetts Press, 2015), 135–47.

A revised version of chapter 3 was published as "Connected Differences: Black German Feminists and Their Transnational Connections in the 1980s and 1990s," in Friederike Bruehoefener, Karen Hagemann, and Donna Harsch, eds., *Gendering Post-1945 German History: Entanglements* (New York: Berghahn, 2019), 229–49.

Portions of the introduction as well as chapters 2 and 4 were published as "Distant Ties: May Ayim's Transnational Solidarity and Activism," in Keisha N. Blain and Tiffany M. Gill, eds., *To Turn this Whole World Over: Black Women and Internationalism* (Chicago: University of Illinois Press, 2019), 74–97.

An early version of chapter 6 was published as "Transnational Feminist Solidarity, Black German Women, and the Politics of Belonging," in Toyin Falola and Olajumoke Yacob-Haliso, eds., *Gendering Knowledge in Africa and the African Diaspora: Contesting History and Power* (New York: Routledge, 2017), 87–110.

ABBREVIATIONS

ADEFRA	Afrodeutsch Frauen/Schwarze Frauen in Deutschland e.V. (Afro-German Women/Black Women in Germany)
AfD	Alternativ für Deutschland (Alternative for Germany)
AFI	African Women's Initiative
AFT	African Women's Theater
AKWAABA	Pan-European Women's Network for Intercultural Action and Exchange
ANC	African National Congress
ARA	African Refugee Association
ARiC	Antirassistisch-Interkulturelles Informationszentrum e.V. (Antiracist-Intercultural Information Center)
AStA	Allgemeiner Studentenaussschuß (Student Union)
ASU	African Student Union
AWA	African Writers Association
BAM	Black Arts Movement
BAZ	Bildungs- und Aktionszentrum Dritte Welt e.V. (Third World Education and Action Center)
BBC	British Broadcasting Corporation
BBWG	Brixton Black Women's Group
BCM	Black Consciousness Movement
BHM	Black History Month

BLM	Black Lives Matter
BLS	Black Liberation Sounds/Black Liberation Sound System
BMA	Black Media Access
BSO	Black Student Organisation
BUC	Black Unity Committee
BT	Bundestreffen (national meeting)
BWEN	Black Women and Europe Network
CDU	Christlich Demokratische Union Deutschlands (Christian Democratic Union of Germany)
CEDAW	United Nations Convention on the Elimination of All Forms of Discrimination against Women
CNA	Committee for the Negro in the Arts
CRC	Combahee River Collective
CRES	Centre for Race and Ethnic Studies
CSU	Christlich-Soziale Union in Bayern (Christian Social Union in Bavaria, sister party to the CDU)
EARESJ	European Action for Racial Equality and Social Justice
EEC	European Economic Community (also EC, or the European Community)
ENAR	European Network Against Racism
ENPAD	European Network of People of African Descent
EU	European Union
EURAFRI	Europa Afrika Zentrum (Europe Africa Center)
FRG	Federal Republic of Germany (or West Germany)
FU	Freie Universität Berlin (Free University of Berlin)
GDR	German Democratic Republic (or East Germany)
IAF	Interessengemeinschaft der mit Ausländern verheirateten Frauen e.V. (later called the Association of Bi-National Families and Partnerships)
IBR	Institute for Black Research
IFAF	Interkulturelle Feministische Antirassismus Forum e.V. (Intercultural Feminist Antiracist Forum)
IPF	Immigrantenpolitisches Forum e.V. (Immigrant Political Forum)
IRNWAD	International Resource Network of Women of African Descent
ISD	Initiative Schwarze Deutsche/Initiative Schwarze Menschen in Deutschland e.V. (Initiative of Black Germans/Initiative of Black People in Germany)

IISF	Interkulturelle Initiative Schwarzer Frauen für Minoritätenrechte und-Studien in Deutschland e.V. (Cross-Cultural Initiative of Black Women for Minority Rights and Studies in Germany)
KOP	Kampagne für Opfer rassistischer Polizeigewalt (Victims of Racist Police Violence)
KT	Koordinationstreffen (planning meeting)
LIT	Literatur Frauen e.V. (Literature Women)
MODEFEN	Mouvement pour la défense des droits de la femme noire (Movement for the Defense of the Rights of Black Women)
OWAAD	Organisation of Women of Asian and African Descent
PAF	Pan African Forum
PCR	Programme to Combat Racism
SDS	Sozialistischer Deutscher Studentenbund (German Socialist Student Association)
SEA	Single European Act
SED	Sozialistische Einheitspartei Deutschlands (Socialist Unity Party, ruling party of the GDR)
SISTERS	Sisters In Struggle to Eliminate Racism and Sexism
SOMFV	Somali Women's Association
SOS	Struggle of Students
SPD	Sozialdemokratische Partei Deutschlands (Social Democratic Party of Germany)
UN	United Nations
UNESCO	United Nations Educational, Scientific and Cultural Organization
WCC	World Council of Churches in Geneva, Switzerland
WUR	Women Under Racism

MOBILIZING BLACK GERMANY

INTRODUCTION

A "Black Coming Out"

We, the Black Germans, want to step out of this state of social invisibility because living under such conditions is hardly pleasant. We are a challenge for our society, which is not prepared for such a task because of its own deranged state of self-consciousness. Hence, it follows that the Black German movement receives its strength and motivation mainly from the desire to find a self-determined identity as Afro-Germans. The individual identity is the prerequisite for living as a person in German society and also for carrying through as a group in the struggle against racism and discrimination of minorities, in other words, using our abilities meaningfully.

—Katharina Oguntoye, "The Black German and the Women's Movement in West Germany" (March 1989)

What does it mean to be a Black German citizen? What did Black German struggles against racism and oppression look like for women, and what shape did Black German politics and activism take in late twentieth-century Germany? When, where, and why did the modern Black German movement emerge, and what was its impact? *Mobilizing Black Germany: Afro-German Women and the Making of a Transnational Movement* answers these questions by sharing a narrative about a group of Black German activist-intellectuals—May Ayim, Jasmin Eding, Helga Emde, Judy Gummich, Katharina Oguntoye, and others—who built and sustained a modern diasporic movement that affirmed their multiple identities while empowering them to challenge discrimination and resist their exclusion and othering from the German nation.[1] In major German cities, Black German women connected despite their own personal differences, forged affective bonds, and "stepp[ed] out" from their "social invisibility" and isolation.[2] These women also engendered new spaces, discourses, and practices that centered their claims of belonging, privileged their antiracist perspectives, and advanced their national and internationalist politics. They did so through grassroots organizing, writing letters, poetry, and prose, and planning cultural and political activities, in which they protested racial injustice and white supremacy across the globe.

Mobilizing Black Germany argues that Black German women played a central role in shaping the intellectual, cultural, and political contours of the modern Black German movement. These women mobilized to address issues that were common in Germany and worldwide and pushed discussions of racialized and gendered oppression to the fore.[3] Black German women's feminist diasporic activism was driven by their "politics and poetics of representation" that produced knowledge, exposed racial inequity, and challenged their erasure from the nation, in turn undermining the status quo.[4] In the context of late postwar Germany, their antiracist politics criticized discriminatory policies and practices, and their poetics epitomized the versatility of Black German cultural forms, reflecting their subjectivities and experiences. They also supported a Black internationalism that enabled them to forge connections and networks within and beyond Germany. These connections were radical forms of affective kinship, in which Black Germans refused to determine lineage and linkage through blood relationships or marriage alone.

Showcasing the unique discursive space that Black Germans constructed and participated in, this book draws on a range of published and unpublished sources, such as correspondences, autobiographical writings, interviews, poetry, newspapers, community-based periodicals, organizational minutes and brochures, and event programs. It also includes archival materials and the private collections of several Black German activists not housed in traditional archives.[5] Together, these sources uncover an overlooked cultural, intellectual, and institutional history of the modern Black German movement of the 1980s to the 2000s, including the activist-intellectuals in its orbit who pushed for a racial identity, gender liberation, and social justice. While there have been several books published about the movement in Germany, mine differs from them because I offer a more detailed account by relying on a diverse array of sources from both sides of the Atlantic.[6] This is the first book to examine the growth and evolution of two prominent membership-driven Black German organizations: the Initiative of Black Germans (Initiative Schwarze Deutsche, ISD) and Afro-German Women (Afrodeutsche Frauen, ADEFRA) as well as the organizational practices, strategies, and events that emboldened its members to seek recognition, basic human rights, and the eradication of racism and discrimination in

Germany and elsewhere. ISD, founded in 1985, and ADEFRA, founded in 1986 with a more concerted feminist emphasis, were the largest Black German organizations in terms of their Black German membership, which also included individuals from the larger Black diaspora in the country. Both groups aimed to represent the community and be inclusive of it, and they gained considerable value in the community, even by individuals who were not active in the larger movement. In later years, these groups gained recognition in the German media and with other institutions and non-governmental organizations. The existence of these organizations proved crucial, considering it was previously difficult to mobilize given how isolated and marginalized some Black Germans were. Their combined efforts represented a new type of Black German activism that took its cues from alternative leftist movements in Germany and global Black freedom struggles.

Black Germans' establishment of local ISD and ADEFRA chapters contributed to new cultural and political moments by creating social and public forums that established a different language to discuss race. This racial grammar changed how race was discussed, shaping ideas about racialized notions of citizenship and what it meant to be German. As cultural-political organizations, ISD and ADEFRA maintained antiracist and feminist agendas, in which their members "invented traditions" by organizing consciousness-raising workshops, historical and sociological seminars, social gatherings, and antidiscrimination protests.[7] Black Germans' work in these organizations also necessitated grassroots internationalist coalition building and solidarity. ISD and ADEFRA feature prominently in this book not only because they catalyzed the movement, but also because they illustrate Black Germans' attempts to think about, identify, and resist the impact of German structural racism. While both groups emerged with and worked alongside other diasporic organizations later referenced in this book, they placed collective Black German organizing on the map and provided a foundation for future antiracist and cultural Black German organizations and initiatives.[8] ISD and ADEFRA made Black Germanness visible in a majority-white nation that failed to acknowledge its colonial past and its afterlife, its long-standing multiracial and multicultural populations, and the persistence of racism and racial violence after the fall of the Third Reich. As Katharina Oguntoye's aforementioned quotation indicated, the modern Black German movement redefined the boundaries of Blackness *and* Germanness, politicizing race and challenging German society to recognize "its own deranged state of self-consciousness."[9]

This book contends that Black German women's activism in the movement entailed a cultural politics of naming, styling, and curating themselves and their histories. Proving that they were thinkers and doers on their own terms, Black German women, including May Ayim (née Brigitte Sylvia Gerund) and Katharina Oguntoye, engaged in acts of knowledge production and self-definition by creating a new lexicon with the designations of "Afro-Germans" (*Afrodeutsche*) and "Black Germans" (*Schwarze Deutsche*). These concepts undercut normative understandings of Germanness and disrupted the fixity of white German identity. These women fashioned identities that used the nation yet pushed beyond it, and their efforts at self-definition were cultural and political interventions. They did so through exchanges among themselves and with Caribbean American feminist lesbian poet Audre Lorde, who was a visiting professor at the Freie Universität Berlin (FU) in 1984. Together these acts resignified their imposed Otherness and made it a foundation for peoplehood, empowerment, and cultural reform.

Black Germans consist of not only individuals of mixed-race descent and individuals with ancestry from Africa, the Caribbean, Europe, Latin America, and the United States, but also other People of Color who understood Black to be a political identity for community building and activism.[10] This was similar to the British context where a political Blackness emerged earlier.[11] Individuals of South Asian, Turkish, and Arabic heritage became involved in the movement, as they, too, endured racism and exclusion in Germany. At times, the label also encompassed overlapping Black diasporas existing in Germany. While Afro-German and Black German are considered synonymous, members in the community prefer the latter designation because it is more inclusive and less reminiscent of colonialism. I use both terms interchangeably throughout the book, but I do give preference to Black German. In addition, Black Germans in the movement were often of mixed-race descent and were raised in white families, orphanages, or foster homes scattered across the postwar Germanys, though the presence of people of African descent on German territory predated this moment.[12] Oftentimes, Afro-Germans were the only Black people in their predominately white neighborhoods with limited or sporadic ties to their Black family members. Some did grow up with their Black relatives or had contact with African Americans owing to their proximity to military bases, especially in the southern part of the country.[13] Others were second or third generation, born to African or Asian immigrants. Considering Germany has no racial categories on its census because of its National Socialist past, it is difficult to ascertain how many Black Germans have lived or currently live in the country. Contemporary estimates for the community are anywhere between 500,000 to 800,000 out of a population of 83.2 million as of 2019.[14]

Dealing with this racist legacy, Ayim and Oguntoye reclaimed their agency by creating positive labels and contesting common derogatory labels such as "darky" (*"Bimbo"*), "colored" (*"Farbige"*), "Negro mixed-breed" (*"Negermischling"*), "mixed-breed children" (*"Mischlingskinder"*), and "occupation children" (*"Besatzungskinder"*).[15] A few of those terms were prominent in the Nazis' policies and discourses, which drew from American Jim Crow legislation.[16] The Nazis implemented the Nuremberg Laws on September 15, 1935, making Jews second-class citizens by revoking their German citizenship, denying them political rights, and prohibiting them from marrying or engaging in sexual acts with people of "German blood." With their first supplementary decree of the laws on November 14, 1935, the Nazis formally established the categories of German, Jew, and half-Jew (*"Mischling"*). They legally defined Jews' racial status, linking Jewishness to birth, blood, and ancestry, but not to religion.[17] The decree also extended to Romani and Sinti as well as Black German populations, although few people of African descent had German citizenship even if they had been born in the country.[18] In 1937 the Nazi regime also sterilized a small population of Black Germans, who were called "The Rhineland Bastards" (*"Die Rheinlandbastarde"*). These individuals were the offspring of French colonial troops and white German women during the Rhineland occupation from 1918 to 1930.[19] Some were subjected to other medical experiments, while others were sent to concentration camps.[20] Those Black Germans who remained in Germany—the majority of whom included men from the colonies—lived increasingly precarious lives.[21] Linking the Nazi past to the postwar present, several of those terms reemerged after the Allied occupation and the presence of African American soldiers and, later, African migrants in the Federal Republic of Germany (FRG, or West Germany), who had relationships with white German women.[22] Such terms were a part of a practice of daily racism whereby some white Germans refused to recognize Black people as fully human subjects and citizens. Thus, Black Germans embodied a paradox for their white compatriots, who believed that one could not be both *Black* and *German*.

The emergence and development of Black German identity proved that Germany was a critical site for the Black diaspora, building on the experiences of African-descended people in the country for centuries. Black German activist-intellectuals positioned themselves within the nation and the global Black diaspora, "forging diaspora" and kinship with African-descended people within and beyond Germany.[23] In many ways, Black Germans' identity (re)making and political movement building epitomizes what Stuart Hall has written in regard to cultural identity and the diaspora. Afro-Germans' identity (re)making was a process that continually evolved through their grassroots organizing and cultural productions and informed their efforts to unveil racism, obtain representation, and resist their imposed liminal citizenship.[24] It also shaped the language and types of knowledge they produced, circulated, and normalized. This book illustrates how Black Germans' community-based events, writing, and politics not only reflected the ways that their perspectives, identities, and movement changed but also how they portrayed themselves in and beyond Germany.

This book also advances our understanding of activism by arguing that their forms of Black intellectualism and internationalism centered discussions of race, racism, and racial identity in Germany and elsewhere in Europe. Black Germans demonstrated how certain values and behaviors informed those categories and contributed to a belief in racelessness.[25] In doing so, they amplified their agential voices, stressing why those topics mattered. *Mobilizing Black Germany* examines community-based magazines and other Black German cultural productions, in which they combined the affective, cultural, and political.

This book maintains that Black Germans were what I call "quotidian intellectuals," who imparted different kinds of knowledge about their individual, collective, and global diasporic histories, creating new vocabularies and meanings of identity, citizenship, and belonging. Quotidian intellectuals refer to ordinary Black German women (and men) who thought, theorized, wrote, performed, and circulated their ideas and knowledge textually, visually, or orally through publications, workshops, conferences, presentations, and other artistic forms in the public sphere. Indeed, they opened other sites for knowledge production and circulation.[26] In both their content and form, Black Germans brought everyday experiences of discrimination to the forefront. They used vernacular cultural forms to destabilize the power of dominant knowledge and representation, to establish the field of Black German studies (BGS), and to bring intellectual and academic inquiry to BGS through their publications and events, countering their archival erasure. Deploying diverse intellectual traditions, these acts were also epistemic interventions that recovered silenced narratives and allowed Black Germans to enter the public sphere. Black German quotidian intellectuals worked in and against dominant discourses and redefined who was understood to be an intellectual and what intellectual work looked like. This is noticeable when we recognize that Black Germans or other African-descended peoples were either included in the public sphere in degrading ways that were based on white Germans' gazes and perspectives, and/or they were excluded from the public sphere because they were not considered to be thinkers. Though some Black Germans were formally educated and others were not, they still spoke their truth to power about race, colonialism, and other topics.

My notion of quotidian intellectuals focuses on a small social group of marginalized, mostly middle-class and lower-middle-class Black Germans who used their intellectualism and internationalism to acquire power and unsettle the late postwar German hegemony while offering new ways of being, feeling, and knowing.[27] Black Germans differed from some of their late postwar white or Turkish German counterparts, who garnered prominence by receiving prestigious literary accolades. Foregrounding their "intellectual activism," Black Germans intertwined language, power, and resistance.[28] In so doing, they showed how their contests about power and knowledge mattered. Undeniably, the normalization of Black German identity through the construction of their movement and the refashioning and curation of a literary tradition allowed a variety of German minority voices to unify and shine while also producing and disseminating cultural knowledge.

THE CULTURAL POLITICS OF RACE

In tracing the everyday acts of Black radicalism that found expression on German soil, this book explores how Black German feminists, straight and queer, openly shared how everyday racism (*Alltagsrassismus*) shaped their lives and those of other German minorities and immigrants.[29] These forms could consist of white Germans touching Black Germans' hair, seeing racist iconography in the media and in public settings, experiencing violent physical attacks, or hearing pejorative words and/or responses that they "didn't look like Germans." They also challenged West Germany's claims to have long expunged racism from its borders. After the Third Reich, the West German government enshrined "equality before the law" and human rights in its 1949 constitution (Basic Law or *Grundgesetz*). But there remained a reluctance to engage the topic of race in the nation, which limited public discussions about the persistence of racism, even as discussions of the Holocaust became slightly more common. This is not to suggest that anti-Semitism disappeared from the postwar landscape.[30] West Germany began to deal with its past (*Vergangenheitsbewältigung*) in the late 1950s and 1960s, which included the prosecution of Nazi war criminals, academics and non-academics writing about the topic, and the 1968 student generation interrogating the Nazi past, though not without some questionable approaches. Cultural or new racism also emerged in postwar West Germany and western Europe and served as an ideological revision of scientific or biological racism predicated on cultural difference, determining who belonged in or out of the national community. This impacted the perceptions and treatment of "guest workers" ("*Gastarbeiter*"), colonial workers, foreign students, and other immigrants.[31]

While instances of anti-Semitism could potentially provoke condemnation by some white West Germans, anti-Black racism remained unaffected.

This occurred because both overt and subtle forms of anti-Black racism were not purged in postwar West Germany, as evinced by the prevalence of blackface, colonial stereotypes, and the (hyper)sexualization of nonwhite bodies in popular images. West German children's and youth literature, for example, depicted people of African descent as ugly, ignorant, exotic, savage, and lazy. Prominent children's books, including Otfried Preussler's 1956 *The Little Water Sprite* (*Der kleine Wassermann*), his 1957 *The Little Witch* (*Die kleine Hexe*), and his 1966 *The Little Ghost* (*Das kleine Gespenst*), contained racist language. West German children's toys such as "Hit Darky" ("*Haut den Bimbo*") from 1950; games such as "Who is afraid of the black man?" ("*Wer hat Angst vorm schwarzen Mann?*"); songs such as "Ten Little Negroes" ("*Zehn kleine Negerlein*"); or everyday consumerism such as chocolate ice cream ("*Eismohr*") and Coca-Cola ("*Negerschweiß*"), racialized people of African descent in the most degrading ways and positioned them as inferior people who never belonged in the nation.[32] Moreover, German (and European) advertising companies readily used the imagery of individuals of African descent to promote commodities such as chocolate or coffee. Europeans made the connection between commodities like chocolate and Blackness by coding them as natural.[33] Aided by a burgeoning mass advertisement culture in the late nineteenth and early twentieth centuries, these companies linked the concepts of modernity, race, nation, and gender in their advertisements to bolster their imperial prestige, appeal to their consumers, and inculcate ideas of civilization, progress, and respectability.[34] Black Germans problematized the colonial entanglements that were embedded in German culture. Witnessing these forms of everyday systemic racism in all aspects of society, they understood that those examples justified their oppression and exclusion in the nation. Instead of remaining silent, they addressed those problems head on by naming race and racism and integrating them into commonplace discussions.

Race was also a taboo subject in the German Democratic Republic (GDR, or East Germany). The term *racism* was not commonly invoked. East German officials outlawed racism in their 1949 constitution and associated its practice with their fascist and colonial pasts and with their West German capitalist counterpart; East Germans both ignored and "forgot" their colonial history.[35] Unlike in West Germany, East Germany placed more Nazi war criminals on trial and reinforced its antifascist legacy, in which many of its leaders were in the resistance, in camps, or in exile. Their engagement with race and racism in the postwar period not only followed developments in Moscow but also internationally, especially with the United Nations Educational, Scientific and Cultural

Organization (UNESCO)'s "Statements on Race," produced in 1950, 1951, 1964, and 1967.[36] Moreover, East Germans also pursued what Quinn Slobodian calls a "racial rainbow," which was "an egalitarian racialist motif" that pervaded their media representations and marked their efforts with anticolonialist solidarity. These representations reflected the government's politics of solidarity (*Solidaritätspolitik*), in which they supported other socialist liberation movements and projected an international antiracist image.[37] The government also celebrated the diversity of its "contract workers" ("*Vertragsarbeiter*") from Angola, Cuba, and elsewhere well into the late 1980s, while denying them certain rights in the country. Although the East German government denounced racism and claimed it did not exist, this did not mean that officials disregarded the value of race as an ideological tool. Both race and racism still had material implications for Black Germans, Jews, "contract workers," and other People of Color.[38]

BLACK GERMAN WOMEN DOIN' IT FOR THEMSELVES

In their responses to different forms of German discrimination (at the individual, state, and federal levels) and global white supremacy, these women consistently pushed for recognition as Black Germans, for equality as citizens and subjects, and for the human rights of all oppressed people.[39] They addressed the state and federal governments' inability to acknowledge and protect minority rights as well as the existence and effects of racism in and beyond Germany. Their willingness to forge an affective community, navigate a diasporic identity, and mobilize against discrimination offered them the potential for agency after enduring years of invisibility, loneliness, and powerlessness. Indeed, they maintained affective ties through their cultural diplomacy writing, workshops, and other events. Black German activist-intellectuals, some of whom were lesbians, also did not hew to heteronormative gender conventions, allowing a variety of queer identities, practices, projects, and relationships to manifest. They also advocated beyond whitewashed queer politics. These feminist activist-intellectuals invested their energy and time to found some of the local chapters of ISD and ADEFRA, and were also leading figures in those organizations. By ushering in their modern movement, they also pursued spatial politics that allowed them to create and reclaim public spaces and embed themselves into the fabric of the nation.[40] Those politics pushed them to see how place and space served as critical tools in their activism and that drove them to transform their environment and alter the meanings of citizenship, identity, and solidarity.

Although this book's emphasis is on the history of ISD and ADEFRA, it does not suggest that all Black Germans were involved in these organizations or the larger Black German movement. Those involved in the movement collaborated with other racialized communities, antiracist activists, and human rights organizations in Germany.[41] Some of them became involved with numerous organizations, including the Antiracist-Intercultural Information Center (Antirassistisch-Interkulturelles Informationszentrum e.V., ARiC), an organization against discrimination and inequality, and Nozizwe: Project for Multicultural Feminist Educational Work, a migrant women's organization, both in Berlin. They benefited from collaborative work and transnational solidarity with others across Africa and the United States. Several Black Germans also worked with pan-European associations such as the Black Women and Europe Network (BWEN), an organization that focused on gendered discrimination in the 1990s, the European Action for Racial Equality and Social Justice (EARESJ), an antiracist organization in the 1990s that dealt with the Europeanization of racist policies, and the European Network Against Racism (ENAR), an antiracist network that advocated for racial equality and pursued legal changes at the European Union level in the late 1990s and 2000s.[42] Involvement in these organizations furthered Black Germans' feminist and antiracist activism on a continental scale. In this way, Black Germans' activism signaled the possibility of making a difference in their nation and beyond.

RECONSIDERING BLACK INTERNATIONALISM, BLACK EUROPE, AND BLACK INTELLECTUALISM

Mobilizing Black Germany joins the scholarship on Black internationalism that has proliferated in the last few decades, offering nuanced interpretations that uncover the narratives of different Black diasporic historical actors. My book departs from existing research by locating Germany as a key site for Black internationalism and extending the periodization of the scholarship through centering articulations of Black internationalism in the post-1970 era. It contends that Black German women's internationalism in the 1980s through the 2000s involved grassroots local and global expressions, in which they invented traditions, articulated feminist discourses, arranged organizational events and political campaigns, and produced writing and art that sought to overturn racism and make society anew. With those diverse mediums, Black Germans created a vibrant political culture that made them feel represented and understood. This type of internationalism intersected with other movements such as "Third World" and/or Women of Color feminism and anti-Apartheid activism and valued collaboration with other Blacks, People of Color, and white allies across Europe and the globe.[43] Black German women's feminism remained expansive, unlike some of their white German counterparts. Black Germans' activism mirrored and intersected with other Black European and European efforts to establish transnational antiracist networks, agendas, and strategies in the 1980s and 1990s.[44] Their practice of internationalism varied, but remained local even as it, at times, propelled them beyond Germany.

Scholars such as Brent Hayes Edwards, Robin D.G. Kelley, William Martin, Tiffany Ruby Patterson, Michael O. West, and Fanon Che Wilkins have theorized about a Black international, in which different activists, artists, and intellectuals of African descent built networks, formed connections, and expressed solidarity with others across the globe based on their common experiences of racism and colonialism.[45] Though critical, these works often ignore or downplay the role women had in shaping Black internationalism. *Mobilizing Black Germany* places gender at the center by arguing that Black German women negotiated feminist and queer politics that motivated them to organize a movement and reimagine their personal and collective identities, their agendas, and their practices.

Examining women's voices, activism, gender, and sexuality, the works of Keisha N. Blain, Carole Boyce Davies, Tanisha Ford, Cheryl Higashida, Marc Matera, Erik S. McDuffie, Barbara Ransby, Tracy Sharpley-Whiting, Quito Swan, Imaobong Umoren, and others have advanced the field in significant ways.[46] This book contributes to this field by emphasizing the vital role that Black German women played in shaping Black freedom struggles in Germany, Europe, and beyond. It also explores Black German women's intellectual activism and how their writing aided the community and shifted German racial and gendered discourses. These women were not only intellectuals and cultural producers, but also arbiters for change in the fight against racism, sexism, capitalism, neo-colonialism, and neofascism at home and abroad.[47]

Much of the scholarship on Black internationalism also sheds light on the experiences of Black diasporic peoples in Europe and dialogues with scholars of Black Europe such as Tina M. Campt, Fatima El-Tayeb, Felix Germain, Paul Gilroy, Kennetta Hammond Perry, and Michelle M. Wright.[48] My book bridges both of these two interrelated fields and shows how Black Germans' diasporic identity was not directly tied to the slave ships during the Middle Passage, as Gilroy and others have emphasized. Instead, *Mobilizing Black Germany* disentangles the Black diaspora from narratives of the Middle Passage, or what Michelle M. Wright calls the "Middle Passage Epistemology." It affirms Wright's interpretation of Blackness not as a category that describes a what, but as a relationship to time (when) and space (where) or *spacetimes,* especially in the post–World War II period.[49] Reconsidering the spacetimes of Blackness, the book recognizes and traces its diverse formulations in Germany. This is important as Germany is still overlooked as a dynamic Black diasporic site because of its short-lived colonialism and early experiences of decolonization.[50] Nevertheless, Black communities have existed in different spacetimes in Germany—a point stressed in the Black German movement. In the 1980s, Black German activist-intellectuals also redefined Blackness, enabling it to achieve a new resonance. For them, Blackness symbolized theirs and others' marginalization in and beyond Germany while also representing a strategic identity and a mode of resistance to and solidarity against that oppression. That said, Blackness was an ontological experience and a political and intellectual practice across time and space. As the movement emerged in cities across Germany, it transformed notions of citizenship, the diaspora, and Europeanness, including Germanness.

Showing how Germany was an important site for transnational political culture, this book uses the modern Black German movement to draw our attention to the strength of diasporic activism and internationalism in late postwar Germany, where Black freedom struggles occurred past the 1970s. Black German women's struggles for gender equality and antiracism exemplified a type of "black left feminism" located in Germany, not unlike in Britain or the United States.[51] Afro-German women's feminist activism overlapped with the emergence of several Third World and/or Women of Color feminist initiatives during the same time. In pursuing their grassroots internationalism in Germany, Black German activist-intellectuals also carved out spaces for themselves and their ideas and utilized them to air their grievances about racism, racial violence, anti-immigration policies, and the reemergence of right-wing populism. They openly called attention to the discriminatory German media, legislation, and politics, and given those dynamics, it was no wonder everyday racism remained a problem. Embracing internationalism, they strengthened their political consciousness and acknowledged similarities and dissimilarities with other marginalized groups worldwide.

Mobilizing Black Germany stresses the need to take seriously the diverse cultural work that Black German women produced, distributed, and normalized, in which they promoted their ideas, writing, and politics of Blackness. They linked their activism, labor, and intellectualism in the movement, and their work validated them in a majority-white polity that continually othered and silenced them.[52] Black German women's writing helped them achieve acclaim, nationally and internationally. For others, writing allowed them to come into their own as readers, thinkers, and artists, in which they gained a new sense of self and direction. In these instances, their intellectual and artistic pursuits provided them with an empowering foundation that gave them a chance to experiment, privileged their voices, and allowed others to engage their works. As

Afro-German women theorized and produced multiple diasporic ideas and images in their larger movement, they contributed to a Black intellectual tradition, one that is often associated with Paulette and Jane Nardal, Claudia Jones, Audre Lorde, and other Black foremothers. But I argue that Afro-German women like Ayim, Oguntoye, and others should also be recognized as critical Black thinkers who were shaped by those foremothers and others and who created alternative discourses and narratives that were independent of white German ones. Yet Black German women did not ignore postwar German intellectual traditions that defined cultural concepts and confronted the status quo. They claimed their cultural inheritances and affirmed their diasporic, German, and European identities. Without a doubt, Black German women pursued cultural and intellectual work that from its inception was political.

A GERMANY WITH BLACKNESS

Centuries of exchange have occurred between Germans and African-descended peoples. From the thirteenth century onward, individuals of African descent have lived, studied, struggled, and worked in Central Europe.[53] Some notable examples include eighteenth-century philosopher Anton Wilhelm Amo's legal studies at the University of Halle and doctoral work at the University of Wittenberg; sociologist W. E. B. Du Bois's studies at the University of Berlin; performer Josephine Baker's La Revue Négre at Berlin's Theatre of the West; Pan-Africanist and communist George Padmore's interlude in Hamburg; and student activist Angela Davis's studies at the University of Frankfurt and Humboldt University.[54] These examples debunked the claims of a Germany without Blacks.[55] Some Black Germans knew of these individuals and drew inspiration from them and others.

Afro-Germans in the movement followed a Black radical tradition in the colonies and the metropole.[56] After Chancellor Otto von Bismarck convened the Berlin or Congo Conference of 1884 and 1885, Germany acquired the colonies of Southwest Africa (now Namibia), East Africa (now parts of Tanzania, Rwanda, and Burundi), Togo (now Togo and parts of Ghana), and Cameroon.[57] These territories provided the sites for earlier forms of Black diasporic mobilization, where colonial subjects agitated for more equality, legal rights, and political autonomy. Scholarship analyzing these earlier instances of activism emphasizes the efforts of men.[58] For example, Rudolf Duala Manga Bell, a Cameroonian king and activist who was educated in Africa and Europe, took up the anticolonialist struggle in Cameroon and Germany. But the German administration later executed him for high treason in 1914. In the German metropole, several elite Duala men from Cameroon—a number of whom were already acquiring an education and training, performing in shows, or working in missionary societies—also inspired anticolonial activism in their homeland. This political resistance and transnational exchange resulted in German officials' restriction of colonial migration from 1893 to 1910. World War I halted migration from the colonies to Germany.[59]

After World War I, some Cameroonians were stranded in Germany, especially as they lost their German protectorate status. With the Treaty of Versailles in 1919, Germany lost all of its colonial possessions, which meant that Cameroon and other colonies became League of Nations Mandates divided between Britain and France. In spite of their liminal positions, former colonial subjects continued to "articulate claims for citizenship, rights, and recognition."[60] In fact, Cameroonian Martin Dibobe, along with seventeen other men, submitted petitions to Germany's Colonial Ministry and the National Assembly in 1919.[61] In the petitions, these men wrote thirty-two demands, arguing for equal rights for Africans and Germans in Germany and highlighting problems with colonialism. They also objected to the imposition of English and French rule and expressed their wish to remain German.

The end of World War I also saw the presence of French colonial troops in the Rhineland, which elicited negative responses. The French occupation was called "The Black Horror on the Rhine" ("*Die Schwarze Schmach am Rhein*"), and the campaign against the occupation relied on racist hysteria and fear regarding French colonial troops' presumed hypersexuality and their alleged rape of white German women.[62] The "Black Horror" campaign galvanized activists and gained national and international prominence. Prominent *Schwarze Schmach* advocates like British journalist Edmund D. Morel and German-American activist Ray Beveridge wrote essays and delivered speeches, garnering considerable attention for the alleged "Black Horror."[63] African American feminist activist Mary Church Terrell challenged the veracity of the accounts of rape and highlighted the campaign's sexualized racism. Terrell's involvement signified a new practice of internationalism in which her activism centered People of Color by connecting campaigns against global racism, sexism, and colonialism.[64] The controversy led to an increased manifestation of anti-Black racism, which caused a great deal of uncertainty for Black Germans and others of African descent in interwar Germany. Interestingly, African American journalists, such as Robert S. Abbott, Joel A. Rogers, and Lewis K. McMillan, also traveled to Germany during that time, but they downplayed the racial oppression that Black Germans and other Blacks experienced there. These journalists represented Germany as liberating and tolerant, which contrasted with their harsh treatment in the United States.[65]

But Black Germans, such as Cameroonian performer and activist Louis Brody (née M'bebe Mpessa), made their voices heard. Brody and others founded the African Aid Association (Afrikanischer Hilfsverein), a self-help organization for African-descended men living in Germany, which remained in existence from 1918 to 1925.[66] Stressing their diasporic consciousness, these men protested the "Black Horror" campaign, affirmed their rights, and attended to the interwar situation of Blacks in Germany.[67] Similar organizations emerged, including the African Fellowship Association (Afrikanischer Kameradschaftsverband) and the Association of German Negroes (Verband Deutscher Neger). There were also several Communist International (Comintern) affiliated organizations in Hamburg and Berlin.[68]

Black Germans' political commitment to fight against inequality and racial discrimination continued throughout the twentieth century. Emily Duala Manga Bell, a Cameroonian anticolonial activist, fought for the rights of her people, especially after the death of her husband Rudolf, mentioned previously. Fasia Jansen, a Black German survivor of the Neuengamme concentration camp, was a songwriter whose songs campaigned for equality. As a peace activist, she remained active in left-wing internationalist and antiracist circles in the 1960s.[69] Some Black German women later involved in the movement, such as Oguntoye, Ika Hügel-Marshall (née Erika Hügel), and others, were active in West German women's and lesbian groups, where they challenged misogyny, sexism, and homophobia.[70]

In Hügel-Marshall's memoir, *Invisible Woman,* published in 1998, she discussed her empowering experiences in the women's movement. Adopting "the personal is political" as her mantra, Hügel-Marshall, along with her fellow feminists, established a women's shelter in Frankfurt—one of the first in West Germany. She protested the criminalization of abortion by participating in "Down with Paragraph 218" marches and accompanied women to the Netherlands to obtain abortions.[71] These events characterized feminist activism in the 1960s and 1970s.

Yet even as they focused on gender equality, West German feminists were often unable to take racism into consideration or embrace ethnic and cultural diversity within their movement. Hügel-Marshall stated in her memoir that, "[Individually] and in groups, we are fighting for equal rights and against oppression. But not against racism. None of my sisters in the women's groups—no one in the entire women's movement, in fact—is interested in hearing the story of black women's struggles. They don't want to see that our society is racist as well as sexist."[72] As the only Black German woman in a feminist group in Frankfurt, she found it difficult to broach topics of racism because when she did her fellow feminist "sisters" quickly dismissed her. They also elided her identity as a Black German woman and were unable to recognize their own racial blind spots.

Oguntoye expressed similar sentiments about being one of the only Black women involved in the lesbian and feminist movements in Berlin. She noted, "I was indeed an 'old activist' and had long been in the women's movement."[73] She acknowledged, "We were always by ourselves. I still remember Yara [Colette Lemke Muñiz de Faria]. She was the first black woman that I met in the sub[cultural scene]. What I mean is that I already knew some [women] in other contexts, but just not in the political movement."[74] Oguntoye also shared, "In the German Womens [sic] scene there is scarely [sic] a handful of Black women who are recognised as Black. We are hopelessly in the minority so that our demand for recognition of our real personalities and our wish to abolish the clichéd picture of us and African culture was simply not fulfilled."[75] Both Ayim and Helga Emde felt excluded at a 1984 feminist congress and a 1989 international women's congress respectively.[76] After experiencing years of exclusion, the Black German movement proved so necessary because it gave those women an opportunity to bring Black feminism into the German fold. In particular, these women's connections with Audre Lorde demonstrate how they could bring intersectional feminist theory into practice, allowing them to determine who they were and reimagine their potential.

Black German women's experiences were not unlike those Black women and Women of Color in the British and U.S. feminist movements of the 1960s through the 1980s, where women took stands against a focus on gender to the exclusion of race, ethnicity, sexuality, and class and recognized overlapping systems of oppression.[77] While Black German women engaged in diverse forms of activism, solidarity with their white German female compatriots remained limited given the latter's inability and unwillingness to think intersectionally and introspectively. Yet, those experiences informed Afro-Germans' future endeavors. Thus, the emergence of the Black German movement afforded Hügel-Marshall, Oguntoye, and others opportunities to be themselves and to fully embrace their gendered and racialized identities.

The political culture of the 1960s and 1970s also influenced Black Germans and their white counterparts. West and East Germany, along with the wider world, took an interest in the U.S. civil rights movement, and covered its major events in newspapers.[78] The presence of civil rights and Black Power leaders and activists, militant African American GIs, entertainers, and foreign students studying, performing, and dissenting in both Germanys transformed the postwar climate.[79] For example, African American activist and author W. E. B. Du Bois, together with his wife, activist Shirley Graham Du Bois, visited East Germany to accept an honorary degree from the Economics Department at Humboldt University and a Peace Medal from the German Peace Council in 1958.[80] After the State Department restored African American performer and communist Paul Robeson's passport, he embarked on a European tour, traveling to East Berlin with his wife Eslanda (Essie) in 1960. While there, he, too, was awarded an honorary degree from Humboldt University and a German Peace Medal. Walter Ulbricht, the East German communist leader of the Socialist Unity Party (Sozialistische Einheitspartei Deutschland, SED), also honored him with the Great Star of Friendship. Robeson also gave several musical performances.[81] He and Essie traveled back to East Germany in 1963, and during that trip, the Council of Ministers awarded Essie the Clara Zetkin medal, acknowledging her important activism.[82] In the SED's official rhetoric, Robeson was a revered hero and served as a symbol of the oppression that "the other America" endured.[83]

Interest in "the other America" did not dissipate. A year after President John F. Kennedy's trip to Frankfurt and West Berlin in 1963, Martin Luther King Jr. traveled to the Cold War Berlins. Willy Brandt, the mayor of West Berlin, instigated his 1964 visit.[84] Provost Heinrich Grüber, the former pastor of East Berlin's St. Mary's Church, also extended an invitation to him. King and Reverend Ralph Abernathy traveled to East and West Berlin. On September 12, King met with Provost Grüber, government officials, and church representatives. The following day, he met with Brandt and attended multiple events, including the signing of the Golden Book of Berlin at city hall, and he spoke at the city's fourteenth-annual cultural festival. King also gave a sermon before twenty thousand Berliners, educating his audience on the U.S. civil rights struggle. Crossing Checkpoint Charlie, King then gave two sermons in communist East Berlin at St. Mary's Church and Sophia Church and spoke to East German and African students at Humboldt University. In comparison to West Germany, his visit in the East garnered very little press, and he did not meet any government representatives, although he maintained a symbolic importance to the regime.[85] King's visit to the postwar Germanys left a significant imprint and is still celebrated.[86]

The Black Power movement also found a receptive audience in the Germanys. There were Black Panther Solidarity Committees in West Germany, in which white student activists mobilized and organized demonstrations for Bobby Seale and other causes. For years, the West German government made it difficult for Black Panther leaders to enter the country, including Kathleen Cleaver, who finally delivered a speech at the University of Frankfurt in 1971. Moreover, activist Angela Davis's arrest in 1970 and imprisonment in 1971 angered West German student activists. The SED also rallied around her and used her case as a symbolic and political tool of solidarity. Angela Davis Solidarity Committees emerged in both Germanys.[87] Spearheaded by Fania Davis, solidarity campaigns existed across the globe. After her release in June 1972, "Angela-mania" continued well after her September 1972 and summer 1973 visits there. Yet in many ways, white East and West Germans were more concerned with improving race relations in the United States than in their own borders. These Germans experienced a cognitive dissonance in which supporting antiracism in the United States allowed them to be ignorant about their own homegrown racism toward Black populations and other communities of color.

Efforts at solidarity with African Americans helped the East German government acquire political legitimacy and position itself internationally. Some African American soldiers even deflected to the East. While West German government officials could not be too critical of their ally, student activists openly addressed racial inequality in the United States and American imperialism in Vietnam. The liberal postwar youth culture of West Germany and the international solidarity politics of East Germany expressed what Moritz Ege and others call "Afro-Americanophilia." Afro-Americanophilia was a common practice among white Germans that involved the appropriation, exoticization, and celebration of Blackness and African American culture.[88] It actually enabled some white Germans to ignore or racially haunt their own Black counterparts and other diasporic populations in the process.[89] Yet these events demonstrate the impact Black freedom struggles had in both Germanys. Afro-Germans were the historical heirs to that Black civil rights tradition and used those previous moments to unify and mobilize against discrimination, demonstrating that Germany was not a racial haven.

Before the official formation of ISD and ADEFRA respectively in 1985 and 1986, which sought to publicize different manifestations of German racism, Black German efforts at Black diasporic activism occurred in a piecemeal fashion. In 1977 an Afro-German lesbian group arose. But the group, according to Oguntoye, "was wrecked under the eyes of the women's scene in Berlin in a very painful way. Out of the fifteen women of that group only one has been ready to do active work in a Black women's community once more." In 1982 a group of Black German youths began meeting in Düsseldorf, although the group also did not last long. For Oguntoye, "The dissolving of a group is traumatic because of the fear of never being able to have a Black community again, which only intensifys[sic] the feeling of isolation. This kind of pain and the danger of the following embitterment was known to all Afro-Germans. To succeed in avoiding this, or at least recovering from it, is our only chance: That is our goal."[90] In addition, the 1980s also brought writers, artists, agitators, performers, and filmmakers from across the Black diaspora to West Germany. For many Black Germans, it was the confluence of peoples, ideas, and events that provided "the fertile ground for a modern Black German movement to evolve."[91] Along those lines, Black Germans relied on a variety of exchanges, connections, and what Jacqueline Nassy Brown refers to as "diasporic resources," which include cultural productions such as art, music, and literature and people, places, ideas, and symbols.[92] Black Germans created visible spaces for their claims of representation, belonging, and intellectualism.

THE POLITICAL BACKDROP TO THE MOVEMENT

Black Germans' different forms of activism were informed by a number of national and international developments concerning race, gender, citizenship, and human rights from the 1980s to the 2000s. As chancellor of West Germany from 1982 to 1990 and reunified Germany from 1990 to 1998, Helmut Kohl of the Christian Democratic Union (CDU) Party tightened immigration laws, ignored German minority rights, and failed to create legislation that would address racism. West Germany ratified the United Nations' (UN) International Convention on the Elimination of All Forms of Racial Discrimination in 1969. It signed the Convention on the Elimination of All Forms of Discrimination against Women (CEDAW) at the 1980 "World Conference of the United Nations Decade for Women: Equality, Development and Peace" in Copenhagen, Denmark, but it did not ratify it until 1985.[93] Yet these actions hardly translated into concrete antiracist and gender equitable initiatives at the federal or state levels. Moreover, the Act on Foreigners of 1990 revised the 1965 law by further regulating entry into Germany and the residence status of foreigners. It also contained new rules on spousal and family reunification and naturalization for second-generation immigrants.[94] While Germany previously had liberal asylum laws, its 1993 Asylum Compromise became more restrictive.[95] In addition, the German Nationality Law, which dated back to 1913, was still intact and based on the notion of *jus sanguinis,* linking German citizenship to blood and descent.[96] The nationality of a child born in Germany was based on that of the father. Although a 1975 law recognized children born of German mothers and foreign fathers as German, each state within the Federal Republic still applied its own citizenship rules. Germany's strong federalist structure delayed changes to its immigration policy in the 1980s and 1990s. Its nationality law was not officially changed until 1999/2000.[97]

Additionally, the reemergence of a xenophobic, nationalist climate was exacerbated after the fall of the Berlin Wall on November 9, 1989. While the fall

of the Wall, the dissolution of East Germany, and the end of the Cold War resulted in the political unification of the Germanys on October 3, 1990, unity
and solidarity did not prevail. Even as, and perhaps because, official rhetoric
claimed that Westerns and Easterns were "one people" (*ein Volk*), bigotry and
provincialism persisted. Overseeing political unification also required Kohl to
overcome multiple problems in the former East, including high unemployment.
The rise of asylum seekers and immigrants in the country from the late 1980s
to 1992 led to intense public debates about multiculturalism, minority rights,
and immigration policies (*Ausländerpolitik*), with ethno-nationalist criticism
coming from across the political spectrum. From the liberal Social Democratic
Party (SPD) to the conservative CDU and Christian Social Union (CSU) par-
ties, various politicians helped engender discourses that claimed foreigners,
especially Muslim and Turkish people, to be irreconcilably different—echoing European-wide sentiments.[98] Some white Germans continued to harbor a
belief that their nation was ethnically homogeneous while also believing that
instances of xenophobia (*Ausländerfeindlichkeit*) were not expressions of racism
because white Germans had already overcome it after World War II.

When Chancellor Kohl claimed that Germany was a "non-immigration
country" in 1982, his statement reflected a common belief that Germany was
a white Judeo-Christian nation. That perspective made the lives of Black Germans, other German minorities, and immigrants difficult. They often endured
verbal attacks and racial violence at the hands of right-wing individuals and
groups.[99] For example, in Eberswalde, a northeastern city, neo-Nazis attacked
and killed Amadeu Antonio Kiowa, an Angolan immigrant, in December 1990.
In Hoyerswerda, a city in the former East, racist riots occurred over several days
and resulted in the attacks on Vietnamese and Mozambican migrants, who
were eventually evacuated from the city in September 1991. In November 1992,
a racist arson attack against two Turkish families resulted in the death of three
people with others seriously injured in Mölln, near Hamburg. Similar incidents
occurred in Solingen, Rostock-Lichtenhagen, Frankfurt an der Oder, and other
cities across reunified Germany.[100] Those racist attacks were troubling, and
debates surrounding this degree of racial violence attempted to explain its root
causes. For many racialized communities, the attacks signified Germany's efforts to maintain its claims to whiteness and homogeneity at frightening costs.
Those incidents illustrated that living in Germany during that time was a matter
of life or death for those same communities.

Internationally, member-states of the European Economic Community
(EEC), originally created with the Treaty of Rome in 1957, had implemented
restrictive legislation on asylum, immigration, and citizenship, leading to a

"Fortress Europe." By the mid-1980s to the 1990s, most western European countries curtailed immigration from Africa, Asia, the Caribbean, Latin America, and the Middle East, particularly Third World countries. European countries prohibited immigration from economic migrants deemed to have evaded the continent's immigration restrictions. These developments coincided with a significant increase in refugee populations.[101] The consolidation of Fortress Europe entailed closing their borders to People of Color, making it difficult for noncitizens to move freely across Europe. The rhetoric of Fortress Europe presumed that an "asylum seeker" was "a subcategory of refugee whose legitimacy had yet to be proven and whose claims were frequently assumed to be suspect." Underpinning these ideas were racial, ethnic, and religious assumptions that overlapped with beliefs and anxieties that these Third World "invaders" violated immigration restrictions.[102] In response, European initiatives sought to disparage, control, monitor, and expel nonwhite people.

These developments corresponded with a rise in pan-European anti-immigrant sentiment and right-wing mobilization.[103] Those efforts paralleled developments to establish a single European market, especially with the ratification of the Single European Act (SEA) in 1987 and the Maastricht Treaty in 1993. The SEA strengthened European political cooperation and supported the free movement of capital, goods, services, and peoples (citizens) among the twelve member-states, and revised the 1957 treaty by pushing for a common market by December 31, 1992. The Maastricht Treaty led to the creation of the European Union (EU), formalizing European citizenship, integration, and intergovernmental cooperation, which had adverse consequences for migrants, refugees, and nonwhite Europeans.[104]

It was against that backdrop that Afro-German women and men created and sustained a diasporic movement to rally against racism in a society that verbally, physically, and discursively marked them as both foreign-born and invisible as German citizens. They attempted to combat discrimination by organizing workshops, protests, and seminars and participating in European antidiscrimination and feminist conferences and human rights organizations. Black Germans felt obligated to collaborate with other communities of color and white allies and engaged in various political causes in Europe and abroad. They pushed for legislative measures that would eradicate racism and ensure women's rights while also attacking exclusionary European policies.

Black German activist-intellectuals' political work has continued down to the present.[105] In 2004, for example, a conservative CSU official in Bavaria, echoed the former Chancellor Kohl, by claiming, "Germany is not a classic country of immigration, and because of its history, geography, and economic conditions, it cannot be one."[106] Similarly, in October 2010, Chancellor Angela Merkel commented on the failure of multiculturalism, stating that "Immigrants needed to do more to integrate."[107] Her remarks came after Thilo Sarrazin, a former central bank official and SPD member, made racist comments about Muslims, Jews, and immigrants. He later published a bestseller on the failure of postwar Germany's immigration policy and other inflammatory ideas about Muslims.[108] Activism against German police brutality grew, especially after the 2005 death of Sierra Leonean asylum seeker Oury Jalloh in a police cell in Dessau.[109] It is little wonder Black German activism has persisted.

TRACING BLACK GERMANS' MOVEMENT MAKING

This book offers a temporal and spatial reframing of narratives of Black freedom struggles by historicizing Black Germans' politics and poetics of representation in their movement, mostly in West and then reunified Germany. It is thematically organized into six chapters that are loosely chronological, beginning in the 1980s and ending in the 2000s. In each chapter, I examine different aspects of Black Germans' efforts to garner recognition and foster a sense of belonging and kinship through their affective expressions, political mobilization, cultural productions, organizational events, and internationalist activity. I illustrate how Black Germans thought, defined, and articulated who they were and what Germany was, unveiling the country's long history of discrimination. The chapters demonstrate that Black Germans also recognized Germany's social organization was based on their exclusion and difference. They used their racial and ethnic differences to mobilize against discrimination and oppression while also acknowledging those differences as constitutive parts of the nation. I conclude with brief reflections on contemporary forms of Black German activism, including the recent Black Lives Matter (BLM) movement in Berlin. The BLM movement continues to draw attention to the persistent racial inequalities and racial violence that African-descended people and communities of color endure in Germany. Though there has been some progress, the concerns that Black Germans grappled with in the 1980s and 1990s still remain today.

The first chapter explores Black German women's correspondences with and personal relationships to Caribbean American author Audre Lorde, who served as a diasporic resource, encouraged Black German women to see how they could be forces for change, individually and collectively. These women also forged alternative kinships to one another that resulted in the creation of an affective, diasporic community and identity. It is through their community that they garnered acceptance as Black Germans and made claims for antiracist reform in Germany.

Chapters 2 and 3 illustrate how Black Germans reimagined possibilities for themselves with their mobilization. They accomplished this by using a variety of diasporic resources, including Lorde, to establish two grassroots organizations, ISD and ADEFRA. With these cultural-political organizations, they experimented by inventing traditions and producing Black spaces for themselves and other marginalized people in Germany. Analyzing Black Germans' national and international efforts at movement making, claim making, and coalition building, I show how their intellectual labor within those organizations and social interactions across the country led them to theorize, produce knowledge, and demand recognition while also challenging daily racism and oppression. These chapters change our perceptions of what intellectualism and intellectuals look like in the German context. Through their organizational activities and publications, Black German quotidian intellectuals cultivated a sense of community with their Black compatriots and others through their intellectual work. Moreover, feminists in ADEFRA practiced a gendered activism and confronted the inherent racism in the white West German women's movement by pursuing Black queer strategies that allowed their feminist politics to flourish and rooted Black feminism in Germany.

Shifting away from detailed analyses of these organizations, chapter 4 turns to individuals, such as May Ayim, Katharina Oguntoye, and others, who created not only an intellectual and cultural foundation for the modern Black German movement with the publication of their critical 1986 volume *Farbe bekennen: Afrodeutsche Frauen auf den Spuren ihrer Geschichte,* but also a political one that was intersectional and feminist. From *Farbe bekennen* onward, Black German women relied on and engendered diasporic resources to write themselves into overlapping public cultures (global Black diasporic and late-postwar German) that ignored and rejected them. Their ideas, ideologies, and writing made them quotidian intellectuals and empowered them to advance their political and cultural agendas. These women's diverse cultural productions (poetry, prose, speeches, spoken-word, and so forth) served as forms of connection and proved instrumental in helping them catalyze their modern movement and establish networks that often took them beyond the borders of Germany. For Ayim, in particular, she gained a wide reputation through her literature at home and abroad, allowing her to become a prominent advocate for the Black German community.

The final two chapters return to ISD and ADEFRA and offer examples of Black Germans' grassroots diasporic activism, intellectualism, and internationalism through three important events. Chapter 5 examines two annual traditions: the national meetings (*Bundestreffen,* BT) in multiple cities and the Black History Month celebrations in Berlin. Affirming their Black internationalism, Black Germans cultivated ties with individuals in and beyond Germany. They also practiced an antiracist ideology that enabled them to confront racism and the afterlives of colonialism in the country, expose the silences surrounding the presence and complexity of Black Germany, and push against instances of continental and global neofascism and white supremacy. I argue that the BHMs encouraged the circulation of knowledge, intellectual exchange, and cultural promotion, changing what constituted intellectual production and ideological expression. In the process, Black Germans and other People of Color produced and decolonized spaces in Berlin, undercutting its traditionally white construction and marking it as Black.

Centering ADEFRA's transnational Black feminist solidarity, chapter 6 analyzes Black German women's participation in the Cross-Cultural Black Women's Studies Summer Institute conferences. After attending several international Cross-Cultural Institutes, Black German women brought the 1991 one to reunified Germany, and they made their concerns about gender inequality, racism, and racial violence clear, sharing their social realities on an international stage. Their involvement with the institute represented their commitment to forge a global feminist solidarity with Women of Color and other allies that advanced a particular type of political Blackness and initiated social change. In this way, they gave Third World feminism a significant forum in Germany.

Mobilizing Black Germany reconstitutes a Black German archive of thought, action, and solidarity, showing the dynamism of Black Germans. By illuminating Black German ideas, practices, and writing, it underscores how they pursued diverse forms of kinship, intellectualism, and internationalism that buttressed their activism. They created an affective community of Germanness *and* Blackness, redefining their parameters. With their "Black Coming Out," Black Germans in and beyond the nation articulated their demands for equality and representation, linking local and global concerns. Black German women were an integral part of this movement. As these women dealt with the intersection of emotions, race, gender, class, sexuality, and discrimination, they emphasized the significance of spatial politics, which recognized how the past informed their present and future. Sharing these Black German narratives of survival, resistance, and internationalism deepens our understanding of the potential of global Black freedom struggles. These narratives are prescient as contemporary Europe is eerily similar to the period in which the movement emerged and evolved.

CHAPTER 1

BLACK GERMAN WOMEN AND AUDRE LORDE

Your strong voice
will no longer be raised
in auditoriums to eager ears
but your words
continue to ring loud and pregnant
in lecture halls, at dinner, among friends and enemies alike.
I miss you.
You always tottered on precipices
thin as wire,
threatening to slice you.

—Yvonne Kettels, "Audre" (September 1992)

On November 17, 1992, Caribbean American feminist poet Audre Lorde died from liver cancer. Since 1984 she had been living and working in St. Croix with her partner Gloria Joseph, though she would travel to the United States and elsewhere to pursue diverse projects. Throughout the world, Lorde's colleagues, friends, and loved ones organized tributes and paid homage.[1] Honoring Lorde, the editors of a Black lesbian magazine *Aché* arranged a November 29 memorial at the Modern Times Bookstore in San Francisco, which two Afro-German women, Yvonne Kettels and Yara-Colette Lemke Muñiz de Faria, attended and presented a eulogy.[2] These women reminisced about their personal experiences with Lorde. Lemke Muñiz de Faria revealed, "The first time I met Audre was some years ago after one of her powerful speeches in Berlin. We were seated opposite each other in a restaurant, sharing a big plate of fish, talking about Ye-manha and cowry shells. It was then that she told me about *Aché* and her dream of it coming together with its German sistah-journal, *Afrekete*; her dream of a coming together of Black Americans and [Black] Germans. Though her dream has not yet come true, a start has been made, otherwise we would not be here together tonight to honor and celebrate [her]."[3] Likewise, Kettels remembered:

the first time I met you—about five years ago—in Berlin at a breakfast gathering for sisters and brothers. We were so few.

Back then I wasn't able to speak to you because my English wasn't developed enough. I guess I was too shy. But we communicated anyway with our hands and feet, connecting as sisters. I wonder how many of you here in the U.S. realize what a great influence Audre had on us, Afro-German women/lesbians and brothers. Did you know that there were strong connections between Audre and Germany?

She was the light in our eyes, rising like the sun, giving warmth and love, sharing the world, her experience, her knowledge, incomparable, unforgettable, strong.[4]

Lemke Muñiz de Faria and Kettels both discussed the transnational kinship between Black Germans and Lorde, stressing how she forged relationships with individuals from across the global Black diaspora. Both women's moments with Lorde showed how they explicitly rooted their emerging sense of community in affective and diasporic practices.

With their recollections, these German women explained that, "Her death hit us hard, even though we knew about her health situation. It is difficult to describe in words what Audre meant to us, Afro-German, Black women/lesbians. . . . And what she will mean to us way beyond her death." Privileging female social bonds, Afro-German women claimed her as their "sister, mother, companion in struggle." Lorde was the first prominent Black intellectual and internationalist with whom many Black Germans had sustained contact, and their kinship with Lorde was critical in their lives and activism. Black German women declared that Lorde's "inspiring power and love. . . . gave us faith and courage to move out of our isolation, to come together and fight against racism, sexism, and homophobia."[5] Moreover, she "led us toward our self-confidence, taught us to use our own experiences and skills to make change happen. Her engagement for Black women worldwide and her encouragement to write and publish a book about ourselves, which turned out to be *Farbe bekennen* (*Showing Our Colours*), changed our lives." Lorde motivated them to believe "in their growing power, in the power of formerly silent Afro-German women and men, young and old, to create and unite change countrywide. In [their] power to bring about international change with other Afro-Europeans, Afro-Asians and

Afro-Americans." These women claimed, "her life's work is a bequest to us." This powerful sentiment is evinced in the stanza at the beginning of this chapter, in which Kettels's entire poem, entitled "Audre," also appeared in the eulogy.[6] The women concluded the eulogy with a conviction to "continue fighting along with all people, who want to create a future together," and with a quotation from Lorde's preface in the volume *Showing Our Colors:* "Women of minorities, companions in struggle. . . . We are greeting you!" More than thirty Black German and Black women signed the eulogy.[7]

Even as they recognized Lorde after her death, Black German women were well aware of her importance while she lived, for they had continuously expressed appreciation and admiration of Lorde in their correspondence and actions. This chapter foregrounds these women's personal connections to Lorde, demonstrating how emotions helped this community to cohere; to feel like Black Germans; and to reconstitute their collective identities. These Black German women represented an "affective community" and used and valued a variety of expressions to describe their lives, feelings, and friendships with Lorde and others, causing their emotions to have a clear place in Germany.[8] They also developed their own norms and practices, demonstrating how emotions served as tools in their refashioning of new transnational, diasporic identities and kinships. For these women, Lorde proved to be a catalyst for the formation, growth, and evolution of the subsequent Black German movement.

Drawn to Lorde and her commitment to advance feminist and antiracist solidarity, engage in Black women's internationalism, and combat multiple forms of oppression, they adapted her ideas on writing, emotions, the diaspora, and community to fit their local and national conditions. Black German women used Lorde as a diasporic resource—albeit one of many—that enabled them to refashion their racial identity, rework notions of belonging, and form a community in a majority-white German society. Afro-Germans lacked a longstanding recognition as a Black diasporic collective, and differed from other diasporic communities in Europe and the Americas.[9] Lorde's arrival in Germany occurred at a moment in the 1980s in which Chancellor Helmut Kohl's government continued to inadequately address racism. Given this climate, Black German women saw Lorde as much more than an ally. She served as a conduit through which they established a diasporic community with their emotions, affinities, and writing. Encouraged by Lorde, these women pursued new Black diasporic projects, developing local, national, and international networks and cultivating affective kinship ties that influenced their claims for belonging and representation in the nation and beyond.

LORDE'S YEARS BEFORE BERLIN

Born on February 18, 1934, in Harlem, New York, Audre Lorde (née Audrey Geraldine Lorde) was the youngest daughter of West Indian immigrants Frederic Byron and Linda Gertrude Belmar Lorde. Her sisters, Phyllis and Helen, were born in 1929 and 1931.[10] Audre's parents maintained a strict working-class household, in which they did not openly share their emotions and tried to keep a racist society at bay. As a result of her strict upbringing, Lorde had difficulties with her parents.

Without a doubt, writing provided Lorde with solace and was an act of self-preservation, especially as she dealt with thorny relationships with her family and managed her own physical disabilities. So shortsighted she was legally blind from a young age, Lorde learned to read and talk about a year before she began school at the age of five. She was also a stutterer.[11] Owing to her disabilities, Lorde began an intimate and intense relationship with words and writing and described learning about poetry through her "mother's strangenesses" and her "father's silences."[12] Her familial relations were often distant and combative and revealed how different she felt from them. As Lorde matured, she later used her outsider status as a source of strength and empowerment and embraced her multiple identities.

Lorde further cemented her relationship to writing by forging connections near and far. She found a "spiritual home" at Hunter High School in New York. Although it was not racially diverse, she established friendships with a group of young white girls, who later called themselves "The Branded." While her connections with women poets satisfied her need for affirmation, love, and "intellectual parity," that community was only supportive of her femaleness not necessarily of her Blackness, and many of those relationships did not extend beyond Hunter.[13] Lorde later experienced a similar dynamic in the women's movement in New York. In spite of her alienation as a Black woman among white women, "writing poetry became an ordinary effort, not a secret and rebellious vice."[14]

Connecting with women abroad, Lorde honed her craft and stimulated her passion for writing. As a student at the National Autonomous University of Mexico (UNAM) from 1953 to 1954, she met and established relationships with women who helped her see "the potential of poetry to connect her feelings with words." Mexico inspired Lorde to affirm her identity as a poet and to gain a "deeper sense of herself as a lesbian."[15] As a dynamic place, Mexico allowed Lorde to evolve, and encouraged her to recognize the importance of exchanging and producing ideas that transcended the boundaries of the United States.

The Harlem Writers Guild also provided Lorde with an intellectual community. Her involvement, although sporadic, exposed her to discourses on Black consciousness and facilitated her writing talents, especially with mentorship from John Henrik Clarke, one of the organizers. Lorde gained a literary home, but still felt isolated from the group's largely cis Black male and heteronormative composition. Moreover, Lorde frequented gay bars, became active in the lesbian scene in Greenwich Village, and avoided the Black nationalist movement in Harlem, practices that did not sit well with some members of the Guild.[16] But through the Guild, she met the famed African American poet Langston Hughes, who published some of her poetry in 1964. Later, in a 1968 letter to the civil rights activist Julian Mayfield, Lorde wrote, "The people I met in the Group and through the CNA [Committee for the Negro in the Arts] were the first creative Black people whose constructive attention and criticism convinced me that I was not merely a quixotic adolescent." She also claimed to "owe more than I can say here as a Black woman and writer, to the encouragement, stimulation and insights gathered in those meetings in the lean years."[17] This Black intellectual space enabled a youthful Lorde to explore and improve her style, language, and consciousness.

After college and other experiences, Lorde returned to school and earned a master's degree in library science from Columbia University in 1961, believing it would better equip her with access to information that she could use to push for social change. Lorde's time at Columbia caused her to be more politically active, especially with the Cold War and nuclear arms race. At Columbia, she continued to explore her sexuality, mostly with women. In 1962, however, she married white attorney Edwin "Ed" Rollins, whom she met at Columbia, and had two children, Elizabeth "Beth" Lorde-Rollins in 1963 and Jonathan Rollins in 1964. After obtaining her degree, Lorde worked at Mount Vernon Public Library. She still managed to juggle the wifely and motherly demands on her, and navigated the sociopolitical climate as well as different relationships with women.[18]

In 1968 Lorde garnered more recognition. She produced her first volume of poetry, *The First Cities,* with the Poets Press, where her childhood friend Diane di Prima was the editor.[19] Poetry increasingly became a subversive form of language for Lorde that enabled her to express and acknowledge the significance of her emotions.[20] That same year, Lorde received a National Endowment for the Arts residency grant to teach a six-week course at Tougaloo College, a Historically Black College and University (HBCU) in Mississippi. It was her first time teaching creative writing, and she gained a newfound energy from her discussions with students that led her to develop her theory of difference.[21] In

Tougaloo she also met one of her partners, Frances Clayton, a white woman who was a visiting professor of psychology from Brown University. It was her experience in Mississippi that motivated Lorde to teach when she returned to New York, and teach she did when Mina Shaughnessy, the director of CUNY's Search for Education, Elevation, and Knowledge (SEEK) Program, hired her as a lecturer. She joined a community of "poet-writer-teachers" that included Toni Cade Bambara, Barbara Christian, Adrienne Rich, and June Jordan, and forged friendships with them.[22] In addition to developing as a teacher, Lorde gained further exposure in African American literary circles, publishing in the *Journal of Black Poetry* and *Negro Digest*. Although Lorde's career had just taken off, in many ways she had already gone through a formative intellectual and emotional passage.

Yet the 1970s was a period of profound transformation for Lorde. Personally, she moved to Staten Island to build a life with Frances and her two children in 1971 and finalized her divorce with Ed in 1975. Though she was happy with Frances and the children, Lorde suffered several health problems, including a benign tumor in her right breast in 1977. A year later, her fears returned when she was diagnosed with breast cancer and underwent a mastectomy.[23] Lorde's cancer prognosis caused her to shift her focus and values and led to her "second life" as a poet, writer, mother, lesbian, and cancer survivor. She also reaffirmed her African diasporic roots by traveling to the Caribbean and Africa. Lorde visited Barbados in 1973 in an effort to reconnect with her father's country, and relished her time there. Always eager to visit Africa, she embarked on a five-week tour of Togo, Ghana, and Dahomey (later the People's Republic of Benin) with Frances and the kids in 1974. She learned about Dahomean religion and mythology, which she would later integrate into her literary work and correspondence. The trip helped her find "a spiritual location; the knowledge of original ancestors; a corporeal reality that was unique, timeless, and complex; and a lust to operate upon the world."[24] In 1978 she traveled to Grenada. It was her first trip to her mother's birthplace. These trips reveal how Lorde embodied the "roots and routes" of the diaspora, and demonstrate her willingness to later use a pronounced Black cultural internationalism in her literature and activism.[25] Her perspectives and practices transcended yet remained within the nation.

Lorde garnered recognition professionally, becoming an associate professor of English at John Jay College and publishing six award-winning volumes in a decade. Her poetry dealt with an array of themes, including racism, emotions, lesbianism, power, and parent-child relationships. Increasingly, she disseminated knowledge through her literature and saw her literature as inseparable from her social protest and politics. Taken together, Lorde's publications reflected her form of intellectual activism. Patricia Hill Collins argues that, "one form of 'intellectual activism' aims to speak the truth to power. This form of truth-telling harnesses the power of ideas toward the specific goal of confronting existing power relations," and "a second strategy of 'intellectual activism' aims to speak the truth directly to the people."[26] Lorde performed these strategies with her teaching, publications, and presentations.

The first half of the 1980s proved busy and fruitful for Lorde. She continued to teach, write, travel, attend conferences, and practice intellectual activism. Her previous experiences with cancer propelled her to write about it, and she produced her first nonfiction book, *The Cancer Journals,* in 1980.[27] Lorde read excerpts from the book at the UN's 1980 Second World Conference on Women in Copenhagen, Denmark, showing her sustained interest in feminist issues and embodying Black women's internationalism through her politics. She used her presentations and other writing to promote social change domestically and internationally.

Lorde did not only write, she also made a foray into publishing as a form of emancipatory politics. In 1980 Lorde, Barbara Smith, Cherríe Moraga, and other feminists and lesbians of color writers came up with the idea for the Kitchen Table: Women of Color Press, which originated from a conversation between Smith and Lorde. The official name, announced in 1981, was chosen because "the kitchen is the center of the home, the place where women in particular work and communicate with each other." Moreover, they "wanted to convey the fact that we are a kitchen table, grass roots operation, begun and kept alive by women who cannot rely on inheritances or other benefits of class privilege to do the work we need to do."[28] The press gave feminist writers of color in the United States a visible platform—one that did not previously exist for them. Yet, it was also international in scope given the themes that their publications explored and their intention to "make connections with and [be] inspired by the global movement of Third World women."[29]

Lorde's productivity, political engagement, and internationalism did not abate. In 1981 she traveled to St. Croix to participate in a Women's Writers Symposium that feminist professor Gloria Joseph organized, which included Adrienne Rich, Toni Cade Bambara, Michelle Cliff, and others. While there, Lorde reexamined her multiple positionalities, especially her identity as an "African-Caribbean-american" woman.[30] She engaged in acts of belonging and influenced others to do the same, forging kinships with Women of Color outside the United States who also dealt with exclusion and resisted discrimination. After the U.S. invasion of Grenada in 1983, Lorde traveled there and later wrote about the impact of imperialism and anti-Black racist violence on the island.

That same year, she was invited to speak at the twentieth commemoration of the 1963 March on Washington because she was "the most prominent black lesbian feminist activist," although there was controversy about her presence at the event because of her sexuality.[31] She also published her biomythography *Zami: A New Spelling of My Name* in 1982 and *Sister Outsider* in 1984, a collection of her essays, letters, and speeches that was emblematic of her intellectual activism. In both, she delivered her truth and produced knowledge to incite change.[32]

Lorde continued to deal with themes that she had encountered in her past. Throughout her career, she remained especially sensitive to the ways in which gender, sexuality, class, and racial prejudice reinforced each other. Both disillusioned and hopeful, she understood how opponents of racism could give voice to class and gender stereotypes, and likewise how the struggle against gender and class prejudices often became ensnared in racism. As a result, she became an early proponent of "intersectional" analyses and activism that attended to multiple interconnected forms of discrimination.[33] Lorde followed in the Black radical and feminist tradition of Claudia Jones, Fasia Jansen, and others. Late in her career, at the age of fifty, she would take her feminism, Black internationalism, and longstanding commitment to writing as a form of self-definition, cultural work, and activism to Berlin, where by her own accounts she had some of the most invigorating years of her life.

LORDE IN THE CITY

Lorde experienced hope, healing, energy, and growth in Berlin. The cosmopolitan city enabled her to form connections with multiple people and shaped her ideas about the diaspora, belonging, and activism.[34] Gloria Joseph, who became her partner after her breakup with Frances Clayton, remembered, "In Germany, Audre experienced a kind of freedom unlike any she had in the States. Here she could dress as she pleased, behave how she wanted without the recognition and fear of disapproval from her black female peers, family, professional colleagues or black male establishment. This is not to say that she did not experience racism, but she could express herself openly and not have apprehensions and fears about the consequences of her actions."[35] Echoing similar sentiments, white German feminist Dagmar Schultz, who helped to bring Lorde to Germany in 1984, noted that, "for Audre, Berlin was a little bit of a playground. In between her work and her reading she just had a good time."[36] Forging relationships with Black Germans and others also supported her as she underwent alternative cancer treatments. She was diagnosed with liver cancer prior to her Berlin trip. While Berlin could be a curative and inspiring space, Lorde recognized it could also be a hard space given the country's inability to fully come to terms with its own racist past and present.

Lorde used Berlin, Germany, and Europe to interrogate her understanding of Blackness and give it new meaning. Her "knowledges, negotiations, and experiences," or what Katherine McKittrick calls "black women's geographies," demonstrate how Berlin as a space allowed Lorde to reimagine herself, her community, her literature, and her activism.[37] She also encouraged Black Germans and other Black Europeans to celebrate and recognize the importance of their Blackness and ties to the Black diaspora in majority-white societies, and helped Black German women reclaim their positions as Black subjects, making their ideas, identities, and struggles legible within Black and German circles. She accomplished this through the diverse places she inhabited such as classrooms, auditoriums, and feminist and/or cultural centers. Before and after her arrival in the country, Black German women readily accepted the knowledge that she imparted in her published works. Yet it was her *presence* in Berlin and across other German cities and her *ability* to consciously form alliances and build community that Afro-German women absorbed and took away from meeting her and then later deployed in their lives and in their movement.

Schultz's early interactions with Lorde at feminist conferences on both sides of the Atlantic prompted Lorde's Berlin visit. Schultz initially met her at the UN's 1980 Second World Conference on Women in Denmark, where she invited Lorde to teach at the John F. Kennedy Institute for North American Studies at the Freie Universität Berlin (FU). She met her again at the 1981 National Women's Studies Association (NWSA) conference in Connecticut.[38] Upon hearing Lorde's and Adrienne Rich's keynote addresses, Schultz felt a call to action. In a 1981 letter to Lorde, she asked her again if she would consider teaching at the JFK Institute and wrote, "I want to tell you how deeply moved I was by your address at the NWSA that is, by your honesty, your willingness to confront and share and, of course, by the beauty and strength of your language, your voice, your presence."[39] Lorde's NWSA speech, "The Uses of Anger: Women Responding to Racism," had provoked some introspection, making Schultz realize how entrenched racism was in German society. She asked if she could publish and translate Lorde's NWSA keynote address and the essay "The Uses of the Erotic: The Erotic as Power" through her Sub Rosa Women's Press.[40]

Underlying Schultz's antiracist perspectives were her personal experiences in the United States. Civil rights and women's movements from 1963 to 1973; an understanding of global feminism as epitomized by Lorde and her writings; and a desire to change the tenor of the German women's movement. Schultz previously confided in a letter to Lorde that, "Some of us hope that these discussions will generate a broader confrontation with racism and anti-Semitism."[41] Her press translated Lorde's and Rich's NWSA speeches, producing the 1983 volume *Power and Sensuality* (*Macht und Sinnlichkeit*), which was the first German-language publication of Lorde's works.[42] Some Black German women, who were also familiar with American scholarship on feminism, positively responded to the German edition.[43] The volume did not prompt a mainstream dialogue about race and racism in Germany. But as some scholars argue, Lorde's presence as a Caribbean American woman in Berlin initiated discussions about racism that had not previously existed.[44]

One of the main reasons for Lorde's sojourn to Germany was meeting Black German women, "for [she] had been told there were quite a few in Berlin."[45] Black German women were moved by the fact that a well-known Black feminist poet wanted to learn about and befriend them. Lorde's stint as a visiting professor in the summer semester of 1984 at the JFK Institute, which involved years of planning and negotiation on the part of FU officials, made a lasting impression on the Black Germans she encountered inside and outside the classroom.[46]

For Afro-German women, such as May Ayim and Katharina Oguntoye, attending Lorde's classes enabled them to acknowledge that they constituted a part of the transnational Black diaspora. Black Germans' white compatriots

Figure 1. "Portrait of Audre Lorde in the Park," photograph by Dagmar Schultz, Berlin, 1984, Freie Universität Berlin, Universitätsarchiv, V/N-47 Audre Lorde, Sig. 92.

constantly asked them to explain their origins and/or called them insulting names, as if being Black and German were incompatible. Prior to Lorde's arrival, some Black Germans had maintained a racial consciousness through reading diasporic literature; listening to music from diasporic artists; and adopting cultural references to freedom movements across the diaspora. Black German women's interactions with her and each other enabled them to further develop their consciousness in a sustained way. Oguntoye, for example, shared how Lorde gave the few Black students in her courses an opportunity to express their thoughts. She also took time to meet with Black female students outside class.[47] Witnessing this change in Black German women, Lorde reflected, "For me, Afro-German means the shining faces of Katerina [sic] and Mai [sic] in animated conversation about their fathers' homelands, their comparisons, joys, disappointments. It means my pleasure at seeing another Black woman walk into my classroom, her reticence slowly giving way as she explores a new self-awareness, gains a new way of thinking about herself in relation to other Black women."[48] Black German women's interactions with one another led to a growing understanding of their diasporic identities and community in Germany.

Though she had initial reservations about traveling to Germany, Lorde "found a mutuality in the women she met there," and felt that she "made a difference in the lives of Afro-German women, many of whom articulated a new sense of self and community." Her time in the country "helped her understand what it meant to claim a consciousness as Afro-European, which was neither conceptually 'African European' nor defined by a scripted blackness."[49] Through her time with Afro-Germans, Lorde saw the multiplicity of Blackness represented, valuing its diverse expressions. Her experiences elucidate how Germany as a space helped her ideas and writing evolve, and reveal how multidirectional influences emerged between Lorde and Black German women.

As a result, these "German women of the diaspora" sought recognition in society by inventing the terms "Afro-German" and "Black German," which encouraged many to position themselves within and feel themselves to be part of the Black diaspora and the German nation.[50] For Black German feminist activist Judy Gummich, "Audre's influence was essential in our seeing ourselves in a positive light, as confident and outspoken Black Germans ready to fight for our rights."[51] As scholars have already shown, Lorde inspired Black German women to document and share knowledge about their individual and collective herstories.[52] Lorde's intellectualism and internationalism had an undeniable influence on Black German women. According to Lorde, "These were women she now saw as real, rather than imagined, allies in global struggles for social change, and she was excited about working with them on their idea for a book [*Farbe bekennen*]."[53]

Connections with Lorde served as a turning point in many Black German women's lives. Whereas other Afro-diasporic communities have inherited a clear sense of common ancestry from their Black parents that often revolved around histories of forced, voluntary, or collective migration, the Afro-German community developed a different legacy that included "direct and indirect routes as a consequence of colonialism."[54] This owed to Germany's short-lived colonial empire, the Third Reich and the Holocaust, the postwar occupations, and the division of Germany. Some Black Germans' limited-to-nonexistent contact with their relatives of African descent also shaped this dynamic. Tina M. Campt has argued that "memory provides the source of the defining tension of diaspora and diasporic identity: the dynamic play of originary and imaginary homes, and the complex networks of relation forged across national, spatial, and temporal boundaries." Because of Black Germans' diversity, they did not possess the common narratives of home, belonging, or community that provided other Black communities with foundational resources that they could use as sources of belonging and identity.[55] In this way, Lorde offered them a model for kinship, self-naming, and intellectual activism.

Although Lorde served as a pivotal figure within the Black German movement, some activists and scholars have found her lionization downplays the role of Black Germans while overemphasizing the role of African Americans in the emergence of the movement.[56] Though some Black Germans have assigned Lorde a symbolic role as the godmother or mother of the movement, others viewed her as just an ally, a mentor, or a friend who supported the movement.[57] Lorde's lionization can be limiting, but we must acknowledge the voices of Black German women, who have allowed these seemingly incompatible images of her to flourish. Their different perspectives add complexity to the history of the connections that Black German women formed with her, in which she could be a *godmother/mother* and a *friend* of the movement. In fact, it does not have to be an either-or dynamic, as both of these roles did coexist, as the letters analyzed in this chapter attest. These characterizations of Lorde reflect Black German women's responses to her and their need to forge Black female relationships that were previously denied to them in their families and in feminist circles. They also show how Black German women in the movement were not monolithic, expressing different ideas about the representation of prominent individuals affiliated with their movement.

Campt also suggests that scholars must examine the asymmetries of power that exist across Black diasporic communities so that we better understand the hierarchies that privilege certain communities over others, especially with regard to Black Europeans. Similarly, Nassy Brown asks "how do power relations within the diasporic space of particular Black communities shape participation in the transnational space of diaspora?"[58] They raise valid points arguing that current scholarship must turn away from privileging African American and heteronormative narratives of the diaspora, in ways that ignore the multiplicity of diasporic experiences and normalize hierarchies within the diaspora.[59] I agree with their assessments, and believe that we need to take Black Germans on their own terms. They offer a compelling case study that represents overlapping diasporic, affective, spatial, and temporal contexts that are and are not completely reflected in the old or new diaspora paradigms. For many in the movement, their lives began in the post–World War II *spacetime* and not the Middle Passage, which anchored them to different Black subjectivities. Given their multiple backgrounds, they already exemplify the diversity of the diaspora. Black Germans' existence and activism also shattered the myth of a (post)racial Germany, especially after the Holocaust.

In many ways, Lorde's life and career affirmed and problematized Michelle M. Wright's Middle Passage Epistemology, referenced in the introduction. She was Caribbean American, but her connection to Afro-Germans and other Black Europeans came from moving in the opposite direction and understanding their particular experiences, which did and did not involve the typical Black Atlantic crossing. Her emphasis on the utility of writing and feelings remained important for Black German women and their larger movement. Through her publications, courses, exchanges, and readings, she elucidated how intertwined poetry and emotions were in women's lives. For Lorde, poetry resided within each woman, and "each one of us holds an incredible reserve of creativity and power, of unexamined and unrecorded emotion and feeling. The women's place of power within each of us is neither white nor surface, it is dark, it is ancient, and it is deep." Lorde stressed the significance of tapping into a reservoir of emotions that existed within women, and that it was critical that women acknowledged this source could be creatively used to deal with sexist, racist, homophobic, and patriarchal societies. She considered poetry to be a form of resistance, survival, and community building. Above all, it helped women identify and validate their ideas, giving "the nameless" a platform where they could be heard. Lorde believed that poetry had the ability "to charter this revolutionary demand" and to turn "our hopes and fears" into a positive act that reflected and reconstituted the materiality of individuals' lives.[60] As Gummich noted, "With her poems, she sang her thoughts into my heart. She strengthened me to fight for our rights together with other Black women/Black people all over the world and to claim our dignity from this society."[61] Lorde's ideas helped Afro-German women as they created their diasporic, affective community in a society that privileged other emotional expressions and that constantly excluded them from claims to Germanness.[62]

But it was not only positive emotions that were constructive for Lorde. She clarified that, "Anger is a very healthy emotion. It helps tell us something, it also helps move us into action for change. That's the way I use my anger. I try to change the things that make me angry in whatever way I can."[63] Lorde used anger as a "liberating and strengthening act of clarification," that she employed to describe her vision of society. "Every woman," she opined, "has a well-stocked arsenal of anger potentially useful against those oppressions, personal and institutional, which brought anger into being. Focused with precision it can become a powerful source of energy serving progress and change."[64] There was utility in channeling anger, which helped Lorde scrutinize intersecting power relations and confront different forms of oppression. Once people verbalized these problems, they could resolve them, opening lines of dialogue and change where there was once silence and inaction. Theorizing on poetry, emotions, the erotic, and women offers an example of Lorde's practice of intellectual activism, in which she shared knowledge and spoke her truth to power. It is no wonder that Lorde's ideas resonated with some Afro-German women.

At her readings, Lorde frequently introduced herself as a "black, lesbian, feminist, warrior, poet, mother, and African Caribbean American woman," using these monikers to show how inextricable her identities, writing, and activism were in her life.[65] Lorde stated, "When I say I am a black feminist, I mean I recognize that my power as well as my primary oppressions come as a result of Blackness as well as my womanness, and therefore my struggles on both these fronts are inseparable." She also noted, "When I say I am a black Lesbian, I mean I am a woman whose primary focus of loving, physical as well as emotional, is directed to women. It does not mean I hate men." As a guest lecturer in Schultz's "Racism and Sexism" seminar at the FU in 1984, Lorde remarked, "As I say as a 49 year old black feminist lesbian socialist mother of two, one including a boy, there is always something wrong with me, there is always some group of people who define me as wrong. It is very encouraging, I learn a lot about myself and my identities that way."[66] She valued her multiple identities and the ability to define herself on her own terms. Afro-German women adopted her ideas, using them to shape their individual and collective identities and goals.

Along with her presence, Lorde's literature and poetry readings imparted experiential knowledge and introspective practices about writing, emotions, and the Black diaspora to Black German women. Lorde did not see poetry as a performance because "it is something we create together that will empower us all," and "it is something that we share and hopefully we each take from this place something that makes us more who we wish to be."[67] Yet, in a sense, her readings throughout Germany and seminars at the FU operated as performances. As Lorde's biographer Alexis de Veaux writes, her "narratives were self-conscious, literary performances; an excavation, and synthesis, of memory, imagination, and truth."[68] Lorde's readings emerged as diverse forms of performance that elicited love, warmth, courage, and solidarity and suffused her feminist and diasporic sensibilities. Her performances were public events and literary and oratory practices that brought people together across cultural and linguistic differences. They served as "acts of transfer," offering Black Germans the tools they needed to claim recognition and challenge discriminatory practices in a majority-white society.[69] With their connections, these women gained more self-awareness and enthusiasm, and it was this confidence and knowledge that they used to mobilize their movement.

Lorde envisioned that her publications served as tools possessed with an affective and curative quality as well as an ideological function. On a basic level, poetry should be written, read, or spoken, but it should also be valued, felt, and applied. Emotional expressions could trigger feelings of love, respect, warmth, or courage, and this was precisely the perspective that informed Lorde's literature. Presenting at the 1988 "The Dream of Europe" (*Ein Traum von Europa*) conference, an international writers' symposium that took place in Berlin, she declared, "I am an African American poet and believe in the power of poetry. Poetry, like all art, has a function: to bring us closer to who we wish to be: to help us [en]vision a future which has not yet been: and to help us survive the lack of that future."[70] Throughout her speech, she sought to incite sociopolitical change by transforming people's feelings through her poetic words. In becoming cognizant of the power of writing, Lorde believed, individuals could tap into an alternative emotional archive, especially in their collaborative projects for social change that helped to dismantle all forms of discrimination.[71] This sentiment was particularly important because conference organizers failed to include any Black European writers.

Feelings and the emotional work that poetry symbolized shaped Lorde's literature and diasporic and feminist politics—aspects that were interrelated in her life. For instance, at a 1987 reading at the Chocolate Factory (*Schokofabrik*), a women's center in Berlin, Lorde said, "I think we need to deal with our feelings and to put them out there to arm them, to give them teeth and hands to work." During this event, Lorde used imagery that personified emotions by giving them corporeal qualities and more urgency. Likewise, at a 1988 reading in Hanover,

Figure 2. "Portrait of Audre Lorde in Cologne," photograph by Ute Weller, Cologne, 1988, Freie Universität Berlin, Universitätsarchiv, V/N-47 Audre Lorde, Sig. 184.

Lorde maintained that it was an individual's responsibility to "use our power in the service of what we believe" and to eradicate injustice in society.[72] Black German women later deployed these ideas in their correspondence to her and in their activism.

In her readings as in her writing, Lorde privileged the centrality of women's kinships. At a 1987 reading of *Zami* in Berlin, she explained, "I wanted to make a lot of connections in this book, connections between women, connections between—it has been the love of women that has kept me alive for so long." She continued, "That loving between women, whether it is bitter, whether it is transient, whether it is painful, whatever, is nourishing and empowering and is an answer to the despair that we have to deal with all the time when we deal with the realities in the rest of our lives. . . . We need each other and ourselves even more."[73] She acknowledged that no matter how those female relationships progressed, they were, nonetheless, empowering and beneficial experiences that helped her endure the vicissitudes of life. Embracing all kinds of relationships—platonic, queer, or familial—sustained women. Black German women appreciated and practiced this approach.

At her presentations, Lorde also stressed the importance of respecting diversity among women. For her, women could advance common objectives through interracial coalitions and international projects. She clarified, "I am interested in making coalitions with anyone who shares a common goal. I work with white women and I am pleased to work with white women when we can work as equals and as peers in situations where we move toward common goals. It is the same way I welcome working with black men. We share common destinies, we share common goals. We have great differences and we need to be able to articulate those differences and work across them."[74] In doing so, women and men could stress their commonalities in constructive ways. Yet unity did not require diverse individuals to be identical to one another. Privileging "connected differences" led to fruitful exchanges and relationships and the promotion of goals that helped to challenge discriminatory practices in society.[75] At a *Schokofabrik* reading, Lorde urged activists in the white German women's movement to "accept antiracism and work against anti-[S]emitism as central to the women's movement or it will die." She reaffirmed that "not because racism and anti-[S]emitism are outside altruistic concerns, but because they are central, central to any kind of movement."[76] Again, at a 1989 reading, she revealed, "No matter what the differences are between us as women, black and white, there are some real battles that we share. . . . [I]f we do not solve the essential questions that lie between us, if we do not recognize the differences of our lives as Black women and white women rest assured we will still be slain."[77] Here again, Lorde recommended that all German feminists pursue intersectional and coalitional politics.

Lorde also facilitated connections between different groups of women within the Black diaspora. She strove to "open lines of communication for instance between Afro-European and Afro-American women, between Afro-European and Afro-American writers." Lorde regarded the cultivation of kinships and political alliances to be just as important as writing communities, believing that they both required dedication and a commitment to activism. She averred, "Well, I hope there is a growing network of women of color happening on an international level, I hope there is a growing network of women of color writers. If I have anything to do about it there will be that kind of network and it will increase. I think it is absolutely necessary that we make contact with each other across national boundaries and if we recognize, here again, there are similarities and there are differences."[78] Black German women adapted those ideas and established community with their Black compatriots in spite of their differences. At a 1990 reading in Stuttgart, for instance, Lorde asked white German women in the audience to leave, and then invited all the Black women to stay and talk with her and each other.[79] Moreover, in *A Burst of Light*, Lorde revealed her elation with her exhilarating, yet exhausting work in Berlin and the connections that Afro-German women had made. She reflected, "I am excited by these women, by their blossoming sense of identity as they're beginning to say in one way or another, 'Let us be ourselves now as we define us. We are not a figment of your imagination or an exotic answer to your desires. We are not some button on the pocket of your longing.' I can see these women as a growing force for international change, in concert with other Afro-Europeans, Afro-Asians, Afro-Americans."[80] Presenting in Dresden, six months after the fall of the Berlin Wall, where she first met Black Germans from the East, Lorde remarked, "More particularly, or more continentally, you must know that you sit here as part of an international community. . . . and this is a[n] [Afro-European] community from which the world has not yet heard."[81] She saw the potential of Black German women and valued their ability to be a political force. Indeed, Lorde practiced what she preached, as she intentionally sought relationships with Afro-German and other Black European women. Those women used their correspondence with her as a form of belonging and as an emotional outlet, developing new ideas and norms in the process.

BLACK GERMAN AND BLACK EUROPEAN WOMEN'S ATTACHMENTS TO LORDE

Forging community through their correspondences, Black German women affirmed the significance of female bonds with Lorde and other Women of Color. These ties helped them survive in a German society that inaccurately imagined itself as white. Given Afro-Germans' heterogeneity, Lorde's ideas about the diaspora and kinship served as a model for members in the Black German movement: a model that embraced differences yet recognized commonality through experiences of marginalization and that sought bonds with communities of color enduring similar predicaments. Their correspondence to Lorde also exemplifies a "covenant of women-bonding." For Lisa McGill, Lorde staged "*Zami*'s community of women by first locating the ways in which she, her lovers, friends, foremothers, and Afrekete form a covenant of women-bonding."[82] Lorde consciously cultivated kinships with women, and so, too, did Black Germans. Yet it is also through their correspondence and practices that these women became an affective community.[83]

Either by typewriter or putting ink to paper, Black German women wrote letters conveying their love, respect, and admiration of Lorde. Writing from the mid-1980s until Lorde's death, Black German correspondences illustrate how important she remained in their lives long after her public appearances and visiting professorship at the FU. Writing to Lorde took courage because of her prominence in feminist, lesbian and gay, and Black diasporic circles and because Black German women wrote in English, not in German, which Lorde could not read or speak fluently. By writing in English, these women connected to this international community, although it is unclear how frequently Lorde responded to them. In several cases, Ayim, Oguntoye, Marion Kraft, and Ika Hügel-Marshall had sustained correspondences and personal interactions with Lorde. Schultz also exchanged letters with Lorde, and she, along with her partner, Hügel-Marshall, and Ayim developed strong personal friendships with Lorde and her partner, Gloria Joseph. Ayim, Hügel-Marshall, and Schultz visited Joseph and Lorde; Joseph and Lorde often stayed with Schultz and Hügel-Marshall on their trips to Berlin.[84] Schultz, Kraft, and Oguntoye even sent letters to Joseph, who also became a significant figure for Black German women in the movement. Friends to the end, Schultz, Hügel-Marshall, and Ayim were present when Lorde succumbed to liver cancer in St. Croix.[85]

Black German women communicated their attachment to Lorde through motherly and sisterly metaphors, common to the period's Black and Euro-American feminist writings. Their growing connections to Lorde transcended cultural, linguistic, and national boundaries. Black German Nicola Lauré al-Samarai, of Palestinian and East German descent, referred to Lorde as "my dearest and so near Audre" and wrote, "Thinking of you, of your warm smile give [sic] me the strength and the power I need to overcome my doubtfulness. So, my dear mothersisterfriend, I want to send you lots of greetings and good wishes to you-hopefully-peaceful island and I hope that you are o.k., that your work is going on and your activities are successful."[86] As a "mothersisterfriend," Lorde drew Lauré al-Samarai in with her warmth and made a familial connection attainable. Marion Kraft, a biracial African American and German woman, claimed in a letter, "You are the 'big sister' I have always longed for, and beyond all possible differences we both must learn to live with and accept, this sisterhood is real."[87] In another letter, Ayim, a biracial Ghanaian and German woman who emerged as one of the movement's most prominent literary voices, claimed, "It was on the 9th November demonstrations where I recited 3 poems. I was wearing your warm embracing jacket[,] Audre[,] and I felt as one of your daughters." Occurring in East and West Berlin as well as other cities, these mass protests on November 9, 1989, were peaceful civic acts that helped to bring the Berlin Wall down. Signifying Lorde's influence, Ayim presented at an event in Berlin, where she introduced herself as a poet for the first time and acknowledged that, "poetry becomes a more and more powerful part in my life."[88] These examples illustrate how Black German women expressed a symbolic filial connection to Lorde. They gained access to a strong Black female figure—a godmother/mother, a sister, a friend, and a mentor—that was previously unavailable in their white German families. Yet extending beyond biology, their attachments to Lorde offered them new familial ties and a sense of acceptance. They privileged radical kinships.

With their correspondences, Black German women also explored alternative forms of intimacy that informed their identities and practice of diasporic belonging. They showed their emotional attachments to Lorde by providing her with personal sketches and poems and showering her with affectionate phrases. Using the salutation "Dearest Audre" in a letter, Ayim also sent her "love and kisses and I wish you can feel it as much as I always feel you in my tough times," and "Audre, I embrace you and kiss you all over."[89] Lorde inspired a sense of affective kinship among Black German women no matter their sexual identity. The women openly revealed their feelings, often ending their letters with "I send my love to you," "In sisterhood," "Much love," "Love Your sister," or "You are with us, Audre, I embrace you Love."[90] Kraft concluded in one letter, "Today, I'm finishing this letter, pointing out again, how glad I am to have made your acquaintance, and how important your work is to me. With love and respect, Marion."[91] With those sentiments, these women relayed their love for Lorde and engaged in a politics of belonging, constituting new customs through their relationships with her and one another. Black German women's emotional expressions also represented their efforts to embrace love or to embody what bell hooks has referred to as an "ethic of love," or considering love as a liberatory act. Practicing their "ethic of love," Black German women built their affective, diasporic community and sought positive change and justice within Germany. Their letters to Lorde afforded them opportunities to embody "love as the practice of freedom" in their personal lives and in their movement.[92]

Lorde's impact remained even after she left Germany, as Black German women revealed that their previous encounters with and relationships to her were heartening. Kraft wrote in a letter:

> Thank you so much for your letter! It arrived on a day I felt particularly bad, and it really did cheer me up!" I would have written much earlier, but as I said, I didn't feel well lately. Returning from a lovely and peaceful holiday in France, I found myself being confronted with the same old tiring stupidities one has to deal with if you are Black *and* German in this country. I was in kind of a depressed mood. . . . I've also been thinking about you very often, and your work, experiences, your strength and your friendship really mean an enormous amount to me![93]

Ayim also shared, "There is always a line in your poems to give me company to help me through. . . . you are very important to me Audre[,] and you will always be!"[94] In another letter, Lauré al-Samarai stated that "Dear Audre, all of us miss you and when we are together we always remember you."[95] Oguntoye, of Nigerian and East German descent, expressed that, "I enjoyed the dinner with you at Dagmar[']s. To see you again was so warm and strengthening."[96] Again stressing Lorde's influence, Kraft wrote, "Your engagement in the question of Afro-German women was really very important, and personally it means a lot for me to have dealt with your writings and to have made your acquaintance!"[97] Lorde was a valuable resource who helped them process their place in the diaspora and a dominant white German context.

Black German women regarded Lorde's personality, literature, and readings as vital gifts of love. Black German Hella Schültheiß treasured Lorde, remarking "I am very happy that you have been here—a wish of my heart was fulfilled. You know, you have taught me a lot through your books, your way of reading and your way of being there and I am very grateful to you—because it is not a matter of course, it's a present, it is love. . . . I write to you and I look at our photographs and I am very glad I've got acquainted with you and I wished you [sic] book something good with you from me, from our group and from Stuttgart."[98] Similarly, Ayim admitted, "We/I(!) miss [you], but you left a lot of warmth and strength to stay here with me/with us. You gave me so much courage these last years."[99] In another letter, Kraft insisted, "Audre, you are one of the very few persons/women in my life who have left a deep impression and brought about changes, and the power to carry on! Yes, you and me are different, too, but what we have in common is our history as Black women, women of the African diaspora, a token, a myth, a tool, a hope, and a vision and a need-to survive."[100] These affective connections offered them diasporic kinships that rooted them. Their attachments to Lorde gave Black German women a positive model of resilience, courage, and power. The women also obtained emotional comfort from Lorde and created their affective community by sharing their common interests and goals and establishing a positive self-image.

Moreover, in a birthday fax, Hügel-Marshall, of African American and German heritage, wrote, "All my knowledge from your works [is] in me and came out of me. Audre you can be very proud. I am sad because I [cannot] write [E]nglish enough to write all my thoughts and feelings in this letter. Have a very nice birthday."[101] Hügel-Marshall derived energy from Lorde and her work, which guided her literary and artistic endeavors. In a letter, Sheila Mysorekar, of Indian and German ancestry, asked, "*How* do you manage to channel you [sic] energy so effectively? I wish you all the best, for love & life & health & writing, and HAPPY BIRTHDAY (since I don't know the date, the wishes come *now*)."[102] Their letters represent how Black German women were

Figure 3. "Audre Lorde with May Ayim, Katharina Oguntoye, Ika Hügel-Marshall, Dagmar Schultz, and other women," photograph by Dagmar Schultz, Berlin-Kreuzberg, April 1990, Freie Universität Berlin, Universitätsarchiv, V/N-47 Audre Lorde, Sig. 184.

"oriented" toward Lorde, especially as she triggered so much love from so many women long after her departure. As Sara Ahmed has noted, "Emotions involve such affective forms of (re)orientation. It is not just that bodies are moved by the orientation they have; rather, the orientation we have toward others shape the contours of space by affecting relations of proximity and distance between bodies. . . . Orientations shape not only how we inhabit space, but how we apprehend this world of shared inhabitance, as well as 'who' or 'what' we direct our energy and attention toward."[103] Black Germans' emotional expressions also contained acts of transfer that provided them with support and confidence to pursue their own projects, produce new ideas, and continue their practice of the ethic of love.

Oguntoye emphasized how Lorde engaged in Black women's internationalism, reaching so many women worldwide. She reflected on her experiences at the 1990 "I am Your Sister: Forging Global Connections Across Differences" conference that took place in Boston, Massachusetts. More than a thousand participants from twenty-two countries came to honor Lorde's life and work.[104] Oguntoye wrote, "I think it was great! It was so exciting to see all the women telling about their lives and how you and your work gave them courage. Also to me you are very precious and I thank you so much for all you did for me and for the Afro-germans [sic]

[and] black people in Germany and for the german womens [sic] movement." She expressed excitement about attending the conference, hearing the testimonies of diverse women, and interacting with Women of Color. The conference offered Oguntoye comfort and helped her practice Black women's internationalist feminism, which confronted global forms of oppression. She recognized Lorde's compassion for human rights in and beyond Germany and confided her hope to maintain a similar zeal. Later in the letter, she delighted in spending time with Lorde in Boston and "was very [proud] to help and enjoyed it a lot."[105]

Black German women also demonstrated the power of bonding and Black women's internationalism by developing stronger diasporic connections with women from across the globe who confronted discrimination. As Oguntoye observed in a letter, "It is quite a motivation to hurry up a bit, that I can meet Jean and other black women in America and [Britain] again. There are so many other women I want to meet. . . . My feeling also tells me that [these] connections are urgently necessary for me to do my work good in Germany and to live my life."[106] Meetings with other Black women and Women of Color motivated Oguntoye to continue her activism. Highlighting the significance of Black women's kinships, Kraft penned, "For me and Helga [Emde] it was a great pleasure to share our ideas and emotions with so many Black women from all over the world! Helga and I have become very close friends (smile), and I think we've only just begun to realize how much we need each other."[107] Kraft appreciated "sharing" her thoughts with other women and developing friendships and networks with them. Her friendship with Emde, in particular, provided her with a sense of camaraderie. Mysorekar expressed a connection to not only her Black German sisters, but also her Black German brothers. She wrote, "Yes, there are Black Germans in the GDR. They are organized and very active. Not only for them, but also for us a totally new world has opened up. In spite of all this reunification talk & 'Germany for Germans'-shouting, I'm hopeful & excited about the link up with our 'brothers and sisters from the East'-our *Black* brothers & sisters!"[108] Mysorekar underscored the attachments that she began to cultivate with her Black German compatriots in the East—relationships that were important with the resurgence of violent ethno-nationalism and xenophobia after reunification.[109] Writing to Lorde again, Kraft stated, "And I want you to discover your own strength, rediscover it for yourself, because to us women around the world, women of the African diaspora, you have given so much, words cannot describe."[110] Through Kraft's ties to Lorde and the global diaspora, she discovered a sense of belonging and persevered in a white German society where she felt othered.

Their letters also highlighted some of the ambivalences and problems that emerged with forging connections to others. Oguntoye stressed, "May [Ayim] and me reading some of *Farbe bekennen* and a group of [J]ewish and non [J]ewish women [Lesbisch-Feministische Shabbeskreis] reporting their results and thoughts. It was a long. . . . but good discussion about [a]nti-Semitism and racism. Problems of understanding and [the ability to] understand became [visible]. . . . I found it difficult to come forward and not [become] involved (verwickelt) into this endless fighting including reproaches and selfdefences [sic]."[111] She revealed how in-fighting, indifference, and the inability to understand each other in a practical way often made cooperation among women difficult. Similarly, Kraft informed Lorde, "Unfortunately, there have been some misunderstandings and quarrels at the latest Black German women's meetings. And here again, I think we must learn to understand and accept differences, and that we need one another."[112] Writing about the tensions within the Black German community, Oguntoye stated, "I had some fights within the afro-german [sic] women's group. The conflict with Helga [Emde] and with Marion [Kraft] exploded. But really sorry I feel for the argument I had with Domenica [Grokte] (one of the twins), because I like her very much. Dose [sic] that mean growing up, to stand through the fights with people one loves?"[113] Black Germans' exchanges and bonds with other Women of Color and each other comprised of a number of emotions and experiences that remained mutually constitutive elements for them. In this way, Black German women continued to form their affective community, tensions and all.

Interestingly, Kraft and Oguntoye detailed some of the hostilities that existed within earlier meetings of the feminist organization ADEFRA, detailed in chapter 3. Lorde was critical in encouraging the group's mobilization. While ADEFRA helped women find a degree of social cohesion, its female composition did not free it from internal strife. A number of concerns emerged about homosexual and heterosexual alliances, generational differences about sexuality, and the collective goals of a variety of women. Ironically, skin color also proved to be a problem, even as Black Germans were discriminated against based on their physical differences.[114] Some were suspicious of their lighter-skinned compatriots, especially those who looked as if they could pass for white. Kraft saw these disputes in ADEFRA as an opportunity to "learn to understand and accept differences" that would allow Black German women to grow with each other.[115] Despite points of disagreement, ADEFRA, along with the Black German female ties fostered by Lorde, remained, relative to much of white German society, supportive of the community and its burgeoning movement.

Later, Oguntoye captured what Lorde's influence upon Black Germans was when she stated, "A person with love as a source of power can achieve anything. This work of resistance, namely the difficult path to be able to accept the good and bad (unpopular) sides, this is the motivation that Audre Lorde's work offers us."[116] Bearing witness, Lorde encouraged Black Germans to learn and adopt what they could to help their communities. At a 1993 memorial celebration held for Lorde in Berlin, Kraft echoed similar sentiments, underscoring, "Her hope was [a] global sisterhood, and that we begin to see one another at the same time we begin to see ourselves. Self-definition and perception of the other is basic to Audre Lorde's work. Above all, we Afro-German women—and men—have benefitted from her gift of a pathway out of our socially-constituted personal and political isolation. We should do everything we can to continue down this path as she would have wished."[117] Both women attributed to Lorde a significant role in the development of the Black German movement.

Lorde's kinships with other Black European women signified her practice of Black women's internationalism. Those women's orientations toward her helped them create affective communities through their textual expressions, in which they thanked her for support, expressed concerns about her health, and explained her profound influence on their lives. In an undated letter, Amsterdam-based South African activist Tania Léon (née Ruth Naomi Léon) wrote, "You will never realize what your visits to Amsterdam meant to me. You contribute to my feeling important."[118] Monique Ngozi Nri, a Nigerian British poet, composed a letter, writing, "I was so sorry to hear that you are ill. Our thoughts are with you and we hope they give you a little strength now that you need it."[119] Afro-Scottish writer Jackie Kay also reflected, "I wanted to thank you Audre for all your support and enthusiasm. You've been a good friend. . . . Actually since 84, we've done pretty well. I've seen you at least once every year. That fills me with such gladness and appreciation."[120] Lorde's friendship contributed to Kay's well-being, giving her comfort and companionship. Likewise, Gloria Wekker, an Afro-Dutch activist and later a professor of anthropology and gender studies at the University of Utrecht, shared in a letter, "I thank you for your fruitfull [sic] gifts to me that will last me a lifetime, for making yourself a *home* of me, for wanting to share the beauty and joy the goddesses offered us."[121] Wekker's orientation to Lorde made her feel a sense of home that allowed her to experience Black joy and appreciate her place in the world.

Lorde also supported Wekker and Léon along with other Afro-Dutch women, such as Tieneke Sumter and José Maas, in their efforts to establish Sister Outsider, a feminist organization for Black and migrant women based in Amsterdam—named after Lorde's collection of essays. In a 2015 interview, Wekker remembered that Lorde "was full of life and joy," and "had an incredible intensity and focus. Being with her felt like basking in her light, and she made me feel beautiful and smart."[122] Owing to Lorde's encouragement, Wekker pursued antiracist work with Sister Outsider and organized civil servants of color in Amsterdam. Lorde even inspired Wekker's decision to pursue a PhD in anthropology at UCLA. These women practiced the ethic of love and used the encouragement that they received from her to embolden them, which proved important given the conservative turn in European politics in the 1980s.

Moreover, Lorde's correspondence represented her ability to engage in a variety of relationships with women in Europe, in which some were platonic while others were erotic. A few letters demonstrate how some relationships with Lorde centered around Black lesbian sexuality. Wekker wrote in a letter, "How I have this feeling of fulfillment [sic] that comes to me when I think of 6/23, and just the thought of you makes me [absolutely] want to take off on a cloud, smile, shake my head at your naughtiness." Their night together in Amsterdam left an impression on Wekker. Lorde was not merely a mentor or friend, but a lover that helped her indulge her desires and find pleasure. She complimented Lorde, "You are quite a lovely lady. I enjoyed all of you, all you's [sic] of you, especially your strong legs and ass!"[123] In another letter, Wekker confided, "I do hope it is possible for me to come and see you. Actually I'll want to do more than that, I'm afraid. Just between you & me."[124] These few examples reveal that the intellectual and the erotic were intertwined in ways that provided a dual sense of pleasurable kinship only available to those who came into intimate—either scholarly or sensually—contact with Lorde.

In addition to expressing affection for Lorde, these women wrote to her to receive intellectual support for their literary work. As Nri recalled, "I have been thinking of you often through last year and today after digging out all my poems which only amount to about 35 after 5 years—I started to re-read *Sister Outsider* and *The Chosen Poems* for a little inspiration and courage to let somebody else see them."[125] In the same letter, Nri also sent along four pages of poems for Lorde to review.[126] Philomena Essed, an Afro-Dutch activist and scholar, sent Lorde her "first paper in English" entitled "Racism in Everyday Experiences of Black Women" and maintained "Comments from you are *most welcome!*"[127] Wekker also recognized the importance of Lorde's feedback in a letter, writing "I send you now the abstract of my article. . . . Can you advise me on which U.S. women's magazine would be interested in publishing it[?]"[128] These expressions demonstrate how these women built trust with Lorde and how she aided them in their creative and intellectual endeavors. Taken together, all of these Black European women embodied an affective community through a constellation of expressions and practices that represented similar sentiments and carried overlapping meanings.

* * *

Audre Lorde's oeuvre, personality, and presence served many important functions in the lives of Black German women, both individually and collectively. Lorde transmitted new ideas and practices that informed Black German women's perspectives about identity, kinship, and activism. She impressed upon these women to explore their emotions and turn to writing as concrete sources for growth, self-definition, and activism. As a result of their exchanges and encounters, Black German women began to exude more self-confidence, gaining a positive understanding of their diasporic identity and learning to feel like Black Germans and, by extension, Black Europeans. These women became an affective community, navigating and using their feelings for empowerment and kinship. Poetry and the emotions that Lorde associated with it also emerged as a tool for establishing new diasporic linkages and relationships. Their ties with one another and other Women of Color provided them with a sense of belonging. Black German women exemplified a variety of emotions and connections—familial, affective, and diasporic—with Lorde and each other. Similarly, Lorde moved and sometimes aroused Afro-Dutch, Afro-Scottish, and Black British women. Shaping their convictions, confidence, and intimacy, she assisted them in their literary pursuits and made them feel as if they and their work mattered.

Their correspondences and relationships to Lorde also helped Black German women enact their membership to the Black diaspora. Lorde's mantra of connected differences proved important for them in the early stages of their movement. Through her mentoring and engagement, Afro-German women developed skills that made them agents of their own destinies by claiming recognition and campaigning against racism and discrimination in Germany and elsewhere. Her influence also inspired them to create cultural and political initiatives that addressed their needs in West and reunified Germany and that continued to exclude and discriminate against them. Lorde's presence and ability to forge bonds in Germany guided Black German women and helped them refashion themselves into empowered Black subjects capable of engendering and disseminating knowledge about their experiences while also producing creative, diasporic spaces that rendered them visible. This was apparent with the groundbreaking 1986 volume *Farbe bekennen: Afro-deutsche Frauen auf den Spuren ihrer Geschichte,* which I examine in chapter 4. Black German women used their newfound motivation and excitement to collectively unify and establish two Black German associations—ADEFRA and ISD—that continued to broaden their sense of solidarity and relieve them of their isolation.

Black German women established a new social fabric through their diasporic community that depended on writing, emotions, "ethic(s) of love," and kinships to retain recognition and build supportive networks and sites of change in Germany. Black Germans owed a profound debt to Lorde, especially as her presence and efforts influenced the making of the modern Black German movement in the 1980s. Lorde's willingness to mentor, support, and connect with these women and others embolden them to mobilize, forge community, construct their narratives, as well as pursue intellectual and diasporic activism. But she was not the only diasporic resource that they had. As the next chapter on ISD demonstrates, these women and men pursued exchanges and connections with many across the Black diaspora in Germany, which also impacted their movement.

THE MAKING OF A MODERN BLACK GERMAN MOVEMENT

As evidenced by their relationship with Lorde, Black Germans gladly forged ties and collaborated with other Black diasporic communities in Germany. Reflecting this tendency was a 1987 interview with Black German activist-intellectuals May Ayim and John Kantara (née John Amoateng) that the African Writers Association (AWA) conducted in its magazine *AWA-FINNABA: An African Literary Cultural Journal*.[1] In the interview, Ayim explained, "We are called 'Initiative Schwarze in Berlin', all of us black Germans feel this isolation and would like to meet. . . . Amongst us are Afro-Germans (in the majority), Afro-British and even Afro-Russians." Kantara reflected, "The reason why people have joined our group, is for me an emotional one, this feeling to get to know other black Germans. Up to now most of us have been living in isolation. What we have lacked is a disciplined and engaged group which will bring us together. As a group we can better react to racism, protect ourselves."[2] Ayim continued, "We are all confronted with marginalization in this society. I'm not sure whether everybody would call this racism. We want to do something against it. We are tired of being alone amongst white people and having always to explain your feelings. You see here in Germany there's no real discussion about racism. They talk of *Ausländerfeindlichkeit,* but seldom call it racism. . . . They [White Germans] would like to see us as a problem. These poor Afro-Germans, they are mixed. They have a problem. We have no problem with our colour, but the society creates difficulties for us." Kantara acknowledged, "There's a certain image, a wrong image society has of us. Seen in a historic view, this image was created during the time of German colonies in Africa. They saw blacks as colonial subjects. Today the society still has these images and w[e] are trying to correct that."[3] As they stressed in the interview, their diasporic organization confronted racism in a German nation that imagined itself as exclusively white and that relied on an "ideology of 'racelessness,' " which was and remains a dominant public discourse that deliberately obscures the persistence of racial thinking and racial practices in Europe.[4] As a result, many white Germans rendered their Black compatriots invisible as Germans or "Others-from-Without," who were presumed to be "primitive savages" or always arriving in, but existing outside the nation.[5] This German imagining excluded them from the national polity.

Ayim and Kantara emphasized the necessity of cultivating affective and diasporic connections to their fellow Black German compatriots and other racialized minorities in Germany. Together these two and other Black Germans ushered in a modern movement through their establishment of a local Berlin chapter of ISD.[6] Additional chapters emerged across Germany. Collectively, Black Germans' efforts at unity and resistance involved the practice of coalitional politics as they campaigned for equality, human rights, and social justice in Germany. While Black German feminists and lesbians are often credited as the pioneers of the movement, Black German men, like Kantara, were also important figures.

This chapter offers the first detailed history of ISD, including some of its local chapters, to demonstrate how Afro-German activist-intellectuals promoted their politics and poetics of representation that affirmed their positions as German and diasporic citizens, in turn making them legible as Black Germans. Uniting across their diverse backgrounds, Black Germans also cultivated a new sense of self that was increasingly rooted in a Black diasporic consciousness. The Initiative, along with its sister organization ADEFRA, examined in chapter 3, resulted in the emergence of the modern Black German movement in the mid-1980s. Both were membership-driven organizations, in which their members hoped to precipitate change by unsettling the German hegemonic order that had long othered and silenced them. They did so by inventing new diasporic traditions that were repetitive symbolic rituals or practices that imparted values and norms and that connected overlapping diasporic pasts with the present.[7] With their local organizations, meetings, and events, Black Germans' invented traditions centered Blackness across different spacetimes.[8] Sharing this sentiment, Black German activist and journalist Sheila Mysorekar wrote, "As Black people, we have had to create ourselves; there was nobody to teach us, no place to go to."[9] Arguably, their new traditions, including consciousness-building workshops, antiracism protests, and other activities, gave them a sense of purpose and substantiated their identities.

Gaining agency, they produced Black spaces symbolically and geographically for themselves, their community, and their allies, proving that Black Germans and other People of Color belonged in the nation. Through spatial politics, they made their groups and organizational events fixtures in society and used diverse locations in urban cities as modes of resistance and survival, which created spaces for cultural reform, inclusivity, and justice. Their spatial politics also integrated diasporic resources from across the globe, showcasing the diversity of Black culture and history and linking them to public settings throughout Germany. As they claimed spaces in the nation, Black Germans also formed intellectual communities, becoming quotidian intellectuals who used vernacular forms to engender alternative discourses on colonialism, racism, and identity and to destabilize traditional German norms and exclusionary practices. These forms of intellectual activism guided their spatial politics. The organizations not only served as cultural and intellectual sites, but also as political and advocacy groups, offering Black Germans and others in the diaspora different levels of support. Though the number of individuals who formally participated in the movement ranged in the hundreds, Black Germans' efforts at grassroots mobilization still constitute a movement because it involved an intergenerational group of people working together to advance their goals and to provoke change in Germany and beyond.

Exploring this new wave of Black German activism from the 1980s to the 2000s not only considers how ISD developed organizationally, but how its members invented traditions and constructed spaces that exemplified Black thought and action in Germany. Their troubling presence (for some white Germans) and movement building constitute a part of a long tradition of Black radicalism. Just like their predecessors throughout the Black diaspora, Black Germans asserted their humanity and political rights and redefined their positions while also opposing different manifestations of white supremacy at home and abroad.[10] While Black Germans' activism mirrored other diasporic movements across the globe, they also differed from them based on their everyday realities of isolation and othering in mostly white postwar German cities. Yet they found acceptance through the ties they forged in their movement.

"WO IST DEINE HEIMAT—ICH MEINE, DEINE RICHTIGE?"[11]: THE ORIGINS OF THE INITIATIVE

In the invitation letter for the first national meeting of Black Germans, held in Wiesbaden near Frankfurt on November 2, 1985, Christiana Ampedu, Helga Emde, and Eleonore Wiedenroth-Coulibaly (née Eleonore Wiedenroth) sarcastically asked Black German readers a familiar question: "Where is your homeland, I mean your real one?" Black Germans were tired of the common belief that "to be German meant to be white" and of everyday encounters with their white German compatriots, in which they answered invasive personal questions, explaining that they were born and/or raised in Germany.[12] In asking this question, they appealed to the common experience of marginalization that their Black compatriots endured in a majority-white society. The meeting was also inspired in part by Christel Priemer's documentary *Germans are white, Negroes cannot be Germans* (*Deutsche sind weiß, Neger können keine Deutschen sein*); the title of the film came from a postcard that the women were sent because of the announced Wiesbaden meeting.[13] Before the November meeting, Wiedenroth-Coulibaly, Emde, Marie Theres Aden, and other Black German women met informally at one another's homes, demonstrating the importance of kitchen-table politics in Germany and signaling that a series of moments led to the launch of the movement.[14] But this initial public meeting allowed Afro-Germans from across the country to unite, socialize, and share their mutual experiences of alienation, exclusion, and frustration.

Over the same period, Ayim, Katharina Oguntoye, and Dagmar Schultz held some of the early research meetings and interviews for the volume *Farbe bekennen*. These exchanges inspired Afro-Germans to seek interpersonal contact. For many Black German women, the volume, published in June 1986, became a medium through which connections and social networking became possible. As Oguntoye later intimated, "Everything really began with *Farbe bekennen*," which "was the trigger, catalyst, and an inspiration for this generation."[15] The importance of the volume was continually referenced in ISD and ADEFRA brochures.[16] As I argue in chapter 4, this pioneering volume served as an epistemic act, enabling Black German women to tell their truths, recover the histories of Black Germans, and introduce knowledge about the gendered and racial inequalities they faced.

The first national meeting in Wiesbaden sparked their modern movement and made them feel like Black Germans. Wiedenroth-Coulibaly, Emde, and Ampedu advertised the event in print, on television, and on the radio in the region. These women later used this event to establish a Black German group in the Hessen and Rhineland-Palatinate areas, located in the west-central and western part of the country, respectively.[17] In a follow-up letter to participants on November 26, the organizers expressed their excitement at the number of Afro-Germans who traveled long distances to take part in the event. Afro-Germans' attendance at the meeting proved that "the idea for such a meeting was not at all wrong."[18]

A few discrepancies exist concerning the number of Black Germans at this event. Some claim that approximately one hundred Black Germans ranging from teenagers to forty-year-olds attended, while others suggest that only thirty or so were there.[19] Regardless of the numbers, the meeting had an affective impact on Black Germans that led many to reassess their lives. The meeting, Emde recalled, "was overwhelming. About one hundred Black people from all over Germany. It was breathtaking. Black people of all shades, sizes and ages. And the most confusing moment for me was hearing the language, German, not English. And only Black people."[20] Emde's recollection rooted Blackness in Germany, allowing her to embrace her Black Germanness and acquire a positive self-worth. For several of these Black Germans, the meeting was the first time they had direct contact with one another. Confirming this point was Black German activist, author, and artist Ika Hügel-Marshall. In fact, she was thirty-nine years old when she met Afro-German and Black people for the first time at the initial 1985 meeting.[21] Their ideas and interactions at this event helped them forge kinships. Disclosing their personal narratives affirmed that they all shared a common predicament. Listening to their fellow compatriots' narratives, however, proved difficult for some, especially as the discussions brought back painful memories of their own pasts. Nonetheless, the meeting opened up possibilities for Black Germans, and the organizers urged participants to write, call, or visit to share their experiences about the meeting and to offer suggestions for future projects.[22]

There is a consensus that the Initiative was established between the years 1985 and 1986. But several discrepancies exist in both the primary and secondary sources about the founding year of the local chapters of ISD that emerged in urban cities. According to Oguntoye, "[Eleonore Wiedenroth-Coulibaly] was also one of the female initiators of the first Afro-German group meeting in Wiesbaden-Frankfurt a.M., that occurred in 1985 and led to the 1986 establishment of ISD in Berlin." She continued, "Then, in 1986 the first meeting of ISD took place and the book *Farbe bekennen* was published."[23] Emde also claimed that the November 1985 meeting in Wiesbaden led to the creation of the Initiative of Black Germans.[24] Recalling the early stages of the group, Jeannine Kantara, an ISD-Berlin activist and later journalist for the prominent newspaper *Die Zeit*, claimed, "A few weeks after the release of *Farbe bekennen* some Afro-Germans from Berlin traveled to Wiesbaden for the national meeting of the Initiative of Black Germans (ISD), which had just been founded in Hessen. Inspired by this meeting, the Initiative of Black Germans e.V. was established in the spring of 1987." Prior to the establishment of ISD-Berlin, specifically "when the Saarland

Broadcasting Service aired the 1986 documentary, 'Germans are white, Negroes cannot be Germans,' " Kantara stated, "we were approximately twenty young [Afro-Germans] in a Berlin backyard apartment who came together in order to watch the movie and discuss it."[25] Some of these inconsistencies have to do with individual members' memories of the movement's initial stages and their involvement in local chapters. They also suggest the urgency of documenting these histories, particularly as the founders age. Here, issues of the past and memory need to be taken into consideration when studying the modern Black German movement. Their recollections and acts of remembrance may mirror other Germans' efforts to navigate and value their past.[26]

ISD afforded Black Germans an opportunity to mobilize, in which they attempted to "find out our own history" and to share goals and insights about multiple topics.[27] At a grassroots level, their activism served as a corrective in German society. They made their presence known and pushed for concrete antiracist changes in language, legislation, and representation. As Black Germans' diasporic activism in ISD blossomed, so, too, did their perspectives and events.

UNDERSTANDING THE INITIATIVE

Nationwide Initiative chapters sought to challenge the marginalization, discrimination, and isolation that Afro-Germans endured in a majority-white environment that still dealt with everyday racism.[28] Several Black German activists have noted, "With the creation of. . . . the Initiative of Black Germans, ISD for short, [we] directly confronted two central illusions within the Federal Republic. The first illusion was: 'Germany is not an immigration country,' and the other: 'There is no racism in Germany.' "[29] Activist-intellectuals attempted to dismantle racist practices and beliefs and demanded inclusion as Black Germans, and supported others of African descent in Germany. This is reflected in the early title of the Berlin group, the Initiative of Blacks in Berlin. In addition to Ayim, Kantara, and Oguntoye, some of the members of this chapter were Nii Addy, Obi Addy, Abenaa Adomako, Angela Alagiyawanna, Daniel Alagiyawanna, Natalie Asfaha, Patricia Elcock, Danny Hafke, Jeannine Kantara, Katja Kinder, Nikolai Kinder, and Mike Reichel. Members' ages ranged from fourteen to thirty. In March 1987 ISD-Berlin's membership list had fifty-two people, and another one from April 1987 included forty-six people. A September 1988 membership list had ninety-five members, but additional individuals, who expressed interest and attended events across the city, could also be involved.[30]

Figure 4. "May Ayim with members of ISD," photographer unknown, 1986, Freie Universität Berlin, Universitäts-archiv, V/N-2 May Ayim (Opitz), Sig. 19.

Black German quotidian intellectuals undermined dominant representation of Germanness and counteracted their invisibility by establishing additional ISD chapters, locating themselves directly in the nation. The ISD-Rhine/Main chapter, established in 1986, included Magdy Abu-Gindy, Peter Croll, Helga Emde, Vera Holzhauser, Daniella Reichert, Eleonore Wiedenroth-Coulibaly, Susan Wright, and Gisela Wright. The ISD-Cologne/Düsseldorf chapter formed in 1986/87. Members included Rita Amoateng, Detlef Brimah, Carla de Andrade Hurst, Themba Kadalie, Theodor Michael, Sheila Mysorekar, Jacqueline Nkobi, and Anita Zwanbun. The siblings Christina, Domenica, and Fidelis Grotke were also members.[31] Between 1988 and 1991, ISD chapters sprung up in ten West German cities, including Kiel, Duisburg, Bielefeld, Mainz, Heilbronn, Stuttgart, and Hamburg/North, and "each group [was] independent and organized according to its needs but all groups accepted the name ISD." In fact, Marie Theres Aden also established the ISD-North group, along with Kwesi Anan Odum, Michael Botsio, and Thomas Hall.[32] By 1992 chapters in Berlin, Hamburg, and Rhine/Main still remained active, and ISD-North Rhine-Westphalia and BLACK (Badische Liga für Afrikanische Connection und Kommunikation) Freiburg groups also emerged. In addition, Black Germans founded BLACK

Heidelberg, BLACK Karlsruhe, and ISD-Bochum groups between 1992 and 1993, further signaling a diasporic orientation, and a Young Black Soul group with Black German youth began meeting in Frankfurt in 1994.[33]

Their efforts to build community did not preclude connections to the East. After the fall of the Berlin Wall, groups also materialized in the former GDR, such as East Berlin, Dresden, and Leipzig, though limited resources and organizational difficulties plagued these groups. Before the Wall fell, the East and West Berlin chapters had already worked together. By 1992 the Nogoma-Leipzig group emerged. Formerly called IG Farbig, the group changed its name given the negative connotation of "*Farbig*," which means "colored." In 1994 ISD-Berlin applied to the World Council of Churches (WCC) in Geneva, Switzerland to acquire funding to assist those groups in the former East. The chapter believed it was necessary given the increasingly public displays of racism and to strengthen support and solidarity networks.[34] Throughout the years, ISD members continued to contact the WCC and its Programme to Combat Racism (PCR), which was established in 1970, for financial support. As more ISD groups emerged, it revealed how the idea of an inclusive Black diasporic community resonated with others across Germany. ISD evolved into a network of community and cultural hubs that centered Black German and Black diasporic experiences and histories. Similar to other social movements, these groups eventually waxed and waned, with members coming and going owing to evolving interests and/or new professional and familial obligations materializing. Nonetheless, through their mobilization, they gained the often-sought recognition from their Black compatriots and other allies. For many this newly found recognition was "a form of 'symbolic dependence' " that shaped their diasporic sense of self and politics.[35]

Women drove many of the local ISD chapters, and some of them were lesbian feminists who saw their campaigns against racism as inextricably linked with their gendered and queer identities. The ISD-Munich chapter, which originated through a reading of *Farbe bekennen*, consisted largely of women, such as Jasmin Eding, Judy Gummich, and others. Later, Ria Cheatom and Mary-Ann Powell joined. But they actively searched for male members. Eventually, Black German men such as Tahir Della (née Thomas Della), Marc Reis, and others became involved.[36] Members in the ISD-Munich chapter expressed their own interests that reflected their individual experiences and pushed for personal connections with one another. They also had strong ties to feminist organizations in Munich. In Bielefeld, two women, one of whom was Marion Kraft, established a group based on the need for political work and an assessment of their personal experiences.[37] Women, several of whom were lesbians, mostly spearheaded the

Frankfurt and Cologne chapters. A number of these women were equally active in ADEFRA chapters. These women-led ISD groups privileged Black feminist perspectives and politics.

During early working group meetings, the members used their local branches to develop projects, evaluate their group's progress, and build their cultural autonomy. At a December 1987 meeting in Berlin, local ISD chapters sent representatives who shared their group's difficulties and accomplishments. ISD-Berlin had been around for a year and a half and relied on previous friendships, personal networks, and advertisements to expand their membership base.[38] ISD-Berlin members disclosed that they established five working groups with different focal points, including a children's and youth group; a women's group; a theater group; a cultural group; and a political group. Each working group devised plans that were then implemented. In fact it was through the cultural group that the idea for the annual Berlin Black History Month event and *afro look,* a Black German magazine, both discussed later in this chapter, developed. The ISD-Frankfurt/Wiesbaden group, also known as ISD-Rhine/Main and in existence for approximately two years by 1987, had organized monthly meetings and social activities.[39] But members of this chapter, who were between the ages of thirty and forty years, criticized themselves for allowing organizational matters to get the better of them, especially as some of the personal exchanges and events had ceased to happen. They decided to forego using local papers to advertise their meetings and activities because of problems that arose with the local press.[40] Whereas ISD-Frankfurt/Wiesbaden avoided the local press, interest in ISD-Cologne/Düsseldorf grew because of their distribution and circulation of flyers and advertisements in regional newspapers. Though the group's monthly meetings initially alternated between Cologne and Düsseldorf, travel proved a problem for some. In spite of this, the local chapter continued to cultivate close personal contacts by meeting and arranging social activities such as meet-ups, and these events would take place either weekly or monthly depending on the group and its activities.[41] These ISD chapters served as a source of socialization, in which Black Germans escaped their isolation. For those without Black parents or siblings, they frequently remained the only Black person in their day-to-day realities (family, work, school, and so forth). Moreover, they also used diasporic resources from Africa, the United States, and other locales and created a diasporic iconography that conveyed cultural meaning and represented their chapters and events in Germany.[42] Debates arose about official local and nationwide logos, as well as brochure and postcard designs. These examples reveal the different strategies Black Germans employed at the local level to build and sustain their movement.

While organizational dynamics differed within the local chapters, each group still exercised considerable autonomy and continued the overarching goals of antiracist work, community building, and empowerment. Its members created a constitution that was continually revised throughout the years. As an organization, the Initiative did not have a strict hierarchal structure with a president or vice president. But each of the chapters had a financial group (*Finanzgruppe*) comparable to a treasurer. The financial groups collected dues and held meetings to ensure transparency and accountability; they also acquired some monetary assistance from the state. The financial groups included a minimum of two people: one person to oversee the bank account and another to check all of the financial records, with the positions preferably occupied by one Afro-German woman and one man.[43] They attempted to maintain gender equity in representation, though some male ISD activists still harbored misogynist, sexist, and homophobic views. Individuals who held this finance position had to be members in their local groups. These groups defrayed the costs for local events and projects.

One of the keys to ISD's success was the occurrence of quarterly planning meetings, or *Koordinationstreffen* (KT) per year in different cities, which began in 1988 and continued into the 2000s.[44] Ideas for the KT emerged at a 1987 working group in Berlin. At these meetings, representatives from the local chapters met to coordinate activities, plan subsequent meetings, and report on their progress. Before the meetings, members of the financial groups were asked to bring reports along with the appropriate documentation to the KT. In addition to managing the budget, the local ISD chapters also discussed their internal group dynamics and long-term goals. At the 1991 KT in Berlin, for instance, ISD chapters debated instituting a speaker's council and a KT secretary. They envisioned that the council not only "would be chosen by the plenary assembly for a year," but it would have "the function of a board of directors and decided on the coordination meetings and represented ISD to other institutions." Moreover, "The Council will consist of three members," in which "at least one man and one woman must be represented." The speaker's council would issue official ISD statements and create a budget listing information about ISD group projects in September for the following year, to be approved at the coordination meeting.[45] The coordination meeting secretary would serve in an advisory board capacity rather than as a decision-making body and would help with the flow of information among the groups as well as the documentation of events within the larger movement. The position was approved in early 1993.[46] These discussions demonstrate how Black Germans' grassroots activism sought to be effective and efficient while also providing a political platform. The KT and the additional positions illustrate ISD members' efforts to provide more structure, stability, and accountability within the group. It reflects how these chapters created an internal governing structure and were far more systematic about their goals and approaches. In the early 1990s, there were conversations about making ISD a legally registered association, in which all the groups would be under one governing organization or remain as separate autonomous organizations. A hybrid of both approaches emerged.[47] As a site for diasporic formation, ISD's day-to-day organizing efforts nationally and regionally were contingent upon the important collective work that took place behind the scenes at these meetings.

As new chapters emerged in urban translocal cities, Black Germans deliberately inserted themselves in cafes, restaurants, and other settings, centering Black geographies and revealing their "rights to the city."[48] These translocal cities remained mostly inclusive and spaces for interconnectivity and solidarity. A number of universities and cultural institutions were located in these cosmopolitan areas and suggest that the Initiative drew their Black German and diasporic membership in part from professionals and students. But they prided themselves on being something more than a "club of intellectuals."[49] Yet in many ways, they were an intergenerational group of intellectuals, activists, agitators, and artists, who theorized and advanced messages that challenged Germany's myth of whiteness and color-blindness. Many of these German cities, such as Berlin and Munich, had long fostered intellectual communities and engendered a public culture from the eighteenth century onward. Black Germans drew on and expanded this culture and history. But they also relied on diasporic resources from South Africa, Nigeria, Britain, and the United States that helped them seize their Black intellectual authority and validate their ideas.

These local chapters represented a Black German spatial form of agency, in which they challenged their "double displacement" and erasure from the nation.[50] Their struggles reflected geographic contests over discursive claims to Black reclamation and ownership in society. In their local chapters, Black Germans engaged their levels of disavowal and mapped themselves into the nation.[51] The social spaces they constructed for their chapters and events shaped their racial and diasporic (re)formation. Their strength and fortitude allowed them to stake alternative claims to place and space and resist the oppressiveness of a majority-white German society. By inhabiting a variety of spaces and centering Blackness, they no longer allowed German racism to displace or silence them. This positioning was similar to other minority communities in Europe and Canada who were often misrepresented or ignored in national narratives.

Black German efforts at resistance enabled them to navigate a Germany that harbored essentialist ideas of citizenship and that validated an unspoken whiteness legislatively and culturally. They challenged these dynamics by confronting the country's colonial amnesia and forgetting, stressing the racist underpinnings of the still-standing German Nationality Law of 1913, and expressing their own version of citizenship that moved through and beyond the nation. Citizenship was always a lived experience for Black Germans. Their spatial acts were significant, since they were constantly read as Black subjects who were visibly non-German or Others-from-Without. ISD chapters also encouraged Black Germans to acknowledge and nurture a sense of self through the collective. They did this by critiquing the use of offensive language and stereotypes, disrupting previous negative connotations of Blackness, and reclaiming their agency. These spatial acts were practices of self-styling that enabled Black German identity to manifest and privileged different types of Black subjectivities that could be political and not just linked to phenotype.[52] As the ISD-Karlsruhe chapter claimed in their brochure, "With concepts such as 'Black German' and 'Afro-German' (based on Afro-American), as an expression of our cultural background, it cannot and should not be limited to origin or skin color alone. In fact, we want Afros to take the conventional hard step to determine their identity for themselves instead of it being determined for them"—a theme echoed by ISD-Rhine/Main.[53] Here, they also recognized the plight of other marginalized People of Color in Germany. Making sense of their environments, Black Germans not only used their local chapters to reimagine social spaces, but they also functioned as sites that allowed them to pursue their politics and poetics of representation and advance their ideas as quotidian intellectuals.

As quotidian intellectuals, they retrieved and shared Black diasporic narratives, engendering epistemic interventions in Germany. In the same *AWA-FINNABA* interview referenced in the beginning of the chapter, Kantara stated, "Marcus Garvey has said: 'A people without a knowledge of their history is like a tree without roots.' "[54] During its formative years, ISD cultivated its roots through several core objectives that involved the collection of Black Germans' personal and collective histories and the implementation of these findings into concrete action. It also arranged contact with other Black compatriots, instilled empowering messages, developed self-help programming, and initiated antiracism projects on national and international levels.[55] Its members embraced their Black German history and their collective memory across different spacetimes, which rooted them in the nation. The focus on disseminating history illustrated its members' willingness to create a space for intellectual inquiry, exchange, and community as well as the production of Black German knowledge at meetings and events in the public sphere. These practices constructed the everyday in content and form and explained German racism. While this intellectual project was important, they were well aware that it would not be enough to change the status quo.

Continuing this intellectualism, members also established a small library of Black authors that included works from Nigerian author Chinua Achebe to African American author Frank Yerby.[56] With this, Black Germans encouraged reading and learning about Black history more broadly, informing their diasporic thinking. They were not unlike their Black British counterparts who maintained similar practices.[57] They did not pursue intellectualism in isolation; their connections to their community, past and present, influenced it. ISD-Rhine/Main's 1989 brochure confirmed this sentiment, noting "To meet as Black Germans/ Afro-Germans, exchange ideas and engage with one another was a new experience for many of us. The isolation, to be surrounded predominantly by whites, without the support of a black community is common to all of us. Otherwise, we are very different, through our socialization, our age, our characters, our interests, our experiences in family life, hetero- or homosexual men or women, and in our connections to our black or white part of our heritage."[58] ISD-Rhine/ Main's members recognized the affective, political, and intellectual function and impact of their group. The group affirmed its members' differences with one another and shared their common experiences of exclusion and isolation. Black Germans' movement building foregrounded their diversity to achieve unity while also fostering intellectualism and distributing relevant materials about their diasporic history and organizational projects and events. All of these efforts formalized and built the field of Black German studies.

Unlike the German student and countercultural movements of the 1960s and 1970s, Afro-Germans were less concerned with theoretical claims about class-consciousness.[59] Though they levied critiques against the capitalist system, there was no effort to establish a Marxist-Leninist revolution, as was the case with some of the chapters of the Black Panther Party and other leftist groups in Germany, Britain, and the United States. Rather, ISD members were preoccupied with articulating an inclusive racial identity based on difference and turning to writing and diasporic politics as tools to challenge multiple forms of discrimination in Germany. The emergence of their movement was also a part of the alternative and new social movement scene of 1980s Germany, which included the Spontis, the Greens, squatters, the women's movement, and the agricultural co-ops. These groups pursued alternative politics and lifestyles, created new literary and artistic practices, and constructed an alternative public sphere, not unlike what Black Germans did through their movement.[60] Therefore, the modern Black German movement constitutes an overlooked history of both the German and Black Left.

In some respects, the Initiative was similar to other Black European organizations that lobbied and focused on the introduction of antiracist and antidiscriminatory legislation and offered cultural activities to shape their community's racial consciousness. Some of these organizations include the Coloured People's Progressive Association (1958), the Committee of African Organizations (1959), the British Black Panthers (1967), African Diaspora (Diaspora Africaine, 1985), Collective for Equal Rights (Collectif Égalité, 1998), Africagora (1999), and the Black Citizen Alliance (Alliance Noire Citoyenne, 2007).[61] Originally, the Initiative was not a lobbying group like the Inter-Racial Friendship Coordinating Council (1959) and the Campaign Against Racial Discrimination (1964), which attempted to hold policymakers in postwar Britain accountable, or the prominent Representative Council of France's Black Associations (Le Conseil Représentatif des Associations Noires, 2005) in France, which formed in response to the 2005 riots in the Parisian suburbs.[62] But local chapters evolved and attempted to change Germany's strict citizenship law and immigration policies, including asylum laws, pushed for antidiscrimination legislation, and demanded more tolerant language in school books, curricula, the media, museums, and everyday parlance, impacting all levels (individual, societal, state, and federal).[63] They also showed how these dynamics were linked to structural racism in Germany. With their diasporic radical diasporic political and intellectual tradition, they centered their experiences.

Initiative quotidian intellectuals undertook collaborative work with Black diasporic communities from different social backgrounds and tried to serve the needs and interests of African and Asian German communities as well as other racialized minorities living in Germany.[64] Black Germans thought that forging solidarities and pursuing coalitional politics would help them combat discrimination and prompt reform.[65] In another brochure, members of the ISD-Stuttgart chapter observed, "We believe that our joint activities reinforce solidarity inwardly and outwardly and strengthens us and gives us the ability to better endure everyday racism."[66] Additionally, ISD "wanted to raise awareness among white Germans with respect to all minorities in this country. This means that the self-image of Germans must be scrutinized and corrected, in which [white Germans] would finally recognize that we live in a multinational society."[67]

An example of this work included their collaboration with the Black Unity Committee (BUC), which was an antiracist coalition in Berlin founded during the first Black History Month (BHM) event in February 1990. It included ISD-Berlin, the Black Media Access (BMA), the Black Arts Movement (BAM), the

Institute for Black Research (IBR), Black Liberation Sounds (BLS), the African Student Union (ASU), and other organizations and individual activists; many of those groups emerged alongside the Black German movement. The BUC formed to address the increased incidents of violence against racialized Others—native and foreign born—after German reunification. Indeed, Berlin as an urban space contributed to translocal solidarity, especially with the rise of ethno-nationalism, and represented the dynamism of Black activism. The group arranged local activities and developed political strategies that demanded that the Senate, the city of Berlin, and the police establish better measures to protect Blacks "against daily racist terror."[68] This racist terror included verbal abuse, violent mob attacks, "lynchings," and murders at transit stops, public institutions, street corners, sporting events from young German white supremacists who wanted "to physically eliminate all non-Germans." These hostilities accelerated after the fall of the Berlin Wall.[69] The BUC also produced the first documentation of racial violence in Berlin and surrounding areas from the period of January to September 1990. The report included newspaper clippings and written statements about minorities who were attacked or killed by neo-Nazis, demonstrating that these incidents occurred frequently in both the East and West. By doing so, they created a collective memory of those racist incidents in the public sphere, signifying the critical role that intellectual activism played.[70]

ISD also collaborated with the Fountainhead Dance Theatre (Fountainhead Tanz Theatre), which was a production, performance, distribution, and teaching unit founded in Berlin by African American professors Donald Muldrow Griffith and Gayle McKinney Griffith, together with three other artists in 1980. Fountainhead hosted events that included ISD members in the 1980s and 1990s.[71] When the Antiracist-Intercultural Information Center (ARiC) Berlin began in 1993, it served as another collaborative partner for ISD, in which they hosted workshops and other events that tackled the problem of discrimination as expressed in German legislation and that promoted racial tolerance.

Moreover, in 2002, ISD together with ADEFRA, coordinated and hosted a "Community- Congress" along with the cooperation of the African Refugee Association (ARA), Black Student Organisation (BSO), Struggle of Students (SOS e.V.), and the Somali Women's Association (SOMFV). The conference allowed men and women in the Black community to meet and attend workshops that featured topics on navigating the European Union's laws, best practices against racism, negotiating people and ideological differences within the Black community, among others.[72] Another congress occurred in 2003. Alliance building remained a key component in many of the Initiative's organizational events, including its own Berlin BHM celebrations, examined briefly in the next section.

This ethos of local collaboration continues to this day. Together with other Black and People of Color organizations, ISD members have worked on the Campaign for Victims of Racist Police Violence (Kampagne für Opfer rassistischer Polizeigewalt, KOP), since it began in 2002, and the "Stop Racial Profiling" campaign that began in 2012. The latter campaign was prompted by a 2010 incident of a young Black German student on a train from Kassel to Frankfurt. Federal police officers profiled him by asking for his identity card in an effort to catch illegal immigrants. He refused and was arrested. He eventually sued the police and won his case in 2012. Both campaigns have sparked broader discussions about racism and whiteness and have sensitized the public to these topics. They have also disclosed the racist practices of the police and judicial proceedings. Actions in these groups have included organizing flash mobs, writing petitions, assisting victims of violence, and documenting and publishing reports on the number of racist incidents. Building on these efforts, the ISD-Frankfurt chapter sponsored an "International Day against Police Brutality" march in the spring of 2018.[73] ISD has worked with many other organizations across Germany.

From its inception, members in ISD thought about and practiced Black internationalism by seeking ties with individuals across the Black diaspora and other People of Color in order to combat racism and other forms of discrimination. For ISD, it was important "to strengthen the self-esteem of its individual members and to assert the rights of Blacks in German society, but [ISD] also aimed to develop contacts with Black movements in other countries." Nationalist and internationalist perspectives guided their cultural diplomacy, shaped their grassroots diasporic politics, and overlapped within the movement.[74] Black German activist-intellectuals also strengthened their commitment to anti-Apartheid and antifascism projects in Germany, organizing demonstrations and lectures. They forged contacts with members of Colours, a group of biracial and People of Color in Bern, Switzerland and members of Pamoja, a Black diasporic Austrian organization in Vienna.[75] Beginning in 1997, ISD and ADEFRA members and other groups in Germany and in the United States initiated a cultural exchange for Black Germans and African Americans, which included a kick-off congress entitled "Showing our Colors" at Howard University. This exchange was a fulfillment of Lorde's dream of an alliance between Black Germans and African Americans.[76] Black Germans also did not foreclose opportunities to work with white allies. ISD members have worked with the European Network Against Racism (ENAR), founded by civil rights activists in 1998 after the European Union (EU)'s 1997 European Year against Racism. ENAR has attempted to end structural racism in the EU. Those endeavors demonstrate that even as

Black Germans focused on developments in Europe, it did not result in them neglecting or relegating their own national or global concerns.

Unsurprisingly, this willingness to collaborate has remained. Recently, Black Germans have organized with the European Network of People of African Descent (ENPAD), a network of organizations for people of African descent in Europe formed in 2014 to raise awareness of anti-Black racism. ENPAD seeks to implement the objectives of the UN International Decade for People of African Descent (2015–2024); the decade's official German launch occurred in 2016.[77] Black Germans have also attempted to secure reparations for the Herero and Nama descendants from the German genocide in 1904 to 1908 and to repatriate the bones collected and housed in Berlin from the genocide back to Namibia. They have worked with the UN, including on the production of parallel reports to the Committee on the Elimination of Racial Discrimination (CERD) in 2015 and with the Working Group of Experts on People of African Descent during their visit to Germany in 2017.[78] Black German grassroots activism and internationalism prevails.

BLACK GERMANS' INVENTED TRADITIONS IN PRACTICE

With their local branches, Black Germans developed new diasporic traditions that established a sense of continuity, sociability, and kinship. These alternative customs fit their local conditions and helped them reimagine their community. The creation of these new rituals maintained a symbolic and practical function and was connected to their spatial politics. But these practices contrasted with other West German political groups that often relegated or ignored Black Germans' concerns with intersectionality and everyday racism. They engendered their new diasporic traditions through their quotidian intellectualism and grassroots activism in four ways.

First, the 1985 Black German meet-up in Wiesbaden began the annual tradition of a national meeting or *Bundestreffen* (BT) in different German cities.[79] As I argue in chapter 5, these national meetings exemplified the importance of Black Germans' construction and maintenance of Black geographies away from the white gaze that they have still maintained. Though they were located in public spaces across Germany, these events were only for Black Germans or other individuals of African descent. The BT enabled them to bond, negotiate their identities, develop their diasporic consciousness, and reclaim their positions within the nation. Through the BT, Black Germans cultivated and maintained friendships to one another that sustained the organization and promoted members' interests as well as the interests of others across the Black diaspora in Germany.

Second, building from their national meetings, ISD-Berlin established the BHM celebrations, beginning in February 1990. These events illustrated their consistent effort to publicly reinsert themselves in the nation. I also maintain in chapter 5 that the BHM events enabled Black German quotidian intellectuals to occupy places that decolonized whiteness and centered their Blackness and the Black diaspora in the nation while also simultaneously underscoring their internationalist solidarity with other People of Color within and outside the diaspora. Creating new meanings of belonging and Blackness, these annual events were sites of intellectualism in the everyday.

Third, in 1988, ISD-Berlin produced a journal entitled *Uncle Tom's Fist* (*Onkel Tom's Faust*) that exemplified Black German quotidian intellectuals in action. It became "the mouthpiece of the ISD-Berlin" and other chapters, but it soon represented the Black German community more generally.[80] While the idea for the journal came from ISD-Berlin's cultural group in the summer of 1987, it also involved the cooperation of members from other chapters. In naming their journal, the editorial team combined the docile and subservient figure of "Uncle Tom" from Harriet Beecher Stowe's *Uncle Tom's Cabin* (1852) with the empowering symbol of the fist, recalling the upraised fists of John Carlos and Tommie Smith at the 1968 Olympics in Mexico City.[81] In the first issue of the magazine, the editorial team stated, "The name *Uncle Tom's Fist* is a metaphor with which we want to symbolize that Blacks will no longer tolerate the racism and oppression of today! We have given Uncle Tom a fist to symbolize that we want to defend ourselves. We do not understand the fist, as one might think, as a sign of authority, but as a sign of an antiracist campaign."[82] They continued, "Uncle Tom was also a member of a minority group, as we are today. He did not have the power or the possibility to raise his voice and indict his slave owners or racism in general." "We want with our magazine," they maintained, "to be the voice of Uncle Tom and to denounce racism wherever it appears."[83] In this way, the editors were explicitly transnational, transcending the borders of the German nation-state to reveal how African American freedom struggles also related to Black Germans' experiences. For them, those transnational linkages were important to emphasize and build upon. Yet, the title was too controversial and militant for some members. Before further disputes emerged, the editors changed the title of the magazine to *afro look: a magazine of Black Germans* (*afro look: eine zeitschrift von schwarzen deutschen*) that same year.[84]

Afro look combined multicultural traditions and maintained antiracist and internationalist perspectives by offering wide-ranging materials on Black

Figure 5. Cover of *Uncle Tom's Fist*
no. 1 (1988), personal photograph in
author's private collection.

Germans and the Black diaspora.[85] The magazine also reflected Lorde's influence, as Black Germans creatively used writing and art to curate their experiences and address injustice. In its early years, *afro look* appeared at least once a year, but starting in 1993, the magazine became a quarterly. After 1997 the issues appeared sporadically until its final one in 1999. With the first few issues of *afro look*, ISD-Berlin's editorial team reached a quantity of fifteen thousand copies. After this, the number declined from one thousand to five hundred copies owing to arrangements made with the Student Union (Allgemeiner Studentenaussschuß, AStA) at the Freie Universität Berlin, where several ISD members were students. At the time, issues averaged three hundred copies sold.[86]

Afro-Germans used the magazine as a form of knowledge production, social justice, and entertainment. In it, they shared information, offered political perspectives, developed their literary skills, and validated theirs and others' experiences of oppression. They promoted their interests, linking local, national, and global developments and emphasized the significance of writing to politicize the movement and establish connections across the diaspora. Afro-German women such as Ayim, Asfaha, Oguntoye, Ricky Reiser, and Regina Stein, along with men including Kingsley Addy, Daniel Alagiyawanna, John Kantara, Mike Reichel, and Roy Wichert contributed graphic designs, poetry, interviews, conference reports, and essays to a burgeoning Afro-German literary scene.[87] Originally, Kantara, along with Asfaha and Wichert, served as the editors of *afro look,* and for a few issues, Wichert served as the sole editor, though he did receive assistance from others. For the 1992/1993 issue, Reiser, Stein, Alagiyawanna, and Adel Oworu joined the editorial team.[88] Throughout the years, the editorial composition shifted again, but Reiser, Elizabeth Abraham, and a few others remained consistent. The magazine was affiliated with ISD from 1988 to 1997 and shared office space with ISD-Berlin until 1993. From 1997 to 1999, Reiser and others published the journal without ISD's institutional or financial support, although some of its members were still involved with it. Under Reiser's tenure, *afro look* acquired more subscribers and sold more copies. But the issue of financial and institutional support for the magazine always remained a problem and was often a topic of discussion at ISD's quarterly meetings.[89]

In addition to *afro look,* other Black German diasporic literature appeared. From 1999–2002, members of ISD-Berlin also published a journal, *Blite,* for

Figure 6. Cover of *afro look* no. 10 (1993), personal photograph in author's private collection.

"youth" between the ages of fourteen and twenty. In 1994 members of ISD-Düsseldorf produced a monthly magazine entitled *Strangers*.[90] ISD-Munich created a regional newsletter entitled *Subculture* that began in the spring of 1990, and ISD-Berlin also sent its members letters, keeping them abreast of events.[91] These mixed-media cultural productions served as alternative intellectual sites that allowed Afro-German quotidian intellectuals to express their feelings, share news, and retain recognition in society, reshaping the boundaries of German national identity and the literary tradition in the process. Black Germans utilized these publications to cultivate their diasporic self and found a sense of amity and unity through their involvement. *Afro look* became a tangible diasporic resource for their fellow Black German compatriots, enabling them to survive and resist in Germany.

The final example of Black Germans' invented traditions highlights how the local groups organized activities that accentuated the histories of Black Germany, Black resistance, and the Black diaspora, previously overlooked narratives in the nation. These diverse events demonstrated how intertwined the local, national, and global became in Black German community grassroots activism. They followed a Black German tradition that did not eschew taboo topics such as race and racism or the rise of ethno-nationalism and xenophobia in Germany and used their events as forms of racial advocacy. Black Germans reimagined their history and identity in the nation by emphasizing their linkages to regions outside Germany such as Burkina Faso and South Africa. Black Germans cultivated a sense of home (or place) and by extension belonging, which did not need to be created through an inward-looking history alone. The ISD-Rhine/Main chapter hosted, for instance, a "Black Consciousness, Black Politics" conference that explored the politics of Thomas Sankara, the president of Burkina Faso from 1983 to 1987.[92] This conference included speakers and panels that explained Sankara's politics, described the history of Burkina Faso and the neighboring country of Mali, and discussed African politics more broadly. The conference ended with a debate about the "contemporary perspective of Black people in a white-dominated world."[93] Their dissemination of non-stereotypical knowledge of Africa counteracted German racist constructions. With this event, the ISD-Rhine/Main group practiced diasporic activism, navigating African current events and demonstrating the important role that intellectualism had in the community.

Moreover, throughout the years, Black Germans offered support to South Africans. Some organized with a group against South African Apartheid in Berlin in 1988.[94] In celebration of its third anniversary, ISD-Berlin organized weeklong events in July 1989, during which the group also hosted a South Africa Day. At its event, members organized a reading with South African women authors; an exhibition and video about the country; and a presentation about South Africa with a discussion session.[95] "Especially for us Germans," Mike Reichel, an activist of ISD-Berlin and later one of the first Black German police officers, wrote, "whether we are black or white, it is important to learn about what is happening in South Africa, as the Federal Republic is one of the main trading partners and supporters of the Apartheid regime."[96] Black Germans, like other Black diasporic groups worldwide, were in solidarity with South African anti-Apartheid activists. Their ability for critical reflection was also key.

The Initiative reimagined the boundaries of German culture and intellectual output through sponsoring events that displayed Black Germans' and other People of Colors' literature, music, and art. ISD-Munich organized a reading with Black German authors, including Angela Alagiyawanna-Kadalie from Dortmund; Nisma Bux from Munich; Michael Küppers-Adebisi (née Michael Küppers) from Düsseldorf; Modupe Laja from Gießen; Sheila Mysorekar from Cologne; and Magali Schmidt from Munich.[97] By sharing their work, these authors gained support and visibility within the community and used the opportunity to cultivate further relationships to other individuals. They also created a body of work that linked them to a Black European intellectual tradition and that shaped a Black German literary canon.

ISD activists also publicly confronted racist incidences in Germany. In the spring of 1991, for instance, a white German electronic group called Time to Time, from a small town near Frankfurt, re-recorded the old German nursery rhyme "Ten Little Negroes" ("*Zehn kleine Negerlein*").[98] In the racist nursery rhyme, the little "negroes" die one by one, a theme that the group embellished by having the children meet an even more gruesome death at the notoriously violent and crime-ridden Zoo train station (*Bahnhof Zoologischer Garten*) in Berlin. The song was a pop hit, reaching number one on the German music charts in May 1991.[99] In a letter, Pastor Austen Brandt, an ISD-Duisburg member, wrote to an attorney and analyzed each stanza of the nursery rhyme, explaining the rhyme's broader racial implications for the Black community.[100] He explained that the song lyrics suggested that Blacks were not considered people, that they were culturally, ethnically, morally, and intellectually unequal, that they were "soulless things" with which one can and may do anything to, that they were objects subjected to derogatory terms, and that they did not belong in the international community and could never be German.[101] Brandt noted that the song upheld a racist image of Black people, which only perpetuated anti-Blackness and unbelonging. The song's anti-Blackness and popularity showed how pervasive these images were in the mainstream. ISD-Duisburg activists campaigned against it by writing letters to the Cologne-based record company, EMI Electrola, and local newspapers and organizing street protests on the song's pronounced racism. Members of the chapter also initiated legal proceedings against the record company.[102] The campaign met with some success, as EMI Electrola stopped producing the song. But it remained on sale as a part of a compilation album.[103]

Additionally, ISD chapters spoke out against racism by writing articles and letters, providing documentation, and organizing protests, including the "It is Time" demonstration on November 14, 1992.[104] Others hosted antiracism workshops, and with some support from the WCC's PCR, the ISD-Frankfurt/Main chapter established an "Anti-Racism Training" (ART), which helped white Germans understand "their own deeply-embedded psychological and social racist biases." Others reviewed encyclopedias, children's books, and public-school textbooks and pressured publishers to expunge racist language and connotations from their publications.[105] This is something still in practice, particularly with recent demands to excise racist language from popular children's books such as *Pippi Longstocking* (*Pippi Langstrumpf*) or *The Little Witch* (*Die kleine Hexe*). These recent calls to revise the language elicited negative pushback from politicians to academics alike.[106] Contributing to progressive Black German traditions, these practices remained politically, intellectually, and emotionally vital to the movement, as they consistently called out racism at home and beyond.

*   *   *

In the words of Oguntoye, the Black German movement "[took] courage (even if from desperation) and the capacity to be open and honest, at least with yourself." She added, "I don't think that it's coincidental that this aspect of the Afro-German movement was first carried by women, and they continue to do so in the main. But in saying this, I don't want to diminish the commitment and development of the men in ISD in any way. On the contrary, I am very proud of them."[107] Her comments reflect the powerful "Black Coming Out," that Black German women and men undertook during the early stages of the movement. They united and worked together to create their local chapters of ISD, forging relationships that sustained them after years of isolation. These friendships took shape at the BT, KT, BHM celebrations, and other organizational activities and projects. The planning and editing of Black German literary magazines, like *afro look,* not only served as a form of kinship and intellectual community but also helped them produce and share knowledge that pushed mixed media approaches and rejected white German frameworks and discourses. Local ISD chapters showed how Black German men and women were quotidian intellectuals and political activists who pursued intellectual activism for the benefit of their community.

Inventing their diasporic traditions, local chapters used their literature, meetings, initiatives, and events to produce spaces for activism and solidarity, pursue political advocacy, challenge their displacement and Otherness, and stake claims to the German nation and the Black diaspora. They also inhabited spaces both figuratively and physically through their writings, activities, and organizations, representing their agency and cultural autonomy. As Ayim clarified, "the Black German [experience]. . . . reflects an ongoing movement of resistance and courage of a not yet strong and visible, but constantly growing Black community."[108] For many, the community was a new (re)source that was empowering and enriching, but it was not without tensions and personal conflict. Black Germans continued to network, becoming relentless in their efforts to achieve equality and more representation in Germany.

Using their experiences as tools for advocacy and activism, Afro-Germans campaigned on a number of issues that emphasized their racial exclusion in German society, spoke out about the persistence of racism, and helped to diminish some of the exoticized and condescending imagery and discourses of Black people in German culture, though they achieved mixed results on this front given some personalities, conflict, and institutional approaches. But one of the significant changes was the inclusion of Afro-German in *Duden,* a prominent German dictionary, in 2006 for the first time. While the labels of Afro-German and Black German are now commonplace, some white Germans still do not accept this community. By elucidating Black German history, the movement deepened awareness about themselves. These quotidian intellectuals creatively crafted alternative traditions that served as forms of social cohesion and that gave them a public platform, remedying their invisibility. As Black German lesbian quotidian intellectuals continued to acknowledge how sutured their racial, gendered, and sexual identities were, they, too, sought more representation and acceptance within the larger movement. They did this through the creation of a Black queer feminist organization that foregrounded the pivotal role that intersectionality played in their lives and activism. In some respects, their critical Black feminist intervention mirrored Audre Lorde's own approach.

CHAPTER 3

ADEFRA, *AFREKETE,* AND BLACK GERMAN WOMEN'S KINSHIP

Just as Black German women, both straight and queer, co-founded ISD, they also rallied together to establish ADEFRA, a new women's organization.[1] Under the auspices of ADEFRA, these women created diasporic, feminist, and intellectual spaces and communities, while affirming their sexualities and identities. They imagined new political possibilities for themselves and the community and pursued spatial politics that centered gender, sexuality, and race. These Black German feminists were also indebted to Third World and/or Women of Color feminists (Audre Lorde, Gloria Joseph, and others) and the global sexual revolution of the late 1960s and the 1970s. Embracing intersectional politics, Black German women insisted on a space within white German feminist and queer discourses. They built on, responded to, and challenged mainstream white German feminists who still ignored the impact that overlapping systems of oppression had on Black women and Women of Color in the nation. As such, ADEFRA emerged as a Black queer feminist project that produced different modes of political action and gave Black feminism room to evolve and thrive in society.[2] Afro-German women made a political intervention that offered other Black women a new entry point into diasporic feminist activism in Germany.

This chapter argues that ADEFRA ushered in the new Black German women's movement that represented their politics and poetics of representation across gendered lines. ADEFRA activist-intellectuals envisaged queer as a claim and an ongoing practice of identity deconstruction, community building, and resistance based on their shared experiences of othering and exclusion.[3] For them, queer was also a multilayered positionality that not only included sexuality, but also their racial (Black) identity, in which both were presumed to be deviant from the German norm. They, too, invented diasporic traditions through ADEFRA. With the emergence of local chapters, Black German women gained representation, resisted their imposed othering, and combated multiple forms of discrimination in Germany and elsewhere, becoming quotidian intellectuals. They accomplished these tasks by engendering spaces, discourses, and narratives and deploying "queer strategies" that allowed them to overturn the heteronormative German order of things.[4] These women also produced knowledge on their and other People of Colors' experiences with German sexism, racism, and homophobia. In the process, Black German feminism gained a stronger presence in cities and the nation. These feminists reinserted themselves into spaces, both literal and metaphorical, that were previously denied to them.

Moreover, ADEFRA and its multigenre literary magazine *Afrekete: Magazine for Afro-German and Black Women* (*Afrekete: Zeitung für afro-deutsche und schwarze Frauen*), published from 1988 to 1990, served as alternative forms of kinship that produced and privileged female bonds that were not based on blood ties or a traditional genealogy.[5] Afro-German women cultivated affective ties that broadened their understanding of belonging and reflected their desire for acceptance; their connected differences strengthened their practices of kinship. After years of isolation in a predominantly white German society, ADEFRA and *Afrekete* opened up spaces for social cohesion and collaboration that Black German women sought. *Afrekete* offered Afro-German women political, cultural, and intellectual connections to one another and other diasporic women, especially with its dissemination to a wider community. Their new social bonds with each other helped them negotiate their gendered and racialized experiences.

Afro-German women's creation of a Black queer feminist project, ADEFRA, was a radical act akin to the work of the Brixton Black Women's Group (BBWG) and the Organisation for Women of African and Asian Descent (OWAAD) in Britain, formed in 1973 and 1978, or the Combahee River Collective (CRC) in the United States, formed in 1974.[6] But unlike those feminist groups in Britain and the United States, Black German women's discussion of oppression mostly addressed race and gender, not so much class. The Black German women's movement recognized that all the dimensions of women's oppression shaped their experiences and constituted a robust Black feminist culture in Germany. ADEFRA activist-intellectuals used Black feminism to mobilize against unjust immigration and asylum policies, demand antidiscrimination legislation, and organize workshops for the betterment of Black German women, other Black women, Women of Color, and the larger Black community. They were committed to collective action with their Black German brothers, as demonstrated in chapter 2.

As ADEFRA and *Afrekete* evolved as important sites within the movement, these women pursued Black intellectualism and internationalism, which empowered them to push beyond whitewashed normative perspectives and practices. As quotidian intellectuals, they embedded their practice of intellectual activism in their organizational events and collaborations, privileging their daily struggles and creating new intellectual and diasporic networks. In many respects, *Afrekete* represented Black German women's queer strategies in practice, considering it did not follow a linear narrative or form in its issues. *Afrekete* mixed genres and writing styles and featured poetry, autobiographical narratives, historical articles, diasporic art, and reports on projects and international feminist conferences. The journal juxtaposed black and white photographs with diasporic symbols and drawings. Featuring contributions from its members and other Black German or People of Color, it reinforced the idea that documenting and disseminating their herstories and publishing their writing and art, in all forms, mattered. *Afrekete* shares a legacy with both white German feminist and lesbian print culture and transnational Black feminist and/or lesbian print culture. *Afrekete* in fact resembled *Aché,* the African American lesbian magazine referenced in chapter 1, in form and content.[7] ADEFRA feminists' literary and diasporic efforts undertaken with *Afrekete* reminds us of what Caribbean theorist Édouard Glissant wrote about Caribbean discourses. In this case, Black German women's "geographic itinerary" entailed a remapping of Black German intellectualism that laid bare all of its nuance and complexity.[8] ADEFRA activist-intellectuals also used *Afrekete* to write themselves into discourses about the German nation and the Black diaspora, shifting understandings of who belonged to each. Each issue centered these women as thinkers, producers, and artists who redefined Black German identity.

It was their awareness of the strength of diasporic feminist mobilizing against white supremacy and patriarchy that informed their Black internationalism and pushed them to attend international antiracist and feminist events and organize similar ones upon their return home. Through their participation in those events, they had vital exchanges with white allies and people within the global Black diaspora, who they then used as diasporic resources. Black German women's ability to produce alternative kinships with their organization, internationalism, and journal represented queer strategies that undermined normalized German ideas and practices.

THE ORIGINS OF BLACK GERMAN FEMINIST MOBILIZATION

In ADEFRA's twentieth-anniversary brochure and celebration in 2006, activist-intellectuals confirmed that the initial meetings with Lorde, her subsequent visits to Germany, and the volume *Farbe bekennen* catalyzed their movement.[9] For many Black German women, Lorde served as a model of Black, lesbian, and feminist intellectual activism.[10] While ISD mobilized against all forms of discrimination and encouraged Black German solidarity between women and men, this commitment was not without controversy. In early meetings, several ISD members perpetuated misogyny, sexism, and homophobia within their organization, alienating some female members.[11] These practices were not uncommon in other left-wing social groups of the 1960s and 1970s, including the German Socialist Student Association (Sozialistischer Deutscher Studentenbund, SDS) and the Black Panther Party in Oakland, California.[12]

At the same time that these grievances developed within ISD, Black German women organized a series of meetings between 1985 and 1987 in Germany, motivating them to create their own feminist and diasporic organization. ISD-Berlin's women's group with Oguntoye also played a significant role. Through her work on *Farbe bekennen*, she met numerous Black women across Germany, and this politicized her in new ways.[13] For Jasmin Eding and others, reading *Farbe bekennen* was inspiring and life-changing. It also provided a means to connect with Oguntoye, who was a proud Black lesbian. Eding eventually contacted her through Orlanda.[14] A December 1986 meet-up in Cologne was important for Oguntoye, Eding, Katja Kinder, Elke Jank (Ja-El), Eva von Pirch, Daniela Toukarzi, the sisters Christina and Domenica Grotke, and others, who were from different regions in Germany. After this meeting, ADEFRA was born. Attendees decided at this meeting that several women, including Oguntoye and Eding, would travel to Utrecht, the Netherlands for an international women's conference. A Black women's theater group organized the conference as a protest against the "Black Pete" ("*Zwarte Piet*") Dutch Christmas tradition. While there, Black German women met and connected with Black feminists from London and Amsterdam, attended theater and writing workshops, saw art performances, and had personal and intellectual exchanges about the conditions of Black women.[15] Meeting Black women in Utrecht was stimulating and helped these women determine next steps for their organization. It would not be their last contact with Black European activists.

Afro-German women, including Oguntoye, Eding, Ja-El, von Pirch, Kinder, Ika Hügel-Marshall, Eleonore Wiedenroth-Coulibaly, and others infused new Black diasporic feminist sensibilities into the larger Black German movement.

Their homage to African culture is evinced in their initial discussions about the name of the organization. During an early meeting, these women contemplated naming the organization Afro-German Lesbians (Afrodeutsche Lesben, ADELE), which they felt sounded too German. They settled on ADEFRA, which means "the women who show courage" in Amharic, the official language in Ethiopia.[16] With this title, they established an "imagined community" to one another, African women, and other Black women in and beyond Germany. Activists' previous political experiences, spontaneity, and improvisation characterized the initial years of ADEFRA.

Similar to ISD, ADEFRA maintained a non-hierarchical structure, engaged in political advocacy work, and pursued cooperation with its Black compatriots. Local chapters sent representatives to ISD's KT (*Koordinationstreffen*), and they also held their own ones two or three times per year. They even organized their own women's BT (*Frauen Bundestreffen*), in addition to the annual meetings that ISD hosted. Diverse chapters of ADEFRA co-organized ISD events (such as the BT, KT, and BHM), sponsored a youth exchange program, and planned countless others.[17] Despite earlier sexist tensions that did not completely disappear, members of local ADEFRA and ISD chapters in Berlin and Munich, for instance, shared bank accounts and worked together. Even though ADEFRA was an organization by and for women, its feminists unbegrudgingly collaborated with and forged solidarity with Black German men in ISD. This cooperation also forced the men to grapple with the themes of misogyny, homophobia, and feminism.[18] As a result, Black German women differed from white German feminists, who often avoided working with white German men.[19] Some of these white feminists criticized Black German women for their unwillingness to separate from the men.

Along these lines, Black German women were similar to their Black feminist counterparts in Britain and the United States. Black British women's engagement with community politics motivated them to work with Black men, and they focused on the intersections of race, class, and gender oppression. In the 1970s, women caucuses formed within British Black Power organizations. These early efforts laid the foundation for the Black British women's movement, especially with the establishment of the BBWG, formerly the Black Women's Group, and OWAAD, both based in London.[20] Jamaican-born Olive Morris was a founding member of the BBWG and also later launched OWAAD with Black British activists Stella Dadzie and Gail Lewis. The BBWG focused on women's issues and produced a newsletter entitled *Speak Out*. OWAAD supported an Afro-Asian unity that campaigned against imperialism, racism, and sexism; they also published a newsletter entitled *FOWAAD!* and planned four feminist conferences from 1979 to 1982.[21] Additionally, African American socialist feminists, like Beverly Smith, Barbara Smith, and Demita Frazier, in the CRC did not segregate from Black men. They also held seven feminist retreats, of which Lorde attended a few, and campaigned against multiple issues in Boston.[22] The CRC feminists recognized that "Black men and women may experience racism differently in the world, but they had common interests in overcoming it—interests that could not be realized in struggles separated along the lines of gender."[23] ADEFRA activists felt similarly as they consistently collaborated with Black German men. The CRC also rejected lesbian separatism.[24] ADEFRA feminists worked with homosexual, heterosexual, cisgender, and/or gender-fluid men and women, and approached solidarity holistically.

The BBWG, OWAAD, and the CRC understood the centrality of class in Black women's lives, and broadened Marxist analysis to include Black women's oppression and their political needs. But this Marxist approach was not common in ADEFRA, though its members were cognizant of class in their lives and when organizing activities. In their country, Afro-Germans did not confront the stark racialized class divisions those in Britain and the United States faced.[25] This owed in part to Germany's social reform policy and social security system. Even before Chancellor Kohl's neoconservative tenure from 1982 to 1998, the government cut some benefits responding to a global recession after the spike in oil prices in 1973 and additional political challenges. But new benefits and social rights emerged, key aspects of the system still remained, and more social spending occurred later in response to unification.[26] Therefore, Black Germans and others were able to earn a better living wage in comparison to their counterparts elsewhere. As a result, Black Germans were generally middle class and/or well-educated, though exceptions did exist. Owing to their social status, they recognized that their plight in Germany differed from others across the Black diaspora.

ADEFRA quotidian intellectuals immersed themselves in radical Black feminist politics that sought to combat all forms of discrimination and that ensured the socialization of their members into a new value system. These women "wanted to show that the Black women's movement had its own experiences, values, and visions based on the need for its own survival strategies." Those feminists also saw their organization as "a forum for Afro-German and Black women: so that we can engage with our black history and culture, develop a collective strength for our black feminist struggle, develop and strengthen our black consciousness and identity in this white society [and] deal with our differences: age, socialization, origin, way of life, lesbian, interests, profession, etc."[27] Their political intervention centered Black queer feminism and made the organization an inclusive Black space from which all individuals in the diaspora in Germany could benefit. With the feminists' project, they pursued queer strategies of belonging, solidarity, and activism.

A BLACK QUEER FEMINIST PROJECT AND COMMUNITY

From the onset, ADEFRA constituted a Black queer feminist project that allowed different Afro-German and other Black women to participate in the articulation of their identities, the pursuit of their intersectional and non-heteronormative politics, and the building of a dynamic community, which was not confined to Germany alone. As ADEFRA's twentieth-anniversary program in 2006 shared, "it was important to note, that Black women, particularly lesbians were the ones who set off the Black movement in Germany," and ADEFRA "quickly gained (in the Black community) the reputation of being a refuge for Black lesbians."[28] According to ADEFRA activist Ekpenyong Ani, there were always concerns about the role of sexuality in the organization. She wrote, "The theme of sexual orientation especially whether ADEFRA was a woman—or lesbian—association, remained a huge question at all times. I can only say, that the lesbians at ADEFRA were always more mobilized, because in a certain way the focus was clear: if you concentrate on women and want to work together with them, then of course, you will find a lot of lesbians."[29] Despite those issues, ADEFRA chapters helped a heterogeneous group of women stake claims of belonging, cultivate new selves and identities, and challenge discriminatory assumptions and practices through their activities. Using ADEFRA, Black German women demonstrated how the intertwining of the Black diaspora, feminism, and queerness could "strengthen and encourage the self-awareness, self-determination, and self-organisation of Black women."[30]

The early ADEFRA founders "were united by the conviction that Black women are entitled to their own space."[31] They physically and symbolically produced spaces for non-normative and gender non-conforming bodies and embraced different embodiments of womanhood that did not exclude "Heteras" or "Hetera-women" (*Hetera-Frauen*).[32] Interestingly, "many black women due to their involvement with ADEFRA became *transitory lesbians;* some for the length of a project, some for the length of a relationship, some always returning, some, it can be said remained beautifully forever."[33] The organization recognized the fluidity and flexibility of women's sexual lives, which was a type of "situational homosexuality." As a result, they encouraged a variety of queer identities to take shape, including bisexual and transgender.[34] ADEFRA reflected dynamics common to queer politics. Cathy Cohen has remarked that, "In queer politics sexual expression is something that always entails the possibility of change, movement, redefinition, and subversive performance—from year to year, from partner to partner, from day to day, and even from act to act."[35] ADEFRA symbolized these types of shifting identities and attachments, and provided its members with the ability to embrace their selves, desires, and motivations on their terms. Black German women also "wanted to be perceived and recognized as part of German society."[36] Working together, they gave Black German feminism a public face and reimagined its political potential; these empowering acts moved different kinds of Black queerness from the margins.

The local communities forged through ADEFRA also provided an affective space that facilitated the navigation of complex emotions based on exclusion and stimulated diverse responses to others that could be emotional or sexual.[37] Socializing with one another provided them with an opportunity to develop what one member described as a "psycho-social consciousness" about their positions and identities.[38] Afro-German women dealt with the accumulation of anger and pain from their experiences in Germany. Their emotional labor covered different facets of their lives. In ADEFRA, these women used the affective spaces and orientations to one another to embrace the messiness of their emotions, identities, and practices, overturning traditional and essentialist norms. Their local chapters served as curative and generative spaces of inclusion and opportunity, though tensions did exist.

As with other social groups, problems arose, particularly as the contrasting and competing views of a variety of women complicated the stability of a collective sense of Black German unity and identity. Kinder shared in an interview, "Even though it was always quite open and already known. We were all out. This was an important step—to make us visible—in the community. The heterosexual women who turned towards ADEFRA sometimes even received stupid looks and comments [because it was presumed they were gay]. But, nevertheless, we have always had a strong standing in the community. This is still the case."[39] Though, in a 2012 interview, Oguntoye observed, "ADEFRA as an Afro-German women's group made us lesbians at times not quite as visible." ADEFRA activist Ani confirmed this sentiment by stating how problems emerged at the 1995 BT because of a lack of respect, insensitive comments, and aggressive actions.[40] Each one of these activists stressed the gender and sexual politics that were embedded within ADEFRA (and ISD) and suggest that multiple overlapping negotiations occurred. While queer women were represented in ADEFRA and some of its founders were lesbians, the presence of straight women contributed to fluctuating power dynamics that mirrored the German feminist movement and impacted how the organization was received and represented.

In *Afrekete*, von Pirch described those undercurrents at early meetings. At a 1987 organizational meeting in Bremen, for instance, debates raged among Black German women. They argued over the general goals of the association: whether it was better to work on women's issues within ISD; whether there would be a splintering of ADEFRA; who would take responsibility for the association; and who did or did not belong to the association? Concerns also emerged about colorism, homophobia, and sexuality.[41] Von Pirch claimed that at the first national Afro-German women's meeting in January 1988, sponsored by ADEFRA-Munich, some of the activists shared that women had different backgrounds from each other, shaping how the association could develop. On the one hand, ADEFRA activists' experiences in the women's movement, which in the case of some members traced back more than fifteen years, had revealed that heterosexual women often sought different goals than lesbians. Unfortunately, von Pirch's article made no mention of the specific women. Some women believed, "A heterosexual Afro-German woman is dominated by men and patriarchal structures that are reflected in her behavior and life, making it difficult to pursue collaborative work." On the other hand, some "thought that this whole [heterosexual/homosexual] division was crap and that the discussion was exhausting, and it did not produce results." Continuing to emphasize this point, von Pirch confirmed that several women noted, "Given the different personalities of women each one must decide for themselves how they live, and this decision should not prevent us from publicly revealing our joint efforts to condemn discrimination, racism, and sexism."[42] Despite attempts to be all-inclusive, dominant positionalities took their toll. Regardless of those tensions, Black German women still made a critical intervention by creating ADEFRA. They also depended on diasporic resources to disrupt normative understandings of identity and sexuality, reject their displacement and marginalization, and reorient themselves to other Black German or Black women.[43]

Across Germany, members of ADEFRA chapters actively arranged workshops, conferences, and other activities that constituted a part of their collective feminist activism and spatial politics. Their efforts at spatial reclamation privileged multiple overlapping systems of oppression in different locations across German cities while also producing Black intersectional spaces within the larger German imaginary. Some chapters, especially ADEFRA-Munich, were more active than others. By 1987 Eding, Gummich, Ria Cheatom, Manu Jaromin, and Buwo (née Gloria Mauermeier) established an ADEFRA-Munich chapter with an office; Tanya Cora, Cassandra Ellerbe-Drück, and Mary-Ann Powell were also active in this chapter.[44] This chapter, which included women from the ages of seventeen to forty, wrote a constitution that other ADEFRA (and ISD) chapters used as a model. Throughout the years, ADEFRA-Munich initiated a number of projects, including a 1988 event with Lorde, a 1992 self-defense workshop, a 1993 conference entitled "Racism," a 1993 "Back to Roots" hair workshop, and more.[45] These activities, among others, occurred across Munich and centered the political and cultural concerns of Black women.

Additional groups emerged in Berlin with Oguntoye and others; in Frankfurt/Wiesbaden with Wiedenroth-Coulibaly, Hügel-Marshall, and Emde, and in Cologne with the Grotke sisters and others. Black German women also mobilized and asserted their presence in Kassel, Gießen, Bielefeld, and Bremen. Many of these chapters collaborated with local feminist or migrant organizations and Women of Color activists. In 1991, ADEFRA-Hamburg began a new stage, which included the work of Arfasse Gamada, Katja Kinder, Netsanet Renisberg, Abigail van Royen, and others; these women also received funding from local and regional intercultural and feminist organizations. Later, Ani, Maisha-Maureen Auma (née Maureen Maisha Eggers), Jelka Lehmann, and other women joined.[46] ADEFRA's quotidian intellectuals organized seminars and conferences; hosted discussion forums; offered direct action against German asylum policies; and campaigned against racist and sexist advertisements, such as the beer company Spaten, in support of Black women and Women of Color. Their monthly meetings became weekly meetings in preparation for those and other events. Members in the Berlin and Munich chapters also worked on the Black Butterfly, a mobile computer school project that gave Black women, especially migrant women, an opportunity to gain computer training.[47] "The key objectives of our work," for ADEFRA feminists revolved around, "the dismantling of racism and sexism—two 'isms' which are closely linked—and the recognition as a social group also within the women's movement."[48] In addition to publishing *Afrekete,* Ja-El and von Pirch of ADEFRA-Bremen also produced films about the lives of Afro-Germans. ADEFRA chapters lost individuals, as members moved, had family obligations, or interests shifted. It also became hard for some within the groups to continue because the work fell to a few, and those women grew exhausted. Even so, Black German women's activism remained tied to their community, and the community occupied the center of their work.

Spearheaded by the Munich chapter, ADEFRA became a nationwide legally registered organization in 1996.[49] In 1998 ADEFRA-Munich closed its office doors, though Eding still arranged activities. By 2000 ADEFRA was formally headquartered in Berlin, as many Black German women moved to the city. All the administrative tasks, board meetings, and major events occurred there, including a 2001 queer event, entitled "Sister's Pride," that was akin to the BT.[50] At this time, Black German feminists Ani and Regina Stein also arranged regular meetings in Berlin. But this is not to suggest that activists in areas outside Berlin still did not organize events. Again, Berlin continued to be a hub for Black diasporic mobilization, as it did in the movement's initial years.

As ADEFRA feminists established new spaces and places for their mobilization and resistance, they also reimagined the notions of home and belonging.[51] Kinder observed that in the early 1980s, "Black female activists were nonexistent in mainstream German society and it is exactly this fact that provided an opportunity to occupy a new space and break down the often quoted symbolic order piece by piece."[52] Eding also expressed that her involvement with ADEFRA made it possible for her to "[find] a home, or rather we created a home for ourselves."[53] Here, home became a malleable and evolving space that was contingent upon their relationships and connections to other Black people. Both of these activists conveyed the significance of ADEFRA, as newly created physical and symbolic locations that enabled them, along with others in the group, to negotiate and promote their identities and interests.

ADEFRA quotidian intellectuals—Eding, Kinder, Ani, Auma, and Peggy Piesche—shared that the organization was a Black queer feminist project because it attended to issues that impacted all women. They also emphasized that ADEFRA was a part of a German lesbian tradition—a fact often overlooked in the historical scholarship on lesbian and gay activism in Germany. In addition, these women, excluding Kinder and Eding, represented a new cohort of ADEFRA feminists. After attending and listening to a 1990 reading Lorde gave in Stuttgart, Ani, who was born in the former East but grew up in East and West Germany, Jamaica, and Nigeria, became involved in ADEFRA-Hamburg.[54] Auma, born in Kenya but raised in Germany, was drawn to ADEFRA-Hamburg after attending a 1993 workshop, "Black Women and Power" (*Schwarze Frauen und Macht*), near Hamburg. There, she met approximately fifty Black female activists from Germany and the Netherlands.[55] "On this day," Auma explained, she "ended a specific search" for a community.[56] Peggy Piesche, from the former East (Arnstadt), attended ADEFRA's first international symposium in 1990 in Munich. After that event, her world changed. "ADEFRA," Piesche declared, "opened up a new world to me in which I can be all I am: black, lesbian, inconvenient."[57] They all made clear that Black women's relationships with one another were mutually supportive and constitutive, serving as a foundation for their feminist activism. As Lorde wrote, "Interdependency between women is the way to a freedom which allows the *I* to be not in order to be used, but in order to be creative. This is a difference between the passive be and the active being."[58] For Lorde, female fellowship engendered new spaces for women to embrace their creative potential and refashion themselves. Her relationships with women shaped her identity, work, and activism. Such interactions, as those highlighted above, and the newly forged ties had a similar impact on Black German women, who contributed to the movement's momentum.

Their community-based Black queer feminist project also operated within and beyond the borders of Germany. Their practice of grassroots international- ism allowed them to assert their Black Germanness and queerness, troubling dominant hegemonies. Black German women formed connections stemming from their participation in feminist conferences in the United States, Canada, Europe, Latin America, and Africa, and they also pursued exchanges and po- litical work with other Black European groups, including the Angelou Center, a Black women-led center in Britain, Sister Outsider, an Afro-Dutch women's group, and SISTERS—Sisters in Struggle to Eliminate Racism and Sexism, a women's network affiliated with the World Council of Churches in Geneva.[59]

This queer strategy was also evident with their hosting of international femi- nist conferences, especially a November 1990 one in Munich. The event showed how their internationalism and solidarity reflected their efforts to promote alternative kinships with diverse individuals and pursue cultural diplomacy. ADEFRA-Munich's international meeting of Black women (*Int. Treffen Schwarzer Frauen*), co-sponsored by Munich-based feminist institutions, was their fifth women's BT. Cheatom, Eding, Gummich, Cora, Powell, Manu Jaromin, Magali Schmid, and Beate Steil organized the event. The four-day symposium, entitled "Risk your life and leave your house" (*Wage dein Leben und verlasse dein Haus*)—a title derived from an African proverb—was open to Black and white Germans and other women across the globe.

Supporting the diversity of women's experiences and confronting discrimi- natory practices, the conference involved Black women and Women of Color networking, sharing their feelings, and exchanging ideas and strategies. At the symposium, Black German quotidian intellectuals sponsored art exhibitions, lectures, and seminars that explored racism, sexism, Afro-German history, and Black women's literature, and continued to challenge mainstream white Ger- man feminist politics. The conference organizers, aware of class and familial dynamics, offered options for shared group meals and childcare. Some of the presentations included "White mother, black child"; "Lesbian Politics-Women's Politics"; and "Differences among women: a critical look at how to deal with others." They also sponsored Black-women-only events, where these women could work through their specific concerns, and some of these workshops in- cluded "Reunification and United Racism" and "The History of Slavery and its Contemporary Meaning."[60] While these seminars showed Black German women's wide-ranging interests, they also represented their ability to share and produce knowledge on gendered and racial topics that were intertwined in their lives, already a normalized practice in their movement.

At this event, as with others, ADEFRA feminists valued building alliances with other women. They sponsored presentations with white and Black feminists alike, including Oguntoye, Hügel-Marshall, Dagmar Schultz, and José Maas, an Afro-Dutch activist. Their commitment to collaborative work remained significant, and organizational brochures constantly referenced their collaboration.[61] ADEFRA feminists recognized, "We as black women have a responsibility to unite and initiate change in the family, in close surroundings [and neighborhoods], regionally and globally. We have the responsibility to survive politically, culturally, and economically. As women, we cannot only think about our immediate space, but we must look after our global community. Our commitment must be 100 percent as we deal with men with whom we live, fathers, brothers, sons, in dealing with sexism and racism."[62] For ADEFRA organizers and participants, the symposium became an opportunity for connections with other Black women, particularly from East Germany, and to learn more about diverse women's situations and survival strategies. This was not the first time a conference was organized to bring women from the East and West together. In fact, the Green Party in Bavaria sponsored a women's congress in July 1990.[63] But through the Munich conference, former-East Black Germans, including Piesche, Carmen Oliver Stanley, Aminata Cissé Schleicher, and Ina Röder, "forged diaspora" through their new contacts.

Underscoring the appeal of the conference, Cheatom, Eding, and Powell—ADEFRA-Munich activists—noted, "For most of the black women (many came from the former East and other European countries), this was the first time that they took part in a meeting exclusively for women. Despite our different ways of life and also partly our different self-image (for example, the label of Afro-German was met with confusion and even a lack of acceptance by our black African, Arabic, French, and Dutch. . . . sisters[)] . . . . the response to the meeting was very positive."[64] Foregrounding their differences and commonalities helped ADEFRA activists establish solidarity networks with Black women from the East and other European countries and further their expansive feminist politics.

Black German women also embedded themselves in other German cities, especially with their 1994 feminist conference near Hamburg. With the theme of self-empowerment for "Black Women/Women of Color in Germany" (*Schwarzer Frauen/Women of Color in Deutschland*), Gummich, Eding, and Jeanine Kantara gave presentations along with other Women of Color quotidian intellectuals.[65] This conference continued to center Black and Women of Color feminism in Germany. ADEFRA quotidian intellectuals, along with additional activists and organizations, planned the "Third National Congress" by and for Black/exiled women, migrant women and Jewish women in 1995, which was in response to the 1994 Hamburg conference and the previous "Ways to Alliances" conferences in 1990 and 1991.[66] They imparted specific knowledge about women's plight and resistance and pushed mainstream feminism discourses to acknowledge intersectionality and racialized sexism. Following a legacy of twentieth-century global feminist activism, these events afforded Afro-German, Black, and other Women of Color activists and participants opportunities to no longer be invisible and engage in meaningful political activism through an intersectional lens. They cleared a path for this type of feminism in the German landscape and aided the next generation of Black activists. Those events and others enabled them to form links that became resources for them, but it was not their only avenue.

KINSHIP IN *AFREKETE*

With *Afrekete*'s creation in 1988, Ja-El and von Pirch relied on multiple diasporic resources to advance their Black queer feminist project. The new magazine was a black and white quarterly, approximately thirty pages in length; some of the issues ranged from forty-five to sixty pages. But the idea for the quarterly changed as it became increasingly difficult to obtain contributions and assistance.

They advertised in mainstream German lesbian and women's magazines, including *Lesbian Stitch* (*LesbenStich*), first published in 1980.[67] *Afrekete* included six issues in total, and each issue centered on a theme that underscored the significance of intersectional and international politics.[68] Moreover, Afrekete was a motif that some African American and Afro-Caribbean authors used in their literary works. According to Henry Louis Gates Jr., Afrekete became a key symbol of the diaspora, serving "as a sign of the disrupted wholeness of an African system of meaning and belief."[69] Their ability to draw inspiration for the magazine's name from Lorde also linked them to her and African indigenous spirituality. Lorde had long integrated African religious entities into her literature and invoked Afrekete in her works and signed some of her letters "in the hands of Afrekete."[70] She used Afrekete as a source of female strength, claiming that the traditional nature of women's power in Africa could inform Black women's consciousness and activism.[71] Black German women's reference to Afrekete connected them to a network of Black women. They integrated diverse Black diasporic styles, symbols, and histories and celebrated Black queerness in all its variety and depth.

Inventing new traditions, *Afrekete* gave Afro-German feminists an opportunity to establish an intellectual community, develop their literary voices, publish

Figure 7. Cover of *Afrekete (Born Free: WANTED!)* 5, no. 4 (1989), Zentrale Bibliothek Frauenforschung, Gender & Queer Studies (Hamburg).

their work, and influence Black German literature. Ja-El and von Pirch, both feminists and quotidian intellectuals, embraced writing as a form of intellectual activism and a medium for survival. They continued the intellectual tradition initiated with *Farbe bekennen,* reflecting their desire to forge diaspora and incite cultural change. Using *Afrekete* as a diverse platform, Black German women expressed their feelings, offered information about Black feminist initiatives and other events, and introduced their readers to Women of Color authors such as Donna Davis and Rosa-Lubia Falk Garcia.[72] *Afrekete* represented how Black German women entwined the local, the national, and the international. The magazine also garnered international attention from individuals in the United States and in Africa.[73] Through *Afrekete*, these quotidian intellectuals challenged the German status quo and made an epistemic intervention by building a diasporic collective for Afro-German and Black women across Germany.

In their first issue, the co-editors established a convivial and welcoming tone, inviting and imploring their "Black, Afro-German Sisters" to participate and shape the direction of the journal and to support it financially.[74] The editors jokingly solicited money by saying, "At AFREKETE we are missing dough,

as cash and money are very rare at ADEFRA."[75] In addition to financial assistance, these Afro-German women also wanted the journal to be culturally viable. They stated, "we call on each of you to use these pages for yourselves and
other women by submitting numerous contributions about whatever lies close
to your heart, soul, stomach (and wherever else a woman desires and would like
to express)." In their call to arms, Ja-El and von Pirch wanted *Afrekete* to foster
a desire for steady participation, support, and creative expression. The significance of contributions and maintaining these links to the community remained
essential for ADEFRA and *Afrekete*'s development and Black Germans' personal
growth. They clarified, "Of course such a goal is impossible to achieve with
only two women. This magazine will only be appealing to ourselves and other
women, if we collectively and individually reassess and redefine our respective
place in this society continually: as women, as Afro-Germans, as Black internationalists."[76] Seeing themselves as part of an international community, their
efforts at "disidentification" were cultural, intellectual, and political acts that
centered Blackness and queerness and offered new survival strategies.[77] Their
internationalism relied on alternative types of bonds that extended outside the
heteronormative and the national. The co-editors, moreover, intended for the
journal to share cultural practices and offer advice about handling their everyday experiences of racism, sexism, and homophobia in Germany. Ja-El and von
Pirch underscored the significance of social bonds among women, considering
it a critical aspect in the vitality of the journal.[78]

Afro-Germans produced alternative discourses by challenging essentialist understandings of Germanness as monoculturally white and by sharing
knowledge about Black Germanness past, present, and future. In this way, they
empowered and amplified the voices of Black German women and established
new values and habits for their community. As a creative and collective outlet,
Afrekete not only functioned as a space of resistance against traditional German othering and erasure, but it was also an alternative space, where cultural
symbols could be reinterpreted, translated, rehistoricized, and read anew. This
rendered Blackness visible across different spacetimes, transforming how it
was understood in German and diasporic contexts.

In many of the issues, Black German contributors explored their archive of
emotions and the dilemma of Otherness in society. For example, in the poem
"White, black—or are they just colors," an unnamed author shared how she
navigated the judgmental and harsh streets of Germany.[79] She also expressed
aggravation about straddling both ends of the emotional spectrum; being
something she was not; and having to defend and define herself according to
people's perceptions. This constant performing (*Theater spielen*) on the street

with individuals who she may or may not know had damaged her self-worth. In a contribution, Hügel-Marshall also explained the need to process all types of emotions. While being a part of ISD and ADEFRA had enriched her life, allowing her to connect with other Afro-Germans and People of Color, it took her a long time to realize that making oneself visible needed to happen both within the larger German society and the Afro-German community. This entailed accepting and respecting the pain and anger that one had suppressed throughout the years and being honest with oneself and the community.[80] By dealing with their positive and negative experiences, Afro-German women disclosed intimate narratives that many of them commonly understood and validated their lived experiences.

Through their magazine, Black German quotidian intellectuals reflected on their perpetual state of marginalization by exposing white Germans' mistreatment and racism toward them in archetypical everyday encounters. In the poem "What do I have to do with Africa?", von Pirch reenacted a scene where a white German woman asked questions that Afro-Germans were long familiar with, such as "where are you from," "are you from Africa," or "when will you return to your country?" Those seemingly innocuous yet inappropriate questions presumed that Black Germans were not included in the nation. These invasive questions were often emotionally grueling and painful. Black Germans' common interactions with their white German compatriots echoed racist German children's songs like "The Ten Little Negroes," which demeaned and othered African-descended people. Instead, Black Germans were considered foreigners "from exotic sounding names of Africa, Latin America, or the Caribbean, or also here in the Federal Republic the beloved, USA."[81] The white German woman's skepticism when the Black German woman stated Berlin proved that she only conceived of German national identity as white.[82] Her poem underscored the quotidian experiences of exclusion that doubly marginalized Afro-German women. First, othering occurred when the white German woman inquired about where the Black German woman came from. In this scenario, this Afro-German woman couldn't be born in Germany because it was considered a white country. Second, rather than establishing a possible connection with the Black German woman, the white German denied her space in the nation by expressing outward disappointment that she came from Berlin. This woman was also incredulous, indicating that racial differences still mattered in post-Holocaust Germany. The white German reified the categories of national belonging and citizenship by excluding the Afro-German from the imagined community. These exchanges also reveal the spatial politics at play in which their white compatriots regularly excised them from the national polity in these encounters. Therefore, face-to-face contact with an Afro-German served as both an intellectual intervention and an act of reclamation. It forced white Germans to become aware of their existence and showed them how Germany (Berlin) was a diasporic space. Yet, as Emde stated in an interview in *Die Tageszeitung* (*taz*), "For the (pains) of the disenfranchised, there is only a band-aid, no healing."[83] Although Black Germans could only experience a temporary relief from their cultural predicament, the magazine still brought Black German women together through their challenging experiences and mutual displacement.

Extending the indictment, von Pirch also impugned white German leftists for their apathy and insensitivity in the same poem. She explored how these German leftists expressed concerns about the plight of people in Africa, yet they ignored the presence and difficulties that African-descended people faced in Germany. Throughout *Afrekete*, Black German women addressed this criticism, expressing frustration because of the hypocrisy in German progressive politics.[84] Rather than align themselves with Black German compatriots in the eradication of racism or inquiring about their experiences as Black women in Germany, white German women concentrated on stereotypical images of African women, such as their colorful clothing or graceful movements as they carried water buckets on their heads. Or, as von Pirch noted in the poem, they remembered German news reports of famines affecting African women and children, the practices of polygamy, or the custom of female genital mutilation.[85] The last two examples from her poem focused on African women's limited rights and oppression in their poverty-stricken, patriarchal African societies and relied on essentialist ideas of a diverse continent and its people. Here, she critiqued white German women's misguided discourses on Africa and gendered Blackness. Though white Germans acknowledged the importance of social equality in Africa or the evils of colonialism in the Third World more generally, they never critically examined its colonial afterlives at home.[86]

Afro-Germans continued to express disillusionment with German liberal activism. When Emde wrote, "I shit on your liberalism. I am a human being," the sentiment resonated with other Afro-Germans, especially as they wanted less discriminatory treatment at home.[87] Although the white German in the poem provided a sympathetic gaze toward the African continent, she overlooked the reality that many Black women suffered in Germany.[88] Von Pirch chided white German women for admiring prominent social activists and musicians such as Winnie Mandela, Angela Davis, or Joan Armatrading while having a limited or superficial engagement with actual individuals of African descent in Germany. Those white German leftists often proclaimed their roles as specialists on Africa and African women, but they never realized that a "German Africa" (*deutsches*

Afrika) also existed in the Federal Republic.[89] Here, these leftists ignored the fact that Germany constituted a physical site for the Black diaspora.

In her contribution to *Afrekete*, von Pirch also admitted that there was a possibility for cross-racial dialogue and bonding with her "white sister" (*weiße Schwester*). Forging a close affiliation with her white sister could yield powerful results, allowing both individuals to learn about their experiences as German women. If the white German woman could put aside her preoccupation and fascination with people on the African continent and acknowledge her Afro-German compatriots, then perhaps a meaningful relationship could develop. A deeper interracial engagement with racism and Germanness could prove a fruitful exercise in creating a multiracial and multicultural German feminist solidarity. Black German women believed that white German women had to rethink their construction and essentialism of Africa and become more invested in tackling similar injustices against Afro-Germans and other People of Color living in Germany. It was only through their awareness and acceptance of difference that tangible changes could occur.

The editors and contributors also emphasized the necessity of bonds in facilitating Afro-German and Black women's survival in society. In a poem, "Invisible Women," Mary-Ann Powell recognized that there was strength in numbers, and the collective efforts and activities of Black Germans symbolized visibility and diversity.[90] Conveying that Afro-German women were no longer alone in their marginality, as they now had one another to rely on for sustenance, comfort, and community, Powell wrote, "Look at your sisters." "You are not alone!" and "You are not invisible."[91] The presence of strong Black ties became necessary for Afro-Germans to form a collective affiliation with one another, and it also assisted them as they confronted exclusionary German practices together. Likewise, von Pirch echoed similar sentiments about meeting and connecting with her Afro-German sister in "What do I have to do with Africa." She wrote, "I meet a Black sister, I ask her: 'where are you from?' She responded: I am Afro-German." Although von Pirch asked "where are you from," this time the dynamics were different, as both of them were Afro-German. Her Black German compatriot disclosed her story, but von Pirch did not disclose her narrative because her Black German sister's story was hers, even though they were different.[92] Here, von Pirch established an emotional relationship with her Black sister in spite of their differences. Cultivating a sense of kinship, they formed connections to one another based on their analogous experiences of oppression and their conscious self-identification as Afro-German. The bond she shared with her Afro-German sister provided her with fellowship and support. In this case, von Pirch imbued a Black diasporic sisterhood with powerful meaning and challenged the negative connotations and perceptions of Blackness, of which there were few positive representations in society, a point continually addressed in *Afrekete*.[93] After years of self-denial and self-hatred about their Blackness, *Afrekete* allowed Black German women to engender positive and empowering images of Black diasporic individuals that changed traditional German beliefs and served them psychologically. Von Pirch also used the word *Geschichte*, which translates as both story and history, to express that Afro-Germans' personal and collective histories intertwined. Writing their narratives enabled them to recover their German and diasporic pasts and foster radical forms of kinship that were queer strategies of belonging. She further confirmed that individual experiences could not be decoupled from the collective, as they were mutually constitutive.

Affective bonds in ADEFRA and *Afrekete* enabled Black German women to transgress boundaries, rupture frameworks, and build community, often reimagining their kin. Sisterhood, for example, was considered affectionate, intimate, queer, and potentially erotic—a theme also evoked in Lorde's work. According to literary theorist Sharon Marcus, "the erotic and sexual can and do intersect, but only the sexual refers to acts that involve genital arousal. Sexual desires are wishes to perform or fantasies about engaging in such acts."[94] Marcus further posited that, "the erotic has no necessary connection to sex acts, to describe a dynamic or relationship as erotic requires no evidence of sex."[95] In an untitled poem written as a monologue and dialogue—not unlike von Pirch's aforementioned poem—Ja-El demonstrated that affectionate relations could shade into the erotic.[96] These relationships provided women with insight and energy, impacting their lives. She writes, "is it not beautiful that we are siblings/ is it not beautiful that we are potentially loving."[97] The connection with a Black German sister enabled her to share affection, as all circuits of love were acceptable and welcomed. The presence of healthy, loving relationships among women remained an important resource for encouragement in an often racist, homophobic, and patriarchal society. The promise of such profound emotional ties with other Afro-German women resulted in a newfound courage. Indeed, the erotic connection among women should always be expressed and never suppressed because it was a "replenishing and provocative source," giving Afro-German women satisfaction, joy, and motivation.[98] These close attachments allowed Afro-German women to access and engender knowledge about their subjectivities. Their organization and magazine also represented the power of Black feminism to be affective, intellectual, creative, political, and spiritual.

Yet, tensions also emerged in Ja-El's poem, as it remained unclear if the other sibling/partner reciprocated the feelings. The voice of the other Black German sister was never present. Within the monologue, the author implored her sibling/partner not to deny the connection because she saw its potential and wanted it to flourish.[99] She did not want to lose the affective and/or erotic bond and experience rejection. In this case, the inability to gain acceptance from white Germans and then the lack of compassion from her own Afro-German sister would be humiliating, disappointing, and devastating. The poem highlighted that the creation of Afro-German female networks would not necessarily be coterminous with harmony.

Afrekete also emphasized the importance of socially valued bonds between women that did not revolve around erotic or queer liaisons. Some Afro-German women made requests in *Afrekete* for leisure or fitness activities such as volleyball, soccer, and basketball with other Afro-Germans.[100] Their journal enabled ADEFRA feminists to express their interest in sponsoring social gatherings and expanding the general scope of the community. In Düsseldorf, for example, there was a German-African circle that met every third Saturday of every month, and advertisements for musical concerts in Munich with Nina Simone and Miriam Makeba, both of whom performed in June 1991.[101] Contributors of *Afrekete* also underscored the significance of cultivating contacts with their white feminist German counterparts and practicing an intellectual activism that centered intersectional and antiracist themes. In doing so, Afro-Germans sought to open dialogue and connected across their differences. At one event, entitled "Workshop in the Schulz," ADEFRA activists used an interracial workshop as an opportunity to invite white German women, form coalitions, and engage in discussions about racism and discrimination in German society. The interracial group of German women discussed the themes of alienation, oppression, and identity, and Afro-German participants exchanged stories about their individual experiences with racism in their daily interactions and the larger German feminist and women's movement. Conflicts arose as some white German participants ignored the problem of racism by suggesting that it was not an issue in Germany.[102]

In *Afrekete*, May Ayim's "Black-white-Monologue" or "Black-I know-Monologue" directly took up the idea that bonds were not always positive, and that solidarity with women did not necessarily result in a feeling of comfort.[103] Channeling the trickster goddess Afrekete, Ayim's poem was a linguistic play with her German mother tongue, especially as her use of *Schwarz-weiß* represents both "Black-white" or "Black I know."[104] Similar to von Pirch's "What do I have to do with Africa," Ayim tackled the idea of Africa as a construct and the hypocrisy of white Germans. After a vacation to East Africa, the poem's white German woman wanted to inform Ayim about the Maasai people. The white German had an imagined ideal of Africa. She deliberately imposed her views of Africanness onto Ayim—wanting her to dance so that the German woman/traveler could remember her experiences abroad. Despite years of friendship, their interaction forced Ayim to question her relationship with her.[105] The friendship and sisterly bond could no longer work because of the lack of openness, empathy, and understanding between them. In addition to Ayim's poem, Emde's "Invisible" also stressed the difficulties of sustaining relationships with women.[106] Emde described the tensions and silences that existed among German women and how damaging they could be. Whenever there was cowardice, fear, malice, and silence within women's relationships, then disharmony would emerge. This became unsettling for Afro-German women especially when it came to problematic white German solidarity and white Germans' inability to be introspective about their own discriminatory beliefs. The illusion of solidarity transformed into the reality of unacceptable difference and racism.

Moreover, the magazine also emphasized the practice of writing and the cultivation of intellectual practices in interracial circles. In an article "First Collective Writing Workshop of Black and White Women," Kraft, an educator, writer, and contributor to *Afrekete*, described how eleven Afro-German women and seventeen white German women gathered in Bielefeld in June 1988, with Lorde present.[107] This diverse group of women, including several ADEFRA quotidian intellectuals, took part in small seminars and exchanged writing techniques and strategies.[108] The workshop enabled these women to discover and learn new ideas and practices about the processes of writing while also forming an intellectual network. At that writing clinic, women also conducted drills, helping to encourage one another to put ink to paper. The Black and white German women who engaged in this creative process also produced mobile circuits of meaning about their identities and their sense of community. The evocative and emotional nature of some of these texts helped those women challenge the immobilizing silences and create kinship through writing. ADEFRA editors also affirmed the importance of kinship through their usage of photographs in their issues. They created a visual archive of Black women's fellowship and bonding. These women also enacted a visual process of recollection and remembrance, as many of the photographs captured them bonding at ADEFRA events or other feminist conferences in and beyond Germany. In those instances, Black women, nationally and internationally, remained important diasporic resources.

TRANSNATIONAL DIASPORIC ROOTS AND ROUTES

Afro-German women involved with *Afrekete* found it necessary to draw connections to communities across the Black diaspora, much as ISD quotidian intellectuals did in *afro look*.[109] The concept of diaspora has enabled local communities across the globe to achieve cohesiveness by offering opportunities for racial consciousness, solidarity, and belonging. For Black diasporic communities in Europe, much like it was for African American women, "race was a sign of perceived kinship ties between blacks in Africa and throughout the diaspora."[110] ADEFRA's *Afrekete* used several diasporic resources and traditions that shaped Black Germans' consciousness and subjectivity. Here, evidence strongly contradicts Jennifer Michaels's claims that, "Afro-German women writers rarely made use of African myths and history in their texts." She has maintained that it was Lorde who forged connections to West African genealogy through her references to mythical women, goddesses, queens, and warriors in her work. Michaels also alleged that African symbolism and metaphors "had little impact on Afro-German women writers, who were divorced from African and African American oral narrative traditions and thus lacked connections to African myths and history."[111] On the contrary, with *Afrekete*, ADEFRA quotidian intellectuals positioned themselves within transnational diasporic communities and used those communities and herstories as a medium for their writing, self-narration, and self-styling. They solidified their ties to the African continent—in this case, Benin and Ethiopia—especially with their use of the titles of Afrekete and ADEFRA.

Afro-German women continued to stress their links to Africa and the diaspora through the layout of the magazine. On the title pages of each issue, von Pirch and Ja-El regularly depicted the image of a woman or women of African descent. The editors represented the "A" in *Afrekete* on their cover pages with a map of the continent embedded within it. Throughout *Afrekete*, the editors and contributors incorporated photographs, Afrocentric imagery, and diasporic symbolism and metaphors. Some of those images included Black people dressed in African or Afrocentric garb and African figures standing or playing the drums often positioned next to poetry.[112] They accentuated their ties to Africa, real and imagined, and depicted figures and animals that relied on African symbolism and cosmologies. Several of the images conveyed an imagined version of Africa, at times essentializing the diverse countries on the continent. But they also reveal Afro-German women's willingness to engage with gendered Black diasporic topics.

In all the issues of the journal, the editors included a series of informative articles, entitled "Goddesses, Symbols, Myths, and Magic," that touched upon the theme of traditionally powerful women in multiple spacetimes—a theme that was also common in the Euro-American feminist tradition of the 1970s and '80s. Written by Ja-El, the series explored different religious figures and cosmologies in Africa and Europe.[113] Black Germans elucidated the matriarchal tradition of female power and spirituality in African history and how these matriarchs were active agents of their destinies. African goddesses had multivalent meanings given the diversity of countries in Africa, and she used this variety to debunk the myth that Africa had always been patriarchal and oppressive to women. She highlighted the ways that African women wielded power and contributed to their societies, maintaining a strong presence throughout the continent. Ja-El recognized that the actions of their African foremothers in the past became crucial to their present and future. For several Afro-German contributors, those African ancestors became necessary and useful diasporic resources. Here, Afro-German women participated in a broader twentieth-century diasporic self-styling culture. The creation of Black diasporic roots was not an uncommon act among individuals of African descent, with some reading diasporic literature, while others wore Afrocentric clothing and natural hair, as was the case with figures such as Angela Davis and others in the "Black is Beautiful" movement. Black German women preserved and publicized aspects of African and diasporic culture and embraced women-identified politics that gave them a sense of agency.

In addition, ADEFRA's editors underscored the critical role of African diasporic womanhood and produced a genealogy of Black women in their poetry and prose. In their first issue, they mourned the death of forty-five-year-old Dulcie September, an anti-Apartheid activist who was killed in Paris on March 29, 1988. September, the head of the African National Congress (ANC) Information Bureau in France, served as the chief representative of the ANC in Switzerland and Luxembourg.[114] She was murdered by a gun with a silencer outside her office in Paris. Kraft wrote a two-page poem entitled "Für Dulcie September," as a dedication.[115] In it, Kraft described September as "A female messenger of freedom in the city of freedom" and her words were "piercing and dangerous weapons for the regime in Pretoria."[116] She expressed her familial and affective bond by calling September sister. Linking her to other women of the diaspora, such as Mmanthatisi, Zora Neale Hurston, and Rosa Parks, Kraft positioned September within a tradition of strong Black women, emphasized the nature of diasporic roots and routes, and recognized Black women as powerful historical agents. In addition to those women, Kraft also referenced the song "Nomzamo." Nomzamo was a small Black township located in the Western Cape of South Africa and Winnie Mandela's first name. Last, she alluded to Lorde's poem "There Are No Honest Poems About Dead Women."[117] Kraft's poem served as an intervention that sought to change popular consciousness about Black women and ensured that their accomplishments would be remembered and documented. She, along with other ADEFRA feminists, continually linked themselves to women in South Africa and other African countries.[118]

Contributors to *Afrekete* also mourned the death of Black women who, though less prominent than September, shared her experiences and a commitment to social justice; they exposed women's erasure. *Afrekete's* issue *Black feminism* (*schwarzer Feminismus*) contained a memorial to their fellow Afro-German sister, Claudia. For them, it was unfortunate that "another Black woman could not survive."[119] Although Claudia committed suicide, the larger racist German society was complicit in her death. Along with a black and white picture of Claudia, they dedicated a translated version of African American singer Tracy Chapman's song, "She's Got Her Ticket," to her. Chapman's song focused on the desire of a woman to flee the hardships of a society, in which subjugation and hatred were ubiquitous. Once again, Afro-German women established kinships among themselves, Claudia, and Chapman. They were all women of the diaspora with intersecting experiences of oppression. Given their unbelonging in Germany, this was an important antiracist and queer strategy.

Throughout *Afrekete,* contributors also linked themselves to enslaved women and explored the historical legacy of slavery. The symbols of colonialism and slavery (ships, markets, and the selling of human chattel) could be related to the broader issues of dislocation, dehumanization, alienation, and racial persecution that individuals across the diaspora endured.[120] Although the Middle Passage was not the central narrative and lineage of the Black German community, those women still positioned themselves within that global history and showed how that past informed their present. Establishing their connections to their diasporic foremothers and sisters (kin) in the publication reinforced Black Germans' bonds to one another and underscored the significance of writing these narratives. Similarly, in a piece entitled "Black Foremothers I," Kraft focused on the rich legacy of Black diasporic foremothers and Black women's intellectualism.[121] In it, Kraft discussed Phillis Wheatley and her book, *Poems on Various Subjects, Religious, and Moral* (1773). Wheatley served as a model for Black writers across the Atlantic, including Ralph Ellison, Toni Morrison, and Alice Walker.[122] Wheatley's ability to command the language and create literary spaces exemplified her Black women's intellectualism. She accomplished what Afro-German women writers set out to do in *Afrekete* and other cultural productions. Kraft claimed that, during the time, it was an adjustment for white males to see an African woman share the same intellectual capacities as whites, but often "her voice was still not audible."[123] She provided a synopsis of Wheatley's life, and mentioned that Wheatley was criticized for her lack of engagement with her African background, the Black race, and the politics of American slavery.

Kraft hardly meant to marginalize or undercut Wheatley's value to Black Germans or the Black diaspora more broadly. Wheatley did not address Africa or her heritage in her poems, but she did claim an African identity that was not tied to a specific region or group, such as Igbo, Kongo, or Yoruba. According to James Sidbury, Wheatley "helped to transform the term [African] so laden with connotations of primitivism and savagery into a source of pride, [which] required her to counter conventional Enlightenment portrayals of Africans' place-or absence of a place-in the progressive universal history of humanity forged by Enlightenment thinkers."[124] Wheatley, along with other African-descended authors, engendered a positive discourse on African identity. In this instance, Black Germans, too, engaged the legacy of Enlightenment and used "The Master's tools" to transform notions of Germanness, in which language helped them braid diverse cultural heritages together and create new meanings. Kraft demonstrated that Afro-Germans were a part of this fertile diasporic history. Her article had a didactic function, familiarizing Black German women with Black diasporic authors and challenging white German cultural power.

For Afro-German women writers, *Afrekete* enabled them to use literature as a site for intercultural and interracial dialogue and female fellowship. These relationships were inseparable from their refashioned identities. Writing also served as a way to psychologically discharge years of trauma, humiliation, sadness, and loss. Therefore, *Afrekete* allowed a collective purging to take place, enabling these minority women to survive. Now, with writing as a collective antiracist project, they were no longer isolated and found solace and community. As Turkish-German author Gülbahar Kültür noted in a *Die Tageszeitung* article about Black German writers, for them, "writing was everyday life management (and survival), self-determination, and an invasion into a closed society: scathing, direct, and linguistically uncomplicated texts in which courage, anger, vitality, and struggle are palpable. It was a new aspect in contemporary German women's literature."[125] Writing was an affective practice that enabled Black German women to forge kinships and create new energizing spaces that dealt with their displacement and erasure; writing could also be a source of joy. These women embraced Lorde's idea that writing "was a vital necessity of their existence."[126] As such, Afro-German women no longer silently waited for recognition. They demanded it.

*   *   *

Local ADEFRA chapters and the journal *Afrekete* represented a critical Black queer feminist project that served as a form of resistance against oppression and exclusion and promoted alternative forms of kinship. This project produced different discourses and narratives that privileged Blackness, womanhood, queerness, and Black internationalism and challenged the status quo. Afro-German creative cultural practices and productions cultivated spaces for multiple women to grow as agents and to reclaim their positions in the nation and the global Black diaspora. They accepted the newly constructed spaces as a way of sustaining themselves and their collective objectives. In particular, AD-EFRA and *Afrekete* became inclusive spaces that enabled Afro-German women to refashion their identities, participate in collective action, and cement bonds to other Afro-Germans and Women of Color. These feminists and quotidian intellectuals also collaborated with one another to address the gendered and racial struggles they suffered. But these alliances were also subject to personality clashes and internal disunion.

Showing Lorde's imprint, *Afrekete* resonated with Afro-German women and other Women of Color because it helped them build a new textual community that privileged a woman-centered Black diaspora. These new literary developments also facilitated the creation of new social bonds, which provided these women with a profound sense of commitment to one another. At the heart of Afro-German women's alternative kinships were affective connections that led to the practice of new forms of belonging. Relying on mutual dependency and amity, they interacted and confided in one another. While the oppression that Afro-German women endured placed them in the margins, they now joined together, publicized their Black Germanness, and demonstrated that their marginality was no longer negative or insignificant. Their relationships to one another symbolized the strength that those Black women possessed. Black German women pursued diverse types of diasporic activism that focused on the interplay among the local, the national, and the international. Regardless of the regional differences among ADEFRA-Munich, -Hamburg, and -Bremen (south and north), these groups initiated collaborative work and crystallized common organizational goals that reverberated throughout Germany. ADEFRA feminists recognized that their relationships and fellowship served as tools for coalition building and knowledge production, creating alliances and networks that were necessary in their activism.

Black German women also used their intellectual activism to destabilize the persistent if often unspoken belief that German national identity was exclusively white and heteronormative, redirecting attention toward their personal and collective herstories in the here and now. Through the power of writing and intellectual activism, Black German quotidian intellectuals, including Oguntoye, Ayim, and others, resurrected the histories of Black Germans by exposing and preserving the legacy of Blackness and the diaspora in Germany with *Farbe bekennen*. *Farbe bekennen* and other Black German cultural productions put Black Germans on the map and urged those near and far to witness the vitality and agency of this diasporic community.

CHAPTER 4

BLACK GERMAN WOMEN'S INTELLECTUAL ACTIVISM AND TRANSNATIONAL CROSSINGS

Prior to the emergence of ISD and ADEFRA, May Ayim and Katharina Oguntoye met and exchanged their stories, both with each other and other Black Germans across Germany. Those exchanges, along with essays and poems, featured in the pioneering volume *Farbe bekennen*, published in 1986. In it, Ayim, Oguntoye, Helga Emde, Eleonore Wiedenroth-Coulibaly, and other women wrote about their Black German (and Black European) experiences, and instantiated Black Germanness, transforming notions of identity and culture. The volume also rehabilitated multigenerational Black German womanhood, disrupting controlling images.[1] Afro-German women's writing in *Farbe bekennen* represented a critical imperative for their white German counterparts to confront their indifference, ignorance, and prejudice. Afro-German women used their experiences and memories as discursive and affective tools to forge connections to one another and circulate knowledge about Black German histories from the pre- and post-1945 periods. Through *Farbe bekennen* and other Afro-German publications, Black German women expressed their truths, excavated their suppressed histories, and publicized their knowledge. These women understood that writing served as an act of self-expression and a catalyst for change.

This chapter argues that Black German women, especially May Ayim as a clear representative, became quotidian intellectuals with the publication of *Farbe bekennen*. The volume characterized a vernacular form of literature based on its queer form and content and bolstered Black knowledge. These women challenged German identity and normative citizenship by normalizing their Black

Germanness and situating themselves within and against German discourses. In the process, they transformed ideas, meanings, and symbols surrounding whiteness and national identity. With their writing, Black German women formed new intellectual practices and pursued an intellectual activism that documented and validated their experiences. As producers of Black knowledge, they designed discourses and narratives that empowered them. Their literature served as the staging ground for their grassroots political activism. Both at home and abroad, they advanced social justice, confronted discrimination, and pushed for antiracist action.

Afro-German women's intellectual activism also positioned them within Germany's already complex late-postwar public sphere.[2] Yet through their literature, Black German quotidian intellectuals also created a women-centered Black public culture and new spaces for their identities and movement in a majority-white culture that both ignored and erased their existence.[3] *Farbe bekennen* and other works opened up spaces for Black literature and Black (women's) history in the nation and represented how the personal, the affective, the public, and the political intertwined in their daily struggles. Their strategies sought to change the face of the nation and symbolized the convergences of Black and feminist issues that demanded attention in Germany. Black German women developed an intellectual tradition that borrowed from Black diasporic, German, and other multicultural customs, reflecting their community's wide-ranging interests and practices. They negotiated overlapping public cultures with their literary interventions and showed how their literature was diasporic just as much as it was German. Exploring Black Germans' production of alternative discourses and narratives serves as a corrective to the persistent falsehood in German history that their small number meant a lack of serious intellectual contributions. *Farbe bekennen* underscored the contributions of these quotidian intellectuals, in which they made their narratives and experiences understood.

Black German women's literature offered opportunities for a series of crossings that enabled their traversal of diverse geographic, cultural, and national borders and that helped them reimagine the diaspora, their Blackness, and their marginality. As such, they were similar to other Black women writers who positioned themselves in multiple spaces to connect with women from across the globe who had been previously "dis-located by time and space."[4] Black German women, including Ayim, Oguntoye, Emde, Wiedenroth-Coulibaly, and others embodied this idea of border crossing. But Ayim stands out in comparison to those other women because she achieved international prominence through her literature. For many, she became the face and voice of the Black German community. Her writing worked to dissolve the socially, culturally, and politically constructed borders that marginalized Black Germans, Turkish Germans, other minorities, and migrant communities in Germany. Initiated in 1986 with *Farbe bekennen* and continued in the post-1989 context, Ayim's writing demonstrates her evolution as a quotidian intellectual. Unquestionably, she brought everyday racialized experiences to the fore in ways that other German discourses did not, bridging the academic with the mundane. She advanced discussions that stressed the complexity of the Third World and the persistence of race and racism, and unveiled the racial impact of the fall of the Berlin Wall on Blacks and People of Color. All of this shaped her Black internationalism.

WOMEN SPEAKING OUT IN *FARBE BEKENNEN*

Written by and for Afro-Germans, *Farbe bekennen* was a feminist and diasporic intervention that signified their practice of the politics and poetics of representation. Featuring Black German women from the ages of sixteen to seventy, the volume reimagined the parameters of Blackness, womanhood, and queerness across different spacetimes, animating new ways of being, knowing, and thinking. The gendered and racial knowledge created in the volume constituted their Black German identities and experiences while also showing the processes of German discrimination that normalized negative ideas of Blackness and/or Otherness. It took Ayim and Oguntoye two years (1984–1986) to write and to conduct research and interviews. Orlanda Feminist Press published the volume; Dagmar Schultz, the head of Orlanda, also served as a co-editor.

In *Farbe bekennen,* Ayim and Oguntoye applied other intellectual strategies and eschewed traditional approaches and linear narrative forms by interweaving poetry, autobiographical texts, historical essays, interviews, and Ayim's research from her master's thesis.[5] Both women's epistemic acts proved crucial and made Black knowledge tangible. Ayim's facility with European, Black, and other intellectuals was impressive. She asserted her analytical voice and used Angela Davis, Simone de Beauvoir, Frantz Fanon, Walter Rodney, Jean Paul Sartre, and others to bolster her claims. As a quotidian intellectual, Ayim transmitted knowledge, challenged the Eurocentric canon, and decolonized German knowledge. The volume also celebrated the contributors' value as Black German subjects and knowledge producers. Illustrative of this was the cover of the volume, in which different generations of Afro-German women appeared together as agents. The title of *Farbe bekennen,* which translates to "acknowledging color," implied "standing by what one is/believes."[6] The women believed in each other and their project, promoted their "textured identities," and embraced alterity and diversity, allowing for flexible negotiations and manifold possibilities in the national polity.[7]

Figure 8. Cover of *Farbe bekennen: Afro-deutschen Frauen auf den Spuren ihrer Geschichte*, 1986, personal photograph in author's private collection.

Before *Farbe bekennen,* Germany saw a proliferation of autobiographies that shifted attention from the self-made man to the female subject's documentation and articulation of personal histories in the 1970s and 1980s. German women authors sought recognition, promoted "the personal is political," and used their writing as a form of consciousness raising.[8] Those women authors also destabilized static notions of the self and practiced different forms of self-representation. *Farbe bekennen* was akin to this literature and stimulated a new Black German writing culture that changed German literature. As with other postwar intellectuals, Black German women emphasized the public substance and character of ideas through their writings; they also were similar to their Black counterparts like Trinidadian London-based activist Claudia Jones or Black British feminist Stella Dadzie, who used their writings to contest European imperialism, white supremacy, and class oppression. *Farbe bekennen* was part of a broad cultural development that aimed at "writing female subjects into literary identity" and giving the unheard Black German woman a voice and a platform.[9]

As demonstrated in chapter 1, Audre Lorde was an empowering figure who encouraged Black German women to produce their own narratives, even telling them at one point that she would not write another word until she heard their herstories. Reflecting on Lorde's impact twenty years later, Oguntoye wrote, "[she] invited us to make our existence and experiences known to the world."[10] Likewise, Black German activist Peggy Piesche explained in 2012 that, "These Black women and lesbians emerged from their social isolation and denial, becoming literally visible and thus wrote themselves into a history whose meaning they recognized through their contact with Audre Lorde."[11] In a 2007 interview, Black German activist Ekpenyong Ani remarked, "I believe that from the beginning Audre very clearly recognized, how important the impetus or challenge of writing for Black people in Germany was. It offered the possibility for us to come into existence and become visible, so that people in general understood that we existed."[12] Black German women recognized how Lorde pushed them to obtain the recognition they needed and deserved. They also began to express themselves publicly, setting the tone of the movement.[13]

Afro-German women connected their local conditions to those within the transnational Black diaspora. Ayim and Oguntoye reinforced this sentiment in *Farbe bekennen*'s introduction, "In disentangling the threads of our histories within Africa and Germany and connecting them to our subjective experiences, we are becoming more sure of our identity, and are able to assert it more aggressively to the outside world. Perhaps, eventually we will not be simply overlooked by a public steeped in ignorance and prejudice."[14] Some Afro-Germans, it should be noted, did not connect their identity to Africa.[15] Notwithstanding, the volume made its contributors' and readers' personal experiences legible and represented an effort to establish a link to the diaspora and other oppressed communities throughout Germany and the globe.

Considering Germany then lacked a cohesive Black community, the Black literature that they read provided them with "a spiritual connection" to other people across the diaspora. Sheila Mysorekar shared, "Now that we have started to write ourselves, we do not only feed on the books that reach us, but we send out messages as well. Now it's our turn to help [spread] the Word." She continued, "[Black Germans] owe very much to Black literature-African- or Asian-America, Caribbean, African and Asian novels, essays, drama, poetry, everything. And it was Black women writers who taught us to assert ourselves as Black German women." She cited authors like Alice Walker, Toni Morrison, Maya Angelou, Paule Marshall, and Ntzoke Shange, as well as Asian American authors Bharati Mukherjee and Amy Tan, whom she labeled Black, considering them all to be inspirational models for Black German intellectualism. Their "books connected us less with our roots in Africa or Asia, but introduced us to the international community of the Black diaspora."[16] Black German women saw early Black women writers as their intellectual ancestors. Serving as diasporic resources, these Black authors helped Black German women engage in acts of self-styling and self-assertion, as they dealt with "the social underpinnings of racism" in Germany.[17] They received resources that they could not obtain from their white relatives.

Diasporic resources abounded in *Farbe bekennen*. Raja Lubinetzki, for instance, underscored the significance of African and African American literature in her development as a writer. Growing up in East Germany, she began writing at the age of fourteen and familiarized herself with Richard Wright's *Native Son*, James Baldwin's writings, and others from the "Black is Beautiful" movement.[18] For Lubinetzki, "through Afro-American and African literature I could at least define myself." Poetry became a habitual and expressive form through which she acquired self-worth.[19] Writing was also a catharsis for her, as she processed some of the vicissitudes of daily life in the East. There, the official rhetoric declared that everyone was a comrade in the struggle against Western capitalism, and officials established gender equity policies in the workplace, though women still endured some hardships especially as they juggled the demands of work and home.[20] Officials also welcomed the recruitment of Africans as a part of their international solidarity politics. Yet racial equality was hardly a reality for those Africans, Black Germans, and People of Color who experienced everyday prejudice.[21] White East Germans claimed, "We don't discriminate against you; if you talk about color, that's your problem."[22] It was clear that, no matter their political ideology, individuals in East and West Germany espoused similar rhetoric about race, silencing their Black German compatriots.

Eleonore Ellen Wiedenroth-Coulibaly, who was of African American and German descent, saw Africa as a cultural point of reference. Her desire to forge ties to Africa was rooted in what she later described as "the myth of international Black solidarity."[23] In "What makes me so different in the eyes of others?" she explained that she often sought contact with people of African descent. Wiedenroth-Coulibaly claimed that, "Blackness opened me up to a new level of community with people. I experienced openness, friendliness, unquestioned acceptance. I was a 'sister'; I belonged." Blackness, and the African continent by extension, offered a refuge from a difficult and depressing life in Germany, and it allowed her to redefine her identity. Upon advice from her African friends and colleagues, she decided to live in Africa, motivated by the belief that "there's no racism there."[24] She reimagined Africa as an ideal space where Afro-Germans no longer endured discrimination, which contrasted with their racist German

Heimat (homeland). Yet moving to her Liberian *Heimat* did not provide Wie-denroth-Coulibaly with a sense of acceptance. Liberian children and adults labeled her "white lady" or European, subjecting her to another kind of exclusion. Her tough experiences throughout different African countries instilled in her a sense of urgency about returning to and surviving in Germany.[25] This resolve informed her activism in the Afro-German movement, especially as she accepted that Germany was her country. Similarly, Julia Berger, of Italian and Afro-German descent, also described that, "In Africa it was bad for me." Berger's experiences in Africa were unpleasant because Africans referred to her as white.[26] These examples indicate that Africa was not a tabula rasa. Africans considered Black Germans to be white/European, and they still experienced exclusion based on skin color. Through their essays and border crossings, Black German women produced knowledge on the complexity of their identities in relation to the African continent.

Farbe bekennen reflected an urge to explain personal experiences with racial and gendered indignities in the private and public realms. Astrid Berger, who was of German and Cameroonian descent and who was Julia's mother, recalled that in school her "teacher looked at me and said out loud: 'This is quite an interesting case!' I was a 'case', not a person—how was I supposed to deal with that?"[27] Berger was often "asked questions like 'Aren't you glad you can stay here?'" For her, it was "hard to tell such a person that I'm German and don't belong anywhere else. By virtue of my black skin I am often in the position of explaining and defending myself, and this has been true for as long as I can remember." As a nurse, she also endured discrimination and racial abuse from patients.[28] Likewise, Angelika Eisenbrandt, of African American and German heritage, shared similar insulting interactions. She disclosed how her white husband exoticized and essentialized her by saying "Fix your hair in a different way. You know, like Blacks who have that really woolly hair." He wanted her "to look African."[29] At her daughter's school, Eisenbrandt dealt with people saying, "how unusual I look" and asking "[my daughter] with surprise: 'What is your mother? She looks so different.' "[30] These narratives reveal the embedded nature of everyday German racism and what the movement publicized and campaigned against.

For several Afro-German women in the volume, Blackness had a negative connotation that caused them to reject this part of their identity. In the article "An 'Occupation Baby' in Postwar Germany," Helga Emde discussed her childhood, where the legacy of National Socialism still shaped her routine interactions. In addition to being the only Black person in her extended family, she had to confront German beliefs that Blackness did not signify beauty. Emde wrote that, "Black means unworthy of existence. And that's exactly how I felt. I always stayed in the most remote corner; I was shy and timid and felt lucky to be asked to play with the other kids—and how! I felt unworthy of existence. I couldn't afford to be conspicuous or else I'd be noticed, not as a sassy little girl but as 'N*****,' 'Moor Head,' 'Sarotti-Moor,'" At the time, "Moor Head," "Negro Kiss," and "Sarotti-Moor" were the names of popular and overtly racialized sweets.[31] While seemingly innocuous for white Germans, these terms were frequently invoked and were painful for Afro-Germans. Emde tried to hide herself because of her Blackness. Yet, Emde's racialized body also made her conspicuous. In this case, a tension existed between Emde's desire for invisibility and her aversion to her visible difference. She further explored this dilemma in her poem "The Cry," which appeared after her essay. Again, Emde wrote about her childhood memories with white German children and adults who excluded her based on her physical appearance. They viewed her as a monolithic "N***** child," who had to behave for both her gender and her race.[32] Venting years of frustrations, her autobiographical article and poetry served as a form of therapy. Those poignant narratives also represented different forms of affective knowledge. In addition, Ayim's essay "The Break" and Oguntoye's poem "Reflection" conveyed similar sentiments about Blackness and exclusion.[33] As a result of their upbringings, *Farbe bekennen* and the larger movement provided Black German women with a much-needed space, where they could be and could process those negative experiences and emotions. Together, the contributions served as diasporic resources for themselves and their Black compatriots.

Farbe bekennen not only initiated what became one of the core intellectual projects of the movement—recovering the collective histories of Black Germans—but it also garnered attention, showing its cultural impact. Contributors promoted the volume across Germany by giving presentations, educating audiences, and forging connections with their Afro-German counterparts in attendance.[34] Similar to other Black Germans, Ayim began to establish herself by handling numerous speaking requests. As quotidian intellectuals, these women occupied diverse spaces to transmit their knowledge and change social dynamics, defying cultural norms and viewpoints. From 1986 to 1987, prominent national and local German newspapers and magazines, such as *Die Tageszeitung* (taz), *Frankfurter Rundschau, Stern, Emma, Zitty, Der Tagesspiegel, Tarantel, LesbenStich,* and *Kieler Rundschau* reviewed the publication.[35] These were diverse publications in terms of their reach, quality, political perspective, and targeted readership. In addition, a series of documentaries on Black Germans aired on different television stations across the country, generating discussions about the existence and diversity of Black Germans and their relegated positions in society.[36]

In 1992 the volume also gained a wider readership across the Atlantic with its publication in English as *Showing our Colors: Afro German Women Speak Out* through the University of Massachusetts Press. It received coverage in the United States and Canada.[37] Black British feminist sociologist Gail Lewis, a longstanding member of the Black British Women's Group, penned the preface to the 1992 British edition of the volume distributed by Open Letters Press in London.[38] Leroy Hopkins has argued that German critics have either ignored Afro-German literary productions or deemed them sociological or foreign, but those aforementioned examples suggest that Afro-German literature had more cultural currency than previously realized, given the events organized and reviews that *Farbe bekennen* received in Germany and elsewhere.[39]

Remaining quotidian intellectuals after *Farbe bekennen,* Afro-German women disseminated their knowledge in multiple venues, where they centered discourses on race and racism and showed the importance of feminist theory *and* practice. They organized reading groups on diverse scholarly texts. Emde published in a variety of German feminist and women-centered journals, including *Afrekete* and the *Contributions to Feminist Theory and Praxis* (*Beiträge zur feministischen Theorie und Praxis*), particularly in the latter's 1988 issue and 1990 special issue on "Divided Feminism: Racism, Antisemitism, and Xenophobia." The special issue featured essays from Ika Hügel-Marshall, Marion Kraft, Sheila Mysorekar, and other feminists from both sides of the Atlantic, including bell hooks. Revealing their willingness to collaborate with other feminists in Germany, Black German women showcased their intellectual and academic engagement and theorized sexism, racism, and Blackness across spacetimes. In the process, they began to change discourses in the mainstream women's movement.[40] Ayim and Oguntoye contributed pieces to a 1989 volume, *Women of Black Africa* (*Schwarz Afrika der Frauen*), sharing their emotions about traveling to their fathers' homelands.[41] For some, their intellectualism grew in and beyond the Black German community and Germany. For example, Emde's intellectual work on Black Germans featured in a 1998 English-language volume for the American Institute for Contemporary German Studies. Mysorekar also published an essay in Carole Boyce Davies's 1995 edited volume on Black women writers.[42] Their combined intellectualism remained a critical and sustaining practice.

Additionally, Oguntoye's and Ayim's initial research in *Farbe bekennen* influenced their future academic and intellectual work. Oguntoye obtained a master's degree in history and published her thesis as *An Afro-German Story: On the Living Situation of Africans and Afro-Germans in Germany from 1884–1950* (*Eine afro-deutsche Geschichte: Zur Lebenssituation von Afrikanern und Afro-Deutschen in Deutschland von 1884 bis 1950*) in 1997.[43] In this book, she produced a historical narrative about

Black Germans' political engagement in the colonies and metropole; this initial work has continued to influence scholars. To this day, Oguntoye still pursues historical projects on Black Germans. Ayim also returned to school to pursue a degree in speech therapy and later a PhD in education at the Freie Universität Berlin with the topic "Ethnocentrism and Racism in Therapy."[44] Ayim later taught as a lecturer at several Berlin-based universities, further imparting knowledge. Whatever the literary venue, Ayim, Emde, Oguntoye, and others demonstrated their intellectual authority on the topics of racism, Eurocentrism, diasporic history, comparative literature, and other themes in their writings. They exemplified the dynamic intellectual culture that Black German women created, in which they held their own as theorists, readers, and writers. *Farbe bekennen* was an impetus and a concrete way for Black German women to express and affirm their identity and ideas and claim spaces within the public sphere.

Through the volume, Ayim, along with others, established a Black German intellectual tradition that relied on diverse German and diasporic customs and ushered in a new generation of Black intellectual thought. Owing to Ayim's work in *Farbe bekennen,* she emerged as one of the most significant figures in the Afro-German community. She became a prominent quotidian intellectual and spokesperson against injustice. Throughout her career, she returned to and built upon her work in *Farbe bekennen.* As demonstrated in the next section, Ayim's early experiences in postwar Germany informed her practices of intellectual activism and Black internationalism.

MAY AYIM'S EARLY YEARS

Brigitte Sylvia Gertrud, nicknamed May, was born on May 3, 1960 in Hamburg to Ursula Andler, a young German woman, and Emmanuel Ayim, a Ghanaian medical student. Ayim wanted to take May back to Ghana for his childless sister, but in Germany, he had no rights to his out-of-wedlock daughter.[45] Her white German mother, like some German mothers of mixed-race children, placed her in an orphanage. She remained at the home for two years until a white German couple from Münster adopted her. She joined the Opitz family that already had children.

Post–World War II German public discourses on gender, race, and class informed the private practices of the family. During her childhood, Ayim felt abandoned by her birth parents and trapped in a loveless family, and her adoptive parents labeled her a "pure-blooded half-breed" (*"reinrassiger Mischling"*).[46] Germans assigned this disparaging term to mixed-race children of African or African American descent in the postwar period. During and after the war, many white Germans viewed Black German children as in but not of the nation, reflecting a belief that Germans were racially homogeneous. Compounding this, German citizenship and national identity, based on a biological notion of whiteness, privileged bloodlines, descent, and paternity.

Ayim's adoptive parents were strict in the hope that she would become a model student in spite of her lineage, which they believed reflected the way-wardness of her German mother and Ghanaian father. She suffered frequent punishment from her parents because of her school performance, behavior, and skin color. Ayim's parents were convinced that with good behavior, she could rise above her "half-breed" status, and they informed her that she must "Always behave nice and proper" because "what people think of you they think of all people of color." Visits every few years from her biological father, nick-named Uncle Emmanuel or Uncle E, informed her negative ideas on Blackness; she remained frightened of him. Ayim longed for whiteness, and "ate soap to become white like her brother." She feared life and harbored suicidal thoughts. Her troubled childhood with the family "made an impression, and the negative events remained clearer in her memory than the positive ones." [47]

Through exchanges with white German teachers and peers, she fostered a belief that Blackness was bad, filthy, and evil. One of Ayim's teachers assigned

Figure 9. "May Ayim in a class photo," photographer unknown, Münster, July 17, 1970, Freie Universität Berlin, Universitätsarchiv, V/N-2 May Ayim (Opitz), Sig. 17.

her the role of a devil in a school play. Children at school and in the neighborhood called her "Moor Head" and "Negro Kiss"—similar to Emde. She also fielded questions from white Germans about when she would return to her homeland and why she spoke German so well. As a result, Ayim developed damaging ideas about her Black identity and longed for acceptance in a nation that imagined itself as exclusively white.

As she grew older, the tensions culminated when she arrived home late one night. This minor transgression resulted in Ayim's parents throwing her out. After this, she maintained sporadic contact with them and her siblings. When she communicated with her parents, they always criticized her and did not support her, claiming that her activism in the community was "a pathological need to overcome her color and Afro-German identity."[48]

On her own at nineteen, Ayim completed her high school exams, studied at a teacher's college in Münster, and transferred to the University of Regensburg, where she majored in education and psychology. Later, she visited Egypt, Ghana, and Kenya, reaching out to her biological father, who was now a professor of medicine in Nairobi. While the trip did not strengthen their relationship, she fostered an important connection to her African roots.

These circumstances and the newfound freedom to explore shaped her writing and her outlook on the meanings of diasporic identity and community. Prevailing against isolation, she welcomed ties to Black Germans and other marginalized communities, and moving to Berlin in 1984 helped her do just that.[49] Her difficulties as an Afro-German woman in an avowedly white postwar German society revealed the necessity of cultivating links with other Black people and People of Color, facing similar struggles. She even reconnected with relatives on a 1986 trip to Ghana, and traveled throughout the world for both work and pleasure. In addition to traveling, Ayim continued to write and perform. Understanding Ayim's commitment to antiracism, feminism, and Black internationalism requires tracing her activism from 1985 to 1996. For more than a decade, she maintained solidarity networks within and beyond Germany that provided her with strategies for survival and resistance.

AYIM'S INTELLECTUAL ACTIVISM IN GERMANY

Despite her hectic schedule, Ayim remained active in the Black German movement. This entailed organizing a variety of conferences, workshops, and projects, including ISD's annual meetings (*Bundestreffen*) and Black History Month celebrations that enabled Black Germans to reclaim spaces within the nation. For Ayim, "Afro-Germans' new visibility improved her quality of life."[50]

Moreover, her activism in ISD and ADEFRA, to a lesser extent, helped her hone organizational skills and build networks in Germany. She also continued to give readings that engaged the themes of racism and sexism.

In addition to the movement, she became involved in other German organizations that championed antiracism and multiculturalism and that attended to internationalist issues. She joined the German branch of the International League for Human Rights (Internationale Liga für Menschenrechte).[51] Ayim became a member of the Antiracist Initiative (Antirassistischen Initiative) and attended their forum, "Action days against racism, sexism, and fascism" (*Aktionstage gegen Rassismus, Sexismus und Faschismus*), held in the spring of 1988 and their subsequent international conference "Against racism, fascism, and sexism" (*Gegen Rassismus, Sexismus, und Faschismus*) in the fall of 1988.[52] Both Berlin-based organizations advocated for human rights through antidiscrimination initiatives. While the available sources tell us that Ayim desired social change and was dedicated to multiple organizations concerned with bigotry and oppression in Germany, we know less about how she interacted with others at these events or how frequently she attended meetings and events. Nonetheless, Ayim's activism outside the Black German movement focused on human rights more broadly and exhibited her commitment to coalition building.

By working with other German minorities, Ayim practiced Lorde's mantra of connected differences and remained true to her vision of activism. She and Nivedita Prasad, an Indian and German activist, organized the 1990 conference, "Ways to Alliances" (*Wege zu Bündnissen*), occurring in Bremen for "ethnic and Afro-German minorities" and planned a 1991 national congress held in Berlin that addressed the plight of immigrant, Jewish, and Black German women. In 1992 they also published *Documentation: Ways to Alliances* with revised conference papers.[53] With the 1990 "The Other Republic" (*Die andere Republik*), a multicultural festival, Ayim engaged with Women of Color and white German antiracists such as feminist Tatjana Böhm, Turkish-German Green Party member Sevim Çelebi, Indian antiracist Sanchita Basu, and Green Party member Ingrid Lottenburger.[54] These conferences advanced ideas about Germany's growing diversity, and signified Ayim's eagerness to build alliances with white Germans and other oppressed communities and to initiate critical dialogues about the problems plaguing Germany. In the 1990s, she also attended meetings for the Black Women's Informal Information and Support Network that included Dionne Sparks, Branwen Okpako, and Auma Obama.[55] She consciously pursued work with Black women. In a 1995 interview, Ayim explained how pleased she was to see that discussions on racism and multiculturalism gradually occurred in Germany and that these developments affected people's opinions, although they had yet to have a full impact in society.[56]

Ayim derived a key source of political and emotional energy from her writing. Her writing was not merely a component of her politics, but it was her politics. It was her poetry, more so than her organizing, that ultimately gave her international acclaim. She gained recognition performing spoken-word nationally and internationally. Performing was therapeutic and validated her experiences and allowed her to support multiple causes. In 1988 she co-founded a Berlin-based literary association, entitled Literature Women (Literatur Frauen e.V., LIT). LIT supported diverse women writers, organized literary events, and pursued research on women. The organization's membership included Schultz, Elsbeth de Roos (Dutch), Ewa Boura (Greek), Sonia Solarte (Colombian), and others, and they organized events with authors such as South African feminist Ellen Kuzwayo.[57] Ayim also read her texts and served as a moderator on a panel about women's literature at the 1988 Women of the World (*Frauen der Welt*) conference entitled "Africa-Women-Weeks" (*Afrika-Frauen-Wochen*) in Berlin.[58] At the 1993 Frankfurt Book Fair, she participated in "Silence is to blame: German is a colorful language" (*Schweigen ist schuld: Deutsch ist eine bunte Sprache*), a conference with

Figure 10. "May Ayim with members of the organization Literatur Frauen, e.V.," photographer unknown, Berlin, 1991, Freie Universität Berlin, Universitätsarchiv, V/N-2 May Ayim (Opitz), Sig. 8.

Women of Color authors.[59] Again, these events demonstrate her commitment to use her writing as a tool for solidarity and advocacy.

At another 1993 panel, she read excerpts from her essay "The Year 1990: Homeland and Unity from an Afro-German Perspective" (*Das Jahr 1990: Heimat und Einheit aus afro-deutscher Perspektive*) in *Distant Ties* (*Entfernte Verbindungen*)—a volume she co-edited and published with Orlanda.[60] In it, she considered the post-Wall climate, "the Wall's shadow had been cast into our East-West brains. People from the two Germanys met one another like twins who know about their common parents but had lived separated from each other since birth. . . . The early excitement of encounter crumbled with unpredictable speed, and the deceitfully won unity suffocated just as quickly under the tight artificial cloak of liberal German folksiness. Of course, you saw the little 'one-Germany' flags and banners waving." She continued, "Who was embracing each other in German-German reunification, and who was embraced, pulled in, bumped out?"[61] After the fall of the Wall, she expanded discourses on East-West and North-South divides by stressing the intersections of identity, racism, and nationalism. For her, East-West programming and initiatives needed to integrate discussions on the North and the South (Third World). Ayim sought to awaken individuals to the illusion of German unity on the ground and cemented her role as a leading Afro-German quotidian intellectual. Connecting with other diasporic writers,

Figure 11. "May Ayim at a reading with Maryse Condé," photographer unknown, Berlin, February 2, 1994, Freie Universität Berlin, Universitätsarchiv, V/N-2 May Ayim (Opitz), Sig. 15.

Ayim served as a moderator for a 1994 Berlin reading of Maryse Condé's newly translated book *The Children of Segu* (*Wie Spreu im Wind*) and later interviewed her and wrote a review of the book.[62] These examples signify her politics and poetics of representation in practice.

Ayim's inclusion of African, African American, and other Black diasporic themes and metaphors also enabled her to position Afro-Germans within a Black intellectual tradition.[63] Through her existential and autobiographical poems, articles, speeches, and spoken-word performances, Ayim used her imposed marginal position to draw attention to Afro-Germans' collective and individual difficulties in German society. In particular, she defied a German epistemic tradition that included men like Georg Wilhelm Friedrich Hegel. Hegel believed the African Other lacked a history and the ability to reason because they were "children," and that Africans could not attain civilization or progress, remaining outside Europe's borders.[64] Ayim's literature established her ability to reason and think philosophically, and her literature located and placed the Black subject within the German nation and European continent more broadly. She also allowed for a more complex understanding of culture and the nation. One that revealed the heterogeneous histories of Black Germans and other minorities in various spacetimes, often outside the spacetime of slavery. As a quotidian intellectual, Ayim captured the *Zeitgeist,* in this case the spirit of the Black German community, demanding a critical assessment of racist discourses and practices in German society, yet comprehending and accepting the differences that existed within and shaped the nation.

In her work, Ayim attended to Germany's colonial and fascist pasts and redirected attention to their afterlives in contemporary society. She explicated that the history of German individuals of color was tied to racist exhibitions and racist colonial projects and showed how Afro-German history predated the postwar period. Indeed, that history had long remained a significant part of German history, though often overlooked and forgotten. She critiqued the discourses that the reunified German government and media advanced by arguing that they sustained a system that indoctrinated a susceptible public. In Ayim's critique, the racist German culture manufactured discourses on integration and multiculturalism that ironically served to silence German minorities, preventing dialogue and transformation from occurring. Throughout her intellectual activism, these and other themes remained central.

In the spirit of other diasporic writers, Ayim's writing was never devoid of political substance that helped her cultivate links.[65] Publishing *Blues in black white* (*Blues in schwarz weiss*) as her first poetry volume in 1995, she proved that her writing and activism remained inseparable.[66] Through her texts and oral performances, Ayim showed the German language's elasticity and melodious sound, pushing its affective reach. In her foreword in Ayim's volume, Maryse Condé noted, "In May's voice I found the echo of other sounds of the diaspora."[67] Throughout the volume, she used multivalent Adinkra symbols and proverbs from Ghana and African American blues traditions, especially with the title and content of her volume.[68] Her first volume was reviewed in several well-known magazines and newspapers in Germany. Indicating her growing reputation, Ayim was also nominated for the *International Who's Who of Contemporary Achievement* in 1995.[69]

Her writing often addressed the themes of identity, marginalization, community, and the global diaspora. In an unpublished English poem, she wrote:

> i am always the other one
>> am the one who does not exist
> i am so obvious
>> that they overlook me
>
>>>> i am the black german
>>>>> i am your contradiction
>>>> i am the part of history
>>>>> that you need to recognize
>>> I AM[70]

Ayim confronted white German society's unwillingness to accept Black Germans, and reinscribed herself (and the community) within the nation. She also embraced the seemingly contradictory nature of her Black German identity and linked it to German history and culture more broadly. Another one of her poems, "Borderless and Brazen" (*grenzenlos und unverschämt*), which tackled racialized issues in reunified Germany, was included in a 1993 special issue of an Afro-Brazilian magazine entitled *Yes to Life* (*Sim da Vida*). Sponsored by the group Black Woman Make Poetry (Mulher negra faz poesia), the magazine also featured works from Caribbean American June Jordan, Zimbabwean Chiny Aradzo, and Afro-Dominican Ochy Curiel.[71]

With the poems "Afro-German I" and Afro-German II," Ayim garnered worldwide esteem. Both poems were written in 1985 while she worked on *Farbe bekennen,* and she performed "Afro-German I" in numerous countries. The poems were published multiple times and took the form of both a dialogue and monologue, in which Ayim at moments disappeared from the conversation.[72] In these poems, she validated Black German subjectivities by re-creating a routine exchange, and confronted white German society's unwillingness to accept Black Germans. Ayim broached topics that Black Germans felt and experienced, and these topics figured prominently in other Afro-German writings, as noted in chapter 3. With the first poem, Ayim depicted a white German woman expressing a degree of incredulousness and fascination about her alleged paradoxical Afro-German identity, declaring:

> You are Afro-German?
> ah, I understand: African and German.
> An interesting mixture, huh![73]

Ayim and other Afro-Germans were "interesting mixtures" rather than normal German citizens. Later, the woman suggested that Ayim "return" to Africa and civilize her people, spreading the ideals of humanity to the "lower culture."[74] Here, too, Ayim recognizes Hegel's philosophical legacy about the African Other.

In "Afro-German II" Ayim continued to focus on Afro-German identity by unsettling the characteristics that white Germans ascribed to African-descended people. She also attended to the lateral differences that linked Black Germans to diverse German minority populations, such as Jewish, Turkish, and the Sinti and Roma. German discriminatory practices, exclusionary discourses, and structural racism impacted all these communities, and afforded opportunities for solidarity.[75] Ayim identified these connected differences with the following lines, the white German interlocutor utters:

> . . . hm, I see.
> You can be glad you're not Turkish, huh?
> I mean: this harassment of foreigners is just awful,
> do you get some of that too, sometimes?[76]

The white German woman perceives Ayim's race as foreign to Germanness and second-guesses whether Ayim could be a native German. She denies her access to German national identity. Wright has maintained, "In short, Afro-German identity is not the *antithesis* in the dialectic of (white) German subjectivity: *it is simply non-existent.*" In Wright's theorization, the Other helped to define the parameters of Europeans' superiority, even though the Other's existence was deemed insignificant.[77] In asking her if she experiences harassment similar to "foreigners," presumed to be Turkish people, the white German's naivete simultaneously marks her as foreign and different from Turks, and Germans by extension. On one level, Ayim can nationally belong as German, but can also unbelong because of her racial identity, which invalidates part of her complex identity. In doing so, the woman casts Ayim as both an "Other-from-Within and an Other-from-Without," and this contradiction shapes her nonexistence in the nation. She claims that Ayim should be lucky that she was not Turkish because they were (and still are) considered "foreigners." Similar, yet different to their positioning of Black Germans, white Germans considered Turkish Germans to not be Germans based on an unspoken belief that whiteness and Judeo-Christian values undergirded Germanness. Therefore, the German woman's observation implied that "foreign" Turkish individuals endured more persecution than Afro-Germans, while ironically harassing and offending Ayim. In this way, xenophobia is more readily accessible as a German discourse than racism.

Discussing xenophobic attacks in society, the white German inquired about Ayim's experiences of racial discrimination but only provided a veneer of sincerity. The white German woman actually downplayed the role of racism in these attacks that occurred before the fall of the Berlin Wall. In doing so, the white German trivialized the experiences of racism that Ayim and other German minorities faced, replying that as a woman, she also had some problems.[78] Wright has posited that, "Ayim also made a point of providing an effective counter-discourse for the Afro-German subject."[79] Uncovering the white German compatriot's ignorance in these autobiographical poems, Ayim's literature and the larger movement's efforts at intellectual activism emphasized instances of everyday German racism and sought to purge society of its racist practices and beliefs. Together, they spatially fixed Black German subjects in the nation.

Through her literature, Ayim performed cultural and social work on behalf of the Afro-German community, in which she outlined their daily struggles that entailed verbal, physical, and visual racial abuse and trauma. In additional poems in Blues in black white, such as "Distant Ties" (entfernte verbindungen), "Blues in Black-White" (blues in schwarz-weiss), "No more rotten gray-for a colorful republic: talk-talk-show for the blah-blah struggle" (gegen leberwurst-grau- für eine bunte republik talk-talk-show für den bla-bla-kampf), and "Autumn in Germany" (deutschland im herbst), Ayim interrogated the concerns of the diaspora, community, racism, and the hypocrisy of German reunification along with its rhetoric of accord and inclusion.[80] Each poem uncovers different aspects of the experiences of People of Color in Germany. She also publicized these developments by publishing in widespread venues such as Die Tageszeitung, Ms. magazine, and others.[81] Ayim recognized that intolerance in post-Wall Germany intersected with others across the world and highlighted the significance of examples of everyday discrimination in global contexts in her writing. Broaching international themes with "Jerusalem" (Jerusalem) and "Please Bosnia-Herzegovina War" (bitte bosnia herzegowina krieg), Ayim transcended German boundaries in an effort to cultivate connections with other marginalized and transnational communities.[82] Ayim wrote poems about well- and lesser-known individuals across the Black diaspora, including

Lorde, Martin Luther King Jr., and Ana Herrero-Villamor, an Afro-Spanish and German woman active in ISD-Berlin who committed suicide.[83] She did this to show how the Israeli occupation, the dissolution of Yugoslavia, and civil rights activism in the United States dealt with common themes of oppression and the physical and symbolic walls of exclusion. Ayim believed these human rights campaigns were interrelated.

Seeking connections to help her survive, Ayim developed relationships and networks outside her native country. Reaching across borders, she became a global citizen who traveled to international forums and conferences. Her transnational activism helped her cultivate bonds to others that informed her work and that gave her renown.

AYIM'S TRANSNATIONAL ACTIVISM

With invitations to perform her spoken-word poetry abroad, Ayim achieved international acclaim. Condé described her as a captivating performer, "[Her] exceptional voice. Unique and already in the hearts of all of us, who are persecuted and thirsty."[84] She used her appeal to bolster her position and to retain recognition. Her literature, presentations, and performances gave her an opportunity to share knowledge about Afro-Germans and to use it to connect with others. These transnational exchanges also fortified her engagement with antiracist and feminist causes across Europe and the globe. At the 1992 "African Women in Europe" conference in London, Ayim saw the event as an opportunity to "creat[e] a space for African women to get together and share their experiences, and strengthen us in and against a Europe which tries to keep us far from each other and away from power and privileges," and she wanted "to develop and improve contact with black movements in other countries."[85] This conference, like others, demonstrated her will to change the policies of Fortress Europe, in which politicians across the continent continued to treat nonwhite Europeans with hostility and increasingly made borders impenetrable to migrants and refugees.

Ayim valued the possibilities for transnational networking and organizing that conferences such as this one offered. Presenting "My pen is my sword: Racism and Resistance in Germany," she again stressed the importance of writing as a medium for community and social transformation for migrants, herself, and Black Europeans. She explained the plight of minorities and their political mobilization in Germany. Although the situation there was "more aggressive and depressing," "white Germans," Ayim noted, "are now waking up and becoming more actively involved in the anti-racist movement." In the talk, she concluded that, "as black women, we try to conquer racism and sexism outside our communities. We might belong to a minority within European countries, but we definitely belong to the struggling majority on this globe."[86]

Ayim recognized how racism and intolerance at the national, continental, and international levels impacted People of Color in Europe. She constantly touched upon these themes at venues, including the 1990 conference on "Exclusion and Tolerance: Modern Racism in the Netherlands and the Federal Republic of Germany," held in Eindhoven, and the University of Warwick and the Technical University of Berlin's 1993 joint conference "Discrimination, Racism and Citizenship: Inclusion and Exclusion in Britain and Germany," where she presented on behalf of ISD.[87] Through her literature, she created awareness of the racialized conditions of Blacks and People of Color in Germany. Each venue was an opportunity to foster critical discussions, to decolonize European knowledge, and to counteract racist developments in the aftermath of the fall of the Berlin Wall.

At the Eleventh International Book Fair of Radical Black and Third World Books in London and this Fair's 1993 one-day conference entitled "Bigotry, Racism, Nazism and Fascism in Europe," which the European Action for Racial Equality and Social Justice (EARESJ) organization also sponsored, she explained the heightened racism after the Berlin Wall, the existent silences regarding Black history, and the inability for antiracist initiatives and public debates to include People of Color in Germany. Ayim also connected with Jamaican-British dub poet Linton Kwesi Johnson, Ghanaian-born British editor and writer Margaret Busby, and Caribbean American feminist author June Jordan, which provided her with sustenance; she developed a strong friendship with Johnson.[88] For years, Ayim, and other Black Germans, including the brothers Nii and Obi Addy and John Kantara, had attended these international book fairs that Black British activist John La Rose organized.[89] Her connection to La Rose and the book fair resulted in her involvement with the EARESJ, of which she was a founding member. These events confirmed that Ayim used her writing and presentations to link with others and agitate for social change.

Participation in these activities was empowering and reinforced Ayim's bonds to women internationally. At the 1994 "Racisms & Feminisms: Differences and Power Relations among Women—Political Solidarity, Feminist Visions" conference in Vienna, she interacted with scholars from the United States such as Trinh T. Minh-ha, Ruth Frankenberg, and Patricia Hill Collins. She attended the panels of other attendees such as British-based sociologist Avtar Brah, Turkish political scientist Dilek Çinar, and Bosnian activist Selena Tufek, with each offering perspectives from their respective countries. These exchanges and her reading from *Distant Ties* positioned her as an important intellectual.[90] Her involvement in these events strengthened her commitment to engage in pan-European dialogues about exclusion and to combat discrimination throughout Europe. To further assist her with these goals, she participated in events for UNESCO, the Council of Europe's Roundtable on "Human Rights and Cultural Politics in a Changing Europe," and the Pan-European Women's Network for Intercultural Action and Exchange (AKWAABA), which represented the cultures and experiences of Black and ethnic minority women.[91] She willingly worked with other Black Europeans on the topic of racism in Europe. Ayim pursued multicultural feminist alliances, becoming a fixture at the international Cross-Cultural Black Women's Studies Summer Institutes, discussed in chapter 6.

Continuing her transnational political activism, Ayim participated in North American and African events that focused on racism's global impact. At the University of Minnesota's 1994 international conference "Xenophobia in Germany: National and Cultural Identities after Unification," she connected with scholars and writers such as Turkish Yüksel Pazarkaya and American Leslie Adelson. Ayim again drew attention to Afro-Germans and issues of intolerance by presenting a keynote speech entitled "Racism and Resistance in United Germany." She had previously given this talk at Carleton College.[92] In her talk, Ayim shared, "There has always been a great reluctance to use the term racism within the German context. The most preferred term is still 'xenophobia' or 'hostility against foreigners,' but these terms deny the fact that all foreigners are not equally subject to attack and that Black Germans are also a target for violence." Later in her talk, she proffered accounts about the alarming climate of 1990s Germany, which saw an upsurge in racial violence. She was disappointed that the "German media barely gave attention to the release of Nelson Mandela" in February 1990. In addition, Ayim "was enraged that noone [sic] talked about the fact that on one side, people welcomed the white citizens of the former GDR whereas, on the other hand, immigration laws for migrants especially from 2/3 of the world- countries, were changed," making it more difficult for them to enter the country.[93] But she ended optimistically, explaining concrete examples of multiracial alliances and antiracism work undertaken in Germany. Ayim's presentation at the University of Minnesota, much like her articles, poetry, and performances, educated audiences about the pressing issues facing Black and People of Color communities and their uphill battle to address the engrained nature of German racism in its everyday and structural forms. After Minnesota, Ayim remained in the United States, traveling to Earlham, DePaul, and other institutions.[94]

Later that year, at the Second Annual Panafest symposium in Accra, Ghana, she enlightened international audiences on the Afro-German experience. Ayim presented a paper entitled "People of African Descent in Europe: The Afro-German Experience," connecting with multiple scholars across the diaspora.[95] It was also at this conference that she became more acquainted with the West African Adinkra symbols that she later incorporated into *Blues in black white*, which emphasizes the importance of these experiences for Ayim and their ongoing value. She also traveled to South Africa in 1995, giving presentations at festivals and universities. As always, Ayim's affective practice of Black internationalism was attuned to intercultural connections and diasporic politics.

While Ayim used these international events to sustain her, life remained difficult. She suffered from depression, receiving psychiatric treatments in 1996. She was diagnosed with multiple sclerosis that same year, just as her career was on the rise. Personal hardships, micro/macroaggressions, and racial exhaustion proved too much. Owing to those issues, she ended her life on August 9, 1996 by jumping off a high-rise building in Berlin-Kreuzberg.[96] Sadly, two days later, Ayim was offered a guest professorship at the University of Minnesota. She left her manuscripts to Orlanda, which published *Borderless and Brazen* (*Grenzenlos und unverschämt*) and *Nightsong* (*Nachtgesang*) in 1997.[97] Unfortunately, conflict emerged, particularly as several Black Germans disliked the idea that she left her work to a white German woman, Schultz, and her press. Moreover, at Ayim's funeral a few activists fought with her adoptive parents. Notwithstanding these dynamics, her death changed the tenor of the movement and shocked many of her friends.[98] As Black German journalist Abini Zöllner remarked, she was a "sharp observer and a voice of the Black community." Another Black German activist-intellectual Nicola Lauré al-Samarai said, "her void is an abyss over which we must learn to tighten our networks."[99] Beyond Germany, friends and peers remembered her, including African American feminist Barbara Smith and Linton Kwesi Johnson, who wrote "Reggae Fi May Ayim" and recorded it on his 1998 *More Time* album.[100]

Ayim left a legacy as a dynamic Afro-German quotidian intellectual. She built networks and connections with Black Germans, other Black people, People of Color, and white allies in Germany and abroad. Moreover, her writing and emotions informed her diasporic and feminist activism. Attending events garnered Ayim international acclaim, which she used to push for recognition for Afro-Germans and to address issues of bigotry in Germany and Europe. Through her work, she demonstrated how local, national, and international events and movements overlapped. Ayim's activism underscores how her embodied Black internationalism impelled her to cross borders, forming ties with others. In this way, she was truly "borderless and brazen."

* * *

Farbe bekennen and Ayim's work were signature moments in the emergence of an Afro-German intellectual tradition that privileged diverse vernacular forms of expression. Constructing an alternative space through their writing, these Black German female quotidian intellectuals informed the general public about the lives of Black women and Women of Color and demanded recognition in German society. Those Afro-German women created a variety of intellectual spaces where they legitimized their knowledge through the production, dissemination, and performance of their literature and art. *Farbe bekennen* also enabled Afro-German women to declare their womanhood and align with women across Germany and the diaspora who faced similar experiences of social exclusion and discrimination. In addition, Afro-German women claimed a positive and empowering connection to African, African American, and Black diasporic traditions while also cultivating new bonds and refashioning identities. While the oppression that these women faced placed them on the margins, they joined together and embraced their marginality as a profound resource. They became quotidian intellectuals agitating for political and social changes in their everyday.

Black German women also employed writing as a way of healing their scars and purging the negativity collectively. Writing served as a catharsis, though not a panacea, especially as women attempted to process their childhood traumas and years of discrimination, and served as an act of self-definition and self-preservation. Writing, intellectualism, and the movement were interdependent. Through writing, Afro-Germans mediated between German and Black diasporic cultures, affirming their textured identities. Black German women used their literature as sites for cultural, emotional, and psychological work that proved necessary in their political mobilization in Germany and beyond.

Farbe bekennen, Ayim, and other quotidian intellectuals fueled Black German literature, including *afro look, Afrekete,* and others. Black German women's autobiographies from individuals who were and were not involved in the movement continue to appear in contemporary society.[101] Among them are Ika Hügel-Marshall, Marie Nejar, Bärbel Kampmann, Abini Zöllner, and ManuEla Ritz.[102] A number of these multigenerational women authors have openly discussed their lives, reflecting upon their personal journeys to self-definition, which for Hügel-Marshall and Ritz involved activism in the Afro-German movement. Afro-German men have also penned their autobiographies, including Hans Jürgen Massaquoi and Theodor Michael.[103] Building on and expanding the Black German literary canon, younger generations of Afro-German authors, including Olumide Popoola, Victoria Toney-Robinson (née Victoria Robinson), Noah

Sow, Philipp Khabo Koepsell, and Schwarzrund, have published works beyond autobiographies.[104] Seeing the importance of Black creativity, some have self-published or created publishing platforms in Germany.[105] Collectively, Black Germans have pursued multiple forms of intellectual activism, continuing the work of the movement, the legacy of *Farbe bekennen,* and, by extension, Ayim.

Much of Ayim's poetry, essays, speeches, and performances documented German racism and decentered simplistic and fixed notions of culture, history, and identity, recognizing that Germany was multicultural and multiracial. Through her intellectual activism, she acknowledged the varieties of Germanness and embedded minority voices in the nation. As a result, she showed that Afro-Germans, not unlike other German minorities, contributed to the nation in significant ways. Ayim reclaimed Hegel's "African Other" as a Black German intellectual and used the dominant language and culture to redefine his/her place. Ayim's works enabled her to question notions of Germanness and to critique the persistent colonial beliefs and rhetoric and the illusion of post-reunification national harmony. From Germany to Ghana, the textual registers in Ayim's literature left the audience and reader with a resounding message about confronting racism and participating in social justice work. Her global activism demonstrated her commitment to forge connections with others, to practice Black women's internationalism, to affirm human rights, and to seek tangible political change.

Ayim has continued to have an important role within the Black German community. The establishment of the May Ayim Award or the International Black German Literary Prize in 2004 signaled the community's willingness to showcase talented community writers nationally and internationally. Michael Küppers-Adebisi and his multimedia project Afrotalk TV Cybernomads, in co-operation with UNESCO and the Haus der Kulturen der Welt (House of World Cultures), organized this first annual Black German Pan-African literary prize that honored writers, poets, and performers.[106] In October 2004, the committee honored an Afro-German poet, Olumide Popoola, along with German-based Brazilian writer Mario Curvello and Afro-German musician MC Santana.[107] Popoola, of Nigerian and German descent, is a London-based writer with a PhD in creative writing. She publishes and tours internationally.[108] The 2004 celebration occurred in conjunction with the exhibition "The Black Atlantic," at the House of World Cultures with scholars Tina M. Campt and Paul Gilroy.[109] In 2011 a new generation of Black German quotidian intellectuals, such as Joshua Kwesi Aikins, helped to rename the street Gröbenufer—named after Otto Friedrich von der Gröben, a colonial official who founded a trading fort in present-day Ghana—to the May-Ayim-Shore (*May-Ayim-Ufer*). It is the first street in Germany to be named after a Black German woman and is not far from where Ayim lived.[110] Afro-Germans' efforts at honoring Ayim and the presence of new Black German authors illustrate how much knowledge production and intellectual activism has remained at the heart of the community.

Ayim, along with other Black German quotidian intellectuals, used their affective, political, and cultural works (on television and in books, newspapers, and so forth) to compel the mainstream public and other Germans to understand the intricacies of racism and power dynamics in their own country. While they used diasporic resources and appropriated different diasporic styles and forms, Black Germans still engendered a literature that was German and multicultural. Constituting multiple forms of intellectual activism, their literature, journals, and initiatives challenged German cultural politics. These Black Germans relied on their textured identities to share new possibilities in German society. One such way that they pushed for social change and pursued activism was through their annual Berlin Black History Month events. These events, much like other Black German organizational initiatives, recovered and animated Blackness, showing how it was a cultural, political, and intellectual mode of their existence.

CHAPTER 5

DIASPORIC SPATIAL POLITICS WITH BLACK HISTORY MONTH IN BERLIN

In 1999 the annual Black History Month event in Berlin celebrated its tenth anniversary and continued an intellectual tradition in the Black German community, evinced by *afro look, Farbe bekennen,* and other publications. For this event, BHM committee members, some of whom were active in ISD and the larger Black German movement, collaborated with activists from local organizations like the Pan African Forum (PAF), Europe Africa Center (Europa Afrika Zentrum, EURAFRI), Immigrant Political Forum (Immigrantenpolitisches Forum e.V., IPF), and additional groups. They organized a month-long series of workshops, panel discussions, literary readings, theater productions, film screenings, children's activities, and social dances that revolved around the theme of "Black People and the New Media" and the legacy of the BHM. A few workshops included "Black History Month Between Fear and Hope," "Black Victims of the Nazi Holocaust," and "Africa's Literature in Dialogue with Europe," all of which reflected the committee's willingness to draw attention to national, continental, and international developments that involved and/or impacted individuals across the Black diaspora.[1] In this way, this BHM, like previous ones, was a clear manifestation of Black diasporic politics and solidarity.

The BHMs provided Black Germans with a sense of belonging with their compatriots and others; the recognition and celebration of Black history within a local German context and a broader European one proved a vital component of the Black German movement precisely because it strengthened their claims of kinship with their nation and the larger diaspora. BHM committee members made these events not only cultural and political, but also intellectual. These were events at which Black Germans and other People of Color produced and circulated knowledge that resuscitated Black diasporic histories in and beyond Europe. Thus, the BHMs represented a culture of everyday intellectualism. Though the BHMs eventually occurred in other cities, such as Hamburg and Frankfurt, the annual events in Berlin emboldened Black Germans to pursue spatial politics that rooted them in the German nation, created physical geographies and intellectual and figurative sites, and showed their resilience and agency.

Beyond a doubt, Black Germans used the BHMs to create "a black sense of place." Katherine McKittrick argues that a "black sense of place can be understood as the process of materially and imaginatively situating historical and contemporary struggles against practices of domination *and* the difficult entanglements of racial encounter. Racism and resistance to racism are therefore not the sole defining features of a black sense of place, but rather indicate how the relational violences of modernity produce a condition of being black in the Americas that is predicated on struggle."[2] Here, she focuses on plantations and prisons in the Americas as representative symbols of a Black sense of place tied to the history of transatlantic slavery, colonialism, and modernity. Though the experience of Black Germans is not located entirely in a narrative of slavery, colonialism, or the Middle Passage, they did engage in a diasporic practice of producing a Black sense of place through their annual BHMs. The lack of traditionally understood Black spaces in the German context was tied to the scattering of Black people across Germany, who often grew up in isolation from others in the diaspora, and was the result of colonization, as it occurred outside Germany's borders, though it permeated those same borders. Therefore, Black Germans' sense of place recognized the entanglements of violence, power, resistance, survival, and colonialism (especially given that Berlin was the location for the Congo Conference of 1884–1885) and produced alternative narratives and discourses that addressed Germany's colonial amnesia and/or forgetting as well as the racist, exclusionary laws to secure Fortress Europe. The BHMs demonstrated how these spatial and cultural voids were in part filled through knowledge while also helping them strengthen their community, politics, and intellectualism. The BHMs not only gave Black geographies room to flourish, both symbolically and physically, but also recast them given their historical absences in a majority-white nation. Black Germans engendered a variety of Black spaces for themselves and others and imbued those figurative and literal locations with new purposes and meanings. As a result, they showed that Berlin and Germany were not monoracial or homogenously white, only constructed as such.

As this chapter demonstrates, Afro-German women and men used the BHMs to produce narratives that decentered German whiteness and constructed an alternative public sphere in Berlin. Black German quotidian intellectuals decolonized the public sphere and public spaces for Black thought and imparted knowledge through their BHM events, which had informative and entertaining functions. The BHMs helped to reconstitute a Black archive in Germany and changed discourses that labeled some German cities as places of urban blight, economic decline, and ethnic conflict. They also claimed these newly created Black national spaces as translocal. In the process of remapping these physical geographies as Black, the BHMs also achieved a symbolic space within the Black German and Black community. This was significant in light of the nation's *Völkerschau* ("Peoples Show/Human Zoo") tradition from the nineteenth to the twenty-first centuries that placed African-descended people in zoos or circuses across the country because of their alleged "natural" or "primitive" state.[3]

Moreover, ISD-Berlin's annual celebrations accentuated and made Black diasporic and Black German culture central to the German experience. As with other movement activities, these celebrations rendered Blackness, and by extension Black Germanness, visible, influencing their identity (re)making, enabling them to achieve more representation, and changing whitewashed cultural politics. In many ways, the BHMs illustrate the when and where or spacetimes of Blackness and how it was constructed, defined, and enacted in Germany. Wright notes that "the only way to produce a definition of Blackness that is wholly inclusive and nonhierarchical is to understand Blackness as the intersections of constructs that locate the Black collective in history and in the specific moment in which Blackness is being imagined—the 'now' through which all imaginings of Blackness will be mediated."[4] The creation of the BHMs brought Blackness from the past into the present in an effort to change the present *and* the future. As the final section of the chapter shows, Black Germans gave space to the varieties of Blackness across different spacetimes while also rejecting hegemonic linear narratives at their BHMs.

BERLIN, THE BHMS, AND MEANING MAKING

As an international urban space with a long history of Black activism, Berlin was an ideal site to help Black Germans create border-crossing translocal and transnational networks and intellectual exchanges that inspired political mobilization and confronted discrimination.[5] Translocally, Berlin included a network of like-minded activist-intellectuals working on common issues, and these individuals disseminated information about their local conditions internationally to create awareness and advocate for social justice. Transnationally, Berlin revived the interconnectivity of peoples and cultures that often worked within, but transcended, the nation.[6] Afro-Germans also explained the experiences of individuals of African descent locally and nationally in Germany and internationally in countries as far away as South Africa. Their diasporic activism remained enmeshed in both local and global currents. The BHMs marked Black Germans' sustained engagement with translocal and transnational social justice in the 1990s.

ISD's Berlin BHM events caused Black Germans to invent new traditions and practice grassroots diasporic activism and Black internationalism. With this activism and internationalism, they made broader sociopolitical connections and campaigned against racial inequalities across Africa and its worldwide diaspora that, at times, mirrored developments in reunified Germany. These annual events also enabled them to speak openly about the reality of extreme ethno-nationalism and racial oppression, including the crimes of everyday racial violence in reunified Germany.[7] The BHMs continued to buttress Afro-Germans' diasporic activism and was similar to the efforts of others across the Black diaspora, such as African American historian and activist Carter G. Woodson and Trinidadian-born journalist and activist Claudia Jones, who both worked to combat global white supremacy. Black Germans also relied on Berlin-based diasporic resources, including Fountainhead Dance Theatre, the African Writers Association (AWA), and the Institute for Black Research (IBR), which impacted the BHMs.

The BHMs were a culmination of activities, including the annual national meeting or *Bundestreffen* (BT), which was already an integral part of the Black German movement. The BT was a fixture that provided Black Germans with affirmation and a safe space, free from the white gaze and dominance. As perhaps one of the most important institutional events signifying Afro-Germans' intellectualism, internationalism, and spatial agency, the BT, which still occurs today, has not received a serious analysis until now, and this present work is the first to examine it.

THE *BUNDESTREFFEN* AND OTHER DIASPORIC RESOURCES

The annual BT was one of Black Germans' first public efforts to construct a meaningful Black sense of place within the German nation, where they learned about their diasporic history, developed their consciousness, and gained acceptance and understanding from their compatriots. They also reclaimed multiple cities, such as Wiesbaden, Munich, and Berlin, as Black, manifesting their physical and metaphoric links to the nation. Afro-Germans, who were usually from local ISD and ADEFRA chapters, collaborated to organize a variety of activities at these national meetings that were for formal members, other Black Germans, or other Black people living in or visiting Germany. In this majority Black space, Black Germans escaped their isolation; they also found a shared sense of happiness and pursued an "ethic of love."[8] Being around their Black compatriots and others was a welcome respite after their often-exhausting racist experiences in German society.

During the early years, the initial meetings focused on self-discovery, enabling Afro-Germans to determine the political perspective and direction of their organization. They considered a number of issues: would ISD be a closed self-organization or an open one, and would the organization represent all Black people in Germany or just a specific Black population? They initially settled on the latter point, but shifted toward a more inclusive diasporic perspective, which was reflected in the name change of the organization from the Initiative of Black Germans to the Initiative of Black Germans and Black People in Germany to the Initiative of Black People in Germany. Black Germans also stressed the need for more time to connect with members in the community. As a result, the BT evolved from a two-day affair like the initial 1985 meeting in Wiesbaden, discussed in chapter 2, to a weekend-long event, with events beginning on Thursday and ending on Sunday.[9]

At the second BT in December 1986, which also occurred in Wiesbaden, a shared sense of spatial agency, kinship, and collaboration remained. Black Germans even invited a few white Germans, who were friends or related to other Black Germans and had an interest in discussing the themes of racism and discrimination.[10] ISD arranged for the press to arrive at the conclusion of the meeting; journalist Rainer Luyken wrote an insensitive article about the meeting in *Die Zeit*.[11] Unfortunately, his article relied upon clichés and stereotypes when describing the BT and its participants, which naturally upset many Afro-Germans and their allies, who wrote counter-responses to him.[12] Not all press coverage, however, was hostile or negative. In a Communist-affiliated German newspaper, entitled *Unsere Zeit,* a feature appeared on Afro-Germans' celebration of the second anniversary of ISD and the movement at the BT. In the article, Black Germans shared that they also sought to "break their 'culture of silence' and to stand up for their rights more."[13]

Some Black German quotidian intellectuals contributed their own BT accounts for the press. In an article in the *Frankfurter Rundschau,* Eleonore Wiedenroth-Coulibaly noted that xenophobia represented an aspect of racism and that discrimination had increased in Germany, but this event allowed Afro-Germans and their local chapters to strengthen their networks and "establish effective public relations." She mentioned that, "Black Germans also want to further solidarity and cooperation with 'other oppressed groups such as foreigners,' because black is the main minority."[14] For them, Blackness was not strictly tied to phenotype. It was a claim and a politically mobilizing strategy that united all marginalized minority communities in the nation. They collectively strategized across their connected differences.

Challenging exclusionary beliefs, practices, and legislation for all Black and other marginalized people in Germany remained an important objective in their movement. These acts also served as a counterpoint to a normalized German whiteness. In addition, for ISD organizers, "The aim of the meeting was, among other things, that the history of Black Germans should not be considered separate, but must be seen as a part of the entirety of German history."[15] Black Germans continued to rewrite their histories and create kinships that were not merely tied to blood relations. As El-Tayeb has noted, "A sense of a continuing African diaspora presence in Germany, the existence of foremothers and forefathers is built around a group of people who rarely shared family ties or even cultures a priori but who are, if not a community of choice, at least one of chosen identification."[16] The BT served as a source of camaraderie and cohesion that sustained Black Germans and aided them in their survival.

ISD and ADEFRA activists wanted the BTs to be an open and inclusive space, where people strengthened their Black German and diasporic bonds and grew into their political consciousness. As the BTs became more popular, organizers managed to arrange a set cost to encourage all social classes to attend. By 1987 the BTs became more structured, with Tahir Della and other members taking on leading roles. These national meetings often took place at hostels, ecological and wellness areas, and cultural institutions across Germany, and they relied on the work of local ISD and ADEFRA groups.[17] With their politics and poetics of representation and intellectual activism in multiple cities and venues, they promoted their Black sense of place throughout the nation. The BTs also grew larger and expanded in scope, in which film screenings and historical seminars took place alongside consciousness raising and political action workshops. These workshops revealed Black Germans' growing political engagement and the movement's momentum.

From health care to slavery, panels at the BT addressed manifold themes that sought to appeal to a wide range of individuals. Organized by ISD-Munich, the September 1989 BT, held near Munich, included panels that not only focused on the topics of racism, prejudices in ISD, and Black European history, but they also featured an exhibition on South Africa, a theater workshop, and a make-up workshop. The latter workshop, along with other BHM hair workshops, proved important for those who did not grow up with Black mothers sharing their knowledge about the application of the correct shade of make-up for their skin tone or the right hair products and practices for their hair.[18] The ordinary coexisted with the exceptional. In addition to formal sessions, Black Germans also sponsored child-friendly events and social activities such as painting, playing sports, or listening to live music.[19] These meetings also afforded participants an opportunity to process and embrace their diasporic identities. During the October 1991 BT, they hosted multiple panels, including one on experimental psychotherapy with Black German psychologist Bärbel Kampmann; another on "Power and Slavery" (*Macht und Sklaverei*); and one on "Information Exchange on the topic of I.S.D" (*Info-Börse zum Thema I.S.D.*). A few activists even hosted a talk show entitled "Black to Future."[20] Thought-provoking sessions were also at the October 1992 BT in Titisee-Neustadt, near Freiburg, and the September 1993 BT in Windischleuba-Thüringen in the former East. These weekend meetings also became an important space for emerging Black German artists, musicians, spoken-word poets, and writers who often introduced and performed their work for the community. For instance, the idea for the 2008 improvisational Black German play, *real life: Deutschland,* was first conceptualized at the 2005 BT, and this play initiated a vibrant Black German theater movement.[21] The diverse programming at these meetings illustrated the range and motivation of Afro-German activists to advance multiple interests within the community, carving out a niche for themselves. As a result, they centered their concerns and narratives in these settings. These annual meetings offered a variety of activities that integrated political, social, intellectual, and psychological themes and helped Afro-Germans stay connected and informed about their history and the larger diaspora.

Undeniably, members of ISD and ADEFRA invented a new diasporic tradition through the BT that reflected their Black internationalist perspectives. At the May 1994 BT, ISD members examined the European Economic Community's signing of the Maastricht Treaty and German reunification as well as the implications that these developments had for Afro-Germans and other People of Color in Europe. The event also highlighted antiracist youth movements in France and England and compared them to German ones. Through this BT, organizers continued to think within yet beyond the nation and acknowledged gendered and racialized dynamics in Germany, such as the presence of multicultural students, the role of Black men, and the socialization of Black girls.[22] In addition, Black Germans saw the utility in organizing these meetings as a vehicle for communicating shared values, training, and shaping further genera-tions of Afro-German youth. They instilled empowering traits and encouraged self-confidence and creativity.[23] Organizers still managed to offer panels geared to an older generation, motivating them to be more politically engaged. The BT workshops and seminars had edifying and ideological functions.

For the tenth BT in 1995, with the theme "Past, Present and Perspectives of the Black existence in Europe" (*Vergangenheit, Gegenwart & Perspektiven Schwarzer Existenz in Europa*), ISD celebrated the movement and used the occasion to assess its history and prepare for the future.[24] During this event, ISD quotidian intel-lectuals exchanged stories about their experiences in the movement. They also hosted a screening of different films representing the movement's history from the last ten years and films about Jack Johnson, Angela Davis, Martin Luther King Jr., and other Black diasporic individuals. Theodor Michael also presented on his survival during the Nazi period, offering details about his negotiation of those racial policies. At this event, as with others, Black German organizers represented their investment in international struggles against injustice and developments across the diaspora and underscored the heterogeneity of the diaspora.[25]

While the BT continued to be a Black diasporic and antiracist space that was welcoming, conflicts and scandal developed among different members in the local chapters, where accusations of fraud, hypocrisy, and infidelity emerged. The diverse personalities that converged at these events led to tensions, frus-trations, and infighting about fame, envy, Black authenticity, solidarity, and activism. At some, smaller cliques existed, which made some attendees feel isolated and excluded. Several male members of ISD also used these meetings as an opportunity to have relations with multiple women. Moreover, white par-ents of Afro-German children could not attend, and if Afro-Germans were in relationships with white Germans, their partners could not attend. This proved disappointing to some.[26]

The BT still has cultural significance in the contemporary movement. In 2015 different members of ISD chapters published *Spiegelblicke,* awkwardly translated as *Mirroring Looks,* to commemorate the thirtieth anniversary of the organization and the movement. The volume included interviews and essays from multiple generations of Black German quotidian intellectuals.[27] Hundreds of Afro-Germans and Black people (from the United States, France, Austria, and other countries) have attended throughout the years, reflecting the inter-national appeal they had gained. While the BT served as one of the precursors to the BHM event in Berlin, which was on a larger scale, Black Germans also built upon earlier grassroots diasporic activism in Berlin.

Several organizations served as diasporic resources and impelled Black Germans to learn from, network with, and engage with many across the diaspora in Berlin. One of those groups included Fountainhead, presented in chapter 2, and in existence since 1980. In March 1986 Fountainhead organized its first Black Cultural Festival. As with ISD and ADEFRA, Fountainhead also evinced a concern with the history of race in Germany, noting in the foreword to the program, "Berlin was the host city of the conference in 1884/85 that consolidated the pattern of colonial rule over Africa and in Germany racism reached its greatest heights as public policy—the denial of not only cultural achievements but also the basic humanity of Black people. On the other hand, Berlin also has examples of resistance to this colonial/imperial legacy. Berlin is now a world city of great cultural diversity including forms of Black Culture."[28] In addition to its festival, Fountainhead organized a Black International Cinema event in 1986.[29] Through these series of events, the group brought diverse people together and underscored the breadth of Black diasporic culture. Fountainhead also sponsored events at the BHMs. Now only under the auspices of Donald Griffith, Fountainhead's Black International Cinema event still occurs annually, garnering additional state and European support.[30]

The AWA, another Berlin-based organization, also attended to Germany's racial past and present. Briefly referenced in chapter 2, the AWA was a group that included writers, performers, and activists in exile from Ghana, South Africa, Uganda, Namibia, Kenya, and Sierra Leone. From 1983 to 1988, they published *AWA-FINNABA,* a literary-cultural journal written in both English and German. It contained poetry, reviews, interviews, editorials, and reports that engaged with Africa, its diaspora, and Germany. Though the journal was short-lived, its eleven issues covered sweeping topics, including South African women writers, Pan-African theorists such as Edward Blyden and Frantz Fanon, among other Black internationalist themes.[31] Aside from publishing, AWA also organized a three-day symposium commemorating the one-hundredth anniversary of the Congo Conference in 1984. Its members also performed poetry, theater, and music at events across Berlin and Germany.[32]

Moreover, the Institute for Black Research (IBR), formerly the Institute for Black Studies, concentrated on antiracism education, activism, and public outreach. The IBR included different activists from minority organizations, who "recognized that there is a chronic lack of information and discussion on racism and eurocentrism in West Germany and West Berlin." They collected information on diverse countries about those topics, initiated dialogues, and informed the German media about these themes.[33] Members of the IBR networked with other international antiracist groups and activists in the Caribbean, the Netherlands, and the United States. The IBR organized discussions comparing racism in Germany and other countries. In 1989 they hosted a talk, entitled "Black power vs white racism in US politics today," with African American scholar Dr. Abdul Alkalimat and another one with London-based activist Wilmette Brown, who presented from her 1983 book, *Black Women and the Peace Movement*. This institute sponsored events with activist-intellectuals, who spoke on the development of Fortress Europe, racism in England, and other topics.[34] Regardless of the number of events and attendees, Fountainhead, the AWA, and IBR were significant for influencing discussions about racism in Germany and elsewhere and pushing individuals and the media to recognize their complicity in upholding systems of oppression and inequality. They offered ample opportunities to promote the spacetimes of Blackness and challenge traditional German myths and narratives. These examples are illustrative of Berlin's fertile ground for grassroots internationalist activism. Given those organizations and others, along with a significant Black population, it is no wonder that many Black Germans saw Berlin as the center of their movement.

THE ANNUAL BLACK HISTORY MONTH CELEBRATIONS

Readily using diasporic resources from the United States, ISD organized their first BHM celebration for a week in February 1990, in which they sought to enlighten the general public about the presence of individuals of African descent in Germany. Underscoring transnational linkages, almost all of ISD's BHM programs referred to Carter G. Woodson, known as the father of Black history in the United States. Nearly all of the sessions in the first BHM focused on Black internationalist themes, including the "Cultural riches in Africa" (*Kulturreiche in Afrika*), the "History of Slavery" (*Geschichte der Sklaverei*), the "Life and Work of Malcolm X" (*Leben und Werk von Malcolm X*), and "The Civil Rights Movement in the US and Martin Luther King" (*Die Bürgerrechtsbewegung in den US und Martin Luther King*).[35] Other ISD and ADEFRA chapters arranged a program that included screenings of fourteen South African films and multiple seminars on racism, colonialism, resistance movements, and more. Black Germans continued this internationalist approach with subsequent BHMs. ISD's BHMs also facilitated the academic study of Black history, furthering the field of Black German studies, along with supporting public outreach.[36] As quotidian intellectuals, Black Germans theorized, shaped, and communicated ideas on a variety of topics that dealt with Africa and its diaspora, often in conjunction with descriptions of racial abuse at the hands of neo-Nazis or daily micro/macroaggressions in society. The BHMs signaled how their intellectual activism was inherently diasporic activism.

The records about the exact origins of the BHM are contradictory. According to the 1990 program, Black Germans Danny Hafke, Roy Wichert, Mike Reichel, and African American Patricia Elcock, all ISD-Berlin members, developed the idea—a claim also echoed in *Spiegelblicke*.[37] They coordinated this first annual celebration with other organizations, including Fountainhead. Likewise, BHM programs from 1991 and 1992 noted that, "Black History Month was launched in February 1990 by the Initiative of Black Germans in Berlin," and "it was a great success."[38] Black German activists Wiedenroth-Coulibaly and Sascha Zinflou have written that the celebrations occurred from 1990 to 2001 in Berlin.[39] In the foreword to the twentieth-anniversary edition of *Farbe bekennen,* however, Oguntoye claimed that the BHM events occurred every February in Berlin from 1988 to 1998.[40] Ayim also wrote that, "Since 1989 ISD with the cooperation of other black groups organized the 'Black History Month' in Berlin."[41] Until two years ago, ISD's web site provided a brief timeline about the event and maintained that it began in 1991. In the 1996 program, the BHM Committee claimed to have been around since 1989.[42] The committee's existence reveals that these events were not haphazardly put together and that ISD's individual members and others worked hard to organize a successful event. The BHMs signified their devotion to the larger Black community not only in Berlin, but across the country.

Analogous BHM events also materialized in other German cities, including Hamburg and Frankfurt. ISD's web site previously noted that these events took place for the first time in Hamburg on a small scale in 1990, under the direction of African American jazz singer and actress Cynthia Utterbach. In *Spiegelblicke,* however, Nigel Asher, a Black German activist and musician active in ISD-Hamburg, suggested that the first BHM celebration took place in 1996 and owed to Utterbach and her circle of friends.[43] In 1998 the first public BHM event took place in the Dennis Swing Club, owned by Trinidadian jazz pianist Dennis Bubsy, and it included multiple diasporic perspectives beyond that of African Americans. From 2007 ISD-Hamburg became a part of the organizing team for the BHM, which also corresponded with a new phase of activism for the group.[44] In February 2013, the BHM tradition began in Frankfurt. There, ISD-Frankfurt activist-intellectuals organized sessions on ISD's new "Stop Racial Profiling" (2012) campaign and included readings and spoken-word performances from Black German authors Olumide Popoola and Philipp Khabo Koepsell.[45] BHM events were important for the Black German community and reflected their members' drive, creativity, and growing agency. These inconsistencies show the incompleteness of this archive and the importance of oral history for providing a richer mosaic of these moments.

Similar cultural events developed before and after the BHMs, in which they drew attention to entrenched racist stereotypes in German society and highlighted Black diasporic peoples' culture and resistance. A few of those events included the Black Film Festival, the African Cultural Days, and the Africa Festival that occurred in Düsseldorf, Munich, Hamburg, and Würzburg. At those events, they screened international films and held musical performances, exhibitions, and discussions on national identities and diasporic politics.[46] In 2012 the Pan-Africanism Working Group, an organization that promotes international understanding and interaction between Germans and Black diasporic people, also hosted a similar BHM event in Munich. Additionally, after the last 2000 BHM event in Berlin, Katharina Oguntoye, in conjunction with her multicultural and immigrant organization Joliba, formed in 1997, coordinated the first Black Bazaar (*Black Basar*) in February 2004 in Berlin. This first bazaar lasted a week, and it continued until 2014.[47] These urban, multicultural spaces enabled ISD activists and participants to stake a claim in the nation and actively engage in translocal and transnational activism that often transcended the borders of Germany. Their efforts at diasporic activism were fundamentally connected to spatial politics that sought reclamation and representation.

The emergence of ISD's BHM instantiated Afro-Germans' Black sense of place. BHM organizers and participants also cultivated connections to one another and other People of Color directly tied to Berlin, and many Black Germans traveled from across the country to attend this annual event. The committee extended BHM invitations to their white compatriots, though they also sponsored several Black-only sessions. They organized events, which could last from a week to almost two months, opened to the public for a modest fee that changed from year to year. From 1990 to 2000, the BHMs established spaces for reflection, covered themes from Christianity to Black women's agency, and offered recommendations from individual wellness to art. Locating their events in Berlin, ISD used places in this major urban, cosmopolitan space, drawing on a legacy of political and sociocultural activism to reach a broad audience. Here, their spatial articulation of belonging was knowingly linked to cosmopolitan translocal spaces. As Wright has argued, "The metropolis (usually but not exclusively Berlin) serves as a refuge from the reactionary and oppressive attitudes that pervade the rural space, although the Afro-German eventually realizes that the same vicious atavistic set of beliefs pervades both locations."[48] Places such as Die Pumpe (The Pump), the KulturBrauerei (Culture Brewery), the Bildungs und Aktionszentrum Dritte Welt e.V. (Third World Education and Action Center, BAZ), and the Werkstatt der Kulturen (Workshop of Cultures) had already obtained recognition within certain circles in the Berlin subcultural movements. Developed in 1987, for example,

Die Pumpe was a cultural and youth center in Berlin-Schöneberg, where theater events and other seminars took place. The BAZ, which is now a children's center, was once a politically active cultural center for migrant and asylum organizations in the 1980s and 1990s in Berlin-Kreuzberg. At one point, ISD-Berlin's office was located there. An old converted brewery in Prenzlauer Berg-Berlin, the KulturBrauerei was the cultural center in the 1990s, where numerous community-based meetings and events occurred that included other artistic and/or minority organizations. Opening in 1993, the Werkstatt der Kulturen was an event center sponsored by the Berlin Senate in Neukölln-Berlin. These community venues were important spaces that valued diversity and that offered the potential for change. Arranging screenings, performances, and workshops at these different neighborhood locations, among others, helped Black Germans feel empowered to reinsert themselves into the fabric of the city.

Representing the interplay between the translocal and the transnational, ISD's BHMs were akin to the Caribbean Carnival in London, which was the forerunner of the Notting Hill Carnival. Since Claudia Jones's deportation from the United States in 1955 and subsequent residence in the United Kingdom, the carnival was one of a series of events that she and her colleagues organized in London, home to a large Caribbean population. After a series of race riots in Notting Hill and Nottingham in 1958, Jones and her journal the *West Indian Gazette* organized the carnival, which was a condensed version of the Trinidad Carnival, "as a gesture of black solidarity and of inter-racial friendship."[49] Similarly, BHMs also provided Black Germans and other racialized communities with a common space to discuss, learn about, and critique the rise of ethno-nationalism in reunified Germany. Moreover, Jones recognized "culture, as a series of normative practices, was an important tool in the community's development as in larger political and economic struggles as a whole. It was through this vision of culture, she felt, that the various black British communities would be educated about each other while developing self-awareness of their own cultural histories." For her, much like it was for the Black German organizers of the BHMs, "putting in place the celebratory, in this case, was an act of cultural affirmation."[50]

In February 1959, Jones, along with the Caribbean Carnival Committee, arranged a number of indoor cultural events such as "masqueraders, steelband musicians (Trinidad All Stars, Dixielanders), live brass bands, calypsonians (Mighty Terror, Sparrow, and Lord Kitchener)." The carnival also included dancers, a queen competition, and the crowning of the carnival queen; the BBC recorded these events. Her *West Indian Gazette* organized concerts with African American activist and performer Paul Robeson, talent shows, forums on the West Indian Federation and China, and marches against racial discrimination and Apartheid.[51] As the carnival continued to grow in prestige, Jamaican writer and theorist Sylvia Wynter and Trinidadian vocalist Mighty Sparrow even participated. These social events were enriching and allowed the West Indian community to unite, comparable to what the BHMs did for Black Germans and other People of Color. A similar sentiment was expressed in the 1998 BHM program, "Especially in a city of many cultures, the BHM presents an opportunity for mutual understanding. It is a reflection of the diversity of black life. . . . We have created a forum for exchange and interaction, and this helps to counteract against prejudices and misunderstandings."[52] A year after Jones's death, the Notting Hill Outdoor Carnival started in 1965.[53] Jones gladly collaborated with others and made the cultural intensely political—a task Black Germans also accomplished with their BHMs.

Through annual BHMs, Black Germans engaged in collaborative work with a number of government entities and local associations concerned with promoting equality, combating multiple forms of discrimination in Germany, and creating awareness about Germany's multicultural heritage and international connections. ISD also applied for and acquired grants from state and federal agencies to fund the event. The BHM committee benefited from private businesses, cultural centers, and civic organizations and welcomed suggestions about exhibitions, performances, workshop themes, and film screenings, as well as the format and design of the BHM program. In 1991 ISD partnered with ADEFRA, the African Women's Initiative (AFI), Nozizwe, Prima Klima Travel, and the Student Union at the Freie Universität Berlin.[54] As the BHM grew in popularity, so, too, did the number of sponsors that helped to organize and present at the annual celebrations, proving these groups' investment. At the 1992 BHM, Nozizwe representatives participated once again, but ISD also garnered support from the Student Unions at both the Freie Universität Berlin and the Technical University, the Evangelical Church Development Service in Stuttgart, the Network in Berlin, the Senate Administration for Cultural Affairs, BMA, EURAFRI, Harambee, *Isivivane*, the People's Art Ensemble, and the Umoja Africa Center, and they had already established partnerships with several of these organizations in other capacities. These entities included diverse cultural groups, several of which were referenced in chapter 2.[55] Other institutions and local businesses such as the IPF, the Filfila Café, the Sikasso Market, and the Tanzania Community Berlin also aided.[56] Together, ISD and its sponsoring organizations and businesses gained opportunities to advertise upcoming organizational activities, to strengthen their membership, or acquire new business. As these alliances demonstrate, ISD remained attentive and open to the specific concerns of different Black diasporic communities.

As ISD worked with these multiethnic communities, Black German quotidian intellectuals understood their struggle against racism to be connected to larger issues concerning equality and human rights. The preoccupation with translocal currents in Berlin, such as increased violence against immigrants and People of Color on the streets in Germany, often dovetailed with transnational currents. With the 1993 BHM, ISD received assistance from the AFI, the IPF, the Network, the Black Liberation Sound System (BLS), and the Liberia Relief Organization.[57] Here, as with other BHMs, ISD aligned with immigrant associations as well as Black and People of Color communities to ensure that the BHM would initiate and elevate relevant and critical discussions about migrants from across the world.[58] The BHMs enabled these sponsoring associations to share and produce knowledge about the impact of marginalization at home and abroad while also debunking racist stereotypes and presumptions in Germany. ISD maintained collaborative partnerships with local groups and campaigned on global issues, such as civil unrest and inequality throughout the African continent and opposition to conservative European politicians such as the National Front leader Jean-Marie Le Pen, who ran for the French presidency in 1974, 1988, 1995, 2002, and 2007. Their ability to blend discussions on discourses about the daily, national, and international currents of racism along with critical attention to issues of migration, whiteness, and intersectionality across Europe and Africa reflected their breadth and ability to bridge the academic with everyday intellectualism. In some instances, these topics had not yet been considered or adopted in mainstream circles.

Privileging Black as a political identity for all individuals of color who were oppressed in Germany, the BHM committee noted in 1996, "We created our self-designation not to be dependent on a particular nationality, place of birth, or passport. Our definition of black is not limited to skin color, but includes all individuals of African-Asian descent affected by racism. From the beginning, our emphasis was on the formation and stabilization of individual identity and the commitment to establishing an antiracist and antidiscrimination society."[59] Through their articulation of a political Blackness, ISD continued to advance multiple intersecting causes of equality that brought disparate communities together, enlightened the public, and counteracted European ignorance and exlusion. They also attempted to avoid claims of Black authenticity in order to foster coalition building across marginalized groups. Their creation of a Black sense of place through these venues, events, and coalitions became meaningful and necessary with German state and federal officials' persistent inaction against bigotry. In centering Blackness *and* humanness, the BHMs enabled

Black Germans to make and unmake different geographies that allowed new spatial politics to flourish and that reimagined their political potential.

The sponsorships at the BHMs showed that multiple organizations, mostly based in Berlin, engaged in cross-ethnic mobilization to draw attention to their unyielding concerns about violent, racist acts, anti-foreign legislation, biased attitudes in the media, and discriminatory practices that denied citizenship to People of Color in Germany. These sponsorships also revealed how local and national dynamics in Berlin were evocative of the political developments in South Africa, Tanzania, and Somalia, to name a few. They signified the willingness of some German state entities and organizations to join ISD in the struggle against different forms of oppression and to encourage tolerance. In this way, allies of multiple nationalities, colors, creeds, orientations, and religions at the BHMs pursued social justice activism in Germany. Solidarity was premised on acknowledging difference and working toward more diversity and equality.

THE SPACETIMES OF BLACKNESS AT THE BHMS

The BHMs represented a convergence of the spacetimes of Blackness, in which the past collided and intersected with the now. With each of the BHMs, Black Germans and other Black organizers showed the diversity and possibility of Blackness at distinct moments. As organizers excavated the overlooked and forgotten narratives of the Black diaspora in Germany, and Europe, and beyond, they presented these narratives using different approaches in a nonlinear fashion. While this act of recovery was similar to that pursued in *Farbe bekennen* and the larger Black German movement, the BHMs also unsettled previous racist notions of a Blackness fixed in time and place by sharing this knowledge. The BHM Committee confirmed this point in their 1996 BHM program, declaring "The specific situation of Black people forms the background of the BHM. In fact, the need for this kind of forum in Germany cannot be over emphasized, considering the fact that limited opportunities are accorded objective information about the present and past of Black people, while on the contrary, much more disinformation is presented regarding prejudiced opinions against them and their cultures." They recognized that nationalism and racism had grown in Germany, making the lives of Black people and People of Color challenging. The BHM committee felt it was their imperative "to disseminate accurate information about the historical, cultural, economic and political development of Black people." By doing so, they could eradicate discrimination and counter the misinformation about the contributions and conditions of African-descended people.[60] The BHM committee accomplished these goals and confirmed that Blackness was everywhere (in eighteenth-century Jena or nineteenth-century Paris). At these events, they also catered to different manifestations of Blackness, which could be therapeutic, artistic, or even political, to name a few. In the process, they recuperated multiple diasporic identities, enabling the Black community to navigate German society.

The collective labor of the BHM committee was contingent upon individual Black Germans, who as quotidian intellectuals supported diverse ambitions through their cultural work at these celebrations. Here, their efforts shaped the fields of Black German studies, Black European studies, African studies, and critical race studies that relied on bottom-up approaches and validated these intellectual and decolonial pursuits. John Kantara, ISD-Berlin co-founder and member, presented a panel entitled "Afro-German History" at the 1990 and 1991 BHMs. Ironically, he used the phrase "A Negro cannot be German" (*Ein Neger kann kein Deutscher sein*) as a point of departure for both seminars. He took the phrase from an anonymous postcard sent to ARD about the film "Germans are white, Negroes cannot be German," as discussed briefly in chapter 2. Through these seminars, he overturned the common view that Afro-German history only began after 1945. At his 1990 presentation, Kantara offered details about Anton Wilhem Amo, an African philosopher, who studied and taught in eighteenth-century Halle and Jena, Germany. Discussing these narratives, Kantara detailed Black Germans' lives under National Socialism and underscored that Germany was a multicultural society. With these seminars, he helped Afro-Germans achieve a better self-image and understand their identity, especially in a society that believed they did not belong.[61]

Likewise, Elke Jank (Ja-El) from the ADEFRA-Bremen chapter presented a seminar, "The Denied Contribution of Black People to the History of Europe," that challenged popular stereotypes of people of African descent as "primitives." She claimed that several Black people were in fact prominent Europeans while others were members of European ruling houses and aristocratic families.[62] ISD-Berlin co-founder Oguntoye's seminars at the 1993 and 1997 BHMs focused on the history of Africans in Germany and Black Germans from 1884 to 1950, drawing on some of her earlier work in *Farbe bekennen*. She also wrote a master's thesis on this topic at the Technical University of Berlin in 1995/1996, later publishing it as *Eine afro-deutsche Geschichte* (*An Afro-German Story*) in 1997.[63] These celebrations showed the intellectual work Black Germans put into them and how their intellectual activism served a larger purpose for themselves and the community.

With the assistance of Black Germans from across the country, the Berlin BHMs contextualized the Black diaspora during different historical moments and shaped the Black public sphere. At the 1992 BHM, for example, Thomas Pforth, from ISD-Duisburg, discussed the legacy of racism as a system of oppression against Blacks. For Pforth, it required time and effort on the part of whites to deal with racism and other systems of oppression because many of them had profited from it. His presentation served as an edifying source for his (assumedly mostly Black) audience, as he claimed that, "Black[s] must leave behind the defensive, their psychological destabilization, isolation, powerlessness in order to influence [and] make decisions. The goal can only be intercultural cooperation."[64] After his seminar at the 1992 BHM, Austen Brandt, another member from ISD-Duisburg and a pastor, presented a lecture entitled, "Black Christianity."[65] Brandt claimed even though many Blacks saw the church in Germany as a form of white power (*als eine Form weißer Macht*), "Black Christianity" has served as a form of resistance and survival for individuals in Africa, North America, and England, and it could offer more possibilities for Blacks in Germany.[66] Brandt also held church services at some of the BHMs, suggesting that some Black Germans still found Christianity to be an important aspect in their lives. Moreover, at the 1992 BHM, Tina M. Campt, an African American graduate student studying in Berlin, and Pascal Grosse, a Black German scholar and activist from the East, offered a presentation entitled, "Aspects of Afro-German History" that provided a "critical review of the background and concept of race as a scientific category, 1900–1960."[67] In addition to this panel, Campt, Grosse, and Black German scholar Yara-Colette Lemke Muñiz de Faria each presented on different aspects of twentieth-century Afro-German history during a seminar at the 1994 BHM.[68] Campt, Grosse, and Lemke Muñiz de Faria interrogated the concept of race in the German context and illustrated how it helped to define national identity, citizenship, and cultural norms, and their presentations were later published in scholarly venues. These workshops illuminated the historical legacy of Black Germans in the nation, revealing their efforts at activism, survival, and resistance across different spacetimes. These activities advanced ISD's aim of employing history as medium for diasporic recovery, consciousness-raising, and critical exchanges.

While ISD underscored the importance of Afro-German history and culture in the West, they also integrated panels that attended to the experiences of Black Germans in the East. During the 1991 BHM, an ISD member from Leipzig presented a workshop, "The Black Community in East Germany Before and After the Fall of the Wall," which considered the development of the Afro-German movement in cities in the former East. The presentation focused on the differences and similarities between East and West and how unification helped to encourage more collaborative work.[69] Similarly, at the 1994 BHM, the panel, "Black Germans in the German Democratic Republic," shed light on the experiences of Afro-Germans in the GDR and their connections to other African countries and African migrants. Reporting on the situation in the former East, Dede Malika Beer, Kerstin Eisner, Pierre Gaulke, and Patrice Poutrus, ISD members, explained the existence of "officially [government] sanctioned antiracism and tolerance (in comparison) to the real instances of xenophobia and racism."[70]

Several BHM panels addressed the impact that heightened ethno-nationalism and racial violence and murder had on the Afro-German community after the fall of the Wall, again communicating the importance of the everyday. It was against this backdrop that Ika Hügel-Marshall's lecture, "Afro-German identity," attributed meaning to and acknowledged subtle distinctions between the concepts of Black German and Afro-German and addressed their meanings during post-reunification. Hügel-Marshall's 1991 presentation detailed what the terms and the movement had done for her personally.[71] For some, the larger Black German movement offered them invaluable support that pushed them to resist. Oguntoye's seminar, "Afro-Germans—Black Germans—Blacks in Germany," at the 1993 BHM also attended to pressing racial concerns for several communities of color in Germany. She explained the concepts of Afro-German, Black, African, and German, underscoring how significant it was to maintain a strong sense of self and identity in spite of the blatant xenophobia and nationalistic fervor in the country.[72] All of these panels challenged Germany's democratic post-Holocaust identity. Black Germans and others in the larger Black community also remade the public sphere, typically an exclusionary site, a Black space that did not ignore or bracket racial difference. Here, difference was privileged, not marginalized. In their Black sphere, their ideas and causes mattered, and they provided alternative understandings of citizenship, identity, belonging, and history. Through these knowledge-producing and processing events, they offered direct public dissent about racism in Germany, Europe, and elsewhere.

In addition to these sociological and historical seminars, ISD also arranged a variety of workshops that recommended constructive forms of self-care in light of the racial violence and racial stress. Afro-German psychologist Bärbel Kampmann, for instance, presented a session at the 1991 BHM entitled, "Psychological problems of Black Germans and therapy as support."[73] Kampmann noted that, "Black Germans live as minorities in a majority white society. Due to this fact [Black Germans] are particularly vulnerable to the contradictions, expectations of behavior, discrimination and isolation, which leave their effects. Traces that often manifest themselves from mental health problems to mental illness."[74] At the 1992 BHM, she also gave a similar presentation, "The Basic Problems of Black Germans," urging Afro-Germans to seek professional assistance when necessary. There was also a stress-management workshop at the 1997 BHM.[75] In addition to psychological and emotional support, self-defense training occurred at a few of the BHMs. At the 1993 BHM, a self-defense course only for People of Color took place and afforded participants an opportunity to learn Karate, Judo, and Jujitsu techniques and to recognize dangerous situations.[76] All aspects of self-care were encouraged and made attendees feel a degree of comfort that they were unable to fully express in a racist society.

Just like with the BT, these annual celebrations enabled Afro-Germans and other People of Color to showcase their creativity in literature, art, music, and theater that focused on their diverse experiences. During the 1992 BHM, Angela Alagiyawanna-Kadalie, Nisma Dux, Michael Küppers-Adebisi, Modupe Laja, Sheila Mysorekar, Magali Schmid, and Eleonore Wiedenroth-Coulibaly, Black German authors and activists, appeared at a reading entitled "Black German Literature." Along with musical accompaniment, they presented their work to a Black audience. Many of these authors had published in the 1992 poetry volume *The Power of the Night (Macht der Nacht)*.[77] Afro-German activist and author, Küppers-Adebisi also recited his poetry with musical accompaniment at the 1993 BHM.[78] At the 1996 BHM, Ayim performed poetry from her 1995 volume *Blues in black white*.[79] Sadly, this would be her last BHM celebration before her death that fall. As an homage to Ayim, the Black community wrote an open letter to her, and also hosted a May Ayim Day with a variety of events celebrating and honoring her life and work at the 1997 BHM.[80] Together, these BHMs gave Black Germans a forum to present their literature and art; the public events were welcoming spaces where their cultural work would be legitimized, appreciated, and understood. Black Germans constantly produced spaces for Blackness and their work and encouraged one another to continue their pursuits at these events.

Diverse local, national, or international groups were also included at BHMs, giving them an opportunity to share their art as forms of cultural education, social cohesion, and Black joy. At the 1991 BHM, ISD, along with Harambee, co-organized a Black Heritage Party in which musical groups performed. At the 1993 BHM, the BLS performed a musical concert along with an unnamed band from Ghana. During the BHM opening celebration in 1996, DJs from Senegal, South Africa, and Uganda spun records, and Ethiopian specialties were provided.[81] With the 1994 BHM, ABATIGAYA, a Rwandan group, sponsored a workshop on dancing and singing from their country, emphasizing ISD's transnational

Figure 12. Programs from the 1994 and the 1996 Black History Month Events in Berlin, personal photograph in author's private collection.

connections.[82] At this same BHM, the African Women's Theater (AFT) performed a staged piece entitled, "Recollection of one's own Foreignness" at the Werkstatt der Kulturen. Seeking to dramatize the everyday experiences of some Black Germans and migrants, the production revolved around an older white German woman's argument with a foreign woman at a bus stop over something trivial.[83] Later in their piece, the group portrayed an episode of acceptance and understanding in Germany. In addition, the People's Art Ensemble arranged a poetry session entitled, "Peoples' Poets Theatre" that introduced jazz poetry as Black art.[84] With these activities, Afro-Germans and People of Color fostered a sense of community and validated their creative potential. These artistic expressions, some of them vernacular, also constituted a part of this Black public sphere.

The BHMs remained a diasporic undertaking that opened up additional opportunities for Black European artists. ISD sponsored Black British artist Dionne Sparks in residence in 1994. Sparks, who was also active in the movement, worked with dyes, textiles, and multimedia, and her work "dealt with the political and historical aspects of Black women's identity." Her exhibition at the Werkstatt der Kulturen was entitled "Conversations Across Seas." Sparks also offered a series of workshops, entitled "Visual Connections," during the months of March and April.[85] Furthermore, in January 1994, the BHM featured an exhibition entitled "Different Colours," including Hafke, Oguntoye, Reiser, Babette Arnold, Dieudonné Otenia, and Henrietta Safo. It was "the first joint exhibition of black artists from both parts of the city."[86] "Different Colours" included paintings and photography from Arnold; paintings from Hafke; photography from Oguntoye; paintings from Otenia; paintings, art design, and collages from Reiser; and ethnically inspired jewelry from Safo. Several of these artists drew from African diasporic and European traditions, and their works ranged "from the rendering of landscapes and inner world of emotions to the artistic condemnation and reflection of racist incidents."[87] The public display of these forms of art provided the artists with recognition within the Black and the white German communities.

The BHMs also provided Reiser, an ISD-Berlin member and an editor of *afro look,* with a chance to feature her Afrocentric artwork in several of the programs.[88] During the 1993 BHM, Reiser also arranged an exhibition entitled "The language of the Media and Racism," in which she collected and collaged numerous newspaper headlines about racial attacks and captured the racial discourses embedded in everyday culture toward Black Germans and other People of Color.[89] Throughout the 1996 BHM program, images of Reiser's art design and borders appeared along with other Afrocentric imagery. With her artwork, she created new diasporic symbols and meanings and rooted them in the German context. Reiser still produces art and much of it maintains a similar focus of incorporating Africa in Germany.

ISD's annual celebrations continued to represent their efforts at diasporic activism. At the BHMs, Black German quotidian intellectuals advocated for change and demonstrated that transnational dynamics helped to constitute the translocal space of Berlin. The translocal and the transnational were in fact relational networks that were not in opposition to one another. Afro-Germans' translocal interventions challenged hegemonic narratives and political systems, creating a confluence of local and global dynamics while also reinforcing transnational diasporic connections.[90] Afro-Germans continued to reimagine their identity, reinvent their traditions in relation to other diasporic and marginalized communities, and compare their struggles to those in other countries fighting against oppressive regimes.

Panels on South African Apartheid often featured prominently. During the 1991 BHM, ISD expressed solidarity with individuals in South Africa and asked participants to provide a small donation for a South African–themed project, the specifics of which were still to be determined.[91] Exiled anti-Apartheid activist Luyanda Mpahlwa and exiled South African artist and one of the editors of *AWA-FINNABA* Vusi Mchunu presented an abridged account of the political struggles in South Africa from the present to the early 1990s. Mpahlwa and Mchunu, who presented in English and German, sought to correct public opinion in Europe that was "strongly influenced by false partially racist or insufficient reports on current problems in South Africa."[92] These men, moreover, explained how "the current war in the Gulf continued to draw attention away from this issue and many people can forget that South Africa is still not free."[93] Following their seminar, Peggy Luswazi, a South African activist in Nozizwe, gave another lecture on South Africa, focusing on its colonial history. She also introduced the audience to "People's Education," a South African project that attempted to create a non-racial and democratic education devoid of Apartheid ideology for all.[94]

ISD's mutual support for South Africa did not fade at subsequent events. Mpahlwa's 1992 lecture "Break the Chains of Apartheid—Change is pain!" discussed current developments in South Africa, again in English and German. Here, Mpahlwa reexamined the history of opposition to Apartheid, including the African National Congress (ANC) and its most recent attempts to unify and democratize the country.[95] I. Schuhmacher from Hamburg and E. Rodtman from Berlin presented a slide seminar about South Africa entitled "Out of the Ruins of Apartheid—The Situation of the Rural Population in South Africa." In their seminar, they clarified that, "despite all of the reforms, the injustice of Apartheid has not yet ended, although Western politicians want to believe it has."[96] Of particular interest to these men were the policies of the 1970s and the difficulties South Africans encountered when returning to their expropriated land. They explained the mission of "Back-to-the-Land"—a campaign initiated by rural and dispossessed South Africans.[97] Similar seminars occurred at subsequent BHMs. ISD's connection to and support of anti-Apartheid activism mirrored their efforts to combat racist practices and legislation in Germany. ISD also offered panels on Mozambique, the southern Sahara, Nigeria, and Somalia, demonstrating their interests in other regions on the continent and allowing Africa to have a nonpatronizing and nondismissive place in the German nation.[98]

ISD and other community organizers also used the film screenings at the BHMs as a didactic tool to impart knowledge to Afro-Germans, other communities of color, and white Germans about key Black figures and their efforts at self-determination, their accomplishments, and their struggles against inequality. The 1991 BHM included multiple film screenings, including a fifteen-minute preview of African American filmmaker Ada Gay Griffin's forthcoming documentary on Audre Lorde entitled *A Litany for Survival*, released in 1995; the film covered Lorde's time in Germany. Addressing Black British identity, *Hear Say*, *Ebony*, and *Black Britains* provided the audience with a glimpse into the world of other Black Europeans.[99] At the 1992 BHM, EURAFRI sponsored a screening of Haitian filmmaker Raoul Peck's *Lumumba: The Death of a Prophet*, describing Patrice Lumumba's rise in politics and tragic death in the Congo. This same BHM also featured a documentary on the life of Jamaican Pan-Africanist Marcus Garvey and a cinematic tribute to African American performer and activist Paul Robeson.[100] At a 1993 "Black Film History" panel, a presenter explained that while Black film was not often recognized in mainstream film history, it has had a long legacy that predated Spike Lee.[101] Moreover, BHM screenings also included films about the 1995 Million Man March in the United States, the Black Panthers and Huey P. Newton, Malcolm X, Le Pen's National Front, Steve Biko, the history of reggae, and other topics.[102] Yet not all of the film screenings were explicitly political, as even comedy and action films featuring African American directors and actors were viewed, including *I am Gonna Git You Sucka* and *Sweet Sweetback's Badasss Song*.[103] The committee organized events that spotlighted the lives of diverse individuals of African descent and that could serve as diasporic resources for participants. They relied on different creative mediums to convey their messages and knowledge.

Panels that elucidated the designation of Black and the concepts of Black consciousness and unity also occurred at the BHMs. Patricia Elcock, at the 1990 BHM, gave a presentation in English and German, entitled "Black Unity." In it, she offered an overview of the differences among Black people and their heritage, living situations, and political and social positions. Elcock urged participants of African descent to recognize and tolerate their differences and to actively forge ties with one another; it is here where the idea for the organization Black Unity Committee emerged.[104] ISD-Berlin member Nicola Lauré al-Samarai also gave a presentation, "Black as a Political Concept," that defined Black as not limited to skin color, but rather connected to all individuals who experienced racism and oppression. She further explained that the popularization of the concept Black derived from Steve Biko, the South African activist, theorist, and founder of the Black Consciousness Movement (BCM) who was killed in jail at the age of 31. Another ISD member Manu Holzer offered similar presentations on Black consciousness and Black solidarity at the 1994 one.[105] At the 1992 and 1996 BHMs, Mahoma Mwangulu, born in Tanzania to parents from Malawi, presented on aspects of Pan-Africanism, explaining its origins and development.[106] Similar events occurred at the last BHM in 2000, but this event also included topics on Germany's African politics and female circumcision in Sudan. These diverse events continually represented ISD's commitment to Black intellectualism and internationalism.

Black Germans also organized and moderated BHM panels that foregrounded women's issues and intellectualism. They encouraged Afro-German women and other Black women to interact and learn from one another. At the 1991 BHM, Nozizwe sponsored a panel entitled "When and where I enter," that paid homage to African American author and activist Anna Julia Cooper and focused on Black women in literature. In their panel, Kenyan activist Gladwell Otieno and Zimbabwean author Tsitsi Dangarembga observed, "A black woman is mostly described in literature not as a member contributing to changes in society, but rather as a supplementary person; sometimes useful, naturally erotic, but nevertheless a minor character. Due to the insight into her imposed role, a Black woman finds in literature a path to an alternative, self-defining, and liberating description of her social reality."[107] They viewed Black women's literature as an empowering source that enabled women to renegotiate and reconfigure their subjectivities. By doing so, Black women challenged their marginal status and shared their literature with others throughout the globe. Black authors and the intellectual communities that they produced allowed them to make critical interventions and confront hegemonic and exclusionary structures and discourses.

During the 1993 BHM, ISD and ADEFRA sponsored "Black Women Days." Several women from the ADEFRA-Hamburg chapter gave presentations, including Katja Kinder and Ilona Ivan. This mini-symposium offered a range of seminars for Black German women, including "Creative and critical perceptions on internalized racism;" "Southern trees bear strange fruits;" "Racism in German children's everyday lives;" "Workshop for parents of Black children and the specific situation of raising children in this country;" and a "Gynecological seminar."[108] The last seminar was important as German society had failed to prioritize Black women's health. At the same BHM, there was also a commemoration service to honor Audre Lorde. Afro-Germans and others from across Germany celebrated and remembered Lorde.[109] Again, these women gave gendered themes and feminist, diasporic perspectives a space within the BHMs. Ayim's 1996 lecture and discussion, "All the women are white, all the blacks are men—but some of us are brave: Racism from the Afro-Feminist Perspective," borrowed its title from African American feminists Barbara Smith, Gloria T. Hull, and Patricia Bell Scott's anthology, and "investigated how racism and sexism manifest in the personal, professional and political fields, and what strategies can evolve to produce individual and collective change."[110] She clarified "that it was not just about white dominance and the mechanisms of social exclusion, but we also needed to look at the weaknesses and promising prospects within the Black community."[111] With the BHMs, these women welcomed the opportunity to create intellectual communities that shaped their Black public sphere and that were cognizant of gender. Their intellectualism attested to their ability to engage complex and wide-ranging themes. It also did not impede their efforts at solidarity with others.

*　*　*

Using the BHM committee, Black Germans and others organized numerous events that centered translocal and transnational issues, showcasing the complexity of the diaspora. The rise of conservativism throughout Fortress Europe, South African Apartheid, the Somalian Civil Wars, the Rwandan genocide, neo-Nazi violence, and harsh immigration regulation impacted Afro-Germans and other communities of color in Germany and inspired their activism. These transnational developments also informed their work on translocal issues. Thus, the annual BHMs afforded Afro-Germans an opportunity to publicize and confront exclusion and discrimination, focusing on issues that could be life or death for them in the everyday.

With their BHMs, Black German and other Black activist-intellectuals pursued spatial politics that enabled them to establish a Black sense of place, both figuratively and literally. At these annual events, organizers and participants engendered alternative discourses and narratives that privileged their experiences and cultures and that encouraged political mobilization. Exemplifying their diasporic activism, these events also enabled Black Germans to produce spaces for themselves and the Black diaspora in the nation. Drawing on multiple diasporic resources, they also fashioned and contributed to a dynamic Black public sphere in reunified Germany as well as stimulated intellectual exchanges and produced and shared knowledge in creative ways.

As they decolonized spaces in Berlin (and beyond with the *Bundestreffen*), Black Germans and other Black communities demanded representation and participated in antiracist and feminist campaigns and projects that counteracted their displacement and acknowledged the diversity of Black people in Germany. Black Germans and others in the community also negotiated space for different types of Blackness and for Blackness to exist in different space-times. They reclaimed Blackness by transforming its negative construction and meaning and demonstrating its value for diasporic communities in the present and future. Afro-German women and men, along with white Germans and other People of Color, used alternative spaces to constitute bonds, inform their political perspectives, and accentuate their transnational activism, and this provided them with a sense of belonging. Black Germans also cultivated transnational solidarity with individuals across Germany, extended their solidarity within the diaspora, and let their activism reach nations worldwide.

With ISD's BHMs, Afro-German men and women developed a significant diasporic tradition, transforming normative belief and practices and giving them room to be heard and acknowledged in Germany. As a result, they manifested their agency and politicized multiple cultural and political issues. Though the BHMs ended in 2000, with Hafke and Reichel still involved, these celebrations still showed how Berlin remained a key city; the BHMs returned in 2009.[112] Berlin also shaped Black German women's transnational intellectual activism, signaling how inherently internationalist some of them were. Black German feminists, in particular, continued this internationalism with their involvement in the international Cross-Cultural Black Women's Studies Summer Institutes. Bringing the 1991 Institute to Frankfurt, Bielefeld, and Berlin, cities across reunified Germany, they affirmed the importance of Black feminist solidarity.

CHAPTER 6

BLACK GERMAN FEMINIST SOLIDARITY AND BLACK INTERNATIONALISM

> If the women's movement is to progress beyond its current malaise and
> lack of direction, it must develop a broader framework within which
> to operate. This calls for a recognition of the links among oppressions
> based on gender, race, class, sexual orientation, and other indexes of
> difference. In this way, white women can begin the process of addressing
> their own racism and thus clear the way for effective alliances with black
> women in our struggles for the self-determination of our peoples.
>
> —Delegates of the 1991 International, Cross-Cultural
> Black Women's Studies Summer Institute (August 22, 1991)

Building from their feminist work in their larger movement, Black German
women organized the Fifth Cross-Cultural Black Women's Studies Summer
Institute in reunified Germany. Beginning on August 2, 1991 and serving as a
"vehicle for international understanding," the institute included more than a
hundred women from six continents, who represented "an assembly of women
activists, theorists, writers, peasants, and workers who [were] concerned about
each other's realities and struggles."[1] It also exemplified the importance of diversity as a unifying tool for community building with Black women from Aote-
aroa/New Zealand to South Africa.[2] Later, one Afro-German attendee observed
that the making of affective connections "to older Black women from all over
the world was. . . . an important personal experience."[3] In an interview, Black
German feminist and professor Marion Kraft, the institute program director,
similarly conveyed that the purpose "of the summer seminar is to build an international network of black women. To be able to find support at different levels,
to gain access to resources, to form centers of information, and looking beyond

the [next] three weeks to give us the chance to create an institution that does not yet exist for us."[4] For Kraft, the institute served important functions for Black German and Black participants from across the globe, and they regularly used the term Black as an inclusive designation for all people who faced oppression and marginalization. Proving its continued importance in the late 1980s and 1990s, a "gendered political Blackness" was also a part of the institute's mission most notable in its title and in the aforementioned excerpt from the delegates.[5] This chapter shifts our focus toward Black and Women of Color feminisms and diasporic activism in Germany, showing how Black German women in the movement continued to theorize and produce knowledge that privileged an inclusive women-centered agenda—similar to work undertaken in *Farbe bekennen* and ADEFRA. In this way, this chapter underscores how these women were the very center of the Black German movement of the late twentieth century. They saw their engagement with other Black and People of Color activist communities as enhancing their intellectual and political work, in which they protested racial injustice and white supremacy across the globe.

As I argue, these women used the 1991 Institute to cultivate connections to Black women with varied backgrounds within and outside Germany that became critical to their feminist and diasporic activism. These women constructed a transnational network that promoted solidarity, extended encouragement, and confronted instances of racism and sexism similar to other Black women internationalists such as Audre Lorde and Eslanda Robeson.[6] This institute, much like previous ones, created spaces where Black feminists could initiate antiracist projects, share survival strategies, and document their challenges in societies that ignored their plight. These women's face-to-face interactions made them feel connected to one another and thereby gave them the strength to overcome silences and fears in their respective societies. The institute represented an affective experience and a cultural moment for them, solidifying trust, encouraging further activism, and affirming perceived commonalities and differences. A closeness remained for some even after the institute ended. For Black Germans, the 1991 Institute also reflected the broader contours of Black European women's transnational activism across Europe during this period, especially with the World Council of Churches' sub-program Women Under Racism (WUR) in the 1980s and later with groups like the Black Women and Europe Network (BWEN) in 1993.[7] The institute represented a persistent international phase within the Black German movement, one that coincided with reunified Germany's attempts to reclaim its place in the global arena. At the same time, Germany was rife with xenophobic violence targeted toward actual and alleged nonwhite foreigners. In continental Europe, deliberate surveillance, harsher borders controls, and exclusionary immigration laws hardened Fortress

Europe. Therefore, the institute helped these women criticize increased racism in the years after the fall of the Berlin Wall and the end of the Cold War in Germany and Europe while also obtaining recognition for themselves as Black Germans and their broader European struggles.

As Black German and Black women asserted their presence in German cities, they claimed the country as a site for different manifestations of Blackness (political or otherwise) and Black feminism—practices already prevalent in the Black German movement. Even more than their British counterparts, Black Germans sought more transnational connections in Europe and across the globe.[8] For some Afro-Germans, these connections proved necessary given their isolating racialized and gendered experiences in late postwar Germany. Finding support at the event, Black German women used cultural tools from and exchanges with Black and Third World feminists in Britain, the Netherlands, the United States, and elsewhere and applied those ideas and tactics to their local and national conditions.

Publicizing their transnational feminist politics, Afro-German and Black participants also used the power of writing to mobilize and sustain their political work, reasserting their intention to transform societies. Delegates produced and unanimously passed the "1991 Resolutions," which addressed issues concerning the legacy of colonialism, globalization, racial injustice, class divisions, and gender inequality. The resolutions served as a rallying call for basic human rights, international justice, and the implementation of new legislative measures on racism and discrimination. While little change occurred, nevertheless, these women's intervention brought media attention to those issues. As evinced by the resolutions, Afro-German women's solidarity politics with marginalized people across the globe emboldened them to confront and combat the material effects of racism and global white supremacy. This document, along with the 1993 edited volume, *Black Women of the World: Europe and Migration (Schwarze Frauen der Welt: Europa und Migration),* based on the event, revealed how these women strengthened their political consciousness by circulating and producing antiracist, feminist knowledge.[9] The 1990s also proved an exciting period for transnational feminist activism and Black freedom struggles. These women's forms of activism, claim making, and Black internationalism are illustrative of diasporic agency and belonging.

BLACK FEMINIST ACTIVISM AND THE EMERGENCE OF THE INSTITUTE

Prior to the Fifth Institute in 1991, several earlier international feminist conferences offered Black and Black German women the opportunity many had been seeking to build transnational alliances and to foreground their concerns. The

United Nations World Conference on Women in Mexico City, Mexico (1975), which inaugurated the UN Decade for Women, led to additional conferences in East Berlin, East Germany (1975), Copenhagen, Denmark (1980), and Nairobi, Kenya (1985). These events "transformed the landscape of transnational feminist organizing" in significant ways. But tensions emerged among white women and Women of Color, as well as First and Third World women.[10] After those conferences and additional feminist ones and book fairs, women across the globe expressed interest in sustaining a human rights dialogue on racism, heterosexism, sexism, classism, and Eurocentrism.

Contemporaneously, a new series of Black and Black women's studies programs developed in the United States, and African American and other feminist scholars founded organizations to explore global feminism and actively participate in Black women's internationalism.[11] These practices have long been a part of Black diasporic women's tools of political engagement and coalition building worldwide.[12] Established in 1987, the Cross-Cultural Black Women's Studies Summer Institute, which was headquartered in New York City and London, served as an example. The institutes mirrored themes from the UN conferences and addressed the collective, intersecting experiences of Black women and Women of Color by sponsoring international conferences in different countries with local host organizations and activists. The goal of the institute was to "foster international cooperation to promote peace, human rights, and development by presenting an opportunity for women of diverse cultures to exchange information, share experiences, identify resources and build links."[13] All the institutes served as a clearinghouse for theoretical and practical information concerning Black women's experiences by supporting research and feminist academic knowledge and mobilizing activists. Along these lines, the previous institutes represented how practices of Black feminism and grassroots internationalism became institutionalized before the one in 1991.

Transcontinental face-to-face exchanges and initiatives in North America drew attention to the issues concerning women with Black diasporic heritage and led to the institute's inception. In 1982 the International Resource Network of Women of African Descent (IRNWAD) was launched at the First International Conference on Research and Teaching Related to Women, held at Concordia University's Simone de Beauvoir Institute in Montreal, Canada, in which women from seventy-one different countries were in attendance.[14] The conference brought together women who had previously attended the 1980 UNESCO meeting in Paris on women's research and the 1980 UN Second World Conference on Women in Copenhagen. The IRNWAD encouraged "women of African descent 'to assume leadership in the research and teaching of the histories and experiences of continental and diasporan African women'" and "to institutionalize this body of study as a legitimate discipline." These representatives made Black and/or Africana women's studies a viable and established field within the academy. The founders of the IRNWAD, moreover, strove "to reverse the international under class status of women of African descent" and "to achieve recognition of issues of women's rights as issues of human rights." By its second international conference in 1985, which occurred in conjunction with the UN Third World Conference on Women in Nairobi, the IRNWAD issued a directive to establish a journal that would be a forum for the exchange of resources, strategies, research, and other skills. It was also at this event that the IRNWAD, along with other African women's groups, formed a Third World/Women of Color Caucus.[15]

Additionally, the members of IRNWAD had already created Black women's studies courses at Concordia University, a Black women's studies minor at Spelman College in Atlanta, and a doctoral program in Africana studies at Atlanta University (now Clark Atlanta University). Dr. Andrée Nicola McLaughlin, a professor from Medgar Evers College in New York, also piloted a cross-cultural Black women's studies curriculum at her home institution. She later co-founded the Cross-Cultural Institute and served as its international coordinator.[16] Cooperation and collaboration with women at the IRNWAD informed McLaughlin's efforts.

Traversing borders, the Cross-Cultural Institute also had transatlantic origins. This owed in part to McLaughlin's tenure as a visiting professor at the University of London's Institute of Education and the Center of Multicultural Education in 1986. While there, women of South Asian and African descent welcomed McLaughlin's emphasis on an intercultural examination of Black women. She also gained knowledge about the Black British experience through her engagement with community-based activists and their organizations. Together, McLaughlin and Noreen Howard, a London-based activist-intellectual, created the first "Cross-Cultural Black Women's Studies Seminar," which took place at the new Women's Studies Summer Institute at the University of London's Institute of Education that they co-founded in 1987.[17]

At the inaugural seminar, entitled "Women's Condition," held in the summer months of July and August, participants focused on the comparative realities of Black women's political struggles and evaluated some of the intellectual underpinnings of Black women's studies. The seminar was a four-week course that included public forums, sessions, film screenings, and discussions on selected readings with countless delegates from Asia, Africa, Europe, North America, and Latin America. The conveners made 80 percent of the events public, affording local, poor, and working-class women an opportunity to learn, engage, and network.[18] McLaughlin confirmed that women "felt it crucial to continue to address the legacies of colonialism and feudalism which impact upon our everyday lives in real ways. . . . issues of economic class, national and racial oppression, gender oppression, differences of ethnicity and religion, and the contradictions of caste, region, skin color, and social class." In an effort to forge connections and foster intercultural understanding, planners included diverse sessions such as "Second-Generation Puerto Rican Women in the USA," "Black Women Organizing in the Eighties in Britain," "Black Women Writers in Japan," "The Education of Black Women," and "Black Women and Feminism in Colombia."[19]

The London Institute also hosted a public talk and roundtable with Gloria Joseph, entitled "Black Women and Feminism: A Global View," that featured U.S.-based feminist academic Jacqui Alexander (Trinidad and Tobago), activist and educator Beryle M. Jones (Canada), researcher Chenzira J. Mutasa (Zimbabwe), researcher Berta Ines Perea Diaz (Colombia), and feminist publisher and author Barbara Smith (United States). The delegates were "enthused and impressed," yet "mindful of their respective circumstances and priorities"—again stressing the importance of connected differences.[20] Having dealt with exclusion in their respective nations, the institute allowed delegates to practice forms of Black internationalism, enhance cultural understanding and dimplomacy, and reshape their political activism. Clarifying the rationale for the institute, McLaughlin acknowledged "the sisters' strong feeling that we could not get an accurate assessment of our condition without looking into the mirror of the world's women that we conceived of a regularly scheduled forum for the cross-cultural study of economically developing women." She also realized the "power of this London exchange" to give Black women a critical platform.[21]

Within the context of the institutes, Black became a transnational political designation as much as a cultural one that was not strictly tied to African descent or skin color. In London McLaughlin recognized the concept of a Black identity as being a "culture, social class, and political class" and observed the theory of "multiple jeopardy."[22] In general, institute delegates understood Black to be "a term to express our cross-cultural identities as black people whether based on culture, political ideas and/or social class, and thus referring to a broad range of national, ethnic, racial, and religious groups."[23] In this way, " 'blackness' does not belong to any one individual or group. Rather, individuals or groups appropriate this complex and nuanced racial signifier in order to circumscribe its boundaries or to exclude other individuals or groups."[24] Black served as an act of performance, an affective bond, a mode of resistance, and a malleable signifier that allowed diverse racialized communities from Latin America, Africa, and Asia to cohere and reimagine their positions and identities.

Subsequent institutes in New York City (1988), Harare, Bulawayo, Zvisha-vane (1989), and Auckland (1991) embodied the interplay among the local, na-tional, and global. Each of the early institutes focused on a theme that stressed specific indigenous undercurrents that affected women in these locales while also emphasizing international dynamics. Broadening the parameters of femi-nism, these institutes helped to unite oppressed individuals worldwide around critical overlapping issues about class, gender, and race and create spaces for networking, communication, and support. These events reveal the importance of Black and Women of Color transnational organizing in which they eschewed white liberal feminism's false universalism, transmitted knowledge about Black communities across the globe, and contributed to the UN's Decade for Women.

This intercultural and internationalist emphasis remained prominent at the July 1988 New York Institute. Bringing together women with more than thirty nationalities and concentrating on the topic of "Women and Communications," the three-week institute sponsored several presentations on the media's repre-sentation and appropriation of Asian and Afro-Colombian women and on the development of national movements in Palestine, El Salvador, and Aotearoa/ New Zealand. Members from feminist organizations in Angola, Zimbabwe, and the Netherlands attended.[25] Presentations and working groups afforded women an occasion to raise their voices and express emotions from motivation and enthusiasm to disappointment. African American feminists Barbara Smith, Audre Lorde, and Sonia Sanchez presented on heterosexual women and the per-sistence of homophobia. Anjuli Gupta, an Indian German, who identified as a "Black feminist" (*Schwarze Feministin*), attended this workshop, professing that, "the exchange gave me energy and inspired many new ideas and encouraged me to continue the fight."[26] The affective reactions of participants influenced their social engagement and encouraged a sense of belonging. Gupta traveled to New York with Katharina Oguntoye and May Ayim, who gave presentations on the origins of the Afro-German movement and Afro-German writing. Kraft and Helga Emde were also supposed to attend, but could not owing to financial difficulties.[27] Prominent figures such as African American writer and activist Toni Cade Bambara, American antiracist activist and scholar Peggy McIntosh, and African American feminist professor Beverly Guy-Sheftall were also in at-tendance.

Showcasing women's innovation and creativity, African American film-maker Ada Griffin of the Third World Newsreel, an independent production and distribution company, hosted an "International Women's Film and Discussion Series" at the institute that featured directors and panelists with distinct back-grounds. Attendees articulated a desire for "the development of an international network so that sometime in the near future an international showing of these women's films and videos could be arranged."[28] It was not only important to collaborate and discuss, but also to maintain these creative connections and share their visual representations on an international stage. These sessions also exemplified Black women's intellectualism, especially as they theorized, exchanged ideas, and imparted knowledge about their experiences personally and collectively, using multiple creative mediums.

The New York event also highlighted how local American issues of injustice related to international instances of bigotry and oppression. Lorde recounted the story of Tawana Brawley, a fifteen-year-old African American girl who accused six white men of raping her in Wappingers Falls, New York in 1987. Delegates participated in a march and penned a statement for Ms. Brawley and her family, and wrote another letter in support of the anti-Apartheid struggle in South Africa.[29] At a press conference at the UN Plaza, delegates also expressed solidarity with Titewahi Harawira, one of the seminar co-conveners and an activist for Māori rights and health services in Aotearoa/New Zealand. The other two seminar co-conveners were Black British activist Gail Lewis and Zimbabwean activist Sekai Holland.[30] Harawira, along with some of her family members, was later arrested in Aotearoa/New Zealand for her indigenous activism. The theme of solidarity continued, especially with the Schomburg Center for Research in Black Culture's art exhibition "In Our Own Image: An International Perspective by Women Artists." The exhibition "portrayed the twin themes of diversity and similarity, reflecting the artists' perceptions of the world, their culture, and themselves."[31] Although the institute fostered multicultural dialogue, some exchanges fell short for non-English speakers and for non-academic women.[32]

These moments of community building were not without problems. A few conflicts emerged at the Third Zimbabwean Institute, entitled "Women and the Politics of Food," held in August 1989.[33] Sekai Holland, the program director, sought "to facilitate [a] forum for women to discuss and define their realities," and encouraged "liaisons to pursue funding for the participation of Pacific, Middle Eastern, Asian, and Amerindian women."[34] Kraft and Dulcie Flower, an indigenous activist from Australia, were the seminar co-conveners. Speaking at the 1989 Institute, McLaughlin described how the event "represent[ed] the combined efforts of women from economically developing nations and communities worldwide," and operated as a collaborative and energizing enterprise. McLaughlin continued, "we are women of diverse nationalities, cultures, religions, ages, experiences, and even ideologies," who are "bonded by a common commitment to empower women in our various struggles for self-determination and autonomy—that is, freedom of the group and the individual."[35] She, in other words, encouraged differences by privileging inclusive Black and feminist identities, identities that were shaped by common struggles against overlapping oppressions.

But as Kraft mentioned in a 1989 letter to Lorde, emotional tensions arose because of participants' inability to respect cultural practices and to listen to one another. Kraft posed a series of questions: "What about our sisters in Azania? What about those women from Uganda, Ethiopia, Panama—who had come a long way? What was the meaning of 'Cross-Cultural'? The fact that some American sisters did not attend the closing meeting, saying they felt 'disrespected'? And even if they were wrong, can we discard their emotions by saying 'they are very young'? How do we deal with differences among ourselves?"[36] Kraft noticed how some participants were unable to acknowledge one another's connected differences. These kinds of cultural tensions among African American, Black diasporic, and other Third World women remained at prominent global feminist gatherings, including the 1985 UN Third Conference on Women in Nairobi. Yet she added that, "the 'Institute' [is] very important. *We* need—as African women, women of the Black diaspora—[a] forum of our own, and I am grateful to the sisters who initiated this." "Zimbabwe," Kraft stated, "*was* an exciting experience, worth all the hardships and frustrations."[37]

As with previous ones, delegates formed solidarity links with local women "through song and dance that reflected the richness of the traditional African cultures and the revolutionary spirit that still exists."[38] The institute gave delegates an opportunity to learn about Zimbabwean history, especially its colonial legacy, liberation struggles, and resettlement after independence. Formal sessions and informal cultural gatherings helped delegates interact with local women who represented different social classes and ethnic groups, such as the Shona and Ndebele, in the independent nation. Zimbabwean women shared that independence did not yield full resettlement, as originally promised, and that the relocation of farm families proved difficult owing to their traditional ethnic beliefs about their ancestors in those areas.[39] Signifying the importance of local activism and coalition building, attendees learned of and participated in grassroots reeducation programs sponsored by Zimbabwean women's clubs. These cross-cultural connections were meaningful and did not overlook the particular oppressions that women faced.

Privileging solidarity, hospitality, and indigenous rights, the Fourth Institute, held in March 1991, organized around the theme of "Human Rights and Indigenous Peoples in the 'Information Age'" in Aotearoa/New Zealand. Some participants met with Māori women, including Harawira, for a fact-finding mission and produced a documentary on indigenous and human rights that featured her and her family.[40] In doing so, they contributed and disseminated knowledge about indigeneity and political agency in the Pacific. With the mission, delegates learned about critical issues concerning the Māori, such as "land, language, culture and power-sharing under the Treaty of Waitangi" (1840) and how "they affect education, health, employment, social welfare, and the goal of Māori sovereignty." Through the tour and exchanges, these women "look[ed] at ourselves and our struggles in new ways, especially as this concerns the struggles of indigenous peoples and the nature of our relationships with each other's struggles."[41] Again, the institute had an emotional impact, fostered connections, and supported creative, collaborative projects. Later, institutes occurred in Caracas, Venezuela (1993), Honolulu, Hawaii (1995), and Johannesburg, South Africa (1998). International symposia and study tours took place in Russia (1999), Costa Rica (1999), Trinidad and Tobago (2001), Japan (2004), and Panama (2006), with Panama as the final one.[42] Kraft attended the 2006 Institute and reunited with McLaughlin; Lily Golden, an Afro-Russian activist and author; and Khosi Mbatha, a South African activist, several individuals from the 1991 Institute. If not without conflicts, these events continued to encourage feminist solidarity and Black internationalism. With these practices, participants showed the significance of forging alternative forms of kinship locally and globally. Through Black German women's activism and involvement in these institutes, they maintained feminist solidarity networks and global contacts, and they used them to develop strategies for survival and resistance and make their voices heard in Germany.

THE FIFTH CROSS-CULTURAL BLACK WOMEN'S STUDIES SUMMER INSTITUTE

The Fifth Institute built on this rich tradition of activism and Black internationalism. Though there were previous conferences that tackled the subjects of racism and anti-Semitism, the Fifth Institute was the first hosted in Germany and dedicated to the topic of Blacks in Europe.[43] The institute shared a commitment to the theme of "Black People and the European Community" (*Schwarze Menschen und die Europäische Gemeinschaft*).[44] It occurred in Frankfurt, Bielefeld, and Berlin with Kraft as the program director and Black German activists Helga Emde and Katharina Oguntoye as regional coordinators; Alem Desta, an Ethiopian lecturer based in the Netherlands, and Melba Wilson, an African American London-based writer, were the seminar co-conveners.[45] May Ayim, Jasmin Eding, Ria Cheatom, Judy Gummich, Ika Hügel-Marshall, Yvonne Kettels, Raja Lubinetzki, Sheila Mysorekar, Eleonore

Wiedenroth-Coulibaly, Ina Röder, Modupe Laja, Yara-Colette Lemke Muñiz de Faria, and Bärbel Kampmann—members of ISD and ADEFRA—attended, presented, and/or arranged activities. ISD-Berlin and ADEFRA-Munich also sponsored it.[46] Kraft and volunteers organized events so that there would be time for meetings, personal exchanges, and excursions to historical and cultural sites in Germany.

The organizers of the 1991 Institute practiced solidarity by using existing Black German networks, such as the Cross-Cultural Initiative of Black Women for Minority Rights and Studies in Germany (Interkulturelle Initiative Schwarzer Frauen für Minoritätenrechte und—Studien in Deutschland e.V., IISF). Founded in 1990, it was an organization Lorde helped to establish.[47] Kraft mentioned in a 2014 article that the institute "was another proof of Audre Lorde's ability to turn the seemingly impossible into reality, to move the Black woman from margin to center—even in Germany."[48] Along with the IISF, Nozizwe, a migrant women's organization, hosted the event. A variety of organizations and institutions including the Department for Multicultural Affairs in Frankfurt, the Protestant Church, SOS Racism (France and Germany), the Association of Bi-National Families and Partnerships (previously Interessengemeinschaft der mit Ausländern verheirateten Frauen e.V., IAF), the WCC in Geneva, and others supported the institute.[49] Women from the ages of eighteen and over were encouraged to attend, and organizers did not dissuade Men of Color or white women from participating, although there were several women only or Black women and/or Women of Color only workshops.[50] The IISF also financed attendee accommodations through fees and previous fundraising efforts. Support from other sponsors covered the expenses of Third World women, offering them a small housing stipend.

The three-week institute came at a pivotal moment in German history, in which the reemergence of ethno-nationalist rhetoric and physical and discursive violence became more pronounced. As McLaughlin opined in a 1992 letter, "Even though German society is in the throes of profound structural change and experiencing an upsurge in racist violence, our German sisters—members of a relatively young Black *national* community—courageously undertook initiatives to conduct the 1991 Institute and to mount a tremendous fund-raising effort. Their endeavors made possible increased national and cultural diversity of delegates in attendance and simultaneous translation at Institute events."[51] Emde was proud to host "the important conference" in "racist Germany" in order to broadcast these developments to others.[52] In this context, Afro-German women constructed sites for support and transnational exchange, and continued to shed light on the plight of Blacks and People of Color in German society. As some "African and American sisters" noted, Black Germans were "well-off and educated, but also more isolated and lonelier than minorities in other states."[53] Several, but by no means all, of the Afro-German participants could be considered a part of the German middle class. Regardless of their social and cultural backgrounds, linking up with other Black participants at the institute encouraged a sense of belonging among Afro-German women, in which they cultivated emotional and social bonds. The creation of these affective communities required alternative practices of intimacy. This institute served as a resource and a mode of Black survival in an increasingly racially hostile environment.

With the first week of sessions, beginning at the University of Frankfurt on August 3 and ending on the 10, Kraft, Emde, and Oguntoye addressed the economic and political development of the European Community and its impact on non-white Europeans and non-European immigrants.[54] A flyer expressed the aims thus: "The [institute] includes an intercultural examination of the history, present and socio-economic situation of Black people in Europe and engages with issues of cultural identity and the campaign that blacks and other minorities wage against xenophobia, eurocentrism, neo-fascism, and racism."[55] Of particular interest to Afro-Germans were "Black Europeans' forms of political and cultural resistance."[56] Moreover, in a newspaper interview, Kraft explained the institute's goals and reminded readers and participants that Black Europeans were complicit in the "global paradigm of oppression." She continued, "Our theme is 'Black people and the European Community,' but a lot of women from the so-called Third World also are participating. These women have completely different problems than we do in western European countries. We live in countries that are directly involved in the exploitation of Third World countries. Therefore to establish a network and then to formulate the common, concrete demands for the UN and individual countries, that is the critical thing that we can do with an event like this."[57] Attendees, German and non-German, explored these themes through a shared feminist engagement.

The institute fostered connections, but it was not without unpleasant experiences of racism, conflict, and organizational glitches. In Frankfurt, participants encountered overt forms of racism. At the University of Frankfurt's bookstore, a South African attendee was told that, "she should remove her dirty fingers" from the merchandise. Moreover, child caretakers returned from a playground complaining that Germans greeted their charges with "Get lost, you N******."[58] A 1992 IISF report mentioned a few tensions at some of the sessions. Some participants, especially Black Germans, believed that having white German women in attendance created the risk that Black women's discussions about racism would be misinterpreted and questioned and seen as a form of exclusion.[59] Some complained that the institute left little time for more personal interactions, while others wanted more involvement from ISD members. Yet the report remarked that, "regardless of these differences, after three weeks of intense work we arrived at a successful conclusion, which was positive."[60]

Inserting themselves in well-known urban spaces, the events reflected the organizers' intersectional perspectives and ambitions and the institute's diversity. Afro-Dutch activist and scholar Philomena Essed and African American activist Melba Wilson were just a few of the prominent figures present in Frankfurt.[61] Barbara Walker, a Jamaican Cologne-based artist, for example, presented an exhibition at the Dietrich-Bonhoeffer House, and Vinie Burrows, an African American Broadway actress, gave a presentation on African myths and histories at the Frankfurt Youth Center.[62] Eva Johnson, an Australian of the Mulak Nation, staged a one-woman show.[63] When events began in Bielefeld on August 11, Burrows performed the production "Sister," which included texts and scenes on the international women's movement.[64] Bianca Tangande, a Dutch artist, opened an exhibition entitled "Images of Oneself," and Māori writer Cathie Dunsford read her poetry.[65] Cameroonian Paris-based journalist, activist, and president of the Movement for the Defense of the Rights of Black Women (Mouvement pour la défense des droits de la femme noire, MODEFEN) Lydie Dooh-Bunya and Black British teacher and writer Beryl Gilroy presented on panels.[66] Several of these participants, including Essed and Dooh-Bunya, were already active in Black European women's organizations and networks. The variety of excursions, workshops, and activities at the institute allowed women to approach their differences creatively and showed how artistic expressions encouraged community. It also illustrated how women used diverse forms of performance to impart knowledge about women.

Beginning on August 17, the events in Berlin centered on the relationship between the European Economic Community (EEC) and the Third World.[67] Emde noted that contact with Black women minorities "offered an example of the political power of women for the future."[68] During the final session, McLaughlin claimed that, "We black women have to meet together the great challenge, the re-creation of the universe."[69] Her optimism reveals just how moving this event was for these women.

The 1991 Institute facilitated Black German ties with feminists in Brazil, the Netherlands, the United States, and beyond. Kinship, emotions, and feminist politics were intertwined, as they had been at past ones. Afro-German women continued to practice both diasporic and post–World War II German traditions that involved establishing transatlantic solidarity with foreign students and activists from Iran, the Congo, and the United States in Germany.[70] Afro-German women witnessed the institute advancing interpersonal connections, intersectional politics, and linkages between the global and the local. Relationships with Black women activists and scholars from abroad served as a critical reference point for Afro-Germans who not only dealt with similar struggles at home, but also tried to tackle injustices internationally.

THE INSTITUTE'S 1991 RESOLUTIONS

United through personal interactions and eager to make a difference nationally and internationally, the delegates produced the "1991 Resolutions" to manifest their collective agency and their Black, diasporic, and feminist politics, which embodied their gendered political Blackness. This appears to be the first time in the institute's history that delegates had created such a revolutionary document, which signified their unflinching willingness to critically reflect and change the world. Given the confluence of intolerant and violent acts across the globe, the delegates signaled their commitment to eliminate oppressive policies, practices, and legislation. In the resolutions, delegates emphasized, "That the fundamental human, national, civil, and democratic rights of black women and their communities have been and continue to be violated."[71] The resolutions, moreover, exposed Black women's conditions and demonstrated that, though the women were from diverse regions, they still faced analogous struggles. Delegates stressed "That the legacies of colonialism, feudalism and imperialism, as well as institutionalized racism, sexism and xenophobia, continue to reproduce social, economic and political inequality." For them, "the violation of our human, national, civil and democratic rights is characterized by the discrimination that we as black women experience in having limited or no access to work, education, housing, or health care because of our gender, race, color, social class, ethnicity, nationality, religion, language, political orientation and/or sexual orientation." They also recognized the prevalence of the sex trafficking of Black women, the mass sterilizations of Black women globally, the economic enslavement of people in the Third World in sweatshops and on the street, among other topics. Again, these Black women embraced their intersectional politics, reflecting on the forms of discrimination and exclusion they endured in their respective nations. They articulated their claims for full-fledged human rights, which was an idea that gained more prominence during decolonization and the 1970s and focused on the morality of individual rights on an international scale.[72]

The resolutions also signified how these women were agents whose unmediated interventions challenged their marginalization and served as counter-discourses against the hegemonic narratives of European colonialism and the policies of Fortress Europe that enforced a rigid border regime, detained im-migrants, and harbored negative attitudes about immigrants and immigration. To be sure, colonial stereotypes and assumptions and oppressive discourses persisted.[73] Moreover, European politicians from across the spectrum imple-mented policies and citizens adopted racist rhetoric and practices that produced a Fortress Europe. In addition, the delegates also described how "the violence of colonialism, which resulted in the near extermination of First Nation peoples, as well as the enslavement and dislocation of Black people globally, continues to be perpetuated in the ongoing oppression and exploitation of Black women and children today." This global history represented a cycle of subjugation that influenced how some attendees and their children lived. Along these lines, participants at the institute were ensnared in structural webs of inequality.

Attendees hoped that their resolutions, nine in total, would "be implemented to eradicate the exploitation, oppression, and violence directed toward Black women and Black people in Africa, the Americas, Asia, Europe, the Middle East, and the Pacific."[74] Delegates exemplified the solidarity of women across the globe who shared and articulated a common vision that remained attentive to women's positions and development and made efforts to improve their condi-tions for the future. In this way, they were not like women leaders from nonprofit organizations, diplomats, and other activists at the previous UN conferences on women. Although these resolutions did not make a strong impact in their respective countries, they did encourage alliances, especially within Europe, among these Women of Color activists. These textual acts symbolized their efforts at knowledge production, helping them reimagine their political work and activism and illustrating their investment in making the plight of women visible. With this document, Black German women demonstrated how they were quotidian intellectuals shaping international discourses and narratives. The resolutions also confirmed the participants' trust of each other despite their differences, as they channeled their common outrage and dissatisfaction toward political action.

Delegates pushed several related causes, including the "recognition of the links among oppressions based on gender, race, class, and sexual orientation, and other indexes of difference."[75] Additionally, the resolutions represented the relationship between the local/national and the international and Black wom-en's internationalism in practice. Resolution #1, put forth by the IISF and en-titled *by the host organization of the 1991 Cross-Cultural Black Women's Studies Summer Institute,* addressed the human rights struggles of migrants and ethnic minorities in Germany and the government's failure to prevent racial discrimination.[76] Re-fusing to decouple national and international issues, the IISF also highlighted parallels with other ethnic minorities. Resolution #2, entitled *on The Unification of Europe 1992*, stated that "consequently, the various, existing European laws tend to restrict the freedom of movement of foreigners outside the EEC and Europeans born outside of Europe but living within the borders of the EEC are in violation of the UN Charter, the Geneva Convention on Refugees, and International Law." For delegates, EEC countries had a "moral obligation to respect their own commitments in the name of the rights of all human beings."[77] With Resolution #3, *on Migrants*, delegates insisted that basic human rights were "not subject to negotiation or tampering" and demanded "that [the] countries of the European Community guarantee the inalienable rights of migrants as well as refugees to legal and political freedom, including the right to be politically and economically active, without fear of arrest, and the right to vote." These women explicitly challenged Fortress Europe's restrictive and discriminatory policies. The delegates further observed that opportunities for asylum in Europe did not spare migrants and refugees from "common oppressions based on racism and social and economic injustice."[78]

With resolutions four through six, delegates articulated their solidarity with Third World, Māori, and South African women and underscored the issues of debt, indigenous sovereignty, and Apartheid. Demanding indemnities from the First World "for all these centuries of exploitation our people [in the Third World] have been forced to bear," Resolution #4 *on External Debt* tackled the question of "Who owes whom?" Delegates wanted wealthy northern "nations to use their resources responsibly and positively to encourage peace and human rights for global development." They also rejected "conditionalities" imposed by the International Monetary Fund and World Bank.[79] With Resolution #5, *on Māori Sovereignty*, delegates urged the Aoteroa/New Zealand government to honor the Treaty of Waitangi from 1840, which guaranteed the Māori Nation full and exclusive rights to lands, forests, and fisheries. Delegates supported the Māori Nation's rights as sovereign people and their opposition to nuclear testing in the Pacific.[80] Promoting feminist sisterhood, Resolution #6, *on Winnie Mandela and South Africa*, "opposed all attempts by the South African government and its police, courts, and media to discredit and destroy her and her work." This Resolution also discussed the legacy of Apartheid and defended the "democratic principle of 'one person, one vote' " for South Africa.[81]

Honoring Black elders at the institute, the women created an international council of women and a transatlantic friendship society that would continue to encourage generational attachments as a means of survival and resistance. With Resolution #7, *on International Council of Elders*, delegates were again cognizant of their diversity, mentioning "First Nation, Third World, refugee, immigrant, and ethnic and national minority women." Elders from these groups would be "accorded every opportunity to attend all Institutes without incurring costs for fees and housing."[82] Resolution #8, *on Afro-German/Afro-American Friendship*, worked to establish a society between Afro-Germans and African Americans, and thereby further expanding opportunities for feminist dialogues and diasporic mobilization.

With their final Resolution #9, *on the Centre for Race and Ethnic Studies (CRES) University of Amsterdam,* delegates wrote "a formal letter to the Board of the University of Amsterdam about its decision to close the Centre for Race and Ethnic Studies (CRES)." They considered the disbanding of CRES—in existence since 1984—as unjust, especially as CRES was one of the first institutions in the Netherlands devoted to intersectional approaches.[83] Given the hostile European climate, institutions such as CRES were invaluable spaces that supported scholarship on "issues in race and ethnic studies."[84]

While all of the resolutions dealt with aspects of feminism, community, and politics, the first and eighth resolutions are significant for demonstrating that Afro-German women bore witness to and stressed the value of personal ties and feminist solidarity. This was a common practice for Black German women as discussed in the previous chapters. Resolutions #1 and #8 affirmed Afro-German women's commitment to draw attention to their marginal positions in society and to foster empowering relationships with diverse Black feminists. In Resolution #1, the IISF drafters bemoaned that Germany "has been and remains a country that considers itself monocultural despite a large and growing number of various ethnic minorities, including Black Germans, and despite millions of immigrant workers, many of whom have been living in Germany for two or three generations and who are still denied basic human, civil and political rights, including the right to vote."[85] As Resolution #1 made clear, Germany was an immigration country, where immigrants', their children's, Black Germans', and other minority political voices were ignored and silenced. The resolution added that "nationalist and even fascist tendencies still exist and have increased since reunification, both in East and West Germany," where "open violence against visible ethnic minorities, people of African descent in particular, have occurred." The ongoing aggression resulted in "racist murder[s]."[86] Afro-German women also confronted Chancellor Helmut Kohl's neoconservative CDU party and politicians from the liberal SPD, demanding that they "put into practice existing UN resolutions against racial discrimination, grant immigrants in this country the right to vote, and actively support regional and national initiatives."[87] For these women, it was important to call out politicians on both sides of the political spectrum, revealing that liberals and conservatives were complicit in systems of oppression in Germany.

With this difficult and violent situation, Afro-German women created an emotional economy in which they could express their feelings and establish trust and camaraderie with other Black women. Without a doubt, emotions do social and political work and become empowering revolutionary tools.[88] Forming affective ties with Black participants enabled Afro-German women to advance political objectives about their marginal status and to construct a new international network of Black and Women of Color feminists and to publicize Afro-German experiences internationally. "Over the past three weeks," Afro-German women noted within the first resolution, "we have had the opportunity to exchange our situations, our ideas and political views with women from all over the world, black women and women of color from all continents, and we do hope that this will be the start of an international network against racism, sexism, and all forms of discrimination."[89] Their first resolution operated as a political, affective, and performative act that situated Afro-German women within multiple activist communities of color. Similarly, with Resolution #8, Afro-German women solidified "the creation of an Afro-German/Afro-American Friendship Society."[90] By doing so, they wanted "to foster historical and cultural linkages between [the] ethnic minority of Black Germans and the Black population of the United States."[91] For Afro-German women, one of "the most important results" of the institute was the Friendship Society and the transatlantic exchanges it would lead to.

The institute and its resolutions gave Afro-Germans the courage and support to redefine and renegotiate their positions in society. These women emphasized this point in the first resolution, "As Black German women and Black women of other nationalities living in Germany, we have decided to make ourselves visible and to make our voices heard. This year's Institute and the ensuing documentation and publication of its contributions and results are important steps forward in this struggle for human rights and dignity."[92] Both the institute and the resolutions also afforded Black German feminists with an opportunity to center their experiences on an international scale, and by so doing, they showed that Black women mattered in Germany.

Furthermore, Marion Kraft and Rukhsana Shamim Ashraf-Khan's 1993 volume, *Black Women of the World,* helped them practice intellectual activism and manifest their collective agency and feminist and diasporic politics. Orlanda, which had previously published *Farbe bekennen* and Lorde's works, printed the volume. The collaborative volume, dedicated to Lorde, who had since died, featured twenty-three revised articles based on institute attendees' presentations and privileged a gendered political Blackness with authors of Asian descent. In the introduction, Kraft and Ashraf-Khan stressed that, "They [minority women] share a commitment to a society without any exclusion, hatred, and violence. Their dialogue across borders is determined by the affirmation of difference as a creative force and the ability to learn from one another."[93] Again, Lorde's idea of connected differences guided the volume, in which they focused on antiracist and intersectional approaches and revealed how differences could be used productively and constructively. For the co-editors, the collection signified an important intervention that entailed underscoring their historical pasts and creating a vision of a new world.[94] The contributors saw their volume (and their work at the institute) as a form of cultural and political work that "tries to inspire and educate women."[95]

The articles and poems by Black German women underscored the significance of "thinking globally and acting locally."[96] Each piece connected national dynamics of social marginalization in Germany to worldwide developments of racial discrimination. Ayim's chapter, for instance, examined the rise of xenophobia and the repression of foreigners and People of Color in reunified Germany and Europe as a whole. These forms of exclusion often involved violent attacks and the enactment of restrictive legislation against immigrants from the Third World.[97] Kraft's contribution illuminated the interplay of sexism and racism for Black German women and how this informed their diasporic and feminist activism. She drew parallels among other women of the Black diaspora in Europe.[98] Mysorekar's chapter offered a comparative analysis on the concept of Black and how it impacted African and Asian diasporic communities in Germany, the United States, and Great Britain in different ways. In spite of these varying contexts, "Racism," she stated, "affects us all, even when it takes on different forms."[99] She encouraged unity between Asians and Africans, which could become a weapon against racism. The volume also incorporated the writings of other Women of Color in Germany and elsewhere, including Elçin Kürsat-Ahlers (Germany) and Elsa Weldeghiorgis (Italy). But together, these Black German contributions sought to campaign for social recognition, human rights (*Menschenrechte*), and human dignity (*Menschenwürde*). Again, these women were quotidian intellectuals producing knowledge and shaping how people understood and engaged those discourses in and beyond Germany.

Black Germans hoped that this new visibility would guarantee that Black women's experiences would be observed, read, and heard in a society that normalized whiteness. Perhaps naively, these Afro-German women thought that their international and national visibility provided them with a political advantage and opened up possibilities for their budding movement. Although the institute gained coverage in several well-known German newspapers, including *Die Tageszeitung (taz)* and *Frankfurter Allgemeine Zeitung (FAZ)*, better introducing society to this Black diasporic community, the publicity did not ensure that Afro-Germans could retain this recognition or that anti-Black racism would abate.

*   *   *

Through the 1991 Cross-Cultural Black Women's Studies Summer Institute, Afro-German women organized events and activities that enabled them to address local and global issues and engage in new forms of diasporic activism. Black Germans and others demanded social recognition from and participated in antiracist and feminist projects that acknowledged the variety of experiences of People of Color in Germany and across the globe. Afro-German women, along with others, developed empowering Black spaces that helped them constitute bonds, accentuating and positioning their activism within their communities and movements. Black Germans cultivated transnational solidarity with individuals throughout Germany, the Black diaspora, and the world. The 1991 Institute also marked Germany as a vibrant Black space, allowing overlapping articulations of Blackness to exist and thrive. Through this space, Black German women become visible agents who showcased the diversity of Germany and the Black diaspora. These Afro-German women and the other attendees of the institute explicitly focused on the experiences of Black women.

Afro-Germans made diasporic and feminist activism culturally relevant within their community and created opportunities to develop their voices and practice Black women's internationalism. The 1991 Institute helped Afro-Germans confront exclusion and discrimination as they continued to concentrate on critical issues in the everyday. The rise of conservatism across Fortress Europe, South African Apartheid, and indigenous rights in Aotearoa/New Zealand motivated Afro-Germans and other participants to produce their resolutions. Engendering alternative discourses through their resolutions, these Black women helped to exchange and disseminate knowledge about their history experiences and articulate ideas about international human rights. Their resolutions signified the participants' commitment to effect social change. These transnational developments also informed Black German women's work on local issues such as migrant rights and the persistence of racism and racial violence in reunified Germany. Afro-German women's involvement in the institute afforded them an opportunity to share their emotions and experiences, promote diasporic knowledge about their struggles, and develop resistance strategies. Confronting multiple forms of discrimination, these Black German women sought feminist connections to broadcast local and international dynamics and Black women's achievements. Even though Afro-German women and their movement were not always successful, this historical moment helped them carve out public diasporic and Black spaces devoted to a gendered political Blackness, diversity, inclusivity, and Third World feminism. These moments still have critical relevance for today as Black women across the globe struggle for recognition, equality, liberation, and justice, negotiating their positions and demanding their rights in societies that render them inconsequential.

EPILOGUE

Black Lives Matter in Germany

Since its inception in 2013, the Black Lives Matter (BLM) movement, founded by three Black women, including two who are queer, has flourished in the United States and across the globe. Protests have taken place in London, Paris, Amsterdam, Vienna, and Copenhagen. BLM has become an international movement, especially as European communities of color campaign for antiracist initiatives, civil rights legislation, equitable treatment as citizens and residents, and the acknowledgment of the instrumental role that race, colonialism, and transatlantic slavery has played and continues to play in these countries.[1] Germany, too, serves as an example of the global reverberations of this movement. After the death of African American Mike Brown in Ferguson, Missouri on August 9, 2014, ISD organized a #FergusonisEverywhere campaign to express solidarity while also highlighting instances of police brutality in Germany with the murders of Sierra Leonean Oury Jalloh in 2005, Congolese Dominique Kouamadio in 2006, and Nigerian Christy Schwundeck in 2011, to name a few.[2] This campaign built on previous activism surrounding the deaths of Angolan Amadeu Antonio Kiowa in 1990, Mozambican Alberto Adriano in 2000, and others and stressed the fact that state and nonstate violence occurred everywhere and that Germany was not immune.[3]

Continuing a Black radical and internationalist tradition, a BLM protest took place in Berlin in June 2017 with thousands of people expressing solidarity and promoting awareness of racial injustice. The event built from the momentum of two earlier BLM marches in Berlin that occurred the previous summer.[4] Initially meeting at the 2016 BLM marches, Mic Oala, Shaheen Wacker, Nela Biedermann, Josephine Apraku, Jacqueline Mayen, and Kristin Lein remained in contact and eventually established a Berlin-based multicultural German feminist collective. With their new group and local connections, they planned the BLM 2017 demonstration as a part of a month-long series of events, which included film screenings, poetry readings, workshops, exhibitions, and more. These events exemplified the diversity of Black activism within the German context. BLM organizers also garnered support from local ISD and ADEFRA groups as well as other People of Color groups, artists, and activist-intellectuals in Berlin. Using these BLM activities, especially the protest, the organizers publicly drew attention to racism and oppression and attempted to gain visibility for Black people and People of Color in Germany and beyond. The different events and the BLM movement in Berlin, more broadly, represented these antiracist, feminist activist-intellectuals' practices of resistance and their ability to create and own spaces of resistance, solidarity, and recognition within a majority-white society. In this way, they demanded and reclaimed their "rights to the city" and continued to make Germany a critical site for Blackness and the Black diaspora—not unlike what Black Germans did with their movement thirty years earlier. Here, too, contemporary forms of political organizing served as acts of disidentification, as those activists also opposed and sought to change the hegemonic power structures, historical silences, and racist ideas and practices entrenched in German society.[5]

Similar to the women at the Cross-Cultural Institutes, these feminists embraced Black as a gendered political identity and advanced intersectional politics and agendas. The women envisioned the German BLM to be a space for individuals to develop new critical methods that would help them acknowledge their overlapping oppressions in order to create an alternative society.[6] They were also not unlike their BLM counterparts in Britain, France, or the United States, in that they encouraged social action by campaigning against state violence and for racial and gender equality and basic human rights.[7]

Much like Black Germans in ISD and ADEFRA, BLM activists in Berlin wanted to transform Germany by underscoring the persistence of racism in a country that has dealt, and continues to deal, with its fair share of racial violence, including the Maji war in Tanzania (1905–1907), the Herero and Nama genocide in Namibia (1904–1908), the Second World War and the Holocaust (1933–1945), the neo-Nazi murder spree (2000–2007), and new attacks against refugees (2015–present).[8] The former three examples relied upon Germans' racist beliefs that Africans, Jews, and other individuals were inferior and subhuman. With the latter two examples, some German politicians, citizens, and neo-Nazis framed non-Black citizens and residents and recent refugees as not belonging in the nation, thereby normalizing their policing, exclusion, and murder. Germany is a nation that remains willfully ignorant about the connection between its racist past and racist present, particularly with the rise of right-wing populist political groups like Alternative for Germany (Alternativ für Deutschland, AfD), founded in 2013.[9] In addition, Black diasporic and communities of color in Germany still struggle with the public perception that they are foreign or immigrants. In essence, they are always arriving, considered to be from somewhere else, nonexistent as Germans.[10] One of the German BLM's intentions, therefore, is to dispel the myth that Germany is no longer a racist country, to help the country acknowledge its amnesia about racism, and to show how much work the country needs to do to dismantle institutional and everyday forms of racism. In this way, these feminists followed the modern Black German movement's tradition of activism that confronted and publicized similar issues. The BLM's month-long events, like earlier ISD and ADEFRA events such as the Berlin BHM celebrations, emphasized the pivotal role that race still plays in society and produced and circulated intersectional knowledge about the global structures of white supremacy and the plight of Black people and People of Color, nationally and internationally.

This younger generation of Black German BLM organizers, such as Wacker, Biedermann, Apraku, and Mayen, built upon a tradition of Black women's radical activism in Germany, demonstrating that Black German women's activism still had a place in the nation. These women acknowledged a shared lineage with the Black German movement of the 1980s and the 1990s, and remarked on how much May Ayim influenced them. Blazing a path much like Ayim, Apraku, along with other activists, has been a prominent figure in the movement to change racist German street names that have been named after colonial figures.[11] Apraku also co-directs the Institute for Discrimination-Free Education in Berlin (IDB), gives tours of the African Quarter in Wedding, Berlin, and tackles other projects. Moreover, those events in Germany also served as sites for intellectualism, empowerment, and community building. Producing and inhabiting spaces that rendered Blackness visible, these Black German women's activism in BLM reflected their efforts to forge solidarity with others and be agents of change.

The recent political activism of BLM illustrates that the campaigns Black German quotidian intellectuals waged in their movement more than thirty years ago still matter and continues to have cultural and political relevance. Those BLM activists demonstrate how racism remains an entrenched problem, at times occupying the center of mainstream discussions among white, Black, and non-Black Germans alike. Those discussions also show the continuing failure of some white Germans to acknowledge Black Germans as compatriots and to listen to their experiences with and read their analyses on discrimination and exclusion in German society.[12] In doing so, many Germans have underwritten and continue to underwrite a national project that ignores and positions Black Germans outside the boundaries of the nation while also rendering their complaints as a misunderstanding, oversensitivity, or divisiveness. Such claims sustain and reaffirm German whiteness, including notions of German citizenship and belonging.

As I have shown in *Mobilizing Black Germany,* these German beliefs and assumptions, long embedded in the fabric of the country, are what compelled Black Germans "to forge diaspora" and to establish their own organizations, ushering in their movement. Several influential Black diasporic individuals, including Audre Lorde, imparted knowledge about turning to emotions and writing as effective and edifying tools for social change and activism. Assuaging years of isolation, Afro-Germans cultivated connections to Lorde, one another, and other People of Color while also creating new empowering designations that countered the negative labels and discourses that had plagued and marginalized them throughout their childhood and adult lives.

Writing themselves into a postwar German public culture and creating a Black public sphere, Black German quotidian intellectuals in the modern movement initiated discussions and produced intellectual work on racism, Blackness, and German colonialism. Black Germans explained how overt and covert forms of racism permeated everyday practices, beliefs, and institutions, proved the persistence of racialization and racist thinking, and defined who had claims to Germanness. Using diverse writings such as *Farbe bekennen, Afrekete, afro look,* and other publications, Black Germans addressed the long history of Blacks in Germany and how their presence informed ideas about identity, citizenship, the nation, and kinship. By so doing, Afro-Germans actively engaged in intellectual, feminist, and diasporic activism and challenged discrimination nationally and internationally. Developments taking place in South Africa and Somalia, for example, were just as important to Afro-Germans as their efforts to confront xenophobia and heightened ethno-nationalism in post-reunification Germany and Fortress Europe. Here, Black German politics in BLM remain enmeshed in the same translocal and transnational dynamics that sparked the initial Black German movement. Forging solidarity with other marginalized communities in and beyond German borders, Afro-Germans established intellectual and international networks that enabled them to survive, resist bigotry and oppression, and advance collective feminist and antiracist projects.

Adapting diverse diasporic resources, Afro-Germans invented new practices, such as the BHM celebrations, the BT, and feminist conferences, that helped them find representation; demanded recognition as German citizens; and made manifest Germany's multiracial and multicultural history and reality. Through these events, Black Germans also pursued spatial politics, embedding themselves in the nation and the global diasporic community. Black German women and men promoted identities, agendas, and politics that framed Blackness and the Black diaspora more generally within the German nation—pushing the margins to the center and underscoring that Black lives always matter in their society.

NOTES

INTRODUCTION

1. The modern Black German movement complicates traditional narratives of the diaspora that deal with the dispersal or scattering of a population, or the return to a "homeland." Afro-Germans situated themselves culturally and politically within the global Black diaspora and Germany.

2. Katharina Oguntoye, "The Black German Movement and the Womens Movement in West Germany," March 1989, box 24, folder 104, p. 3, Audre Lorde Collection, Spelman College Archives, Atlanta, Georgia (hereafter cited as Lorde Papers). The missing apostrophe in the title of Oguntoye's paper was an error in the original. See also Katharina Oguntoye, "Die Schwarze Deutsche Bewegung und die Frauenbewegung in Deutschland," *Afrekete (schwarze überlebens-Kunst)* 4, no. 2 (1989): 33, *Frauenforschungs-, -bildungs- und-informationszentrum*, Berlin, Germany (hereafter cited as FFBIZ). On affective communities, see Leela Ghandi, *Affective Communities: Anticolonial Thought, Fin-de-Siecle Radicalism, and the Politics of Friendship* (Durham, N.C.: Duke University Press, 2006).

3. This book mostly focuses on the Federal Republic of Germany (West and reunified Germany) with limited discussions of the German Democratic Republic (East Germany). I use Germany more broadly rather than write West, East, and reunified Germany, though I reference specific activities in those areas when necessary. I also use Berlin, adding specificity only when necessary.

4. Feminist diasporic activism enabled Black German women to address racism, homophobia, sexism, and patriarchy, while also reclaiming new notions of liberation and humanness. Annette Joseph-Gabriel's notion of "the politics and poetics

of liberation" informed my idea of "the politics and poetics of representation." See Annette Joseph-Gabriel, "Beyond the Great Camouflage: Haiti in Suzanne Cesaire's Politics and Poetics of Liberation," *Small Axe* 20, no. 2 (2016): 1–13.

5. There are certain limits to traditional German state archives, in which none of the Berlin-based ones had any source materials about the modern Black German movement. As a result, I contacted several members in the movement, and some of them graciously shared their materials. I also found traces of the movement at feminist and lesbian archives in other German cities. Several historians have spoken about the silences and violence of Black women in the historical archives. See, for example, Marisa Fuentes, *Dispossessed Lives: Enslaved Women, Violence, and the Archive* (Philadelphia: University of Pennsylvania Press, 2016). Saidiya Hartman, "Venus in Two Acts," *Small Axe* 26 (2008): 1–14.

6. See Denise Bergold-Caldwell, Laura Digoh, Hadija Haruna-Oelker, Christelle Nkwendja-Ngnoubamdjum, Camilla Ridha, and Eleonore Wiedenroth-Coulibaly, eds., *Spiegelblicke: Perspektiven Schwarzer Bewegung in Deutschland* (Berlin: Orlanda, 2015); Natasha Kelly, ed., *Sisters and Souls: Inspirationen durch May Ayim* (Berlin: Orlanda, 2015); Peggy Piesche, ed., *Euer Schweigen schützt Euch nicht: Audre Lorde und die Schwarze Frauenbewegung in Deutschland* (Berlin: Orlanda, 2012); AntiDiskriminierungsBüro (ADB) Köln and cyberNomads (cbN), eds., *The BlackBook: Deutschlands Häutungen* (Frankfurt am Main: IKO-Verlag für Interkulturelle Kommunikation, 2004).

7. On "invented traditions," see Eric Hobsbawm, "Introduction: Inventing Traditions," in *The Invention of Tradition*, eds. Eric Hobsbawm and Terence Ranger (Cambridge, U.K.: Cambridge University Press, 2012), 1. An invented tradition describes "a set of practices, normally governed by overtly or tacitly accepted rules of a ritual or symbolic nature, which seek to inculcate certain values and norms of behaviour by repetition, which automatically implies continuity with the past. In fact, where possible, they normally attempt to establish continuity with a suitable historic past."

8. Some of those groups include Each One Teach One (EOTO) e.V., Der braune Mob e.V., and Joliba e.V. EOTO is a library, archive, and cultural space founded in 2012, and serves as an archive for Black Germany, inclusive of the movement. Founded in 2001, Der braune Mob is the first Black media watch group. Joliba is a multicultural and immigrant organization founded in 1997 and contains some materials from the movement.

9. Oguntoye, "The Black German Movement and the Womens Movement," 3. Throughout the book, I capitalize "Blackness" and "Black" because they refer to a particular cultural group and experience. I also capitalize "Women of Color," "Men of Color," and "People of Color" but not "communities of color." I also do not capitalize "white," which is not a proper noun. See Kimberlé Crenshaw, "Mapping the Margins: Intersectionality Identity Politics, and Violence Against Women of Color," *Stanford Law Review* 43, no. 6 (1991): 1244, n6.

10. I use mixed-race and recognize it is a socially constructed category, but I have elected not to place it in quotation marks. On racialized identities, see Marlene Daut, "Introduction: The 'Mulatto/a' Vengeance of 'Haitian Exceptionalism,'" in Daut, *Tropics*

of Haiti: Race and the Literary History of the Haitian Revolution in the Atlantic World, 1789–1865 (Liverpool: Liverpool University Press, 2015), 45–48.

11. On political Blackness in Britain, see Stuart Hall, "Old and New Ethnicities, Old and New Identities," in *Culture, Globalization and the World System,* ed. Anthony King (London: Macmillan, 1991), 41–68. Some scholars have also linked a political Blackness to the Négritude movement of the 1930s, the Bandung Conference of 1955, and the Tricontinental Conference of 1966. See Brent Hayes Edwards, *The Practice of Diaspora: Literature, Translation, and the Rise of Black Internationalism* (Cambridge, Mass.: Harvard University Press, 2003); Anne Garland Mahler, *From the Tricontinental to the Global South: Race, Radicalism, and Transnational Solidarity* (Durham, N.C.: Duke University Press, 2018).

12. See Katharina Oguntoye, May Opitz/Ayim, and Dagmar Schultz, eds., *Farbe bekennen: Afro-deutsche Frauen auf den Spuren ihrer Geschichte* (Berlin: Orlanda, 2006); May Opitz, Katharina Oguntoye, and Dagmar Schultz, eds., trans. Anne Adams, *Showing Our Colors: Afro-German Women Speak Out* (Amherst: University of Massachusetts Press, 1992); Peter Martin, *Schwarze Teufel, edle Mohren: Afrikaner in Geschichte und Bewusstsein der Deutschen* (Hamburg: Junius, 1993); Mischa Honeck, Martin Klimke, and Anne Kuhlmann, eds., *Germany and the Black Diaspora: Points of Contact, 1250–1914* (New York: Berghahn, 2013).

13. Felicitas Jaima, "Adopting Diaspora: African American Military Women in Cold War West Germany" (PhD diss., New York University, 2016); Sara Lennox, "Introduction," in *Remapping Black Germany: New Perspectives on Afro-German History, Politics, and Culture,* ed. Sara Lennox (Amherst: University of Massachusetts Press, 2016), 5, n19. Couples in the United States and Denmark adopted some of these mixed-race children.

14. Marion Kraft, "Re-presentations and Re-definitions: Black People in Germany in the Past and Present," in *Children of the Liberation: Transatlantic Experiences and Perspectives of Black Germans of the Post-War Generation,* ed. Marion Kraft (Oxford, U.K.: Peter Lang, 2019), 12. See also Patricia Mazón and Reinhild Steingröver, eds., *Not so Plain as Black and White: Afro-German Culture and History, 1890–2000* (Rochester, N.Y.: University of Rochester Press, 2005), 2.

15. Depending on the context, *"Neger"* can be translated as either "Negro" or "N*****." Nonetheless, it still is offensive to individuals in the Black German community.

16. James Whitman, *Hitler's American Model: The United States and the Making of Nazi Race Law* (Princeton, N.J.: Princeton University Press, 2017).

17. Michael Burleigh and Wolfgang Wippermann, *The Racial State: Germany 1933–1945* (Cambridge, U.K.: Cambridge University Press, 1991).

18. Fatima El-Tayeb, *Schwarze Deutsche: Der Diskurs um "Rasse" und nationale Identität, 1890–1933* (Frankfurt am Main: Campus, 2001).

19. Tina M. Campt, *Other Germans: Black Germans and the Politics of Race, Gender, and Memory in the Third Reich* (Ann Arbor: University of Michigan Press, 2004); Iris Wigger, *The "Black Horror on the Rhine": Intersections of Race, Nation, Gender and Class in 1920s Germany* (New York: Palgrave, 2017). On sterilizations, see Reiner Pommerin, *Sterilisierung der*

Rheinlandbastarde: Das Schicksal einer farbigen deutschen Minderheit, 1918–1937 (Düsseldorf: Droste Verlag, 1979).

20. Clarence Lusane, *Hitler's Black Victims: The Historical Experiences of Afro-Germans, European Blacks, Africans, and African Americans in the Nazi Era* (New York: Routledge, 2003).

21. Katharina Oguntoye, *Eine afro-deutsche Geschichte: Zur Lebenssituation von Afrikanern und Afro-Deutschen in Deutschland von 1884 bis 1950* (Berlin: Hoho Verlag Christine Hoffmann, 1997); Robbie Aitken and Eve Rosenhaft, *Black Germany: The Making and Unmaking of a Diaspora Community, 1884–1960* (Cambridge, U.K.: Cambridge University Press, 2013).

22. Yara-Colette Lemke Muñiz de Faria, *Zwischen Fürsorge und Ausgrenzung: Afrodeutsche "Besatzungskinder" im Nachkriegsdeutschland* (Berlin: Metropol, 2002); Heide Fehrenbach, *Race after Hitler: Black Occupation Children in Postwar Germany and America* (Princeton, N.J.: Princeton University Press, 2005). Similarly, white Austrian women also pursued relationships with African American, Moroccan, and Senegalese soldiers during the Allied occupation in Austria (1945–1955). On the Austrian Allied occupation, see Walter Sauer, *Expeditionen ins afrikanische Österreich: Ein Reisekaleidoskop* (Vienna: Mandelbaum, 2014); Ingrid Bauer, " 'Leiblicher Vater: Amerikaner (Neger)': Besatzungskinder österreichisch-afroamerikanischer Herkunft," in *Früchte der Zeit: Afrika, Diaspora, Literatur und Migration,* eds. Helmuth Niederle, Ulrike Davis-Sulikowski, and Thomas Fillitz (Vienna: WUV Universitätsverlag, 2001), 49–67.

23. See Frank Guridy, *Forging Diaspora: Afro-Cubans and African Americans in a World of Empire and Jim Crow* (Chapel Hill: University of North Carolina Press, 2010).

24. Stuart Hall, "Cultural Identity and Diaspora," in *Identity: Community, Culture, and Difference,* ed. Jonathan Rutherford (London: Lawrence & Wishart, 1990), 222; Stuart Hall, "The Work of Representation," in *Representation: Cultural Representation and Signifying Practices,* ed. Stuart Hall (Walton Hall, U.K.: Open University Press, 1997), 13–74. See also Michelle M. Wright, *Becoming Black: Creating Identity in the African Diaspora* (Durham, N.C.: Duke University Press, 2003), 26.

25. Fatima El-Tayeb, *European Others: Queering Ethnicity in Postnational Europe* (Minneapolis: University of Minnesota Press, 2011); David Theo Goldberg, "Racial Europeanization," *Journal of Ethnic and Racial Studies* 29, no. 2 (2006): 331–64. The discourse of racelessness is sustained by the normalization of an unspoken whiteness. On whiteness in the German context, see Uli Linke, *German Bodies: Race and Representation After Hitler* (New York: Routledge, 1999); Maisha Eggers, Grada Kilomba, Peggy Piesche, and Susan Arndt, eds., *Mythen, Masken und Subjekte: Kritische Weißseinsforschung in Deutschland* (Münster: Unrast, 2005).

26. In the Gramscian sense, Black Germans might resemble "organic intellectuals," but they were not tied to a historical materialist tradition within a Marxist framework. Owing to their positionalities, they were not at the forefront of mainstream theoretical intellectual work per se, nor was their intellectualism predicated on this. They also did not forge unity with "traditional intellectuals," as Gramsci imagined for the working class. But Black Germans did transmit their ideas about colonialism, produce specific

racialized knowledge, and engage with German and non-German intellectuals. See David Forgacs, ed., *The Gramsci Reader: Selected Writings 1916–1936* (New York: New York University Press, 2000); Stuart Hall, "Cultural Studies and its Theoretical Legacies," in *Stuart Hall: Critical Dialogues in Cultural Studies*, eds. David Morley and Kuan-Hsing Chen (London: Routledge, 1996), 261–74. On the public sphere, see Jürgen Habermas, trans., Thomas Burger with the assistance of Frederick Lawrence, *The Structural Transformation of the Public Sphere: An Inquiry into a Category of Bourgeois Society* (Cambridge, Mass.: MIT Press, 1991); Nancy Fraser, "Rethinking the Public Sphere: A Contribution to the Critique of Actually Existing Democracy," *Social Text* 25/26 (1990): 56–80. On decolonizing knowledge, see Grada Kilomba, *Plantation Memories: Episodes of Everyday Racism* (Münster: Unrast, 2010), 25–36.

27. Traditionally, Germany has had a robust middle class, which included the *Wirtschaftsbürgertum,* an economic middle class, and the *Bildungsbürgertum,* an educated and professional middle class. The *Kleinbürgertum* or lower middle class also became prominent in the late nineteenth and twentieth centuries, but were not considered a part of the middle class proper. Class lines blurred in the twentieth century, especially after the World Wars. Germany's strong social programs, including state welfare and health care, also contributed to this dynamic. Black Germans in the movement constitute a part of the educated, professional, and lower-middle/middle classes; some could rely on extended family kinship networks. On the European middle classes, Jürgen Kocka, "The Middle Classes in Europe," *Journal of Modern History* 67, no. 4 (1995): 783–806.

28. By intellectual activism, I mean their development of alternative analyses and truth-telling to multiple audiences. On intellectual activism, see Patricia Hill Collins, *On Intellectual Activism* (Philadelphia: Temple University Press, 2012).

29. On everyday racism, see Kilomba, *Plantation Memories*; Philomena Essed, *Understanding Everyday Racism: An Interdisciplinary Theory* (London: Sage Publications, 1991).

30. On Jews in the FRG, see Atina Grossmann, *Jews, Germans, and Allies: Close Encounters in Occupied Germany* (Princeton, N.J.: Princeton University Press, 2007); Michael Brenner, ed., trans., Kenneth Kronenberg, *A History of Jews in Germany Since 1945: Politics, Culture, and Society* (Bloomington: Indiana University Press, 2018).

31. I place quotation marks around "guest workers" because the term is considered derogatory toward some. Beginning in 1955, "guest workers" in West Germany came from Italy, Spain, Greece, Turkey, Portugal, Yugoslavia, Japan, Morocco, Tunisia, and Korea. Rita Chin, *The Guest Worker Question in Postwar Germany* (New York: Cambridge University Press, 2007), 37, n14. See also Neil MacMaster, *Racism in Europe, 1870–2000* (New York: Palgrave, 2001); Rita Chin, Heide Fehrenbach, Atina Grossmann, and Geoff Eley, eds., *After the Nazi Racial State: Difference and Democracy in Germany and Europe* (Ann Arbor: University of Michigan Press, 2009).

32. My intention is not to offend anyone with the use of these entrenched racist German concepts. But I do use them to show the linguistic pervasiveness of German racism and its material and affective impact. Opitz, Oguntoye, and Schultz, *Showing Our Colors,* 126–33; Rosemarie Lester, *Trivialneger: Das Bild des Schwarzen im westdeutschen Illustriertenroman* (Stuttgart: Akademischer Verlag, 1982). Moor ("*Mohr*") was a

term used to describe Black people; it was originally associated with religion in the sixteenth and seventeenth centuries. On moors, see Kate Lowe, "The Black Diaspora in Europe in the Fifteenth and Sixteenth Centuries, with Special Reference to German-Speaking Areas," in Honeck, Klimke, and Kuhlmann, *Germany and the Black Diaspora,* 38–56. *"Negerschweiß"* literally translates into Negro sweat and remained a postwar term for the American commodity.

33. See Silke Hackenesch, *Chocolate and Blackness: A Cultural History* (Frankfurt am Main: Campus, 2017).

34. David Ciarlo, *Advertising Empire: Race and Visual Culture in Imperial Germany* (Cambridge, Mass.: Harvard University Press, 2011); Dana S. Hale, *Races on Display: French Representations of Colonized Peoples, 1886–1940* (Bloomington: Indiana University Press, 2008); Anne McClintock, *Imperial Leather: Race, Gender, and Sexuality in the Colonial Context* (New York: Routledge, 1995).

35. Quinn Slobodian, "Socialist Chromatism: Race, Racism, and the Racial Rainbow in East Germany," in *Comrades of Color: East Germany in the Cold War World,* ed. Quinn Slobodian (New York: Berghahn, 2015), 26, 30. See also Jeffrey Herf, *The Divided Memory: The Nazi Past in the Two Germanys* (Cambridge, Mass.: Harvard University Press, 1997); Britta Schilling, *Postcolonial Germany: Memories of Empire in a Decolonized Nation* (Oxford, U.K.: Oxford University Press, 2014). Schilling argues "Germans' collective memory of colonialism was at times discontinuous, with gaps, disruptions, changes of emphasis, and moments of 'forgetting,' especially after 1945" (9).

36. Slobodian, "Socialist Chromatism," 27.

37. Ibid., 28–31; Maria Höhn and Martin Klimke, *A Breath of Freedom: The Civil Rights Struggle, African American GIs, and Germany* (New York: Palgrave, 2010), 123–41.

38. On racism in East Germany, see Peggy Piesche, "Making African Diasporic Pasts Possible: A Retrospective View of the GDR and Its Black (Step-)Children," in Lennox, *Remapping Black Germany,* 226–42; Jan Behrends, Thomas Lindenberger, and Patrice Poutrus, eds., *Fremde und Fremd-Sein in der DDR: Zu historischen Ursachen der Fremdenfeindlichkeit in Ostdeutschland* (Berlin: Metropol, 2003); Mike Dennis and Norman LaPorte, eds., *State and Minorities in Communist East Germany* (New York: Berghahn, 2011). Beginning in 1967, "contract workers" in East Germany were from Hungary, Poland, Algeria, Cuba, Mozambique, Vietnam, Mongolia, Angola, and China. African students and activists from the Mozambique Liberation Front (FRELIMO) and the South West African People's Organisation (SWAPO) were also there. See Mike Dennis, "Asian and African Workers in the Niches of Society," in Dennis and LaPorte, *State and Minorities in Communist East Germany,* 87–123; Sara Pugach, "African Students and the Politics of Race and Gender in the German Democratic Republic," in Slobodian, *Comrades of Color,* 131–56; Gregory Witkowski, "Between Fighters and Beggars: Socialist Philanthropy and the Imagery of Solidarity in East Germany," in Slobodian, *Comrades of Color,* 73–94; Meghan O'Dea, "Lucia Engombe's and Stefanie-Lahya Aukongo's Autobiographical Accounts of *Solidaritätspolitik* and Life in the GDR as Namibian Children," in *Rethinking Black German Studies: Approaches, Interventions and Histories,* eds. Tiffany N. Florvil and Vanessa D. Plumly (New York: Peter Lang, 2018), 105–34.

39. See Samuel Moyn, *The Last Utopia: Human Rights in History* (Cambridge, Mass.: Harvard University Press, 2012).

40. On Black geographies, see, for example, Katherine McKittrick, *Demonic Grounds: Black Women and the Cartographies of Struggle* (Minneapolis: University of Minnesota Press, 2006); McKittrick, "On plantations, prisons, and a black sense of place," *Social & Cultural Geography* 12, no. 8 (2011): 947–63; Camilla Hawthrone, "Black Matters are Spatial Matters: Black Geographies for the Twenty-First Century," *Geography Compass* 13, no. 11 (2019): 1–13.

41. On other forms of Black German activism, see Fatima El-Tayeb, " 'If You Can't Pronounce My name, You Can Just Call Me Pride': Afro-German Activism, Gender, and Hip Hop," *Gender & History* 15, no. 3 (2003): 460–85.

42. See The European Network Against Racism, "1998–2018, A Short History," June 2018, https://www.enar-eu.org/The-European-Network-Against-Racism-1998 -2018-a-short-history; Sharmilla Beezmohun, "A Timely Intervention—Or Before Its Time?: A Short History of European Action for Racial Equality and Social Justice," in *Afroeuropean Cartographies,* ed. Dominic Thomas (Newcastle, U.K.: Cambridge Scholars Publishing, 2014), 16–24; Pamela Ohene-Nyako, "The Black Women and Europe Network against 'Fortress Europe' in the 1990s," unpublished paper, 2019 African American Intellectual History Society Conference, pp. 1–11. Cited with the author's permission.

43. I use "Third World" instead of "Global South" throughout the manuscript in keeping with the terms that were prevalent during the period.

44. See Daniel Gordon, "French and British Anti-Racists Since the 1960s: A rendez-vous manqué?," *Journal of Contemporary History* 50, no. 3 (2015): 606–31.

45. Edwards, *The Practice of Diaspora;* Tiffany Ruby Patterson and Robin D.G. Kelley, "Unfinished Migrations: Reflections on the African Diaspora and the Making of the Modern World," *African Studies Review* 43 (2000): 11–45; Michael O. West, William Martin, and Fanon Che Wilkins, eds., *From Toussaint to Tupac: The Black International since the Age of Revolution* (Chapel Hill: University of North Carolina Press, 2009).

46. Keisha N. Blain, *Set the World on Fire: Black Nationalist Women and the Global Struggle for Freedom* (Philadelphia: University of Pennsylvania Press, 2018); Blain and Tiffany M. Gill, eds., *To Turn the Whole World Over: Black Women and Internationalism* (Urbana: University of Illinois Press, 2019); Carole Boyce Davies, *Left of Karl Marx: The Political Life of Black Communist Claudia Jones* (Durham, N.C.: Duke University Press, 2008); Tanisha Ford, *Liberated Threads: Black Women, Style, and The Global Politics of Soul* (Chapel Hill: University of North Carolina Press, 2015); Cheryl Higashida, *Black Internationalist Feminism: Women Writers of the Black Left, 1945–1995* (Urbana: University of Illinois Press, 2011); Marc Matera, *Black London: The Imperial Metropolis and Decolonization in the Twentieth Century* (Oakland: University of California Press, 2015); Erik S. McDuffie, *Sojourning for Freedom: Black Women, American Communism, and the Making of Black Left Feminism* (Durham, N.C.: Duke University Press, 2011); Barbara Ransby, *Eslanda: The Large and Unconventional Life of Mrs. Paul Robeson* (New Haven, Conn.: Yale University Press, 2013); Tracy Denean Sharpley-Whiting, *Negritude Women* (Minneapolis: Uni-

versity of Minnesota Press, 2002); Quito Swan, "Giving Berth: Fiji, Black Women's Internationalism, and the Pacific Women's Conference of 1975," *Journal of Civil and Human Rights* 4, no. 1 (2018): 37–63; Imaobong Umoren, *Race Women Internationalists: Activist-Intellectuals and Global Freedom Struggles* (Oakland: University of California Press, 2018).

47. On Black Power in and beyond Europe, see Anne Marie Angelo, " 'Black Oppressed People All over the World Are One': The British Black Panthers' Grassroots Internationalism, 1969–1973," *Journal of Civil and Human Rights* 4, no. 1 (2018): 64–97; Nico Slate, ed., *Black Power Beyond Borders: The Global Dimensions of the Black Power Movement* (New York: Palgrave, 2012); Maria Höhn, "The Black Panther Solidarity Committee and the Trial of the Ramstein 2," in *Changing the World, Changing Oneself: Political Protest and Collective Identities in West Germany and the U.S. in the 1960s and 1970s*, eds. Belinda Davis, Wilfried Mausbach, Martin Klimke, and Carla MacDougall (New York: Berghahn, 2010), 215–40.

48. Tina M. Campt, *Image Matters: Archive, Photography, and the African Diaspora in Europe* (Durham, N.C.: Duke University Press, 2012); El-Tayeb, *European Others*; Felix Germain, *Decolonizing the Republic: African and Caribbean Migrants in Postwar Paris* (East Lansing: Michigan State University Press, 2016); Paul Gilroy, *The Black Atlantic: Modernity and Double-Consciousness* (Cambridge, Mass.: Harvard University Press, 1993); Kennetta Hammond Perry, *London is the Place for Me: Black Britons, Citizenship, and the Politics of Race* (New York: Oxford University Press, 2015); Michelle M. Wright, *Physics of Blackness: Beyond the Middle Passage Epistemology* (Minneapolis: University of Minnesota Press, 2015). See also Florvil and Plumly, *Rethinking Black German Studies*; Olivette Otele, *African Europeans: An Untold History* (London: Hurst, forthcoming 2020); Cassander L. Smith, Nicholas Jones, and Miles P. Grier, eds., *Early Modern Black Diaspora Studies: A Critical Anthology* (New York: Palgrave, 2018).

49. Wright, *Physics of Blackness*, 3–5.

50. Black Germans represent what the diaspora is *and* what it is not, especially when we consider the legacy of slavery, colonialism, and decolonization. See Darlene Clark Hine, Trica Danielle Keaton, and Stephen Small, eds., *Black Europe and the African Diaspora* (Urbana: University of Illinois Press, 2009), which includes Germany in its discussion.

51. Natalie Thomlinson, *Race, Ethnicity and the Women's Movement in England, 1968–1993* (London: Palgrave, 2016), esp. 64–103; Tracy Fisher, *What's Left of Blackness: Feminisms, Transracial Solidarities, and the Politics of Belonging in Britain* (London: Palgrave, 2012); McDuffie, *Sojourning for Freedom*. On Black feminism in Europe, see Akwugo Emejulu and Francesca Sobande, eds., *To Exist is to Resist: Black Feminism in Europe* (London: Pluto Press, 2019).

52. On Black women's intellectualism, see Brittney Cooper, *Beyond Respectability: The Intellectual Thought of Race Women* (Urbana: University of Illinois Press, 2017); Mia Bay, Farah Griffin, Martha Jones, and Barbara Savage, eds., *Toward an Intellectual History of Black Women* (Chapel Hill: University of North Carolina Press, 2015); Kristin Waters and Carol B. Conaway, eds., *Black Women's Intellectual Traditions* (Burlington:

University of Vermont Press, 2007). See also Davies, *Left of Marx*. In it, Davies pushes us to recognize the connections between activism and intellectualism.

53. See Honeck, Klimke, and Kuhlmann, *Germany and the Black Diaspora*; Larry Greene and Anke Ortlepp, eds., *Germans and African Americans: Two Centuries of Exchange* (Oxford: University Press of Mississippi, 2011); Maria Diedrich and Jürgen Heinrichs, eds., *From Black to Schwarz: Cultural Crossovers between African America and Germany* (Münster: LIT, 2010); Carol Blackshire-Belay, Leroy Hopkins, and David McBride, eds., *Cross Currents: African Americans, Africa, and Germany in the Modern World* (Columbia, S.C.: Camden, 1998).

54. On these individuals, see Marilyn Sephocle, "Anton Wilhem Amo," *Journal of Black Studies* 23, no. 2 (1992): 182–87; Kenneth Barkin, "W.E.B. Du Bois' Love Affair with Imperial Germany," *German Studies Review* 28, no. 2 (2005): 285–302; Hakim Adi, "Pan-Africanism and communism: the Comintern, the 'Negro Question' and the first International Conference of Negro Workers, Hamburg 1930," *African and Black Diaspora* 1, no. 2 (2008): 237–54; Nancy Nenno, "Femininity, the Primitive, and Modern Urban Space: Josephine Baker in Berlin," in *Women in the Metropolis: Gender and Modernity in Weimar Culture*, ed. Katharina von Ankum (Berkeley: University of California Press, 1997), 141–67; Angela Davis, *Angela Davis: An Autobiography* (New York: Random House, 1988).

55. Sander Gilman, *On Blackness without Blacks: Essays on the Image of the Black in Germany* (Boston: G.K. Hall, 1982). See also Reinhold Grimm and Jost Hermand, eds., *Blacks and German Culture* (Madison: University of Wisconsin Press, 1986).

56. Some scholars trace Black German radicalism to the Enlightenment period. See Kevina King, "The Black Radical Tradition in Germany," unpublished paper, 2019 German Studies Association Conference, pp. 1–8. Cited with the author's permission.

57. Bradley Naranch and Geoff Eley, eds., *German Colonialism in a Global Age* (Durham, N.C.: Duke University Press, 2014); Eric Ames, Marcia Klotz, and Lora Wildenthal, eds., *Germany's Colonial Pasts* (Lincoln: University of Nebraska Press, 2005); Pascal Grosse, *Kolonialismus, Eugenik und bürgerliche Gesellschaft in Deutschland, 1850–1918* (Frankfurt am Main: Campus, 2000); Sara Lennox, Sara Friedrichsmeyer, and Susanne Zantop, eds., *The Imperialist Imagination: German Colonialism and its Legacy* (Ann Arbor: University of Michigan Press, 1999). Germany also acquired territory in China and the Pacific.

58. Oguntoye, *Eine afro-deutsche Geschichte*, 76–109; Aitken and Rosenhaft, *Black Germany*, 22–87; Stefan Gerbing, *Interventionen von Kolonisierten am Wendepunkt der Dekolonisierung Deutschlands 1919* (Frankfurt am Main: Peter Lang, 2010).

59. Aitken and Rosenhaft, *Black Germany*. Cameroonians were not the only people of African descent in Germany.

60. Tobias Nagl, "Counterfeit Money/Counterfeit Discourse: A Black German Trickster Tale," in Lennox, *Remapping Black Germany*, 106.

61. Paulette Reed-Anderson, *Rewriting the Footnotes: Berlin und die afrikanische Diaspora* (Berlin: Die Ausländerbeauftragte des Senats, 2000), 46–49; Aitken and Rosenhaft, *Black Germany*, 129–31; Gerbing, *Interventionen von Kolonisierten*, 47–56. Owing to the

efforts of Oguntoye and others, a commemorative plaque was erected in October 2016 to pay homage to Martin Dibobe in Prenzlauer Berg, Berlin. In July 2019, organizers erected another plaque to honor the eighteen signatories of the 1919 petitions.

62. Wigger, *"Black Horror on the Rhine";* Campt, *Other Germans,* 31–62; Sally Marks, "Black Watch on the Rhine: A Study in Propaganda, Prejudice and Prurience," *European Studies Review* 13, no. 3 (1983): 297–334.

63. Julia Roos, "Nationalism, Racism and Propaganda in Early Weimar Germany: Contradictions in the Campaign against the 'Black Horror on the Rhine,' " *Germany History* 30, no. 1 (2012): 45–74; Roos, "Women's Rights, Nationalist Anxiety, and the 'Moral' Agenda in the Early Weimar Republic: Revisiting the 'Black Horror' Campaign against France's African Occupation Troops," *Central European History* 42, no. 3 (2009): 473–508; Jared Poley, *Decolonization in Germany: Weimar Narratives of Colonial Loss and Foreign Occupation* (Oxford, U.K.: Peter Lang, 2007).

64. On Terrell's Black internationalism, see Noaquia N. Callahan, "A Transnational Infatuation: African American Progress and 'the Negro Problem' on the International Stage at the Turn of the Twentieth Century," unpublished paper, 2015 German Studies Association Conference, p. 2. Cited with the author's permission. Also see Reed-Anderson, *Rewriting the Footnotes,* 30–32. Claude McKay and Alain Locke also commented on this situation. See Jonathan Wipplinger, "Germany, 1923: Alain Locke, Claude McKay, and the New Negro in Germany," *Callaloo* 36, no. 1 (2013): 106–24.

65. Robbie Aitken, "Embracing Germany: Interwar German Society and Black Germans through the Eyes of African American Reporters," *Journal of American Studies* 52 (2018): 447–73.

66. On the *Afrikanischer Hilfsverein,* see Leroy Hopkins, "Race, Nationality and Culture: The African Diaspora in Germany," in *Who Is a German? Historical and Modern Perspectives on Africans in Germany,* ed. Leroy Hopkins (Washington, D.C.: American Institute of Contemporary German Studies, 1999), 6–15; Peter Martin, "Der Afrikanische Hilfsverein von 1918," in *Zwischen Charleston und Stechschritt: Schwarze im Nationalsozialismus,* eds. Peter Martin and Christine Alonzo (Hamburg: Dölling and Galitz, 2004), esp. 73–80.

67. Oguntoye, *Eine afro-deutsche Geschichte;* Christian Rogowski, "Black Voices on the 'Black Horror on the Rhine'?," in Lennox, *Remapping Black Germany,* 118–34.

68. Philipp Khabo Koepsell, "Literature and Activism," in *Arriving in the Future: Stories of Home and Exile: An Anthology of Poetry and Creative Writing by Black Writers in Germany,* eds. Asoka Esuruoso and Philipp Khabo Koepsell (Berlin: epubli, 2014), 37–39. On those communist organizations, see Adi, "Pan-Africanism and communism," 237–54; Aitken and Rosenhaft, *Black Germany,* 194–230.

69. Campt, *Other Germans,* 163–64; Sharon Dodua Otoo, "But Some of Us Are Brave," *migrazine.at online magazin von migrantinnen für alle* no. 1 (2013), http://www.migrazine.at/ artikel/some-us-are-brave-english.

70. In a fall 2011 conversation with Katharina Oguntoye, she mentioned that there was only a small subset of Afro-German women who had this experience and knowledge.

71. Ika Hügel-Marshall, trans. Elizabeth Gaffney, *Invisible Woman: Growing Up Black in Germany* (New York: Continuum, 2001), 97, 98. See also Ika Hügel-Marshall, *Daheim Unterwegs: Ein deutsches Leben* (Berlin: Orlanda, 1998). I refer to the English translation throughout. Paragraph 218 of the German constitution outlawed abortion. In East Germany, abortions until twelve weeks of pregnancy became legal in 1972, and West Germany decriminalized abortion in 1976. On German feminism and gender, see Friederike Brühöfener, Karen Hagemann, and Donna Harsch, eds., *Gendering Post-1945 German History: Entanglements* (New York: Berghahn, 2019); Myra Ferree, *Varieties of Feminism: German Gender Politics in Global Perspectives* (Stanford, Calif.: Stanford University Press, 2012); Atina Grossmann, *Reforming Sex: The German Movement for Birth Control and Abortion Reform, 1920–1950* (New York: Oxford University Press, 1995).

72. Hügel-Marshall, *Invisible Woman,* 98. On Hügel-Marshall's autobiography, see Michelle M. Wright, "In a Nation or a Diaspora? Gender, Sexuality and Afro-German Subject Formation," in Diedrich and Heinrichs, *From Black to Schwarz,* 265–86; Sonya Donaldson, "(Ir)reconcilable Differences?: The Search for Identity in Afro-German Autobiography" (PhD diss., University of Virginia, 2012), chapter 2; Deborah Jansen, "The Subject in Black and White: Afro-German Identity Formation in Ika Hügel-Marshall's Autobiography *Daheim unterwegs: Ein deutsches Leben,*" *Women in German Yearbook* 21 (2005): 62–84.

73. Katharina Oguntoye quoted in Peggy Piesche, "Rückblenden und Vorschauen: 20 Jahre Schwarze Frauenbewegung," in Piesche, *Euer Schweigen schützt Euch nicht,* 23.

74. Oguntoye quoted in Piesche, "Rückblenden und Vorschauen," 21–22. See also Ika Hügel-Marshall, "Lesbischsein läßt sich verleugnen, Schwarzsein nicht," in *Lesben, Liebe, Leidenschaft: Texte zur feministischen Psychologie und zu Liebesbeziehungen unter Frauen,* ed. JoAnn Loulan (Berlin: Orlanda, 1992), 298–307.

75. Oguntoye, "The Black German Movement and the Womens Movement," 4.

76. May Opitz, "Betrifft Frauenkongreß, 26. März 1984," box 21, p. 3, May Ayim Archive, Universitätsarchiv Freie Universität Berlin, Germany (hereafter cited as Ayim Archive); Helga Emde, "Internationaler Frauenkongreß in Frankfurt/Main vom 5.-8. 10.1989," *Afrekete (Born Free: WANTED!)* 5, no. 4 (1989): 14–15, Zentrale Bibliothek Frauenforschung, Gender & Queer Studies, Hamburg, Germany (hereafter cited as ZBFG&QS).

77. See Gloria T. Hull, Patricia Bell Scott, and Barbara Smith, eds., *But Some of Us Are Brave: All the Women Are White, All the Blacks Are Men* (New York: CUNY Press, 1983); Cherríe Moraga and Gloria Anzaldúa, eds., *This Bridge Called My Back: Writings by Radical Women of Color* (Albany: State University of New York Press, 2015); Kimberly Springer, *Living for the Revolution: Black Feminist Organizations, 1968–1980* (Durham, N.C.: Duke University Press, 2005).

78. Natalia King Rasmussen, "Friends of Freedom, Allies of Peace: African Americans, The Civil Rights Movement, and East Germany, 1949–1989" (PhD diss., Boston University, 2014), 107–64; Höhn and Klimke, *A Breath of Freedom,* 90; Mary Dudziak,

Cold War Civil Rights: Race and the Image of American Democracy (Princeton, N.J.: Princeton University Press, 2000).

79. Höhn and Klimke, *A Breath of Freedom*; Martin Klimke, *The Other Alliance: Student Protest in West Germany and the United States in the Global Sixties* (Princeton, N.J.: Princeton University Press, 2010); Quinn Slobodian, *Foreign Front: Third World Politics in Sixties West Germany* (Durham, N.C.: Duke University Press, 2012).

80. Rasmussen, "Friends of Freedom, Allies of Peace," 97–103.

81. He lost his passport from 1950 to 1958 because of the Red Scare. On Robeson's East German performances and race, see Kira Thurman, "Singing in the Promised Land: Black Musicians in the German Democratic Republic," in *Singing Like Germans: Black Musicians in the Land of Bach, Beethoven and Brahms,* forthcoming manuscript, chapter 6. Cited with the author's permission. The SED were the ruling party in East Germany.

82. Rasmussen, "Friends of Freedom, Allies of Peace," 131; Umoren, *Race Women Internationalists,* 113. Zetkin played a prominent role in the German Communist Party and the Comintern in the 1920s while also advocating for women's rights.

83. Höhn and Klimke, *A Breath of Freedom.*

84. Brandt was mayor from 1957 to 1966, and later became the West German chancellor from 1969 to 1974.

85. Höhn and Klimke, *A Breath of Freedom*, 102; Marcia Chatelain and Britta Waldschmidt-Nelson, "Introduction Untold Stories: The March on Washington—New Perspectives and Transatlantic Legacies," *German Historical Institute Bulletin Supplement* 11 (2015): 5–14.

86. See Donald Muldrow Griffith and Fountainhead Tanz Theatre, *A Complexion Change: Transnational & Intercultural Diplomacy* (Berlin: Commissioner for Integration Tempelhof-Schöneberg, 2014), 3–132, which celebrated the anniversary of King's 1964 visit.

87. Rasmussen, "Friends of Freedom, Allies of Peace," 107–64; Klimke, *The Other Alliance*, 108–42; Katrina Hagen, "Ambivalence and Desire in the East German 'Free Angela Davis' Campaign," in Slobodian, *Comrades of Color,* 157–87. See also Jamele Watkins, "Black Rose from Alabama: Solidarity Campaigns with Angela Davis in Europe," unpublished paper, 2019 African American Intellectual History Conference, pp. 1–11. Cited with the author's permission.

88. Moritz Ege, *Schwarz werden: "Afroamerikanophile" in den 1960er und 1970er Jahren* (Bielefeld: Transcript, 2007); Priscilla Layne, *White Rebels in Black: German Appropriation of Black Popular Culture* (Ann Arbor: University of Michigan Press, 2018).

89. On diasporic haunting, see Kimberly Alecia Singletary, "Everyday Matters: Haunting and the Black Diasporic Experience," in Florvil and Plumly, *Rethinking Black German Studies,* 137–67.

90. Oguntoye, "The Black German Movement and the Womens Movement," 8.

91. Koepsell, "Literature and Activism," 42.

92. Jacqueline Nassy Brown, *Dropping Anchor, Setting Sail: Geographies of Race in Black Liverpool* (Princeton, N.J.: Princeton University Press, 2005), 42.

93. In contrast, East Germany ratified the Convention on the Elimination of All Forms of Racial Discrimination in 1973 and signed CEDAW in July 1980, ratifying it almost immediately.

94. See Der Bundesminister des Innern (Hans-Gerd Pracht), "Das neue Ausländergesetz," 1990, Bonn, box 22, n.p., Ayim Archive.

95. Patrice Poutrus, "Asylum in Postwar Germany: Refugee Admissions Policies and their Practical Implementation in the Federal Republic and the GDR between the late 1940s and the mid-1970s," *Journal of Contemporary History* 49, no. 1 (2014): 115–33.

96. France, for example, practiced *jus soli* and was based on birthright citizenship. Rogers Brubaker, *Citizenship and Nationhood in France and Germany* (Cambridge, Mass.: Harvard University Press, 1994). See also El-Tayeb, "'Blood Is a Very Special Juice: Racialized Bodies and Citizenship in Twentieth-Century Germany," *International Review of Social History* 44 (1999): 149–69; Victoria Robinson, "Schwarze Deutsche Kräfte: Über Die Absurdität der Integrationsdebatte," *360°: Das Studentische Journal für Politik und Gesellschaft* (2007): 1–10.

97. Deniz Gökturk, David Gramling, and Anton Kaes, eds., *Germany in Transit: Nation and Migration, 1955–2005* (Berkeley: University of California Press, 2007), 4; Mathias Bös, "The Legal Construction of Membership: Nationality Law in Germany and the United States," *Program for the Study of Germany and Europe, Working Paper Series* no. 005 (Cambridge, Mass.: Minda de Gunzberg Center for European Studies, Harvard University, 2000), 11. This change allowed for the naturalization of foreign nationals who lived or were born in Germany. Additional changes to the law occurred in 2005, 2007, and 2014.

98. The CSU only operates in Bavaria and is the sister party to the CDU. See McMaster, *Racism in Europe*; Fatima El-Tayeb, *Undeutsch: Die Konstruktion des Anderen in der postmigrantischen Gesellschaft* (Bielefeld: Transcript, 2016).

99. See Eleonore Wiedenroth-Coulibaly and Sascha Zinflou, "20 Jahre Schwarze Organisierung in Deutschland—Ein Abriss," in AntiDiskriminierungsBüro and cyberNomads, *The BlackBook*, 142; Noah Sow, *Deutschland Schwarz Weiss: Der alltägliche Rassismus* (München: Goldmann, 2008).

100. Roger Karapin, *Protest Politics in Germany: Movements on the Left and Right Since the 1960s* (University Park: Pennsylvania State University Press, 2007), 161–218; Hermann Kurthen, Werner Bergmann, and Rainer Erb, eds., *Antisemitism and Xenophobia in Germany after Unification* (New York: Oxford University Press, 1997). Even before the fall of the Wall, foreigners and nonwhites were the target of racial violence in both Germanys.

101. Matthew Carr, *Fortress Europe: Dispatches from a Gated Continent* (New York: New Press, 2016), 22.

102. Carr, *Fortress Europe*, 22.

103. Elizabeth Buettner, *Europe after Empire: Decolonization, Society, and Culture* (Cambridge, U.K.: Cambridge University Press, 2016), 318–21; Danielle J. Walker, "Report on a Council of Europe Minority Youth Committee Seminar on Sexism and Racism in Western Europe," *Feminist Review* 45 (1993): 120–28. See also John La Rose, ed., *Racism Nazism Fascism and Racial Attacks: The European Response* (London: New Beacon Books, 1991).

104. Buettner, *Europe after Empire;* Erik Jones, Anand Menon, and Stephen Weatherill, eds., *The Oxford Handbook of the European Union* (Oxford, U.K.: Oxford University Press, 2012). Those member-states included France, West Germany, Italy, Belgium, Luxemburg, the Netherlands, the United Kingdom, Ireland, Denmark, Greece, Portugal, and Spain.

105. Black diasporic activism also occurred in Austria. See Araba Evelyn Johnston-Arthur, "'I resist because I exist . . .': Widerstandsstrategien gegen die Bedrohung der eigenen Existenz durch Rassismus," *Nachrichten und Stellungnahmen der Katholischen Sozialakademie Österreichs* 5 (2002): 1–3; Nancy Nenno, "*Here to Stay:* Black Austrian Studies," in Florvil and Plumly, *Rethinking Black German Studies,* 71–104.

106. Gökturk, Gramling, and Kaes, *Germany in Transit,* 4.

107. "Chancellor Merkel says German multiculturalism has 'utterly failed,'" *Deutsche Welle,* October 17, 2010, http://www.dw.de/chancellor-merkel-says-german-multiculturalism-has-utterly-failed/a-6118859; Matthew Weaver, "Angela Merkel: German multiculturalism has 'utterly failed,'" *The Guardian,* October 17, 2010, http://www.guardian.co.uk/world/2010/oct/17/angela-merkel-german-multiculturalism-failed. In 2015 Merkel stated that multiculturalism was a sham.

108. Thilo Sarrazin, *Deutschland schafft sich ab: Wie wir unser Land aufs Spiel setzen* (München: Deutsche Verlags-Anstalt, 2010). In April 2013, the UN ruled that with Sarrazin's book and his other statements, Germany broke an international antiracism accord, and it had ninety days to comply with the committee's demands. See "UN takes Germany to task for 'racist' Sarrazin," *The Local,* April 19, 2013, http://www.thelocal.de/society/20130419–49241.html.

109. Eddie Bruce-Jones, *Race in the Shadow of the Law: State Violence in Contemporary Europe* (Abingdon, U.K.: Routledge, 2017).

CHAPTER 1. BLACK GERMAN WOMEN AND AUDRE LORDE

1. Hundreds of condolences came from across the globe. Alexis De Veaux, *Warrior Poet: A Biography of Audre Lorde* (New York: W.W. Norton, 2004), 366.

2. "A Eulogy for Audre Lorde: From Afro-German Women," *Aché* 5, no. 1 (1993), box 52, folder 742, p. 7, Lorde Papers. Co-founded by Lisbet Tellefsen and Pippa Fleming, *Aché* was the longest-running African American lesbian magazine published from 1989 to 1993. On *Aché,* see Angela Bowen, "Black Feminism," in *Lesbian Histories and Cultures: An Encyclopedia,* ed. Bonnie Zimmerman (New York: Taylor & Francis, 2000), 118.

3. "A Eulogy for Audre Lorde," 7.

4. Ibid.

5. Ibid.

6. Ibid., 8. I acquired Kettels's permission to use her poem.

7. Ibid., 7–8. The following Black German and Black women signed the eulogy: "May Ayim, Katharina Oguntoye, Ajoke Sobanjo, Guy St. Luis, Kim Everett, Ina Roder, Peggy, Peppa Gabriel, Abenna Adomako, Muna El-Khawad, Elisabeth Abraham, Elke Jank, Eva V. Pirch, Ria Cheatoh, Judy Gummich, Jasmin, Gabriela Willbold, Tina

Campt, Ika Huegel, Helga Emde, Marion Kraft, Katja Kinder, Zariama Harat, Patricia Saad, Nicola Laure Al-Samarei, Farida Corinna, Marion Gottbrath, Sarah Schnier, Natalie Asfaha, Yvonne Kettels, and Yara-Colette Lemke Muniz de Faria." Several of the women's names are misspelled.

8. Ghandi, *Affective Communities*. On emotions studies, see Barbara Rosenwein, *Emotional Communities: In the Early Middle Ages* (Ithaca, N.Y.: Cornell University Press, 2006); Sara Ahmed, *The Cultural Practice of Emotions* (Abingdon, U.K.: Routledge, 2004); Maria Stehle and Beverly M. Weber, "German Soccer, the 2010 World Cup, and Multicultural Belonging," *German Studies Review* 36, no. 1 (2013): 103–24.

9. Tina M. Campt, "The Crowded Space of Diaspora: Intercultural Address and the Tensions of Diasporic Relation," *Radical History Review* 83 (2002): 102.

10. Originally from Barbados, Frederic had previously been married with children before marrying Linda Belmar in Greenville, Grenada in 1923, and they moved to New York about a year later.

11. Audre Lorde, *Zami A New Spelling of My Name: A Biomythography* (Freedom, Calif.: Crossing Press, 1994), 21.

12. De Veaux, *Warrior Poet*, 17.

13. Ibid., 26–27, 31; Karla M. Hammond, "Audre Lorde: Interview," in *Conversations with Audre Lorde*, ed. Joan Wylie Hall (Oxford: University of Mississippi Press, 2004), 34.

14. Lorde, *Zami*, 83. In 1952, Lorde published in the *Harlem Writers Quarterly* and *Seventeen*.

15. De Veaux, *Warrior Poet*, 53.

16. Ibid., 39. The Guild evolved from the Committee for the Negro in the Arts in 1950. The CNA was a Black leftist and communist cultural institution that fought for African American artists, actors, musicians, and writers who were blacklisted by Hollywood and the House Un-American Activities Committee during the Cold War. On the Guild and the postwar Black Left, see Higashida, *Black Internationalist Feminism*; Dayo Gore, *Radicalism at the Crossroads: African American Women Activists in the Cold War* (New York: New York University Press, 2011); Mary Helen Washington, "Alice Childress, Lorraine Hansberry, and Claudia Jones: Black Women Write the Popular Front," in *Left of the Color Line: Race, Radicalism, and Twentieth-Century Literature of the United States*, eds. Bill V. Mullen and James Smethurst (Chapel Hill: University of North Carolina Press, 2003), 183–204.

17. Audre Lorde quoted in Rebeccah Welch, "Black Art and Activism in Postwar New York, 1950–1965" (PhD diss., New York University, 2002), 195.

18. De Veaux, *Warrior Poet*, 68, 70, 76, 80, 84.

19. Audre Lorde, *The First Cities* (New York: Poets Press, 1968).

20. Karla Jay, "Speaking the Unspeakable: Poet Audre Lorde," in Wylie Hall, *Conversations with Audre Lorde*, 111–12; Ilona Pache and Regina-Maria Dackweiler, "An Interview with Audre Lorde," in Wylie Hall, *Conversations with Audre Lorde*, 168.

21. De Veaux, *Warrior Poet*, 96. See also Mari Evans, "My Words will be There," in Wylie Hall, *Conversations with Audre Lorde*, 72. Frances M. Beal, Stuart Hall, Paul Gilroy, and others have also theorized this idea of difference.

22. De Veaux, *Warrior Poet*, 102–3.

23. Ibid., 121–22, 189, 222–24.

24. Ibid., 134–38, 151.

25. See Gilroy, *The Black Atlantic*.

26. Collins, *On Intellectual Activism*, xxii.

27. Audre Lorde, *The Cancer Journals* (San Francisco: Spinsters Ink, 1980).

28. Barbara Smith, "Breaking the Silence that Audre Challenged," in *The Wind is Spirit: The Life, Love and Legacy of Audre Lorde,* ed. Gloria Joseph (New York: Villarosa Media, 2016), 133; Barbara Smith, "A Press of Our Own Kitchen Table: Women of Color Press," *Frontiers: A Journal of Women Studies* 10, no. 3 (1989): 11; De Veaux, *Warrior Poet*, 275–77.

29. Smith, "A Press of Our Own Kitchen Table," 12.

30. De Veaux, *Warrior Poet*, 337. Lorde deliberately spelled America in the lower case.

31. Ibid., 323–27; Susan Cavin, "An Interview with Audre Lorde," in Wylie Hall, *Conversations with Audre Lorde*, 101–2.

32. Audre Lorde, *Sister Outsider: Essays and Speeches* (Trumansburg, N.Y.: Crossing Press, 1984).

33. While Lorde practiced and wrote from this perspective, the Combahee River Collective (CRC) also employed critical intersectional analyses in the 1970s. But legal theorist and activist Kimberlé Crenshaw coined the term "intersectionality" in 1989. See "The Combahee River Collective Statement," in *How We Get Free: Black Feminism and the Combahee River Collective,* ed. Keeanga-Yamahtta Taylor (Chicago: Haymarket Books, 2017), 15–28; Kimberlé Crenshaw, "Demarginalizing the Intersection of Race and Sex: A Black Feminist Critique of Antidiscrimination Doctrine, Feminist Theory and Antiracist Politics," *University of Chicago Legal Forum* 1 (1989): 139–67.

34. Place and space were important to Lorde as evinced by her writings. A few examples include: Lorde, "Notes from a Trip to Russia," in Lorde, *Sister Outsider,* 13–35; Lorde, "Grenada Revisited: An Interim Report," in Lorde, *Sister Outsider,* 176–90; Lorde, *A Burst of Light: Essays* (Ithaca, N.Y.: Firebrand Books, 1988). See also Stella Bolaki and Sabine Broeck, eds., *Audre Lorde's Transnational Legacies* (Amherst: University of Massachusetts Press, 2015).

35. Gloria Joseph, ed., *The Wind is Spirit: The Life, Love and Legacy of Audre Lorde* (New York: Villarosa Media, 2016), 148.

36. Dagmar Schultz quoted in Gloria Joseph, *The Wind is Spirit,* 145.

37. McKittrick, *Demonic Grounds,* x.

38. Dagmar Schultz, "Audre Lorde-Her Struggles and Her Visions" (Berlin: Heinrich Böll Stiftung and Gunda Werde Institut: Feminismus und Geschlechterdemokratie, n.d.): 1, http://dagmarschultz.com/downloads/audre_lorde.pdf; de Veaux, *Warrior Poet,* 295–96; Katharina Gerund, "Sisterly (Inter)Actions: Audre Lorde and the Development of Afro-German Women's Communities," *Gender Forum* 22 (2008): 56.

39. Dagmar Schultz letter to Audre Lorde, July 17, 1981, box 5, folder 117, p. 1, Lorde Papers; Schultz letter to Audre Lorde, September 12, 1981, box 5, folder 117, p. 1, Lorde Papers.

40. Schultz letter to Lorde, July 17, 1981, 2; de Veaux, *Warrior Poet,* 296. Founded in 1974, Sub Rosa Women's Press focused on women's health and politics and was formerly Women's Self Publishing (*Frauenselbstverlag*). Schultz became a co-owner in 1982. Sub Rosa Women's Press eventually became Orlanda Feminist Press (*Orlanda Frauenverlag*).

41. Schultz letter to Lorde, July 17, 1981, 2.

42. Dagmar Schultz, ed., *Macht und Sinnlichkeit: Ausgewählte Texte,* trans. Renate Stendhal, Marion Kraft, Susanne Stern, and Erika Wisselinck (Berlin: Orlanda, 1993); Sara Lennox, "Divided Feminism: Women, Racism, and German National Identity," *German Studies Review* 18, no. 3 (1995): 482.

43. See Oguntoye, "The Black German Movement and the Womens Movement," 4.

44. Lennox, "Divided Feminism," 482, 501; El-Tayeb, *European Others,* 63. See also Katharina Gerund, "Visions of (Global) Sisterhood and Black Solidarity: Audre Lorde," in Gerund, *Transatlantic Cultural Exchange: African American Women's Art and Activism in West Germany* (Bielefeld: Transcript, 2013), 175–91; Katharina Oguntoye, "Mein Coming-out als Schwarze Lesbe in Deutschland," in *In Bewegung bleiben: 100 Jahre Politik Kultur und Geschichte von Lesben,* eds. Gabriele Dennert, Christiane Leidinger, and Franziska Rauchut (Berlin: Querverlag, 2007), 161; *Audre Lorde-The Berlin Years 1984– 1992,* directed by Dagmar Schultz with Ika Hügel-Marshall and Ria Cheatom (New York: Third World Newsreel, 2012), DVD. In it, white German feminists Ilona Bubeck and Traude Bührmann recall Lorde's influence on the German women's movement.

45. Lorde, *A Burst of Light,* 56–57; Audre Lorde letter to Dr. Horst Hartwich, December 10, 1983, vol. 60, n.p., The Audre Lorde Archive, Universitätsarchiv Freie Universität Berlin, Germany (hereafter cited as Lorde Archive). See also Dr. Horst Hartwich Freie Universität Official letter to Audre Lorde, October 4, 1982, vol. 60, n.p., Lorde Archive; Hartwich Freie Universität Official letter to Lorde, November 12, 1982, vol. 60, n.p., Lorde Achive; Westhusen Official Letter to the Präsidenten der Freien Universität Berlin Zentrale Universitätsverwaltung (Frau Handschuhmacher), January 5, 1983, vol. 60, n.p., Lorde Archive.

46. She taught "Contemporary Black Literature," "The Poet as Outsider," and "Contemporary Women's Poetry." At the time, May used her adopted last name of Opitz.

47. Oguntoye, "Mein Coming-Out als Schwarze Lesbe," in Dennert, Leidinger, and Rauchut, *In Bewegung bleiben,* 162–63; Oguntoye quoted in Piesche, "Rückblenden und Vorschauen, in Piesche, *Euer Schweigen schützt Euch nicht,*" 24.

48. Lorde, *A Burst of Light,* 57

49. De Veaux, *Warrior Poet,* 344.

50. Lorde, "Foreword to the English Language Edition," in Opitz, Oguntoye, and Schultz, *Showing our Colors,* vii.

51. Judy Gummich, "Afro-German: A New Spelling of My Identity," in Joseph, *The Wind is Spirit,* 171.

52. On Lorde's influence in Germany, see Maureen Maisha Eggers, "Knowledges of (Un-) Belonging: Epistemic Change as a Defining Mode for Black Women's Activism in Germany," in Lennox, *Remapping Black Germany,* 33–45 ; Piesche, ed., *Euer Schweigen*

schützt Euch nicht; El-Tayeb, *European Others,* 43–80; Carol Blackshire-Belay, "The African Diaspora in Europe: African Germans Speak Out," *Journal of Black Studies* 31, no. 3 (2001): 264–87; Carolyn Hodges, "The Private/Plural Selves of Afro-German Women and the Search for a Public Voice," *Journal of Black Studies* 23, no. 2 (1992): 219–34.

53. De Veaux, *Warrior Poet,* 344–45.

54. El-Tayeb, *European Others,* 50.

55. Campt, "The Crowded Space of Diaspora," 101–2.

56. El-Tayeb, *European Others,* 64. See also Anne Adams, "The Souls of Black Volk: Contradiction? Oxymoron?" in Mazón and Steingröver, *Not So Plain as Black and White,* 209–32.

57. During a conversation with Ria Cheatom in August 2011, she remarked that Lorde was "the mother of the movement." See Ria Cheatom, interview, Sound recording. Berlin-Schöneberg, August 8, 2011, the author's private collection, Real audio, MP3. See also *Audre Lorde-The Berlin Years 1984–1992* for interviews with a few Black German activists such as Judy Gummich, Marion Kraft, and Jasmin Eding, in which they reflected similar sentiments. On the other hand, Ika Hügel-Marshall saw Lorde as a "homegirl and mentor," but not the mother of the movement. See Hügel-Marshall, "That is the Whole Truth," in Joseph, *The Wind is Spirit,* 150.

58. Campt, "The Crowded Space of Diaspora"; Brown, *Dropping Anchor, Setting Sail,* 42. Wright has also advanced these ideas in her works. See Wright, *Physics of Blackness.*

59. Other scholars have also suggested moving beyond the "Black Atlantic" perspective, see Jayne O. Ifekwunigwe, "'Black Folk Here and There': Repositioning Other(ed) African Diaspora(s) in/and 'Europe,'" in *The African Diaspora and The Disciplines,* eds. Tejumola Olaniyan and James H. Sweet (Bloomington: Indiana University Press, 2010), 313–38; Paul Tiyambe Zeleza, "Rewriting the African Diaspora, Beyond the Black Atlantic," *African Affairs* 104, no. 414 (2005): 35–68.

60. Lorde, "Poetry is Not a Luxury," in Lorde, *Sister Outsider,* 38.

61. Gummich, "Afro-German," in Joseph, *The Wind is Spirit,* 173.

62. On postwar German emotions, see Anna Parkinson, *An Emotional State: The Politics of Emotion in Postwar West German Culture* (Ann Arbor: University of Michigan Press, 2015).

63. "Reading and discussion in Dagmar Schultz'[s] seminar 'Racism and Sexism' at the JFK Institute of North American Studies at the Free University of Berlin," July 7, 1984, vol. 6, p. 5, Lorde Archive. Lorde discussed the significance of other "negative" emotions such as pain and fear in her works. See Nina Winter, "Audre Lorde," in Wylie Hall, *Conversations with Audre Lorde,* 9–17.

64. Lorde, "The Uses of Anger: Women Responding to Racism," in Lorde, *Sister Outsider,* 127, 128–29.

65. Lorde used these monikers at public engagements in Germany and elsewhere. See "Press Conference (Berlin, 1990)," 1990, vol. 23, p. 3, Lorde Archive; "Lesung in der Schoko Fabrik," November 20, 1987, vol. 12a, p. 2, Lorde Archive; "Interview with Audre Lorde in Zürich by Radio Lora," 1984, vol. 30, p. 1, Lorde Archive; Pache and Dackwei-

ler, "An Interview with Lorde"; Charles H. Rowell, "Above the Wind: An Interview with Audre Lorde," August 29, 1990, box 52, folder 755, pp. 68–77, Lorde Papers.

66. "Reading and discussion in Dagmar Schultz'[s] seminar," July 7, 1984, 7. Lorde was already fifty, not forty-nine, when she began teaching in Berlin.

67. "Reading in Dresden," May 29, 1990, vol. 24, p. 2, Lorde Archive; "Lesung in der Schoko Fabrik," November 20, 1987, vol. 12b, p. 7, Lorde Archive. See also "Audre Lorde Reading in Frankfurt/M.," November 13, 1987, vol. 13, pp. 1–2, Lorde Archive.

68. De Veaux, *Warrior Poet,* 13.

69. See Diana Taylor, "Acts of Transfer," in Taylor, *The Archive and the Repertoire: Performing Cultural Memory in the Americas* (Durham, NC: Duke University Press, 2003), 2–3.

70. The Dream of Europe conference occurred from May 25–29, 1988. Draft remarks by Audre Lorde, "The Dream of Europe," n.d., box 17, folder 061, n.p, Lorde Papers; Dieter Esche letter to Audre Lorde, March 22, 1988, box 51, folder 700, p. 1, Lorde Papers. See also Bolaki and Broeck, *Audre Lorde's Transnational Legacies,* 23–26; "Ein Traum von Europa," *Kongress Zeitung,* May 25–29, 1988, folder Lorde Lichtflut 1988, Orlanda Frauenverlag (hereafter cited as Orlanda); "Ein Traum von Europa," flyer, folder Lorde Lichtflut 1988, Orlanda.

71. On the emotional archive, see Ann Cvetkovich, *An Archive of Feelings: Trauma, Sexuality, and Lesbian Public Cultures* (Durham, N.C.: Duke University Press, 2003), 7–8.

72. "Lesung in der Schoko Fabrik," 7; "Reading in Hanover," May 16, 1988, vol. 15, p. 1, Lorde Archive; "Audre Lorde: A New Spelling of Our Name," *Sojourner* 10, no. 5 (1985), box 51, folder 659, p. 17, Lorde Papers. Beginning in the 1980s, the *Schokofabrik,* also known as the *Schoko,* was located in a former chocolate factory in Kreuzberg. German feminists led this project with the goal of supporting young girls, lesbians, and women.

73. "Audre Lorde Reading in Berlin 'Araquin,' " July 1, 1987, vol. 8a, pp. 1–3, Lorde Archive.

74. "Reading at BAZ (Berliner Aktions Zentrum of people of color)," July 1984, vol. 10, p. 11, Lorde Archive; "Reading in Hanover," 1.

75. Lorde emphasized this idea in many of her works. See Lorde, *Sister Outsider*; Audre Lorde and James Baldwin, "Revolutionary Hope: A Conversation Between James Baldwin and Audre Lorde," *Essence* (1984): 72–74, 129–30, 133.

76. "Lesung in der Schoko Fabrik," 8.

77. "Lesung im Büchergarten," June 25, 1989, vol. 7, p. 2, Lorde Archive.

78. "Interview with Audre Lorde by Dagmar Schultz," 5–6.

79. See "Reading in Stuttgart," May 18, 1990, vol. 25, p. 7, Lorde Archive. See also ADEFRA-München, "Rundbrief Mai '91," May 1991, p. 2, The Private Collection of Ria Cheatom (hereafter cited as Cheatom Collection).

80. Lorde, *A Burst of Light,* 57.

81. "Reading in Dresden," May 29, 1990, 4.

82. Lisa McGill, *Constructing Black Selves: Caribbean American Narratives and the Second Generation* (New York: New York University Press, 2005), 150.

83. Ghadhi, *Affective Communities*.

84. This connection still remains, as Joseph traveled from St. Croix to attend Schultz's film premiere of *Audre Lorde—The Berlin Years, 1984–1992* at the Berlinale Film Festival in February 2012. For more on these relationships, view the film. Joseph died in August 2019.

85. De Veaux, *Warrior Poet*, 365.

86. Nicola Lauré al-Samarai letter to Audre Lorde, August 2, 1990, box 3, folder 073, p. 1, Lorde Papers.

87. Marion Kraft letter to Audre Lorde, October 17, 1988, box 3, folder 069, p. 4, Lorde Papers.

88. May Ayim letter to Audre Lorde, November 14, 1991, box 3, folder 094, p. 1, Lorde Papers.

89. May Ayim card to Audre Lorde, May 10, 1991, box 3, folder 094, p. 1, Lorde Papers.

90. See additional examples including "I send my love to you"—Katharina Oguntoye letter to Audre Lorde, November 12, 1986, box 3, folder 093, p. 3, Lorde Papers; "In sisterhood"—Marion Kraft letter to Audre Lorde, March 6, 1988, box 3, folder 069, p. 2, Lorde Papers; "Much love"—Ika Hügel fax to Audre Lorde, February 18, 1992, box 5, folder 118, p. 1, Lorde Papers; "You are with us . . ."—Lauré al-Samarai letter to Audre Lorde, December 4, 1990, box 3, folder 073, p. 5, Lorde Papers.

91. Marion Kraft letter to Audre Lorde, July 12, 1986, box 3, folder 069, p. 3, Lorde Papers.

92. bell hooks, "Love as the Practice of Freedom," in hooks, *Outlaw Culture: Resisting Representations* (New York: Routledge, 2006), 243–50.

93. Marion Kraft letter to Audre Lorde, September 20, 1986, box 7, folder 161, p. 1, Lorde Papers.

94. Ayim card to Lorde, May 10, 1991, 1.

95. Lauré al-Samarai letter to Lorde, December 4, 1990, 2.

96. Katharina Oguntoye letter to Audre Lorde, August 4, 1986, box 3, folder 093, p. 4, Lorde Papers.

97. Marion Kraft letter to Audre Lorde, December 20, 1986, box 3, folder 069, p. 1, Lorde Papers. Black German male activist John Kantara also recognized the importance of Lorde by sending her a speech he had given at the 7th Annual International Book Fair on Radical Black and Third World Books in London. But Black German men did not write her as much.

98. Hella Schültheiß letter to Audre Lorde, August 8, 1990, box 5, folder 115, n.p., Lorde Papers. I am unable to determine her full ancestry. But she was a lesbian involved in the Black German movement.

99. Ayim letter to Lorde, November 14, 1991, 1.

100. Kraft letter to Lorde, October 17, 1988, 4.

101. Hügel fax to Lorde, February 18, 1992, 1.

102. Sheila Mysorekas [sic] letter to Audre Lorde, September 3 (year unknown), box 3, folder 086, p. 4, Lorde Papers.

103. Sara Ahmed, *Queer Phenomenology: Orientations, Objects, and Others* (Durham, N.C.: Duke University Press, 2006), 2–3.

104. See also "I am Your Sister: Forging Global Connections Across Differences," flyer, Cheatom Collection; "I am Your Sister: Forging Global Connections Across Differences," letter, May 12, 1990, pp. 1–2, Cheatom Collection.

105. Katharina Oguntoye letter to Audre Lorde, October 18 and 22, 1990, box 3, folder 093, p. 3, Lorde Papers.

106. Oguntoye letter to Lorde, October 18 and 22, 1990, 3.

107. Kraft letter to Lorde, October 17, 1988, 1.

108. Sheila Mysorekar letter to Audre Lorde, International Women's Day 1990?, n.d., box 3, folder 086, p. 1, Lorde Papers.

109. Karapin, *Protest Politics in Germany;* Dennis and LaPorte, *State and Minorities;* Kurthen, Bergmann, and Erb, *Antisemitism and Xenophobia in Germany*. For a comparison of the anxiety and fear that emerged after the fall of the Berlin Wall and the contemporary refugee problem on New Years Eve 2015 in Germany, see Vanessa Plumly, "Refugee Assemblages, Cycles of Violence, and Body Politic(s) in Times of 'Celebratory Fear,'" *Women in German Yearbook* 32 (2016): 163–88.

110. Kraft card to Lorde, December 9, 1991, 1.

111. Oguntoye letter to Lorde, August 4, 1986, 1–2. The Lesbian-Feminist Sabbath Circle (Lesbisch-Feministische Schabbeskreis) was a secular, Jewish, feminist, and lesbian group established by (Ben) Maria Baader, Jessica Jacoby, and Gotlinde Magiriba Lwanga in Berlin from 1984 to 1989. See Michaela Baetz, Gabriele Dennert, and Christiane Leidinger, "Chronik der Antisemitismusdiskussionen in der (Frauen- und) Lesbenbewegung der BRD der 80er Jahre," in Dennert, Leidinger, and Rauchut, *In Bewegung bleiben,* 175.

112. Kraft letter to Lorde, October 17, 1988, 1.

113. Katharina Oguntoye letter to Audre Lorde, October 26, 1988, box 3, folder 093, p. 2, Lorde Papers.

114. Nicola Lauré al-Samarai im Gespräch mit Aktivistinnen Katja Kinder, Ria Cheatom und Ekpenyong Ani, "'Es ist noch immer ein Aufbruch, aber mit neuer Startposition': Zwanzig Jahre ADEFRA und Schwarze Frauen/Bewegungen in Deutschland," in *Re/visionen: Postkoloniale Perspektiven von People of Color auf Rassismus, Kulturpolitik und Widerstand in Deutschland,* eds. Kien Nghi Ha, Nicola Lauré al-Samarai, and Sheila Mysorekar (Münster: Unrast, 2007), 349.

115. Kraft letter to Lorde, October 17, 1988, 1.

116. Katharina Oguntoye, "Portrait: Audre Lorde," *afro look: Eine Zeitung von Schwarzen Deutschen* 3 (1989): 18, the author's private collection.

117. Marion Kraft quoted in Schultz, "Audre Lorde—Her Struggles and Her Visions," 4.

118. Tania Léon letter to Audre Lorde, n.d., box 3, folder 74, n.p., Lorde Papers. Léon also worked at Flamboyant, a center with a library and information for and about Black and migrant women, formed in 1986.

119. Monique Ngozi Nri letter to Audre Lorde, July 14, 1986, box 3, folder 92, n.p., Lorde Papers.

120. Jackie Kay letter to Audre Lorde, March 21, 1988, box 3, folder 64, pp. 1, 5, Lorde Papers.

121. Gloria Wekker letter to Audre Lorde, July 22, 1986, box 5, folder 138, p. 1, Lorde Papers.

122. Gloria Wekker and Cassandra Ellerbe-Dueck, "Naming Ourselves as Black Women in Europe: An African American-German and Afro-Dutch Conversation," in Bolaki and Broeck, *Audre Lorde's Transnational Legacies*, 58. Sister Outsider was founded in 1984 and disbanded in 1986. See also Gianmaria Colpani and Wigbertson Julian Isenia, "Strange Fruits: Queer of Color Intellectual Labor in the Netherlands in the 1980s and 1990s," in *Postcolonial Intellectuals in Europe: Critics, Artists, Movements, and Their Publics*, eds. Sandra Ponzanesi and Adriano José Habed (London: Rowman & Littlefield, 2018), 213–30.

123. Wekker letter to Lorde, July 22, 1986, 2.

124. Wekker letter to Lorde, February 15, 1987, n.p.

125. Monique Ngozi Nri letter to Audre Lorde, January 18, 1987, box 3, folder 92, p. 1, Lorde Papers.

126. Jackie Kay letter to Audre Lorde, April 29, 1985, box 3, folder 64, n.p., Lorde Papers.

127. Philomena Essed letter to Audre Lorde, July 14, 1984, n.p., Lorde Papers.

128. Gloria Wekker letter to Audre Lorde, January 28, year unknown, box 5, folder 138, n.p., Lorde Papers.

CHAPTER 2. THE MAKING OF A MODERN BLACK GERMAN MOVEMENT

1. Based in Berlin, *AWA-FINNABA* was an African literary magazine produced from 1983 to 1988. I discuss the AWA in chapter 5. John Amoateng later assumed his wife Jeannine's last name Kantara, who he met through ISD-Berlin.

2. African Writers Association, "Speak your mind," *AWA-FINNABA* no. 9 (1987): 53. See also "Wir wollen aus der Isolation heraus," in May Ayim, *Grenzenlos und unverschämt* (Berlin: Orlanda, 1997), 45–48.

3. African Writers Association, "Speak your mind," 53–54.

4. El-Tayeb, *European Others*, xvii. For more on racialization in Europe, see Goldberg, "Racial Europeanization"; Gloria Wekker, *White Innocence: Paradoxes of Colonialism and Race* (Durham, N.C.: Duke University Press, 2016); Paul Gilroy, *"There Ain't No Black in the Union Jack": The Cultural Politics of Race and Nation* (Chicago: University of Chicago Press, 1991); Etienne Balibar and Immanuel Wallerstein, eds., *Race, Nation, Class: Ambiguous Identities* (London: Verso, 1991).

5. Wright, *Becoming Black*, 190–91. Wright claims that other diasporic communities in the United States and Britain are seen as "Others-from-Within." People who are

born and are physically part of the nation, but are excluded and presumed to be inferior and unable to integrate into society. See also El-Tayeb, *European Others*; Eggers, Kilomba, Piesche, and Arndt, *Mythen, Masken und Subjekte*.

6. While the acronym remains the same, ISD is now called Initiative of Black People in Germany (Initiative Schwarze Menschen in Deutschland e.V.) or ISD Bund e.V. Over the years, ISD underwent several name changes before settling on this more inclusive title.

7. Hobsbawm, "Introduction," in Hobsbawm and Ranger, *The Invention of Tradition*, 1.

8. Wright, *Physics of Blackness*.

9. Sheila Mysorekar, " 'Pass the Word and Break the Silence': The Significance of African-American and 'Third World' Literature for Black Germans," in *Moving Beyond Boundaries: International Dimensions of Black Women's Writing*, vol. 1, eds. Carole Boyce Davies and Molara Ogundipe-Leslie (New York: New York University Press, 1995), 80.

10. On Black radicalism, see Cederic Robinson, *Black Marxism: The Making of the Black Radical Tradition* (Chapel Hill: University of North Carolina Press, 2000); Robin D.G. Kelly, *Freedom Dreams: The Black Radical Imagination* (Boston: Beacon Press, 2002).

11. When I originally examined May Ayim's personal materials, they were in private hands. While most of those materials are now housed at the Freie Universität Berlin, there are still a few folders that are not. Therefore, I have listed those materials as The May Ayim Papers. Quoted in Christiana Ampedu, Helga Emde, and Eleonore Wiedenroth, "Invitation letter," n.d., folder May Projekt Afro-Deutsche/Zeitungsartikel über Afro-deutsche-Schwarze in den Medien, n.p., The May Ayim Papers (hereafter cited as Ayim Papers). See also Eleonore Wiedenroth-Coulibaly, "Die multiplen Anfänge der ISD," in Bergold-Caldwell et al., *Spiegelblicke*, 28–32.

12. Ampedu, Emde, and Wiedenroth, "Invitation letter." On Black Germans' experiences with white Germans, see Robinson, "Schwarze Deutsche Kräfte," 4; Sow, *Deutschland Schwarz Weiss*, esp. 252–63; Tupoka Ogette, *exit Racism: rassismuskritisch denken lernen* (Münster: Unrast, 2017).

13. Ika Hügel-Marshall, "ADEFRA—Die Anfänge: Ein Gespräch mit Ria Cheatom, Jasmin Eding und Judy Gummich," in *Kinder der Befreiung: Transatlantische Erfahrungen und Perspektiven Schwarzer Deutscher der Nachkriegsgeneration*, ed. Marion Kraft (Münster: Unrast, 2015), 324.

14. Wiedenroth-Coulibaly, "Die multiplen Anfänge der ISD," in Bergold-Caldwell et al., *Spiegelblicke*, 29.

15. Oguntoye quoted in Piesche, "Rückblenden und Vorschauen, in Piesche, *Euer Schweigen schützt Euch nicht*," 23; Katharina Oguntoye, "Vorwort zur Neuauflage 2006," in Oguntoye, Ayim/Opitz, and Schultz, *Farbe bekennen*, 8.

16. For a few examples, see ISD Rhine-Main (Wiesbaden), "ISD Initiative Schwarze Deutsche (wir über uns)," 1989, p. 4, Cheatom Collection; ISD-München, "ISD Initiative Schwarze Deutsche (wir über uns)," 1989, p. 4, Cheatom Collection.

17. "Die Situation der schwarzen Deutschen," *Frankfurter Rundschau*, October 30, 1985, n.p.; "Schwarze Deutsche treffen sich," *Wiesbadender Kurier*, October 30, 1985, p. 5; "Heute Afro-Deutsche," *Allgemeine Zeitung*, October 21, 1985, folder May Projekt

Afro-Deutsche/Zeitungsartikel über Afro-deutsche-Schwarze in den Medien, n.p., Ayim Papers; Wiedenroth-Coulibaly, "Die multiplen Anfänge der ISD," in Bergold-Caldwell et al., *Spiegelblicke,* 29.

18. Christiana, Eleonore, Nadja, and Sunny letter to November 2 participants, November 26, 1985, folder May Projekt Afro-Deutsche/Zeitungsartikel über Afro-deutsche-Schwarze in den Medien, n.p., Ayim Papers. The letter also mentioned a list of attendees, but this list was not included.

19. Wiedenroth-Coulibaly, "Die multiplen Anfänge der ISD," in Bergold-Caldwell et al., *Spiegelblicke,* 30; Helga Emde, "I too am German—An Afro-German Perspective," in *Who Is a German? Historical and Modern Perspectives on Africans in Germany,* ed. Leroy Hopkins (Washington, DC: American Institute of Contemporary German Studies, 1999), 40. Journalist Dietrich Haubold wrote that there were approximately thirty Afro-Germans in attendance. See Dietrich Haubold (Saarländischer Rundfunk) letter to "The Initiative," November 13, 1985, n.p. and Dietrich Haubold, " 'Wo ist dein richtiges Heimatland?': Hautfarbe schwarz, Nationalität deutsch—Probleme einer Minderheit," folder May Projekt Afro-Deutsche/Zeitungsartikel über Afro-deutsche-Schwarze in den Medien, pp. 1–5, Ayim Papers. Several Afro-Germans found Haubold's article to be insensitive and inaccurate. ISD members wrote him, challenging him on his racism. See "The Initiative" response letter to Dietrich Haubold, November 29, 1985, folder May Projekt Afro-Deutsche/Zeitungsartikel über Afro-deutsche-Schwarze in den Medien, n.p., Ayim Papers.

20. Emde, "I too am German," in Hopkins, *Who Is a German?,* 40.

21. Ika Hügel-Marshall, "Die Situation von Afrodeutschen nach dem Zweiten Weltkrieg (am Beispiel meiner Autobiographie: *'Daheim unterwegs. Ein deutsches Leben'*) und heute," in Niederle, Davis-Suilowski, and Fillitz, *Früchte der Zeit,* 75–84, esp. 80.

22. Christiana, Eleonore, Nadja, and Sunny follow-up letter to November 2 participants, November 26, 1985, n.p.

23. Oguntoye, "Vorwort zur Neuauflage 2006," in Oguntoye, Ayim/Opitz, and Schultz, *Farbe bekennen,* 7; Oguntoye, "The Black German Movement and the Womens Movement," 2.

24. Emde, "I too am German," in Hopkins, *Who Is a German?,* 39. See also Hopkins, "Race, Nationality and Culture," in Hopkins, *Who is a German?,* 12–15.

25. Jeannine Kantara, "Die Geschichte der Zeitschrift *afro look* und die Anfänge der ISD Berliner Frühlingserwachen," in Diallo and Zeller, *Black Berlin,* 166.

26. Work on German historical memory is rich, and this is, by no means, an exhaustive list. See Campt, *Other Germans;* Alon Confino, *Germany as a Culture Remembrance: Promises and Limits of Writing History* (Chapel Hill: University of North Carolina Press, 2006); Michael Geyer and Konrad Jarausch, *Shattered Past: Reconstructing German Histories* (Princeton, N.J.: Princeton University Press, 2003); Anne Fuchs, Mary Cosgrove, and Georg Grote, eds., *German Memory Contests: The Quest for Identity in Literature, Film, and Discourse Since 1990* (Rochester, N.Y.: Camden House, 2006).

27. African Writers Association, "Speak your mind," 55.

28. Initiative Schwarze Deutsche und Schwarze in Deutschland e.V. (ISD-Berlin), brochure, n.d., n.p., Cheatom Collection.

29. Wiedenroth-Coulibaly and Zinflou, "20 Jahre Schwarze Organisierung," in AntiDiskriminierungsBüro and cyberNomads, *The BlackBook,* 135.

30. I am able to recognize these individuals as members of ISD based on letters, minute meetings, a few membership lists, among other sources that I collected, though it is still difficult to gauge how many individuals regularly attended meetings and events in this group and others. See ISD-Berlin, "Mitglieder (Stand: 09.03.87)" and ISD-Berlin, "I.S.D.-Mitglieder (Stand: 25.04.87)," folder Literatur, e.V. Aktuelles, Ayim Papers; "I.S.D. Berlin e.V. Mitglieder/Interessenten (Stand: 12.09.88)," box 6, n.p., Ayim Archive.

31. Sadly, Grotke died in May 2019, and Michael died in October 2019.

32. "I.S.D.-Gruppen in der BRD," *Onkel Tom's Faust* no. 1 (1988): 40; ISD, "Verteilung der Spende des Weltkirchenrates," December 8, 1988, folder ISD-Ko-Treffen, p. 3, Cheatom Collection; Oguntoye, "The Black German Movement and the Womens Movement," 2; Wiedenroth-Coulibaly, "Die multiplen Anfänge der ISD," in Bergold-Caldwell et al., *Spiegelblicke,* 30, 32.

33. ISD, "Koordinationstreffen 04/92," Hamburg, November 14–15, 1992, folder ISD Ko-Treffen, n.p., Cheatom Collection; ISD, "Anwesenheitsliste Koordinationstreffen Leipzig (8.-10.1.1993)," folder ISD Ko-Treffen, p. 1, Cheatom Collection; "2. Koordi/ 94 in FFM," folder ISD Ko-Treffen, p. 4, Cheatom Collection; ISD-NRW e.V., "ISD in Bochum, Initiative Schwarze Deutsche & Schwarze in Deutschland," n.d., folder ISD Liga, n.p., Ayim Papers.

34. Initiative Schwarze Deutsche und Schwarze in Deutschland (Fidelis Dusine-Grotke), "Antrag auf Unterstützung," May 24, 1994, folder ISD-Ko-Treffen, p. 3, Cheatom Collection.

35. Megan Watkins, "Desiring Recognition, Accumulating Affect," in *The Affect Theory Reader,* eds. Melissa Gregg and Gregorty J. Seigworth (Durham, N.C.: Duke University Press, 2010), 272, 273.

36. ISD, "Protokoll der Arbeitsgruppen zum Thema," 2. Now living in Berlin, Della remains active in the contemporary movement. Other men such as Roy Adomako, Thomas Pforth, Michael Küppers-Adebisi (née Michael Küppers), Yonas Endrias, Patrice Poutrus, Alexander Weheliye, and Austen Brandt were also involved in ISD, but not all in the Munich group. This is not an exhaustive list.

37. Ibid., 2.

38. "May [Ayim] and Mike [Reichel] letter to Helga Emde," March 4, 1987, folder Literatur e.V. Aktuelles, n.p., Ayim Papers.

39. ISD, "Protokoll der Arbeitsgruppen zum Thema 'Bundesweite Zusammenarbeit der Initiativen schwarzer Deutscher-Ziele und Möglichkeiten,' 2 Bundestreffen der Initiativen schwarzer Deutscher vom 5.-6. Dezember 1987 in Berlin," folder ISD Ko-Treffen, p. 1, Cheatom Collection.

40. ISD, "Protokoll der Arbeitsgruppen zum Thema," 1.

41. Ibid.

42. See ISD, "Koordinationstreffen der Initiativen Schwarze Deutsche in Frankfurt/ Main 26./27.03.1988," folder ISD Ko-Treffen, n.p., Cheatom Collection.

43. ISD, "Protokoll des Finanztreffens," October 15, 1988, folder ISD Ko-Treffen, n.p., Cheatom Collection.

44. See, for example, folder ISD Ko-Treffen, Cheatom Collection.

45. ISD, "Anhang Konzeption für eine Geschäftsordnung der Initiative Schwarze in Deutschland/ Koordinationstreffen," folder ISD Ko-Treffen, pp. 1–2, Cheatom Collection.

46. Ibid., 1.

47. "Koordi/ 94 in FFM," folder ISD Ko-Treffen, pp. 21–22, Cheatom Collection.

48. McKittrick, *Demonic Grounds*, xxi–xxiv, 1–64; Henri Lefebvre, "The Right to the City," in *Writings on Cities,* eds. and trans. Eleonore Kofman and Elizabeth Lebas (Cambridge, U.K.: Wiley-Blackwell, 1996), 147–59. Wright has also posited that the metropolis served as a counter-discourse for Afro-German and Black British communities. See Wright, *Becoming Black,* 224–25. On translocality, see El-Tayeb, *European Others;* Arjun Appardurai, *Modernity at Large: Cultural Dimensions of Globalization* (Minneapolis: University of Minnesota Press, 1996), 178–99.

49. The Initiative letter to Dietrich Haubold, November 29, 1985.

50. Fatima El-Tayeb, "Blackness and Its (Queer) Discontents," in Lennox, *Remapping Black Germany,* 252.

51. McKittrick, *Demonic Grounds,* 3, 102–6.

52. On Black European attempts to self-style, see Marleen de Witte, "Heritage, Blackness and Afro-Cool: Styling Africanness in Amsterdam," *African Diaspora* 7 (2014): 260–89.

53. ISD-Karlsruhe, "ISD Initiative Schwarze Deutsche wir über uns," n.p., Cheatom Collection; ISD-Rhine/Main, "ISD Initiative Schwarze Deutsche wir über uns," p. 2, Cheatom Collection.

54. African Writers Association, "Speak your mind," 55.

55. ISD, "Einige Punkte zur Vorstellung der Initiative Schwarzer Deutscher (Afro-Deutsche)," n.d., n.p.

56. See Initiative Schwarze Deutsche, "Die kleine Bibliothek: Literatur von schwarzen Autorinnen/Autoren in deutscher Übersetzung," 1993, folder ISD Liga, pp. 1–24, Ayim Papers; Initiative Schwarze Deutsche, "Die kleine Bibliothek: Literatur von schwarzen Autorinnen/Autoren in deutscher Übersetzung," 1995, pp. 1–31, the author's private collection. This intellectual tradition continues with Each One Teach One (EOTO) e.V. in Berlin, which currently includes the archive of the late ISD activist Vera Heyer as well as book collections from Ricky Reiser and Eleonore Wiedenroth-Coulibaly.

57. On thinking Black in Europe, see Rob Waters, *Thinking Black: Britain, 1964–1985* (Oakland: University of California Press, 2019), 51–92.

58. ISD-Rhine/Main, "ISD Initiative Schwarze Deutsche wir über uns," brochure, 1989, p. 2, Cheatom Collection.

59. See Belinda Davis, Wilfried Mausbach, Martin Klimke, and Carla MacDougall, eds., *Changing the World, Changing Oneself: Political Protest and Collective Identities in West Germany and the U.S. in the 1960s and 1970s* (New York: Berghahn, 2010); Timothy S. Brown, *West German and the Global Sixties: Anti-Authoritarian Revolt, 1962–1978* (New York: Cambridge University Press, 2013).

60. Sabine von Dirke, *"All Power to the Imagination!": The West German Counterculture from the Student Movement to the Greens* (Lincoln: University of Nebraska Press, 1997); Belinda Davis, "What's Left? Popular and Democratic Political Participation in Postwar Europe," *American Historical Review* 113, no. 2 (2008): 363–90.

61. Anne-Marie Angelo, "The Black Panthers in London, 1967–1972: A Diasporic Struggle Navigates the Black Atlantic," *Radical History Review* 103 (2009): 17–35; Perry, *London is the Place for Me*, 126–52; Trica Danielle Keaton, Tracy Denean Sharley-Whiting, and Tyler Stovall, eds., *Black France/France Noire: The History and Politics of Blackness* (Durham, N.C.: Duke University, Press, 2012).

62. See Perry, *London is the Place for Me*, 126–52; Brett Bebber, "'Standard Transatlantic Practice': Race Relations and Anti-Discrimination Law Across the Atlantic," *Journal of Civil and Human Rights* 4, no. 1 (2018): 5–36; Allison Blakely, "The Emergence of Afro-Europe: A Preliminary Sketch," in Hine, Keaton, and Small, *Black Europe and the African Diaspora*, 21.

63. On diasporic activism in Germany, see Asoka Esuruoso, "A Historical Overview," in Esuruoso and Koepsell, *Arriving in the Future*, 18–21; Noaquia Callahan, "A Rare Colored Bird: Mary Church Terrell, Die Fortschritte der farbigen Frauen, and the International Council of Women's Congress in Berlin, Germany 1904," *German Historical Institute Bulletin Supplement* 13 (2017): 93–110.

64. ISD, "Protokoll des. 1. Treffens der Afro & Schwarzen Deutschen in Düsseldorf am Rhein, May 24, 1987," folder ISD Ko-Treffen, p. 2, Cheatom Collection.

65. ISD, "Einige Punkte zur Vorstellung der Initiative."

66. ISD-Stuttgart, "ISD Initiative Schwarze Deutsche Stuttgart wir über uns," 1991, n.p., Cheatom Collection.

67. ISD, "Einige Punkte zur Vorstellung der Initiative."

68. Black Unity Committee, "Black Unity Committee (BUC)," n.d., box 22, n.p., Ayim Archive; "The Black Unity Committee (BUC) in Berlin, Germany," *Isivivane* no. 3 (1991), box 19, p. 43, Ayim Archive.

69. "The Black Unity Community (BUC) responds to the heatwave of racism in Germany," *Isivivane* no. 4 (1991): 22.

70. Black Unity Committee, untitled document, n.d., box 22, n.p., Ayim Archive; Black Unity Committee, ed. *Dokumentation: Rassistische Überfälle in Berlin und Umgebung- Im Jahr der Deutschen-Deutschen Vereinigung* (January–September 1990), box 22, n.p., Ayim Archive.

71. See Fountainhead Dance Theatre, "Black Cultural Festival," March 3–23, 1986, box 6, pp. 1–22, Ayim Archive; Fountainhead Dance Theatre, "Black International Cinema," February 8–10 and 12–13, 1987, box 6, pp. 1–24, Ayim Archive.

72. "Community-Tagung: Selbstorganisation Schwarzer Menschen in Deutschland," October 18–20, 2002, n.p., Cheatom Collection.

73. Kevina King, "Black, People of Color and Migrant Lives Should Matter: Racial Profiling, Police Brutality and Whiteness in Germany," in Florvil and Plumly, *Rethinking Black German Studies,* 169–96; *Kampagne für Opfer rassistischer Polizeigewalt* (KOP), ed., *Alltäglicher Ausnahmezustand: Institutioneller Rassismus in deutschen Strafverfolgungsbehörden* (Münster: edition assemblage, 2016); "Germany March 15: Day of Action Against the Normalization of Racist Police Violence," *Decolonial International Network,* April 4, 2018, https://din.today/newsletter/2018_04/germany-march-15-day-of-action-against-the-normalization-of-racist-police-violence/. On German state violence, see Bruce-Jones, *Race in the Shadow of the Law.*

74. See, for example, ISD-Rhine/Main, "ISD Initiative Schwarze Deutsche wir über uns," 5; ISD-München, "ISD Initiative Schwarze Deutsche-München wir über uns," 1989, p. 5, Cheatom Collection; ISD-Karlsruhe, "ISD Initiative Schwarze Deutsche wir über uns," n.p., Cheatom Collection; Ayim and Oguntoye, "Preface to the English Edition," in Opitz, Oguntoye, and Schultz, *Showing Our Colors,* xvi.

75. ISD, "Koordinationstreffen der Initiativen Schwarze Deutsche in Frankfurt/Main 26./27.03.1988," folder ISD Ko-Treffen, n.p., Cheatom Collection; Colours, "Events '92," n.p., Cheatom Collection. I have been unable to locate additional information on Colours. Pamoja was created in 1996 in Vienna, Austria. See also Araba Evelyn Johnson-Arthur, " 'Es ist Zeit, der Geschichte selbst eine Gesalt zu geben' . . . Strategien der Entkolonisierung und Entmachtigung im Kontext der modernen afrikanischen Diaspora in Österreich," in *Re/visionen Postkoloniale Perspektiven von People of Color aus Rassismus, Kulturpolitik und Wiederstand in Deutschland,* eds. Kien Nghi Ha, Nicola Lauré al-Samarai, and Sheila Mysorekar (Münster: Unrast, 2007), 423–42.

76. "African American–Black German: Cultural Community X Change 1997," n.p., Cheatom Collection; "African American–Black German: Cultural Community Youth X Change 1999," n.p., Cheatom Collection. See also Hügel-Marshall, "Die Situation von Afrodeutschen nach dem zweiten Weltkrieg," 83.

77. A People of African Descent (PAD) Week occurred in November 2019, in which Each One Teach One e.V. in Berlin organized a three-day Black congress with more than thirty Black diasporic groups based in Germany. See Femi Awonyi, "Congress Pushes for more recognition of Black People in Germany," *African Courier,* November 30, 2019, https://www.theafricancourier.de/europe/congress-pushes-for-more-recognition-of-black-people-in-germany/.

78. European Network for People of African Descent, "#Be The Change Network," April 8, 2018, http://bethechangenetwork.tumblr.com/quickabout; Keisha Fredua-Mensah and Jamie Schearer, "Initiative Black People in Germany (ISD): Enriching the Public Discourse by highlighting Colonial Continuities," *Migrant Tales,* December

12, 2016, http://www.migranttales.net/initiative-black-people-in-germany-isd -enriching-the-public-discourse-by-highlighting-colonial-continuities/; Initiative Schwarze Menschen in Deutschland e.V., "Parallel Report to the UN Committee on the Elimination of Racial Discrimination on 19th-22nd Report submitted by the Federal Republic of Germany Under Article 9 of the International Convention on the Elimination of All Forms of Racial Discrimination," March 2015, pp. 1–21; "Statement to the media by the United Nations' Working Group of Experts on People of African Descent, on the conclusion of its official visit to Germany, 20–27 February 2017," https://www.ohchr.org/EN/NewsEvents/Pages/DisplayNews .aspx?NewsID=21233&LangID=E.

79. Wiedenroth-Coulibaly, "Die multiplen Anfänge der ISD," in Bergold-Caldwell et al., *Spiegel Blicke*, 29.

80. ISD-Berlin, "In eigener Sache," *Onkel Tom's Faust* no. 1 (1988): 3, the author's private collection.

81. On this protest and Black athletes, see Amy Bass, *Not the Triumph but the Struggle: The 1968 Olympics and the Making of the Black Athlete* (Minneapolis: University of Minnesota Press, 2002). By 1853, Stowe's novel was the most popular American fiction in Germany. See Heike Paul, "Mobility between Boston and Berlin: How Germans Have Read and Reread Narratives of American Slavery," in *Cultural Mobility*, ed. Stephen Greenblatt (New York: Cambridge University Press, 2009), 131.

82. ISD-Berlin, "In eigener Sache," 3.

83. Ibid., 3.

84. Jeannine Kantara, "Die Geschichte der *afro look*," in Diallo and Zeller, *Black Berlin*, 160; Leroy Hopkins, "Speak, so I might see you! Afro-German Literature," *World Literature Today* 69, no. 3 (1995): 536.

85. On *afro look*, see Kantara, "Die Geschichte der *afro look*," in Diallo and Zeller, *Black Berlin*, 160–62; Francine Jobatey, "*Afro Look*: Die Geschichte einer Zeitschrift von Schwarzen Deutschen" (PhD diss., University of Massachusetts-Amherst, 2000); Hopkins, "Speak, so I might see you!"; Anne Adams, "afro look: magazine of blacks in Germany; An Africanist Analysis," in *Africa, Europe and (Post)Colonialism: Racism, Migration and Diaspora in African Literatures*, eds. Susan Arndt and Marek Spitezok von Brisinski (Bayreuth: Bayreuth University, 2006), 257–78.

86. Jobatey, "*Afro look*," 24, 25.

87. ISD-Berlin, "Impressum," 2.

88. ISD, *afro look* no. 8 (1992/1993): 2, the author's private collection.

89. Personal conversation with Ricky Reiser, fall 2011, Berlin, Germany.

90. Kantara, "Die Geschichte der *afro look*," in Diallo and Zeller, *Black Berlin*, 162. On *Blite*, see Oliver Seifert, "Bericht über das Jugendprojekt 'Blite'—eine Quartalzeitschrift von Schwarzen Jugendlichen," in AntiDiskrimierungsBüro and cyberNomads, *The BlackBook*, 163–66; Hopkins, "Race, Nationality and Culture," in Hopkins, *Who Is a German?*, 21. See also *Strangers*, box 2, Ayim Archive.

91. ISD, "Protokoll vom 3. Koordinationstreffen in München vom September 1–2, 1990," folder ISD Ko-Treffen, p. 2, Cheatom Collection.

92. ISD-Rhine/Main, "Schwarzes Bewußtsein-Schwarze Politik," program, November 12–14, 1993, n.p., Cheatom Collection.

93. ISD-Rhine/Main, "Schwarzes Bewußtsein-Schwarze Politik."

94. "Sonstiges—Manwachengruppe für Südafrika—gegen Apartheid," *Onkel Tom's Faust* no. 1 (1988): 31. See also Heike Hartmann and Susann Lewerenz, "Campaigning against Apartheid in East and West Germany," *Radical History Review* 119 (2014): 191–204.

95. ISD-Berlin, "Südafrika-Tag: Der ISD," folder Literatur e.V. Aktuelles, n.p., Ayim Papers.

96. ISD-Berlin, "Südafrika-Tag."

97. "Einladung zur Lesung Schwarzer-deutscher Literatur," January 4, 1992, n.p, Cheatom Collection.

98. Time to Time consisted of Martin Recke, Udo Weller, and Stefan Grino. Kalpana Vora, "Blacks Outraged by Song," *The European,* 1991, The Private Collection of Ricky Reiser (hereafter cited as Reiser Papers); Sandra Ebert, "10 Kleine Negerlein: Dieser Schlager ist dumm und rassistisch," *Express,* May 11, 1991, Reiser Papers; "Null & Nichtig: Kein Negerlein" *Rheinische Post,* May 21, 1991, Reiser Papers.

99. "Der Musikmarkt Top 15: Deutsche Bestseller," May 1, 1991, Reiser Papers.

100. Austen P. Brandt letter to Staatsanwaltschaft in Duisburg, May 25, 1991, pp. 1–4, Reiser Papers.

101. Brandt letter to Staatsanwaltschaft, 4.

102. ISD-Duisburg letter to Herr Helmut Fest EMI Electrola, May 8, 1991, n.p., Reiser Papers.

103. Thorsten Keller, "Disco-Hit vom Markt genommen: 'Zehn kleine Negerlein' als rassistisch kritisiert," *Kölner Stadt-Anzeiger,* May 16, 1991, Reiser Papers.

104. See SprechenInnenrat der I.S.D., "Erklärung des SprecherInnenrates der Initiative Schwarze Deutsche & Schwarze in Deutschland I.S.D.—BRD zu den rassistischen Ausschreitungen gegenüber Flüchtlingen," September 6, 1992, n.p., Cheatom Collection; "Kurzansprache auf der Demo in Bonn am 14.11.92," folder ISD Ko-Treffen, Cheatom Collection.

105. Emde, "I too am German," in Hopkins, *Who Is a German?*, 41.

106. See Dialika Neufeld, "It's Time to Remove Racism from Children's Books," *Spiegel Online,* January 23, 2013, http://www.spiegel.de/international/germany/why -racism-should-be-removed-from-books-for-children-a-879628.html.

107. Oguntoye, "The Black German Movement and the Womens Movement," 10.

108. May Ayim, "Racism and Resistance in United Germany," unpublished talk, Carleton College, May 10, 1994, box 10, p. 4, Ayim Archive.

CHAPTER 3. ADEFRA, *AFREKETE,* AND BLACK GERMAN WOMEN'S KINSHIP

1. ADEFRA also went through a few name changes. It is now referred to as *Schwarze Frauen in Deutschland e.V.* (Black Women in Germany). Now there are two ADEFRA subgroups: Generation ADEFRA e.V.-Schwarze Frauen in Deutschland and ADEFRA

Roots, both based in Berlin. Generation ADEFRA consists of Maisha-Maureen Auma, Deborah Moses-Sanks, Ekpenyong Ani, Katja Kinder, and Peggy Piesche. ADEFRA Roots includes Ria Cheatom, Judy Gummich, and Jasmin Eding.

2. See El-Tayeb, "Blackness and Its (Queer) Discontents," in Lennox, *Remapping Black Germany*; Brittney Cooper, *Eloquent Rage: A Black Feminist Discovers Her Superpower* (New York: St. Martin's Press, 2018), 22. Cooper argues that Black feminism is fundamentally queer.

3. El-Tayeb, *European Others*. On queer communities of color, see E. Patrick Johnson and Mae G. Henderson, eds., *Black Queer Studies: A Critical Anthology* (Durham, N.C.: Duke University Press, 2005); Fatima El-Tayeb, "'Gays who cannot properly be gay': Queer Muslims in the Neoliberal European City," *European Journal of Women's Studies* 19, no. 1 (2012): 79–95.

4. El-Tayeb, *European Others*, xiii; El-Tayeb, "Blackness and Its (Queer) Discontents," in Lennox, *Remapping Black Germany*, 253.

5. El-Tayeb, "Blackness and Its (Queer) Discontents," in Lennox, *Remapping Black Germany*, 253–54. From the second issue onward, it was entitled *Afrekete: Magazine by Afro-German and Black Women* (*Afrekete: Zeitung von afro-deutschen und schwarzen Frauen*).

6. Keeanga-Yamahtta Taylor, *How We Get Free: Black Feminism and the Combahee River Collective* (Chicago: Haymarket Books, 2017); Beverly Bryan, Stella Dadzie, and Suzanne Scafe, *The Heart of the Race: Black Women's Lives in Britain* (London: Virago, 2018).

7. Natalie Thomlinson, "'Second-Wave' Black Feminist Periodicals in Britain," *Women: A Cultural Review* 27, no. 4 (2016): 432–45; Julie Enszer, "'Fighting to create and maintain our own Black women's culture': *Conditions*, 1977–1990," *American Periodicals: A Journal of History of Criticism* 25, no. 2 (2015): 160–76. See also *Aché* 2, no. 1 (1990): 1–32.

8. Édouard Glissant, trans. Michael Dash, *Caribbean Discourse: Selected Essays* (Charlottesville: University of Virginia Press, 1989), 4.

9. ADEFRA-München, untitled brochure, April 1993, n.p., Cheatom Collection.

10. ADEFRA, *20 Jahre Schwarze Frauenbewegung in Deutschland/20 Years of Black Women's Activism in Germany* (Berlin: Museum Europäischer Kulturen, 2006), 7.

11. See Eva von Pirch, "Black Magic Women: 1. Bundestreffen Afro-deutscher Frauen in Januar 1988," *Afrekete: Zeitung für afro-deutsche und schwarze Frauen (. . . . über was uns angeht)* 1, no. 1 (1988): 7, ZBF&GQS.

12. Ferree, *Varieties of Feminism*, 53–83; Robyn Spencer, "Engendering the Black Freedom Struggle: Revolutionary Black Womanhood and the Black Panther Party in the Bay Area, California," *Journal of Women's History* 20, no. 1 (2008): 100–102.

13. ADEFRA, *20 Jahre Schwarze Frauenbewegung in Deutschland*, 7; von Pirch, "Black Magic Woman," 7–8; Hügel-Marshall, "ADEFRA—Die Anfänge," in Kraft, *Kinder der Befreiung*, 324.

14. Denise Bergold-Caldwell, "Black to the Future: Ein Gespräch zwischen Katharina Oguntoye, Jasmin Eding und Abenaa Adomako," in Bergold-Caldwell et al., *Spiegel Blicke*, 34.

15. Piesche, "Rückblenden und Vorschauen," 19–20; ADEFRA, *20 Jahre,* 7; Bergold-Caldwell, "Black to the Future," in Bergold-Caldwell et al., *Spiegel Blicke,* 34–35.

16. Bergold-Caldwell, "Black to the Future," in Bergold-Caldwell et al., *Spiegel Blicke,* 35. See also Ekpenyong Ani, "Die Frau, die Mut zeigt—der Verein ADEFRA Schwarze Deutsche Frauen/Schwarze Frauen in Deutschand," in AntiDiskriminierungsBüro and cyberNomads, *The BlackBook,* 145; Lauré al-Samarai, " 'Es ist noch immer ein Aufbruch, aber mit neuer Startposition,' " in Ha, Lauré al-Samarai, and Mysorekar, *Re/visionen,* 348.

17. See "African American—Black German: Cultural Community X Change 1997"; Hügel-Marshall, "ADEFRA—Die Anfänge," in Kraft, *Kinder der Befreiung,* 325.

18. ISD (Mike Reichel), "Verteilung der Spende des Weltkirchenrates," December 8, 1988, folder ISD-Ko-Treffen, n.p., Cheatom Collection. See also Hügel-Marshall, "ADEFRA—Die Anfänge," in Kraft, *Kinder der Befreiung,* 323.

19. Ferree, *Varieties of Feminism,* 53–83.

20. Bryan, Dadzie, and Scafe, *The Heart of the Race,* 148; Thomlinson, *Race, Ethnicity and the Women's Movement,* 64. See also Heidi Safia Mirza, *Black British Feminism: A Reader* (London: Routledge, 1997).

21. On Black British feminism and Olive Morris, see Fisher, "Transnational Black Diaspora Feminisms," 65–91; Bryan, Dadzie, and Scafe, *The Heart of the Race;* Tanisha Ford, "We Were the People of Soul," in Ford, *Liberated Threads: Black Women, Style, and The Global Politics of Soul* (Chapel Hill: University of North Carolina Press, 2015), 123–57; "OWAAD," in *Sisterhood and After: An Oral History of the Women's Liberation Movement,* The British Library, http://www.bl.uk/learning/histcitizen/sisterhood/clips/race-place-and-nation/civil-rights/143178.html.

22. "Barbara Smith," in Taylor, *How We Get Free,* 50–51, 55.

23. Taylor, "Introduction," in Taylor, *How We Get Free,* 7.

24. "The Combahee River Collective Statement," in Taylor, *How We Get Free,* 21.

25. In Germany, Africans are classed either as those with means to travel to Europe or refugees and/or asylum seekers who are working-class, with some exceptions. I think their Blackness rather than their multicultural identity reinscribes class and ethnic hierarchies. This causes them to differ from some biracial Afro-Germans.

26. Lutz Leisering, "Germany: Reform from Within," in *International Social Policy: Welfare Regimes in the Developed World,* eds. Pete Alcock and Gary Craig (New York: Palgrave, 2001), 161–82.

27. ADEFRA-München, untitled brochure.

28. ADEFRA, *20 Jahre,* 3; Ekpenyong Ani, Jasmin Eding, Maisha M. Eggers, Katja Kinder, and Peggy Piesche, "Schwarze Lesben im geteilten Feminismus," in Dennert, Leidinger, and Rauchut, *In Bewegung bleiben,* 298–99.

29. Ekpenyong Ani quoted in Lauré al-Samarai, "Es ist noch immer ein Aufbruch" in Ha, Lauré al-Samarai, and Mysorekar, *Re/visionen,* 353.

30. ADEFRA, *20 Jahre,* 5.

31. Ibid., 3.

32. Lauré al-Samarai, "Es ist noch immer ein Aufbruch," in Ha, Lauré al-Samarai, and Mysorekar, Re/visionen, 354.

33. Ani et al., "Schwarze Lesben im geteilten Feminismus," in Dennert, Leidinger, and Rauchut, In Bewegung bleiben, 298–99.

34. See Leila Rupp, "Sexual Fluidity 'Before Sex,' " Signs 37, no. 4 (2012): 849–56. See also ADEFRA, e.V., "Sister's Pride," Berlin, June 1–5, 2001, folder ADEFRA ISD ect., n.p., Cheatom Collection. The misspelling of etcetera was in the original. For a period, ADEFRA also included transwomen with its title: ADEFRA—Black Women/Transwomen in Germany (ADEFRA—Schwarze Frauen/Transfrauen in Deutschland).

35. Cathy Cohen, "Punks, Bulldaggers, and Welfare Queens," in Johnson and Henderson, Black Queer Studies, 23.

36. ADEFRA-München, untitled brochure.

37. Ani et al., "Schwarze Lesben im geteilten Feminismus," in Dennert, Leidinger, and Rauchut, In Bewegung bleiben, 299.

38. Lauré al-Samarai, "Es ist noch immer ein Aufbruch," in Ha, Lauré al-Samarai, and Mysorekar, Re/visionen, 348.

39. Katja Kinder quoted in Piesche, "Rückblenden und Vorschauen," in Piesche, Euer Schweigen schützt Euch nicht, 20.

40. Oguntoye quoted in Piesche, "Rückblenden und Vorschauen," in Piesche, Euer Schweigen schützt Euch nicht, 20; Lauré al-Samarai, "Es ist noch immer ein Aufbruch," in Ha, Lauré al-Samarai, and Mysorekar, Re/visionen, 353.

41. Von Pirch, "Black Magic Women," 7.

42. Ibid., 8.

43. El-Tayeb, "Blackness and Its (Queer) Discontents," in Lennox, Remapping Black Germany, 253; El-Tayeb, European Others, 70–80; Piesche, "Rückblenden und Vorschauen," in Piesche, Euer Schweigen schützt Euch nicht, 22. See also Ahmed, Queer Phenomenology, 107.

44. ADEFRA, 20 Jahre, 7.

45. Hügel-Marshall, "ADEFRA—Die Anfänge," in Kraft, Kinder der Befreiung, 325, 327; ADEFRA and IISF, e.V. in cooperation with FrauenAnstiftung, "Rassismus: Geschichte und Hintergründe, Auswirkung und Strategien," program, February 19–21, 1993, pp. 1–10, Cheatom Collection; ADEFRA-München, "Back to Roots: Eine fantastische Reise durch tausendundein Haar," program, July 23–25, 1994, folder ISD Liga, Ayim Papers. In 1994 they also created a cultural center called Zami. See ADEFRA-München, "Zami: Zentrum für Schwarze Deutsche/Schwarze in Deutschland (Kontakt- und Informationszentrum) Konzeptionsentwurf," May 1994, pp. 1–10, Cheatom Collection.

46. ADEFRA, 20 Jahre, 8. In the late 1980s, there was also an Afro-German gay men's group entitled, "The Hot Chocolates," that Carl Camurça organized in his Berlin apartment. But it has been difficult to obtain additional information about the group.

47. ADEFRA brochure, n.d., folder ADEFRA ISD ect., n.p.; "Newsletter der Initiative Schwarze Menschen in Deutschland- ISD-Bund e.V.," January 26, 2001, folder ADEFRA ISD ect., n.p., Cheatom Collection.

48. Ria Cheatom, Jasmin Eding, Mary Powell, and Ulrike Gerhart, "Wage Dein Leben Verlasse Dein Haus!: ADEFRA München über sich und das 5. Afro-deutsche Frauenbundestreffen," *Kofra: Zeitschrift für Feminismus und Arbeit (Rassismus von Frauen)* 10 (1991): 21, Cheatom Collection. See also Eva von Pirch in ADEFRA, *20 Jahre,* 16; Ani, "Die Frau, die Mut zeigt," in AntiDiskriminierungsBüro and cyberNomads, *The BlackBook,* 146.

49. ADEFRA, *20 Jahre,* 8; Hügel-Marshall, "ADEFRA—Die Anfänge," in Kraft, *Kinder der Befreiung,* 325, 328.

50. ADEFRA e.V., "Sister's Pride."

51. On notions of Black German *Heimat* and kinship after 1989, see Vanessa Plumly, "BLACK-Red-Gold in 'der bunten Republik': Constructions and Performances of Heimat/en in Post-Wende Afro-/Black German Cultural Productions" (PhD diss., University of Cincinnati, 2015).

52. ADEFRA, *20 Jahre,* 5. See also "'Es ist noch immer ein Aufbruch, aber mit neuer Startposition," in Ha, Lauré al-Samarai, and Mysorekar, *Re/visionen,* 347–60.

53. ADEFRA, *20 Jahre,* 7.

54. Ibid., 3. A short biography of Ani was included in the 2008/2009 art exhibition and exhibition program. Bundeszentrale für politische Bildung and Initiative Schwarze Menschen in Deutschland, ed., *Homestory Deutschland. Schwarze Biografien in Geschichte und Gegenwart* (Berlin: bpb, 2009). See also "Es ist noch immer ein Aufbruch," in Ha, Lauré al-Samarai, and Mysorekar, *Re/visionen,* 347–60.

55. ADEFRA, *20 Jahre,* 2.

56. Auma quoted in Ibid.

57. Ibid., 8–9.

58. See Lorde, "The Master's Tools Will Never Dismantle the Master's House," in Lorde, *Sister Outsider,* 111. Lorde also detailed this point in *Zami,* the title of which comes from "a Carriacou name for women who work together as friends and lovers" (255). She continued to unpack this theme in many of her speeches and writings, including *The Black Unicorn* and poems such as "Outlines," "Woman," and "Love Poem."

59. Hügel-Marshall, "ADEFRA—Die Anfänge," in Kraft, *Kinder der Befreiung,* 327, 332–34; Pamela Ohene-Nyako, "Black Women's Transnational Activism and the World Council of Churches," *Open Cultural Studies* 3 (2019): 219–31.

60. ADEFRA in Cooperation mit FrauenAnstiftung und Kofra program, "Int. Schwarzer Frauen Treffen: 'Wage dein leben verlasse dein haus,'" November 1–4, 1990, pp. 1, 2, Cheatom Collection; Hügel-Marshall, "ADEFRA—Die Anfänge," in Kraft, *Kinder der Befreiung,* 326.

61. ADEFRA, "Int. Schwarzer Frauen Treffen," 3.

62. Cheatom, Eding, Powell, and Gerhart, "Wage Dein Leben Verlasse Dein Haus!," 21.

63. See "Ver-Einigung macht stark?: Frauen BRDDR Frauen Frauenkongreß," July 28–29, 1990, n.p., Cheatom Collection.

64. Cheatom, Eding, Powell, and Gerhart, "Wage Dein Leben Verlasse Dein Haus!," 22.

65. See ADEFRA-Hamburg in Kooperation mit der Frauen Anstiftung e.V, "Bundesweiter Kongreß: Schwarzer Frauen-Women of Color in Deutschland," September 2–4, 1994, pp. 1–4, Cheatom Collection; ADEFRA-Hamburg in Kooperation mit der Frauen Anstiftung e.V, "Programminhalte," Lauenburg, September 2–4, 1994, folder ISD Liga, n.p. Ayim Papers.

66. "3. Bundesweiter Kongreß von und für Schwarze/im Exil lebenden Frauen, Migrantinnen und Jüdinnen (SEFMIJ)," October 3–6, 1995, box 54, n.p., Ayim Archive.

67. See *LesbenStich* 10, no. 4 (1988), 25; *LesbenStich* 10, no. 1 (1989): 5, Spinnboden Lesbenarchiv und Bibliothek, Berlin, Germany (hereafter cited as Spinnboden).

68. Apparently, a seventh issue was produced, but not published. I have been unable to find it, and my emails to one of the editors remained unanswered.

69. Henry Louis Gates Jr., *The Signifying Monkey: A Theory of Afro-American Literary Criticism* (New York: Oxford University Press, 1988), 4–5. On the African origins of Afrekete, see Luis Nicolau Parés, "Transformations of the Sea and Thunder Voduns in the Gbe-Speaking Area and in the Bahian Jeje Candomblé," in *Africa and the Americas: Interconnections during the Slave Trade*, eds. J. C. Curto and R. Soulodre-La France (Trenton, N.J.: Africa World Press, 2005), 69–93.

70. See Lorde, *The Black Unicorn* and *Zami*.

71. Lorde, "An Open Letter to Mary Daly," in Lorde, *Sister Outsider,* 66–71.

72. Von Pirch in ADEFRA, *20 Jahre*, 16.

73. While I have been unable to find circulation figures for *Afrekete*, I suspect the numbers were in the low hundreds or fewer than a hundred.

74. Elke Jank and Eva von Pirch, "Einladung," *Afrekete* (. . . . über alles, was uns angeht) 1, no. 1 (1988): 1, ZBF&GQS.

75. Jank and von Pirch, "Einladung," 1.

76. Ibid., 2.

77. See José Esteban Muñoz, *Disidentifications: Queers of Color and The Performance of Politics* (Minneapolis: University of Minneapolis Press, 1999). Muñoz argued that disidentification was a strategy that minority subjects used to negotiate their positions in majority societies and that allowed them to work both within and against the dominant ideology.

78. Jank and von Pirch, "Vorwort," *Afrekete* (. . . . über alles, was uns angeht), 2.

79. "weiß, schwarz—oder sind es nur Farben?," *Afrekete* (*schwarze überlebens-Kunst*) 4, no. 2 (1989): 8, Cheatom Collection.

80. Ika Hügel, "Der kleine Unterschied bei den Päckchen, die wir ja schließlich alle zu tragen haben," *Afrekete* (*schwarze überlebens-Kunst*) 4, no. 2 (1989): 20.

81. Von Pirch, "Was habe ich mit Afrika zu tun," *Afrekete* (. . . . über alles, was uns angeht) 1, no. 1 (1988): 19.

82. Von Pirch, "Was habe ich mit Afrika zu tun," 19. See also Crawley, "Challenging Concepts of Cultural and National Homogeneity," 241–319. Crawley analyzed the same poem, though our analyses differ slightly given my discussion of emplacement.

83. Helga Emde quoted in Gülbahar Kültür, "So dumm sind die Deutschen," *Die Tageszeitung*, March 7, 1988, reprinted in *Afrekete (.... über alles, was uns angeht)* 1, no. 1 (1988): 6.

84. A few examples of these themes include: Helga Emde, "Liebeslied für die weiße Frau," *Afrekete (schwarze überlebens-Kunst)* 4, no. 2 (1989): 2, Cheatom Collection; "Mich ärgert das," *Afrekete (schwarzer Feminismus)* 2, no. 3 (1988): 17, ZBF&GQS; Magli (Schmid), untitled poem, *Afrekete (Born Free: WANTED!)* 5, no. 4 (1989): 7, ZBF&GQS. See also Ayim, "They're People Like Us," in Opitz, Oguntoye, and Schultz, *Showing Our Colors,* 137–38 and additional articles in the volume.

85. Von Pirch, "Was habe ich mit Afrika zu tun," 19–20.

86. See Slobodian, *Foreign Front;* Klimke, *The Other Alliance*.

87. Helga Emde quoted in "So dumm sind die Deutschen," 6.

88. Von Pirch, "Was habe ich mit Afrika zu tun," 20.

89. Ibid., 20.

90. Mary-Ann Powell, "Invisible Woman," *Afrekete (Kunst, Politik, USW)* 6, no. 2 (1990): 13, ZBF&GS. See also Veronica von Roon, "Identität," *Afrekete (Kunst, Politik, USW)* 6, no. 2 (1990): 13.

91. Powell, "Invisible Woman," 13.

92. Von Pirch, "Was habe ich mit Afrika zu tun?," 20.

93. Kültür, "So dumm sind die Deutschen," 6.

94. Sharon Marcus, *Between Women: Friendship, Desire, and Marriage in Victorian England* (Princeton, N.J.: Princeton University Press, 2007), 113.

95. Marcus, *Between Women,* 114.

96. Elke Jank, untitled poem, *Afrekete (.... über alles, was uns angeht)* 1, no. 1 (1988): 10. See also Tanya, untitled poem, *Afrekete (Kunst, Politik, USW)* 6, no. 2 (1990): 27.

97. Jank, untitled poem, 10.

98. Lorde, "The Use of the Erotic," Lorde, *Sister Outsider,* 54.

99. Jank, untitled poem, 10.

100. Ibid., 27. See also *Afrekete (schwarzer Feminismus)*, 44; *Afrekete (Kunst, Politik, USW)*, 40–41; *Afrekete (Born Free: WANTED!)*, 55–57.

101. *Afrekete (Kunst, Politik, USW)*, 41; ADEFRA, "Rundbrief Mai 91," 3.

102. "27.2.88 workshop im schulz," *Afrekete (.... über alles, was uns angeht)*, 14–16.

103. May Opitz, "Schwarz-weiss-Monolog," *Afrekete (schwarzer Feminismus)*, 26; Ayim, *Blues in schwarz weiß* (Berlin: Orlanda, 1995), 75.

104. *Weiß* as an adjective and color means "white," but *weiß* is also a form of the verb to know (*wissen*), and I know translates into *ich weiß*.

105. Ayim, "Schwarz-weiss-Monolog," 26.

106. Emde, "Unsichtbar," *Afrekete (schwarzer Feminismus)*, 36.

107. Haus Neuland Verein für Familienbildung, "Einladung zur ersten gemeinsamen Schreibwerkstatt Schwarzer und Weisser Frauen," June 3–5, 1988, pp. 1–4, Cheatom Collection.

108. Marion Kraft, "Erste Gemeinsame Schreibwerkstatt Schwarzer und Weisser Frauen," *Afrekete: (schwarzer Feminismus)* 2, no. 3 (1988): 18.

109. See Ricky Reiser, "Josephine Baker," *afro look* no. 8 (1992/1993): 8–9; Reiser, "Interview mit Spike Lee," *afro look* no. 9 (1993): 16–17, the author's private collection. See also Francine Jobatey, "Black German Literature," in *The Feminist Encyclopedia of German Literature*, eds. Friederike Eidler and Susanne Kord (Westport, Conn.: Greenwood Press, 1997), 53; Jobatey, "*Afro Look*," 130–58.

110. Evelyn Higginbotham, "African-American Women's History and the Metalanguage of Race," *Signs* 17, no. 2 (1992): 268. See also James Clifford, "Diasporas," *Cultural Anthropology* 9, no. 3 (1994): 302–38.

111. Jennifer Michaels, "Audre Lorde and Afro-German Women Writers," *German Studies Review* 29, no. 1 (2006): 35.

112. *Afrekete (schwarzer Feminismus)*, 3.

113. See Elke Jank, "Göttinnen, Symbole, Mythen, und Magie," *Afrekete (. . . . über alles, was uns angeht)*, 21–22; Jank, "Göttinnen, Symbole, Mythen, und Magie," *Afrekete (schwarzer Feminismus)*, 38–39; Jank, "Göttinnen, Symbole, Mythen, und Magie," *Afrekete (Born Free: WANTED!)*, 43–45; Jank, "Göttinnen, Symbole, Mythen, und Magie," *Afrekete (Kunst, Politik, USW)* 6, no. 2 (1990): 23–25; Jank, "Göttinnen, Symbole, Mythen, und Magie," *Afrekete (schwarze überlebens-Kunst)*, 31–32; Jank, "Göttinnen, Symbole, Mythen, und Magie," *Afrekete* 3, no. 1 (1989): 32–34, FFBIZ.

114. On Dulcie September, see "The Case of 'Dulcie September': The Truth Commission Files," http://www.withmaliceandforethought.com/pdf/dulcie_september.pdf.

115. Marion Kraft, "Für Dulcie September," *Afrekete (. . . . über alles, was uns angeht)* 1, no. 1 (1988): 3–4.

116. Kraft, "Für Dulcie September," 3.

117. Ibid., 4. On this poem, see Lorde, *The Collected Poems of Audre Lorde*, 409.

118. For some references to South Africa, see *Afrekete (schwarzer Feminismus)*, 4–5; *Afrekete (Born Free: WANTED!)*, 23, 32–33, 36, 40, 51–53; *Afrekete (schwarze überlebens-Kunst)*, 38.

119. *Afrekete (schwarzer Feminismus)*, 1.

120. See also Sakae, untitled poem, *Afrekete (schwarzer Feminismus)*, 37; *Afrekete (. . . . über alles, was uns angeht)*, 24; *Afrekete (schwarzer Feminismus)*, 14, 24, 40; Emde, "Frankfurt gegen Rassismus-Schwarze Deutsche-," *Afrekete (Kunst, Politik, USW)*, 3–5; *Afrekete (Kunst, Politik, USW)*, 7, 13, 15.

121. Marion Kraft, "Schwarze Vor-Mütter (I)," *Afrekete (schwarzer Feminismus)*, 41.

122. Ibid., 41–42.

123. Ibid., 41.

124. James Sidbury, *Becoming African in America: Race and Nation in the Early Black Atlantic* (New York: Oxford University Press, 2007), 6–7, 17–38.

125. Kültür, "So dumm sind die Deutschen," 6.

126. Lorde, *Sister Outsider*, 37.

CHAPTER 4. BLACK GERMAN WOMEN'S INTELLECTUAL ACTIVISM AND TRANSNATIONAL CROSSINGS

1. On Black womanhood, see Hazel Carby, *Reconstructing Womanhood: The Emergence of the Afro-American Woman Novelist* (New York: Oxford University Press, 1987); Cooper, *Beyond Respectability*.

2. See Sean Forner, *German Intellectuals and the Challenge of Democratic Renewal: Culture and Politics after 1945* (Cambridge, U.K.: Cambridge University Press, 2014); Michael Geyer, ed., *The Power of Intellectuals in Contemporary Germany* (Chicago: University of Chicago Press, 2001); Keith Bullivant, ed., *Beyond 1989: Re-reading Germany Literature since 1945* (Providence, R.I.: Berghahn, 1997).

3. On the Black public sphere, see Elsa Barkley Brown, "Negotiating and Transforming the Public Sphere: African American Political Life in the Transition from Slavery to Freedom," *Public Culture* 7 (1994): 102–46; V.P. Franklin, *Living Our Stories, Telling Our Truths: Autobiography and the Making of the African American Intellectual Tradition* (New York: Oxford University Press, 1996). See also Eggers, "Knowledges of (Un-) Belonging."

4. Carole Boyce Davies, "Introduction: Migratory Subjectivities: Black Women's Writing and the Re-negotiation of Identities," in Davies, *Black Women, Writing and Identity: Migrations of the Subject* (New York: Routledge, 1994), 4.

5. "Liste von TeilnehmerInnen," n.d., folder Farbe bekennen, n.p., Orlanda; Helga Lukoschat, "Nicht weiß und nicht schwarz," *Die Tageszeitung,* June 28, 1986, n.p., Orlanda. At the University of Regensburg, Ayim wrote a thesis entitled "Afro-Deutsche: Ihre Kultur- und Sozialgeschichte auf dem Hintergrund gesellschaftlicher Veränderungen." See also Ayim, *Grenzenlos und unverschämt* (Berlin: Orlanda, 1997), 169–70, 174; Ayim, trans. Anne Adams, *Blues in Black and White: A Collection of Essays, Poetry, and Conversations* (Trenton, N.J.: Africa World Press, 2003), 153–54.

6. Orlanda, "Rights Information," June 1986, folder Farbe bekennen, Fotos, Rezensionen, p. 1, Orlanda.

7. Tina M. Campt, "Afro-German Cultural Identity and the Politics of Positionality: Contests and Contexts in the Formation of a German Ethnic Identity," *New German Critique* 58 (1993): 117.

8. Barbara Kosta, *Recasting Autobiography: Women's Counterfictions in Contemporary German Literature and Film* (Ithaca, N.Y.: Cornell University Press, 1994), 5, 35; von Dirke, *"All Power to the Imagination!,"* 90. On women and autobiography, see Sidonie Smith and Julia Watson, eds., *De/Colonizing the Subject: The Politics of Gender in Women's Autobiography* (Minneapolis: University of Minnesota Press, 1992).

9. Kosta, *Recasting Autobiography,* 10.

10. Oguntoye, "Vorwort zur Neuauflage 2006," in Oguntoye, Opitz/Ayim, and Schultz, *Farbe bekennen,* 5.

11. Peggy Piesche, "Gegen das Schweigen: Diasporische Vernetzungen Schwarzer Frauen in transnationalen Begegnungen: Eine Würdigung," in Piesche, *Euer Schweigen schützt Euch nicht,* 11.

12. Ani quoted in Lauré al-Samarai, "Es ist noch immer ein Aufbruch" in Ha, Lauré al-Samarai, and Mysorekar, *Re/visionen,* 352.

13. Though they did not register the same impact as *Farbe bekennen,* other works about being Black in Germany preceded the volume. See Gisela Fremgen, ed.,. . . . *und wenn du dazu noch Schwarz bist: Berichte schwarzer Frauen in der Bundesrepublik* (Bremen: Edition Con, 1984); Guy (Nzingha) St. Louis, *Gedichte einer schönen Frau* (1983; Rastatt: Pabel-Moewig, 1988).

14. Opitz and Oguntoye, "Editors' Introduction," in Opitz, Oguntoye, and Schultz, *Showing our Colors,* xxii; Oguntoye and Ayim, "Vorwort der Herausgeberinnen," in Oguntoye, Opitz/Ayim, and Schultz, *Farbe bekennen,* 18.

15. On this idea, see Aija Poikane-Daumke, *African Diasporas: Afro-German Literature in the Context of the African American Experience* (Münster: LIT, 2006). For more on Afro-German literature, see also Stephanie Kron, *Fürchte Dich nicht, Bleichgesicht!: Perspektivenwechsel zur Literatur Afro-Deutscher Frauen* (Münster: Unrast, 1996).

16. Mysorekar, "'Pass the Word and Break the Silence,'" in Davies and Ogundipe-Leslie, *Moving Beyond Boundaries,* 83, 82. The bolded text was Mysorekar's emphasis. See also El-Tayeb, *European Others,* 62–76.

17. Oguntoye and Opitz, "Editors' Introduction," in Opitz, Oguntoye, and Schultz, *Showing our Colors,* xxii; Oguntoye and Opitz/Ayim, "Vorwort der Herausgeberinnen," in Oguntoye, Opitz/Ayim, and Schultz, *Farbe bekennen,* 17.

18. Raja Lubinetzki, "I never wanted to write," in Opitz, Oguntoye, and Schultz, *Showing our Colors,* 218; Katharina Birkenwald, "Ich wollte nie schreiben," in Oguntoye, Opitz/Ayim, and Schultz, *Farbe bekennen,* 225. Lubinetzki used an alias when the volume was initially published. See also El-Tayeb, *European Others,* 65.

19. Ibid., 218; ibid., 226.

20. On women in East Germany, see Donna Harsch, *Revenge of the Domestic: Women, the Family, and Communism in the German Democratic Republic* (Princeton, N.J.: Princeton University Press, 2006); Hagemann, Harsch, and Brühöfener, *Gendering Post-1945 German History.*

21. Piesche, "Making African Diasporic Pasts Possible," in Lennox, *Remapping Black Germany,* 226–42; Piesche "Irgendwo ist immer Afrika . . . Blackface' in DEFA-Filmen" and "Funktionalisierung und Repräsentation von multikuturellen Images in DDR-Comics," in AntiDiskriminierungsBüro and cyberNomads, *The BlackBook,* 286–91 and 292–97; Slobodian, *Comrades of Color.*

22. Lubinetzki, "I never wanted to write," in Opitz, Oguntoye, and Schultz, *Showing Our Colors,* 219; Birkenwald, "Ich wollte nie schreiben," in Oguntoye, Opitz/Ayim, and Schultz, *Farbe bekennen,* 226.

23. Ellen Wiedenroth, "What makes me so different in the eyes of others?," in Opitz, Oguntoye, and Schultz, *Showing Our Colors,* 170; Ellen Wiedenroth, "Was macht mich so anders in den Augen der anderen?," in Oguntoye, Opitz/Ayim, and Schultz, *Farbe bekennen,* 177.

24. Wiedenroth, "What makes me so different in the eyes of others?," in Opitz, Oguntoye, and Schultz, *Showing Our Colors,* 170; Wiedenroth, "Was macht mich so anders in den Augen der anderen?," in Oguntoye, Opitz/Ayim, and Schultz, *Farbe bekennen,* 177. Wiedenroth also published this piece in a magazine. See Ellen Wiedenroth, "Was

macht mich so anders in den Augen der anderen?" *Die Brücke: Rundbrief des Military Counseling Networks* 2 (1989): 6, Ayim Papers.

25. Poikane-Daumke, *African Diasporas*, 51, 52. She analyzed the same passage of Wiedenroth and included an interview with her.

26. Julia Berger, "I do the same things as others do," in Opitz, Oguntoye, and Schultz, *Showing Our Colors*, 198; Berger, "Ich mache dieselben Sachen wie die anderen," in Oguntoye, Opitz/Ayim, and Schultz, *Farbe bekennen*, 204. Berger did not specify where in Africa.

27. Astrid Berger, "Aren't you glad you can stay here?," in Opitz, Oguntoye, and Schultz, *Showing Our Colors*, 114; Berger, "Sind sie nicht froh, daß sie immer hier bleiben dürfen?," in Oguntoye, Opitz/Ayim, and Schultz, *Farbe bekennen*, 124.

28. Ibid., 118; ibid., 128. Berger died in the fall of 2011.

29. Angelika Eisenbrandt, "All of a sudden I knew what I wanted," in Opitz, Oguntoye, and Schultz, *Showing Our Colors*, 193; Eisenbrandt, "Auf einmal wußte ich, was ich wollte," in Oguntoye, Opitz/Ayim, and Schultz, *Farbe bekennen*, 199.

30. Ibid., 195; ibid., 201.

31. While these terms are terribly offensive, I am staying true to the words of Black Germans at the time of this publication and its later translation. Helga Emde, "An 'Occupation Baby' in Postwar Germany," in Opitz, Oguntoye, and Schultz, *Showing Our Colors*, 101, 102; Emde, "Als 'Besatzungskinder' im Nachkriegsdeutschland," in Oguntoye, Opitz/Ayim, and Schultz, *Farbe bekennen*, 111, 112. In the 1980s, the first two terms were changed to "Chocolate Kiss" ("Shokokuss") and "Foam Kiss" ("Schaumkuss"), and the last term was the name of a German chocolate company, Sarotti, based in Berlin. On this tradition, see Ciarlo, *Advertising Empire*; Hackenesch, *Chocolate and Blackness*.

32. Emde, "The Cry," in Opitz, Oguntoye, and Schultz, *Showing Our Colors*, 111; Emde, "Der Schrei," in Oguntoye, Opitz/Ayim, and Schultz, *Farbe bekennen*, 121. See also Emde, "The Revolutionary," in Opitz, Oguntoye, and Schultz, *Showing Our Colors*, 110; Emde, "Der Revolutionär," in Oguntoye, Opitz/Ayim, and Schultz, *Farbe bekennen*, 120.

33. Oguntoye, "Reflection," in Opitz, Oguntoye, and Schultz, *Showing Our Colors*, 215; Oguntoye, "Spiegel," in Oguntoye, Opitz/Ayim, and Schultz, *Farbe bekennen*, 214; Opitz, "The Break," in Opitz, Oguntoye, and Schultz, *Showing Our Colors*, 204–9; Opitz/Ayim, "Aufbruch," in Oguntoye, Opitz/Ayim, and Schultz, *Farbe bekennen*, 210–15.

34. See a few examples: "Lesung mit Autorinnen von Farbe bekennen: Afrodeutsche Frauen auf den Spuren ihrer Geschichte," flyer, October 3, 1986, Frankfurt-Oberwursel, folder Farbe bekennen, Fotos, Rezensionen 1986, Orlanda; "Lesung mit Audre Lorde und den Autorinnen von Farbe bekennen: Afro-deutsche Frauen auf den Spuren ihrer Geschichte neu erschienen im Orlanda Frauenverlag," June 10 and June 13–14, 1986, folder Farbe bekennen, Fotos, Rezensionen 1986; "Über Grenzen: Lesung mit Helga Emde, Ika Hügel, Marion Kraft und Raja Lubinetzki," March 5, 1988, Frauenkulturhaus-Bremen, folder Farbe bekennen, Fotos, Rezensionen 1986, Orlanda.

35. See Doris Hege, "Farbe bekennen," *Theorie Geschichte Politik;* "Schwarze Deutsche," *Emma,* 1986, pp. 52–53; "Rassismus," *päd extra,* October 1987; Nora Räthzel, *Das Argument,* July 1987, pp. 470–71; H.M., "Farbe bekennen," *Peripherie* Nr. 25/26, 1987, pp. 191–92; Elke Wiechmann-Kubitzek, "Farbe bekennen," *Ika,* August 1987; Dorothee Nolte, " 'Ich bin die einzige Schwarze in meiner Famillie': Fremd im eigenen Land: Afrodeutsche Frauen bekennen sich zu ihrer Geschichte," *Der Tagesspiegel* nr. 12, October 5, 1986, p. 4; Monica Weber-Nau, "Was ist aus den 'Toxis' geworden?: 'Besatzungskinder' in der Bundesrepublik," *Frankfurter Rundschau,* August 2, 1986; "Farbe bekennen," *Tarantel* nr. 18, January/Febuary 1987; Dietrich Haubold, "Die Afro-Deutschen: Eine Minderheit sucht ihre Identität," *Saarländischer RF,* July 1987, p. 12, Orlanda. Other magazines included *Sozialmagazin, Baseler Zeitung/Magazin, Peripherie, Wir Berlinnerinnen,* and *Das Argument.*

36. *Ein bißchen schwarz ein bißchen weiß, oder was es heißt ein deutscher "Neger" zu sein,* Christel Priemer (Germany: ARD, 1984), DVD; *Deutsche sind weiß, Neger können keine Deutschen sein!,* Christel Priemer (Germany: ARD, 1986), DVD; *Schwarze Frauen bekennen Farbe: Lebensgeschichten aus einem kalten Land,* Christel Priemer (Germany: ARD, 1992), DVD. See also Christel Priemer, *Schwarze Frauen bekennen Farbe,* ARD, June, 22, 1992; Monika Mengel, "Farbe bekennen-weiße Feministinnen und Rassismus, ein Bücherbericht," WDR III, September 20, 1993, folder Farbe bekennen, Fotos, Rezensionen 1986, pp. 1–20, Orlanda; Letter Familie Wondrejz to ARD Broadcast about the program "Schwarze Frauen bekennen Farbe," June 25, 1992, folder Farbe bekennen Korrespondenz 1986, Orlanda; "Deutsch sein heißt nicht immer weiß zu sein," folder Farbe bekennen Korrespondenz 1986.

37. Reviews appeared in the *Women's Review of Books, African Women, Ms.* magazine, *Wasafiri: Focus on Writing in Britain, Sojourner: The Women's Forum,* among others. Based in Toronto, Canada, *Tiger Lily* magazine for racialized, immigrant, and refugee women also reviewed the book. See, for example, Sabine Broeck, "On the edge of the margin," *Women's Review of Books* 10, no. 2 (1992): 7–8; Nana Ama Amamoo, "Showing our Colors," *African Women* (1993): 52–53; Jogamaya Bayer, "Showing our Colors," *Wasafiri: Focus on Writing in Britain* 12 (1993): 67–68.

38. Gail Lewis, "Preface to the UK Edition," in *Showing Our Colours: Afro-German Women Speak Out,* eds., Katherina Oguntoye, May Opitz/Ayim, and Dagmar Schultz (London: Open Press, 1992), vii–x. Unfortunately, I do not have evidence of its reception in the UK.

39. Leroy Hopkins, "Writing Diasporic Identity: Afro-German Literature Since 1985," in Mazón and Steingröver, *Not So Plain as Black and White,* 185. Fischer, a Frankfurt press, also published the volume in 1992, placing it in its women in society series.

40. See Emde, "Der Tanz," *Beiträge zur feministischen Theorie und Praxis* 23 (1988): 148; "Geteilter Feminismus: Rassismus, Antisemitismus, Fremdenhaß," *Beiträge zur feministischen Theorie und Praxis,* 13, no. 27 (1990): 5–160.

41. Gabriela Mönnig, ed., *Schwarz Afrika der Frauen* (München: Frauenoffensive, 1989), 255–66, 267–79.

42. For citations of these works, see footnote 19 and footnote 9 in chapter 2.

43. See footnote 21 in the book's introduction for a full citation of Oguntoye's book.

44. May Ayim, "Erster Zwischenarbeit für die Dissertation zum Thema: Ethnozentrismus und Rassismus in Therapiebereichen," June 1992, folder Ayim Nachtgesang 1997, n.p., Orlanda. At this time, she began publishing and performing under the name Ayim.

45. Silke Mertins, "Blues in Black and White: May Ayim (1960–1996)—A Biographical Essay," in Ayim, *Blues in Black and White,* 144. See also Maggie MacCarroll, "May Ayim: A Woman in the Margin of German Society" (MA thesis, Florida State University, 2005), 1–16, 26–59; *Hoffnung im Herz Mündliche Poesie,* directed by Maria Binder (New York: Third World Newsreel, 1997), DVD; *Blues Schwarzweiss: Vier schwarze deutsche Leben,* directed by John A. Kantara (Berlin, 1998), Videocassette.

46. Mertins, "Blues in Black and White," in Ayim, *Blues in Black and White,* 144.

47. Ibid., 142–44; May Opitz, "The Break," in Opitz, Oguntoye, and Schultz, *Showing Our Colors,* 204, 207.

48. Mertins, "Blues in Black and White," 144–45.

49. Chantal-Fleur Sandjon, "Der Raum zwischen gestern and morgen: May Ayim," in Diallo and Zeller, *Black Berlin,* 241–47. See also Kelly, *Sisters and Souls.*

50. Dr. Annette Wierschke, "Interview with May Ayim Opitz (Berlin)," July 2, 1995, box 24d, p. 9, Ayim Archive.

51. "Einladung zur Mitgliederversammlung," March 8, 1996, folder ISD Liga, Ayim Papers.

52. Antirassistischen Initiative, "Aktionstage gegen Rassismus, Sexismus und Faschismus Veranstaltungshinweise," April 24–May 8, 1988, box 6, n.p.; "Selbstdarstellung der Antirassistischen Initiative e.V.," n.d., box 6, n.p., Ayim Archive.

53. May Ayim and Nivedita Prasad, eds., *Dokumentation Wege zu Bündnissen* (Berlin: AStA, 1992).

54. Die Grünen Bündnis 90, "Die andere Republik," October 13–14, 1990, Berlin, box 22, Ayim Archive.

55. See, for example, Tsisti Dangarembga, "Informal Newsletter of the Black Women's Informal Information and Support Network," n.d., box 10, n.p., Ayim Archive. Sparks is an artist. Okpako is a director and writer and well-known for her films *The Education of Auma Obama* (*Der Geschichte der Auma Obama,* 2011) and *Dirt for Dinner* (*Dreckfesser,* 2000). Obama, who is Barack's half-sister, studied German and obtained a PhD from the University of Bayreuth in 1996.

56. Wierschke, "Interview with May," 9.

57. Literatur Frauen e.V., box 20, Ayim Archive. See also Verein zur Förderung der Frauenliteratur und -Forschung Berlin e.V., "Antrag," Berlin, n.d. folder Literatur e.V. Aktuelles, pp. 15–16, Ayim Papers; Dagmar Schultz and Hildegard Günther, "Tagesordnung der Gründungsversammlung des Vereins zur Förderung der Frauenliteratur und- Forschung Berlin e.V.," Berlin, folder Literatur e.V. Aktuelles, n.p., Ayim Papers;

Hildegard Günther letter to May Opitz, September 15, 1988, Berlin, folder Literatur e.V. Aktuelles, n.p., Ayim Papers.

58. Frauen der Welt, "Project: 'Afrika-Frauen-Wochen'," February 5–March 20, 1988, box 6, p. 3, Ayim Archive.

59. "Schweigen ist schuld: Deutschland ist eine bunte Sprache," October 10, 1993, n.p., Ayim Archive.

60. Literatur Frauen, "Zwischen den Zeiten, zwischen den Welten," flyer, January 12, 1993, box 24, Ayim Archive; Ayim, "Das Jahr 1990: Heimat und Einheit aus afro-deutscher Perspektive," in *Entfernte Verbindungen: Rassismus, Antisemitsmus, Klassenunterdrückung*, eds. Ika Hügel, Chris Lange, May Ayim, Ilona Bubeck, Gülsen Aktas, and Dagmar Schultz (Berlin: Orlanda, 1993), 206–22. It was published in English as "1990: Home/land and Unity from an Afro-German Perspective," in Ayim, *Blues in Black and White*, 45–59.

61. Ayim, "1990," in Ayim, *Blues in Black and White*, 45, 46.

62. Institut Français, "Lesung: Maryse Condé," February 24, 1994, box 24a, n.p., Ayim Archive; Ayim, "Maryse Condé über ihr Leben-eine eigene Vorstellung," *Umbrüche* 10 (1994), box 10, pp. 60–63, Ayim Archive.

63. Ayim read Frantz Fanon's *Black Skin, White Masks;* Toni Morrison's *The Bluest Eye;* Jean Paul Sartre's *Reflexions sur la question juive;* Cherríe Moraga and Gloria Anzaldúa's *This Bridge Called My Back,* and others. While conducting research, I stumbled upon one of Ayim's card catalogs. In it, she took notes from readings and referenced books and poems. On one index card, she even critiqued Fanon by asking: "Where is the black woman?" ("Wo bleibt die schwarze Frau?"). See May Ayim, brown wooden box of index cards, card catalog, Ayim Papers.

64. Ayim discussed Hegel in Opitz, Oguntoye, and Schultz, *Showing Our Colors*, 25–26; Oguntoye, Opitz/Ayim, and Schultz, *Farbe bekennen*, 42–43. See also Wright, *Becoming Black*, 8–16, 27–64. Hegel never traveled to Africa and supported European imperialism and the Atlantic slave trade.

65. See Marion Kraft, *Kurt Tucholsky und seine publizistischen Arbeiten aus der Zeit der Weimarer Republik* (Frankfurt am Main: University of Frankfurt, 1976); St. Louis, *Gedichte einer schönen Frau;* Raja Lubinetzki, *Magie: Gedichte und Grafik* (Berlin: Künstlerbuch, 1985).

66. Ayim, *Blues in schwarz weiss*.

67. Maryse Condé, "Grußwort," in Ayim, *Blues in schwarz weiss,* 7.

68. These visual symbols represent aphorisms, and the Akan of Ghana and the Gyaman of Cote d'Ivoire in West Africa use them. Ayim discussed this lineage in *Blues in black white*. Ayim used this book: Haus Der Kulturen Der Welt, *Adinkra: Symbolic language of the Ashanti/Adinkra: Symbolsprache der Ashanti* (Berlin: Movimento Drück, 1993), Ayim Papers. See also Karin Schestokat, "May Ayim: Texte und Themen," in *Literatur und Identität: deutsch-deutsche Befindlichkeiten und die multikulturelle Gesellschaft,* ed. Ursula E. Beitter (Frankfurt am Main: Peter Lang, 2000), 219–21; Karein Goertz, "Showing

Her Colors: An Afro-German Writes the Blues in Black and White," *Callaloo* 26, no. 2 (2003): 30.

69. See Barbara von Korff Schmissing, "Blues in schwarz-weiß," *Der ev. Buchberater,* December 1995, p. 364; Schnüss, "Poesie Schwarz-Weiss: Lustvoll gereimt," *Bonner Stadtmagazin,* September 1995, p. 33; Gerlinde Holland, "Blues in schwarz-weiß," *Stadt Revue,* November 1996, p. 141. See also folder May Ayim *Blues in schwarz weiss* 1995, Orlanda; J. M. Evans letter to May Opitz, July 29, 1994, Ayim Papers. Her brief biography would be included in the 1995 publication.

70. May Opitz "Afro-German," in Dagmar Schultz Letter to Audre Lorde, March 23, 1986, box 5, n.p., Lorde Papers. The unpublished poem was written in English. Dagmar Schultz granted me permission to cite this poem.

71. Sim da Vida, "Negras USAM Poesia Para Combater Racismo," October 1993, Rio de Janiero, box 24a, n.p., Ayim Archive.

72. Ayim, "afro-deutsch I" and "afro-deutsch II" in Ayim, *Blues in schwarz weiss,* 18–19, 25. In *Becoming Black* Wright argued that "In 'Afro-German I' and 'Afro-German II,' Ayim uses a strategy also located in Du Bois [*The Souls of Black Folk*] and Aimé Césaire [*Notebook of a Return to My Native Land*]: ventriloquism. Yet she uses it to different ends, to reveal the illogical spatial and temporal assumptions that emerge from those subjects who are unable to comprehend, much less speak, the material, performed truth of diasporic identities that do not so easily align with monologic definitions of race and nation" (197).

73. Ayim, "afro-deutsch I," 18.

74. Ibid. Wright and others have also analyzed this poem. See Wright, *Becoming Black,* 192–94; Wright, "Others-from-within from Without," 299–301; Schestokat, "May Ayim," 221–22. My discussion of "Afro-German I" dialogues with these scholars' analyses. But Wright assumed the German interlocutor was a man rather than a woman, and Schestokat engaged with Homi Bhabha's idea of hybridity and Molefi Asante's ideas about cultural and social dislocation.

75. See also Karin Obermeier, "Afro-German Women: Recording Their Own History," *New German Critique* 46 (1989): 175.

76. Ayim, "afro-deutsch II," 25.

77. Wright, *Becoming Black,* 8, 30–32, 191.

78. Ayim, "afro-deutsch II," 25; Ayim, "afro-german II," 16.

79. Wright, "Others-From-Within from Without," 303.

80. Ayim, "entfernte verbindungen," 28–29; "blues in schwarz weiss," 82–83; "gegen leberwurstgrau- für eine bunte republik talk-talk-show für den bla-bla-kampf," 62–65; and "deutschland im herbst," 68–70.

81. "Bibliographie," n.d., folder Ayim Grenzenlos und unverschämt 1997, Orlanda.

82. Ayim, "jerusalem," 87 and "bitte bosnien herzegowina krieg," 92–94.

83. "die zeit danach," 53–54; "soul sister," 56–57; and "ana" 47–49. Ana Herrero-Villamor, a twenty-two-year-old poet and spoken-word artist, was found dead in her apartment in 1992. See "Beerdigung von Ana Herrero-Villamor," November 11, 1992,

Berlin-Charlottenburg, box 18, n.p., Ayim Archive. See some of Herrero-Villamor's poetry in Piesche, *Euer Schweigen schützt Euch nicht*. See also "community" 99–101, where Ayim references Steve Biko, Malcolm X, Marcus Garvey, Sojourner Truth, Rigoberta Menchu, Mahatma Gandhi, and others. For Ayim's other forms of writing, see Ayim, Suandi, Jamilia, and Rose Tuelo Brock, eds. *Akwaaba* (London: Pankhurst Press, 1995), Ayim Papers; Ayim, "Grenzenlos und unverschämt," *Isivivane* no. 2 (1990), box 9, p. 8, Ayim Archive; Ayim, "Das Jahr 1990: Heimat und Einheit aus afro-deutscher Perspektive," in Lange et al., *Entfernte Verbindungen*, 206–22.

84. Condé, no title, 1995, folder Ayim Grenzenlos und unverschämt 1997, Orlanda.

85. Bisi Adeleye-Fayemi, Nana Ama Amanoo, and Jerusha Arothe-Vaughan, "African Women in Europe: Report of Conference convened by Akina Mama Wa Afrika London," October 30–31, 1992, box 4b, p. 25, Ayim Archive.

86. Adeleye-Fayemi et al., "African Women," 25.

87. "Veröffentlichungen," n.d., n.p., Ayim's Papers; Czarina Wilpert invitation to May Ayim, October 15, 1993, box 46, n.p.; Technische Universität Berlin und University of Warwick, "Diskriminierung, Rassismus, und Staatsbürgerschaft in Grossbritannien und Deutschland," program, box 46, n.p. Ayim Archive.

88. 11th International Book Fair of Radical Black and Third World Books, "1993 Brochure and Programme," March 21–27, 1993, box 4a, p. 16, Ayim Archive. Ayim's poetry was also published in Busby's 1992 volume *Daughters of Africa*.

89. On the history of this book fair, see Sarah White, Roxy Harris, and Sharmilla Beezmohun, eds., *A Meeting of the Continents: The International Book Fair of Radical Black and Third World Books—Revisited: History, Memories, Organisation and Programmes 1982–1995* (London: New Beacon Books, 2005).

90. "Racisms and Feminisms" conference, October 29–30, 1994, box 24, n.p., Ayim Archive.

91. "May Ayim Veröffentlichtes Gesamtwerk: Inhaltsverzeichnis/Bibliographie," February 1997, Folder Ayim Nachtgesang 1997, Orlanda; Pan-European Women's Network for Intercultural Action and Exchange, "Programme of Activity," n.d., box 19, n.p., Ayim Archive; AKWAABA, "Pan European Women's Network for Intercultural Action and Exchange Newsletter," 2, no. 3 (1994), box 19, n.p. Ayim Archive. Ayim also received letters from the Black Women's European Alliance and the Black Women and Europe Network. It is unclear if these organizations eventually became AKWAABA.

92. University of Minnesota, "Xenophobia in Germany: National and Cultural Identities after Unification, May 11–14, 1994," program, box 10, n.p., Ayim Archive; the German and Russian Departments at Carleton College, "May Ayim: Afro-German Writer and Poet—Christopher U. Light Lecturer," program, Northfield, Minnesota, May 9–11, 1994, box 10, pp. 1–3, Ayim Archive.

93. Ayim, "Racism and Resistance in United Germany," 8, 9.

94. See Margaret Hampton fax to May Ayim, March 2, 1994, box 46, p. 2; May Ayim letter to Inca Rumold, February 25, 1994, box 46, n.p., Ayim Archive; Inca Rumold letter to May Ayim, February 14, 1994, box 46, n.p.

95. 2nd Pan-African Historical Theatre Festival (Panafest '94), "The Re-emergence of African Civilization," December 12–16, 1994, box 10, p. 3, Ayim Archive.

96. Orlanda, "Wir trauern um unsere Autorin May Ayim," n.d., pp. 1–3, Cheatom Collection.

97. May Ayim, *Grenzenlos und unverschämt* (Berlin: Orlanda, 1997); Ayim, *Nachtgesang* (Berlin: Orlanda, 1997).

98. Mertins, "Blues in Black and White," 156.

99. Abini Zöllner, no title, August 25, 1996, folder Ayim Grenzenlos und unverschämt 1997, Orlanda; Nicola Lauré al-Samarai, no title, August 23, 1996, folder Ayim Grenzenlos und unverschämt 1997.

100. See, for example, Kader Konuk and Nancy Jancovich, "With Love, In Memory and in Honour of May Ayim," *Journal of Gender Studies* 6, no. 1 (1997): 72–73; Barbara Smith card to Dagmar Schultz, August 23, 1996, box 56, n.p., Ayim Archive; Linton Kwesi Johnson, "Reggae Fi May Ayim" in Ayim, *Blues in Black and White*, 1–3.

101. On *afro look* and *Onkel Tom's Faust*, see Hopkins, "Speak, so I might see you!" 533–38; Hopkins, "Writing Diasporic Identity," in Mazón and Steingröver, *Not So Plain as Black and White*, 183–208; Adams, "afro look," 257–78; Jobatey, "*Afro Look*." See also *Weibblick: Informationsblatt von Frauen für Frauen (Schwarze deutsche Frauen, Rassismus in der Sprache, weiße Frauen mit schwarzen Kindern)* 13 (1993): 1–49.

102. See Hügel-Marhsall, *Daheim Unterwegs*; Marie Nejar, *Mach nicht so traurige Augen, weil du ein Negerlein bist: Meine Jugend im Dritten Reich* (Hamburg: Rowohlt, 2007); Harold Gerunde, *Eine von uns: als Schwarze in Deutschland geboren* (Wuppertal: Peter Hammer, 2000); Abini Zöllner, *Schokoladenkind: Meine Familie und andere Wunder* (Berlin: Rowohlt, 2003); ManuEla Ritz, *Die Farbe meiner Haut: Die Anti-Rassismustrainerin erzählt* (Freiburg: Verlag Herder, 2009). Harold Gerunde, who was Bärbel Kampmann's husband, wrote the book after she died of cancer in 1999. On Afro-German autobiographies, see Tina Bach, "Schwarze Deutsche Literatur: Eine Einführung," *freitext* 18 (2011): 19–23; Reinhild Steingröver, "From Farbe bekennen to Scholadenkind: Generational Change in Afro-German Autobiographies," in *Generational Shifts in Contemporary German Culture*, eds. Laurel Cohen-Pfister and Susanne Vees-Gulani (Rochester, N.Y.: Camden, 2010), 287–310; Ekpenyong Ani, " 'Say it loud!': Afro-Diasporische Lebensgeschichten im deutschen Kontext," May 2006, https://heimatkunde.boell.de/2006/05/01/say-it -loud-afro-diasporische-lebensgeschichten-im-deutschen-kontext; Nicola Lauré al-Samarai, "Unwegsame Erinnerungen: Auto/biographische Zeugnisse von Schwarzen Deutschen aus der BRD und der DDR," in *Encounters/Begegnungen*, eds. Marianne Bechhaus-Gerst and Reinhard Klein-Arendt (Münster: LIT, 2004), 197–210.

103. See Hans Massaquoi, *Destined to Witness: Growing up Black in Nazi Germany* (New York: Harper Collins, 1999), which was first published in English; Massaquoi, *Neger, Neger Schornsteinfeger! Meine Kindheit in Deutschland* (München: Fretz & Wassmuth, 2000); Massaquoi, trans. Ulrike Wasel und Klaus Timmermann, *Hänschen klein, ging allein…: Mein Weg in die neue Welt* (Frankfurt am Main: Fischer, 2004). There was also

a 2006 television show in Germany based on his book. See also Theodor Michael, *Deutsch sein und schwarz dazu: Erinnerungen eines Afro-Deutschen* (München: Deutsche Taschenbuch, 2013); Theodor Michael, trans. Eve Rosenhaft, *Black German: An Afro-German Life in the Twentieth Century* (Liverpool, U.K.: Liverpool University Press, 2017). This list is not comprehensive, considering Thomas Usleber, Charles Huber, Gert Schramm, and others have also written memoirs.

104. See Olumide Popoola, *This is not about sadness* (Münster: Unrast, 2010); Popoola, *When we Speak of Nothing* (London: Cassava Republic Press, 2017); Victoria Robinson, *Schanzen-Slam* (Berlin: Anais, 2009); Sow, *Die Schwarze Madonna: Afrodeutscher Heimatkrimi* (Norderstedt: Books on Demand, 2019); Philipp Khabo Koepsell, *The Afropean Contemporary: Literatur- und Gesellschaftsmagazin* (Berlin: epubli, 2015); Koepsell, *Die Akte James Knopf* (Münster: Unrast, 2010); Schwarzrund, *Biskaya: Afropolitaner Berlin-Roman* (Vienna: Zaglossus, 2016). Nadine Golly, Natasha Kelly, Olivia Wenzel, and Chantal-Fleur Sandjon, to name a few, also publish.

105. Launched by Berlin-based Black British writer and activist Sharon Dodua Otoo in the fall of 2012, *Witnessed* is a diasporic literary project in Germany, in which authors contribute English-language works. See Sandrine Micossé-Aikins and Sharon Dodua Otoo, *The Little Book of Big Visions: How to be an Artist and Revolutionize the World*, Witnessed ed. 1 (Münster: Edition Assemblage, 2012); Olumide Popoola, *Also By Mail: A Play*, Witnessed ed. 2 (Münster: Edition Assemblage, 2013); Nzitu Mawakha, *Diama: Images of Women of Colour in Germany*, Witnessed ed. 3 (Münster: Edition Assemblage, 2013). Otoo has also published her own literature in both English and German, and won the prestigious Ingeborg-Bachmann literary prize in 2016. See also Sharon Dodua Otoo, *Synchronicity* (Münster: Edition Assemblage, 2014); Otoo, "The Unpublished Interview," unpublished paper, 2019 Black Women Writers presentation, pp. 1–19. Cited with the author's permission.

106. Michael Küppers, "professional kultur®evolution inna germany," in AntiDiskriminierungsBüro and cyberNomads, *The BlackBook*, 154; Piesche, "Gegen das Schweigen," in Piesche, *Euer Schweigen schützt Euch nicht*, 14. Küppers runs the project with his wife Adetoun, who is also an activist.

107. See Peggy Piesche, Michael Küppers, Ani Ekpenyong, and Angela Alagiyawanna, eds., *May Ayim Award: Erster internationaler schwarzer deutscher Literaturpreis 2004* (Berlin: Orlanda, 2004).

108. Popoola wrote poems in *afro look*. See also Olumide Popoola and Beldan Sezen, eds., *Talking Home: Heimat uns unserer eigenen Felder* (Amsterdam: Blue Moon, 1999); Popoola and Annie Holmes, *Breach* (London: Peirene Press, 2016).

109. Paul Gilroy and Tina M. Campt, eds., *Der Black Atlantic* (Berlin: House of World Cultures, 2004).

110. I was present at the August 29, 2011 official dedication ceremony for Ayim in Berlin-Kreuzberg. Aikins also published a report about colonial street names in Berlin in 2008. Google Germany honored Ayim with a Doodle in February 2018.

CHAPTER 5. DIASPORIC SPATIAL POLITICS WITH BLACK HISTORY MONTH IN BERLIN

1. Black History Month, "10 Jahre BHM in Berlin," program, January 31–February 27, 1999, 9, 11, 26, 30, the author's private collection.

2. McKittrick, "On plantations, prisons, and a black sense of place," 949–50. She used the italics. She also notes "A black sense of place is therefore tied to fluctuating geographic and historical contexts" (949).

3. There was an "African village" held in Augsburg, Germany in July 2005, and ISD immediately criticized it and considered it a part of this *Völkerschau* tradition. On the *Völkerschau,* see Andrew Zimmerman, *Anthropology and Antihumanism in Imperial Germany* (Chicago: University of Chicago Press, 2001); Jürgen Zimmerer, *Kein Platz an der Sonne: Erinnerungsorte der deutschen Kolonialgeschichte* (Frankfurt am Main: Campus, 2013).

4. Wright, *Physics of Blackness,* 14.

5. El-Tayeb, *Europeans Others,* 7. On Black activism in Berlin, see Reed-Anderson, *Rewriting the Footnotes;* Reed-Anderson, *Menschen, Orte, Themen: Zur Geschichte und Kultur der Afrikanischen Diaspora in Berlin* (Berlin: Senatsverwaltung für Arbeit, Integration und Frauen-Die Beauftragte für Integration und Migration, 2013); Oumar Diallo and Joachim Zeller, eds., *Black Berlin: Die Deutsche Metropole und ihre Afrikanische Diaspora in Geschichte und Gegenwart* (Berlin: Metropol, 2013).

6. On translocal spaces, see El-Tayeb, *Europeans Others,* xxxvii; Appardurai, *Modernity at Large.* The scholarship on transnationalism is rather extensive. I only cite a few examples here: "AHR Conversation: On Transnational History," *American Historical Review* 111, no. 5 (2006): 1441–64; Robin D. G. Kelley, " 'But a Local Phase of a World Problem': Black History's Global Vision, 1883–1950," *Journal of American History* 86 (1999): 1045–74; Andrew Zimmerman, *Alabama in Africa: Booker T. Washington, the German Empire, and the Globalization of the New South* (Princeton, N.J.: Princeton University Press, 2010).

7. Witnessing a sea change in Germany, Audre Lorde and Gloria Joseph wrote a letter to Chancellor Kohl, sharing what this meant for People of Color and how they felt unsafe in the country after the fall of the Berlin Wall. The letter was reproduced several times in German newspapers and American journals. See Joseph and Lorde, "Black Women Find Racism Rampant in Germany," *Off Our Backs* 22, no. 10 (1992): 18.

8. hooks, "Love as the Practice of Freedom," 243–50.

9. Tahir Della im Gespräch mit Hadija Haruna-Oelker, "'Wir wollten Schwarze Gemeinschaft auf vielen Ebenen erlebbar machen,'" in Bergold-Caldwell et al., *Spiegelblicke,* 40, 42.

10. "Hallo Sisters und Brothers, Freaks und Froots!," letter, n.d., folder Literatur e.V. Aktuelles, p. 2, Ayim Papers.

11. "Hallo Sisters und Brothers, Freaks und Froots!," n.d., 2.

12. Ibid. See also R. Luyken, "Schwarzsein ist nicht genug," *Die Zeit,* December 26, 1986, folder Literatur e.V. Aktuelles; Dagmar Schultz letter to *Die Zeit,* January 20, 1987, folder Literatur e.V. Aktuelles.

13. "Ausländerhaß trifft auch Deutsche: Zweites bundesweites Treffen der 'Initiative Schwarze Deutsche,' " *Unsere Zeit (UZ)-DKP Zeitung,* December 17, 1986, folder May Projekt Afro-Deutsche/Zeitungsartikel über Afro-deutsche/Schwarze in den Medien, n.p., Ayim Papers.

14. Michael Meinert, "Eine Frau: Wir werden oft totgeschwiegen. . . . : 'Initiative Schwarze Deutsche' tagte/ 'Kampf gegen Rassismus in allen Bereichen,' " *Frankfurter Rundschau,* December 9, 1986, no. 285, folder May Projekt Afro-Deutsche/Zeitungs- artikel über Afro-deutsche/Schwarze in den Medien, p. 13, Ayim Papers.

15. "Ausländerhaß trifft auch Deutsche," n.p.

16. El-Tayeb, "Blackness and Its (Queer) Discontents," in Lennox, *Remapping Black Germany,* 252–53.

17. See, for example, "II Bundestreffen der Initiativen schwarzer Deutscher von 5.-6. Dezember 1987 in Berlin," folder Ko-Treffen, Cheatom Collection; Della im Gespräch mit Haruna-Oelker, " 'Wir wollten Schwarze Gemeinschaft,' " in Bergold-Caldwell et al., *Speigelblicke,* 40; ISD, "4 Bundestreffen der Initiative Schwarze Deutsche," Düssel- dorf, September 16–18, 1988, folder Literatur e.V. Aktuelles, n.p., Ayim Papers.

18. ISD-München, "Einladung ISD-Bundestreffen 1989," invitation, München, October 8–10, 1989, folder Literatur e.V. Aktuelles, n.p., Ayim Papers.

19. ISD-München, "Einladung ISD-Bundestreffen 1989."

20. ISD, "6.-I.S.D.-Bundestreffen-1991," program overview, Verden, October 11–13, 1991, folder ISD Liga, n.p., Ayim Papers.

21. On Black German theater, see Jamele Watkins, "The Drama of Race: Contem- porary Afro-German Theater" (PhD diss., University of Massachusetts, 2017), esp. 53–93.

22. ISD, "Einladung zur 9. Bundestagung der Initiative Schwarze Deutsche und Schwarze in Deutschland vom 11. bis 15. Mai 1994," invitation, Finnentrop, folder ISD Liga, n.p., Ayim Papers.

23. ISD, "Einladung zur 9. Bundestagung."

24. ISD, "10. Bundestreffen 3.-6. August 1995 Berlin—Vergangenheit, Gegenwart & Perspektiven Schwarzer Existenz in Europa," program, n.p., Cheatom Collection.

25. ISD, "10. Bundestreffen 3.-6. August 1995 Berlin."

26. This is based on informal discussions with individuals at the 2009 BT that I attended.

27. See Bergold-Caldwell et al., *Spiegelblicke.* See also Marie-Sophie Adeoso, "Afro- deutsche Vielfalt," *Frankfurter Rundschau,* February 25, 2016, http://www.fr.de/kultur/ literatur/schwarze-bewegung-afrodeutsche-vielfalt-a-378901; Juli(a) Rivera, *mEin Viertel 100—25 Jahre Bundestreffen* (Berlin, 2011). Born in East Germany, Rivera is a gen- der-fluid Black German activist, who lives in Toronto and Berlin. The film was the first Black German documentary about the community.

28. Fountainhead Dance Theatre, "Foreword," in "Black Cultural Festival," 4–5.

29. Fountainhead Dance Theatre, "Black International Cinema," 1–24.

30. See Fountainhead Dance Theatre, "XXXI. 2016 Black International Cinema Berlin," program, Berlin, May 13–15, 2016, p. 48, the author's personal collection.

31. See African Writers Association, *AWA-FINNABA* no. 9 (1987): 4–76.

32. Vusi Mchunu, "AWA-FINNABA and the Berlin Congo Conference," *AWA-FINNABA* no. 5 (1985): 14–16. See also Koepsell, "Literature and Activism," 42.

33. Institute of Black Studies, "Programm," 1989, Berlin, folder Literatur, e.V. Aktuelles, n.p., Ayim Papers. I am uncertain when the name change occurred.

34. Institute of Black Studies, "Programm."

35. ISD, "Black History Month 17.-25. Februar 1990 Programm," Berlin, folder Literatur e.V. Aktuelles, 1.

36. See Wiedenroth-Coulibaly and Zinflou, "20 Jahre Schwarze Oranisierung," in AntiDiskriminierungsBüro and cyberNomads, *The BlackBook*, 140.

37. ISD, "Black History Month Programm 17.-25. Februar 1990," 1; ISD, "Programm Black History Month 1991," 1. Reichel and Hafke remained involved with the BHMs through financing, planning, and editing of the program until the last one in 2000. Sadly, Reichel committed suicide in the fall of 2017.

38. ISD, "Black History Month '92," Berlin, p. 1, Ayim Papers.

39. Wiedenroth-Coulibaly and Zinflou, "20 Jahre Schwarze Organisierung," in AntiDiskriminierungsBüro and cyberNomads, *The BlackBook*, 134.

40. Oguntoye, "Vorwort zur Neuauflage 2006," in Oguntoye, Opitz/Ayim, and Schultz, *Farbe bekennen*, 8.

41. May Ayim, "Die Afro-deutsche Minderheit," in *Ethnische Minderheiten in der Bundesrepublik Deutschland: Ein Lexikon,* eds. Cornelia Schmalz-Jacobesn and Georg Hansen (Munich: Verlag C.H. Beck, 1995), 51.

42. See ISD, "Vorwort," in "Black History 1996: Schwarze Visionen," Berlin, folder ISD Liga, p. 3, Ayim Papers; I.S.D. Initiative Schwarze Deutsche Berlin, "Hallo Ihr AFROSda draußen!" August 1989, folder Literatur e.V. Aktuelles, Ayim Papers.

43. Those friends included Love Newkirk, Iris Moore, and LaToya Manly-Spain.

44. As of 2020, that specific link on the BHMs is no longer available on ISD's web site. Nigel Asher, "Die Geschichte des Black History Month in Deutschland," in Bergold-Caldwell et al., *Spiegelblicke,* 46, 47.

45. See ISD and Heinrich Böll Stiftung, "Black History Month 2013," http://www.netzwerk-gegen-diskriminierung-hessen.de/fileadmin/Faltblatt_BlackHistory Month_Racial_Profiling.pdf; Camilla Ridha and Eleonore Wiedenroth-Coulibaly, "Impressionen vom Black History Month in Frankfurt am Main," in Bergold-Caldwell et al., *Spiegelblicke,* 51–55.

46. See, for example, ISD-Düsseldorf, "Black Film Festival '89," Düsseldorf, June 23–25, 1989, folder Literatur e.V. Aktuelles, n.p., Ayim Papers; Initiative Schwarze Deutsche, "Black Film Festival," flyer, June 12–15, 1990, n.p., Cheatom Collection; Sokoni, e.V., "3. Afrikanische Kulturtage," program, October 18–November 22, 1991, Hamburg, n.p., Cheatom Collection; Black Media Access, "Afrika Festival Würzburg," *African Programme Afro-Kulturkalender* 55 (1995), folder ISD-Liga, p. 4, Ayim Papers.

47. Ricky Reiser, "Re: Black History Month," email correspondence with the author, April 10, 2019.

48. Wright, *Becoming Black*, 224.

49. Quoted in Davies, *Left of Karl Marx*, 173. See also Bill Schwarz, " 'Claudia Jones and the *West Indian Gazette*': Reflections on the Emergence of Post-colonial Britain," *Twentieth Century British History* 14, no. 3 (2003): 269; Perry, *London is the Place for Me*, 89–125.

50. Davies, *Left of Karl Marx*, 175.

51. Ibid., 180, 177.

52. ISD, "Vorwort," in "Black History Month 1998 Programm," Berlin, January 30–March 4, 1998, p. 4, the author's private collection.

53. Schwarz, "'Claudia Jones and the *West Indian Gazette*,' " 275; Davies, *Left of Karl Marx*, 182.

54. ISD, "Antrag auf finanzielle Unterstützung des Black History Month 1991," folder ISD Liga, pp. 1–4, Ayim Papers; ISD, "Programm Black History Month 1991."

55. ISD, "Black History Month '92," 2–4.

56. ISD, "Black History Month '93," Berlin, box 18, p. 4, Ayim Archive.

57. ISD, "Black History Month '93," 1.

58. ISD, "Vorwort" in "Black History 1996: Schwarze Visionen," 3–4.

59. ISD, "Black History 1996: Schwarze Visionen," 12. See also ISD, "Black History Month '94: Die Farben Afrikas," Berlin, p. 6, the author's private collection.

60. Black History Month Committee, "Foreword," in "Black History 3. Februar-3. Marz 1996 (Schwarze Visionen)," folder ISD Liga, p. 4, Ayim Papers.

61. John Amoateng, "Afro-Deutsche Geschichte," in "Black History Month 17.-25. Februar 1990 Programm," 1; Amoateng, "Afro-Deutsche Geschichte," in "Programm Black History Month 1991," 3. On Amo, see Sephocle, "Anton Wilhelm Amo," 182–87; Martin, "Der Schwarze Philosoph," 308–28. Much of Amo's philosophical works have been lost, and he is a forgotten German Enlightenment figure.

62. Elke Jank, "Der verleugnete Beitrag schwarzer Menschen zur Geschichte Europas," in "Black History Month 1991," 8.

63. Katharina Oguntoye, "Im Windschatten der deutschen Geschichte—zur Geschichte von AfrikanerInnen und Afro-deutschen in Deutschland seit 1884," in "Black History Month '93," 14; Katharina Oguntoye, "Die Geschichte der Afrikaner und Afro-Deutschen in Deutschland von 1884 bis 1950," in "Black History Month '97," 30, Cheatom Collection. See the introduction footnote 21 for a full citation of Oguntoye's book.

64. Thomas Pforth, "1492 Vergangenheit, 1992 Gegenwart und 1993 Perspektive Schwarzer Existenz in Deutschland," in "Black History Month '92," 17.

65. Austen P. Brandt, "Schwarzes Christentum," in "Black History Month '92," 17.

66. Brandt, "Schwarzes Christentum," 17.

67. Campt and Grosse, "Aspekte Afro-Deutscher Geschichte," in "Black History Month '92," 18.

68. Campt, Grosse, and Lemke Muñiz de Faria, "Schwarze Deutsche und Schwarze in Deutschland, 1920–1960: Aspekte ihrer gesellschaftlichen Wahrnehmung," in "Black History Month '94," 31.

69. N.N., "Die Schwarze Community in der DDR vor und nach dem Fall der Mauer," in "Programm Black History Month 1991," 9.

70. Beer, Eisner, Gaulke, and Poutrus, "Schwarze Deutsche in der DDR," in "Black History Month '94," 16.

71. Ika Hügel, "Afro-Deutsche Identität," in "Programm Black History Month 1991," 5.

72. Oguntoye, "Afro-deutsche—Schwarze Deutsche—Schwarze in Deutschland," in "Black History Month '93," 6.

73. Bärbel Kampmann, "Psychische Probleme Schwarzer Deutscher und Therapie als Hilfestellung," in "Programm Black History Month 1991," 5.

74. Kampmann, "Psychische Probleme Schwarzer Deutscher," in "Programm Black History Month 1991," 5.

75. Kampmann, "Basisprobleme Schwarzer Deutscher," in "Black History Month '92," 13; Dr. Lula Lewes, "Streßmanagement," in "Black History Month '97," 20.

76. Mario Santiago, "Selbstverteidigungsworkshop," in "Black History Month '93," ISD, Berlin, p. 14, Ayim Papers.

77. Among them were Alagiyawanna-Kadalie, Küppers, Laja, Mysorekar, and Schmidt. "Schwarze Deutsche Literatur," in "Black History Month '92," 13. ISD-München, ed. *Macht der Nacht: eine Schwarze Deutsche Anthologie* (München: ISD, 1991–92).

78. Michael H. Küppers, "Return of the Native," in "Black History Month '93," 12. In 1989 he studied postmodern literature with Fredric Jameson and African American literature with Henry Louis Gates Jr. at Duke University, and in 1996 he was the first Afro-German lyricist and poet at the Goethe Institute in New York.

79. Ayim, "Blues in schwarz weiss: Lesung in deutscher Sprache," in "Black History 1996," 20.

80. See ISD, "May Ayim Opitz von der Black Community Berlin," in "Black History Month '97," 6–7; "May Ayim Tag," in "Black History Month '97," 34.

81. See Harambee and ISD, "Black Heritage Party," in "Programm Black History Month 1991; "Concert & Party Black Liberation Sound System & Live Music from Ghana," in "Black History Month '93," 8; ISD, "'Schwarze Musik' in der 'Weißen Rose': Eröffnungsparty zum Black History Month," in "Black History 1996," 14.

82. ABATIGAYA, "Tänze und Gesang aus Ruanda mit ABATIGAYA," in "Black History Month '94," 27.

83. Afrikanisches Frauentheater, "Theateraufführung: Erinnerung an die eigene Fremdheit," in "Black History Month '94," 29.

84. People's Art Ensemble, "People's Poets Theatre," in "Black History Month '92," 18.

85. Sparks, "Black History Month-Artist in Residence," in "Black History Month '94," 33.

86. "Different Colours," in "Black History Month '94," 11.

87. Ibid., 11.

88. In 1995 Reiser also created the Black Calendar *(Schwarzer Kalendar)* together with Vera Heyer and Pierre Gaulke, which included the birth dates of significant individuals and political events throughout the Black diaspora. See Reiser, Heyer, and Gaulke, "Kalender mit Daten Schwarzer Persönlichkeiten aus Politik, Kunst, Literatur, Kultur" (Berlin, 1995), the author's private collection.

89. See Ricky Reiser, "Mediensprache und Rassismus," in "Black History Month '93," 5.

90. Stuart Hall, "The Local and the Global: Globalization and Ethnicity," in *Dangerous Liaisons: Gender, Nation, and Postcolonial Perspectives,* eds. Anne McClintock, Aamir Mufti, and Ella Shehata (Minneapolis: University of Minnesota Press, 1997), 173–87.

91. ISD, "Black History Month 1991," 1.

92. Luyanda Mpahlwa and Vusi Mchunu, "Südafrika Heute und die Geschichte des politischen Kampfes," in "Black History Month 1991," 2.

93. Mpahlwa and Mchunu, "Südafrika Heute und die Geschichte des politischen Kampfes," 2.

94. Peggy Luswazi, "Erziehung zur Befreiung—ein Weg aus der Kolonialisierung des Geistes," in "Black History Month 1991," 2. Her name is misspelled in the program; I have corrected it here.

95. Luyanda Mpahlwa, "Break the Chains of Apartheid—Change is pain!" in "Black History Month '92," 9. See also Abdul Ilal, "Südafrika—Dominanz oder Partnerschaft?," "Black History 1996," 30.

96. I. Schuhmacher and E. Rodtman, "Aus den Ruinen der Apartheid—Situation der Landbevölkerung in Südafrika," in "Black History Month '92," 9.

97. Schuhmacher and Rodtman, "Aus den Ruinen der Apartheid," 9.

98. For some instances of this, see Abdul Illal, "Demokratie und Versöhnung in Mosambik," in "Black History 1996," 17; Dr. Shungu M. Tundanonga-Dikunda, "Nachhaltige Entwicklung contra Entwicklung Afrikas südlich der Sahara," in "Black History 1996," 19; Stephania A.A. Evboikuokha, "Die Völker und Sprachen Nigerias" in "Black History 1996," 28; Nur Weheliye, "Friedensperspektive in Somalia," in "Black History 1996," 30.

99. Ada Gay Griffin, "Audrey [sic] Lorde," in "Black History Month 1991," n.p.; Michael Maynard, "FireIce," in "Black History Month 1991," n.p. Lorde's first name was misspelled in the program. See also "The Black History Month Programme, Berlin February 23–March 10th, 1991," *Isivivane* no. 4 (1991): 23.

100. EURAFRI, "Lumumba: Tod eines Propheten," in "Black History Month '92," 5; ISD, *Marcus Garvey* and *Paul Robeson—A Tribute to an Artist,* in "Black History Month '92," 9.

101. F. R. Brownman, "Schwarze Filmgeschichte," in "Black History Month '93," 13.

102. ISD, *Million Men March,* in "Black History 1996," 30; ISD, *Black Panthers—Huey P. Newton,* in "Black History Month '94," 27; ISD, *Malcolm X,* in "Black History 1996,"

29; IPF, *Sweet France,* in "Black History Month '93," 10; ISD, *The Life and Death of Steve Biko,* in "Black History Month '94," 12; HARAMBEE, "History of Reggae Music and Rasta-Movement," in "Black History Month '94," 22.

103. "I'm Gonna [Git] You Sucka!" and "Film Sweet Sweetback's Badasss Song," in "Black History Month '94," 16, 21.

104. Patricia Elcock, "Black Unity," in "Black History Month 17.-25. Februar 1990 Programm."

105. Nicol Laure-Al Samarei [sic], "Schwarz als Politischer Begriff," in "Black History Month 1991," 9; Manu Holzer, "Schwarzes Bewußtsein-Black Consciousness Eine Überlebensnotwedigkeit," in "Black History Month '94," 18; Holzer, "Schwarze Solidarität kennt keine Grenzen oder. . . ." in "Black History Month '94," 20.

106. ISD, "Das Programm: The Events," in "Black History Month '92," 5; Mahoma Mwaungulu, "Pan-Afrikanismus," in "Black History 1996," 21. He co-founded the Pan-African Forum e.V. in 1997. Mwaungulu died in 2004, and was later honored at the 2009 BHM.

107. Gladwell Otieno and Tsitsi Dangarembga, "'Wann and wo ich eintrete': Schwarze Frauen in der Geschichte—am Beispiel der Literatur," in "Black History Month 1991," n.p.

108. "Schwarze Frauentage im Rahmen des BHM 1993," in "Black History Month '93," 16; "Schwarze Frauentage," program, February 26–28, 1993, box 18, n.p., Ayim Archive.

109. "Gedenkfeier zu Ehren Audre Lordes," in "Black History Month '93," 9; "Celebration of Life: Audre Lorde-Memorial Celebration," February 6, 1993.

110. Smith, Hull, and Scott, *But Some of Us Are Brave.*

111. May Ayim, "Alle Frauen sind weiß, alle Schwarzen sind Männer—Aber manche von uns sind mutig: Rassismus aus afrofeministischer Perspetive," in "Black History 1996," 24. For other BHM events by and/or on Black diasporic women, see Charlotte Burrows, "Schwarze Frauenbewegung in den USA," in "Black History Month '93," 10; Ilona Ivan, "Black Women in Jazz," in "Black History Month '94," 20; ADEFRA and ISD, "Black Women Support Network," in "Black History Month '94," Berlin, 18.

112. See "Die Geschichte des Black History Month in Deutschland," *Heritage Newsletter* 7/8 (2003), https://blackhistorymonthberlin.wordpress.com/die-geschichte-des-black-history-month-in-deutschland/.

CHAPTER 6. BLACK GERMAN FEMINIST SOLIDARITY AND BLACK INTERNATIONALISM

1. Ulrike Helwerth, "Black Coming out," *Die Tageszeitung,* August 25, 1991, n.p., Cheatom Collection; Dora Hartmann, "Neues Europa-neuer Feminismus?: Schwarze Frauen über Rassismus und Sexismus," *Bielefelder Stadtblatt,* August 15, 1991, n.p., Cheatom Collection; "Strategien gegen den Rassismus: Frauen-Seminar über Schwarze in Europäischer Gemeinschaft," *Frankfurter Allgemeine Zeitung,* August 5, 1991, n.p., Cheatom Collection; " 'Schwarze Frauen stehen in Europa ganz am Rande': Interkulturelles

Sommer-Seminar für Frauenstudien," *Frankfurter Rundschau,* August 5, 1991, no. 179, Cheatom Collection; Dr. Phyllis E. Jackson, "The Cross-Cultural Black Women's Studies Summer Institute: A History, 1987–1990," June 1, 1990, box 14, p. 3, Ayim Archive. Jackson served as the institute historian and editor, but died suddenly early in 1990.

2. Delegates were from Aotearoa/New Zealand, Brazil, Canada, Ethiopia, Eritrea, France, Great Britain, India, Italy, the Netherlands, Nigeria, Norway, Pakistan, Panama, Peru, the Philippines, South Africa, Trinidad and Tobago, Uganda, the United States, Venezuela, and Zimbabwe. On centering difference and commonality within feminist organizing, see Chandra Talpade Mohanty, *Feminism without Borders: Decolonizing Theory, Practicing Solidarity* (Durham, N.C.: Duke University Press, 2003).

3. Interkulturelle Initiative Schwarzer Frauen für Minoritätenrechte und Studien in Deutschland, "Black World: Eine Boschüre von Schwarzen Frauen vol. 1. (Juli 1992), Ordentliche Jahres-Vereinsversammlung vom 31.1. bis 2.2. 1992 in Köln," p. 2, Cheatom Collection.

4. Hartmann, "Neues Europa-neuer Feminismus?," 7. Kraft received her PhD in 1994 from the University of Osnabrück.

5. This also included white women. On similar practices in the Black British feminist movement, see See Nydia Swaby, "'Disparate in Voice, Sympathetic in Direction': Gendered Political Blackness and the Politics of Solidarity," *Feminist Review* 108, no. 1 (2014): 11–25; Julia Subdury, *"Other Kinds of Dreams": Black Women's Organisations and the Politics of Transformation* (London: Routledge, 1998).

6. De Veaux, *Warrior Poet;* Ransby, *Eslanda.*

7. See Ohene-Nyako, "Black Women's Transnational Activism"; Ohene-Nyako, "The Black Women and Europe Network." After the Black European Women's Congress in 2007, another Black European women's organization, the Black European Women's Council (BEWC), emerged. For more on the BEWC, see Cassandra Ellerbe-Dueck, "The Black European Women's Council: 'thinking oneself into the New Europe,' " *African and Black Diaspora* 4, no. 2 (2011): 145–60.

8. Carmen Faymonville, "Black Germans and Transnational Identification," *Callaloo* 26, no. 2 (2003): 367.

9. Marion Kraft and Rukhsana Shamim Ashraf-Khan, eds. *Schwarze Frauen der Welt: Europa und Migration* (Berlin: Orlanda, 1993).

10. Jean Quartet and Benita Roth, eds., "Human Rights, Global Conferences, and the Making of Postwar Transnational Feminisms," *Journal of Women's History* 24, no. 4 (2012): 20. The literature on the International Women's Year (IWY) of 1975, the UN Conferences on Women, and transnational feminism is extensive. See, for example, Myra Marx Ferree, "Globalization and Feminism: Opportunities and Obstacles for Activism in the Global Arena," in *Global Feminism: Transnational Women's Activism, Organizing, and Human Rights,* eds. Myra Marx Ferree and Alli Mari Tripp (New York: New York University Press, 2006), 3–23; Jocelyn Olcott, "Cold War Conflicts and Cheap Cabaret: Sexual Politics at the 1975 United Nations International Women's Year Conference," *Gender & History* 22, no. 3 (2010): 733–54; Jutta Joachim, *Agenda Setting, the UN, and NGOs: Gender Violence and*

Reproductive Rights (Washington, D.C.: Georgetown University Press, 2007); Lois West, "The United States Women's Conferences and Feminist Politics," in *Gender Politics in Global Governance,* eds. Mary Meyer and Elisabeth Prügl (New York: Lanham, Rowman & Littlefield, 1999), 177–94. For a discussion on socialist feminist activism, see Kristen Ghodsee, *Second World, Second Sex: Socialist Women's Activism and Global Solidarity during the Cold War* (Durham, N.C.: Duke University Press, 2019). There was also a National Women's Conference in Houston, Texas (1977).

11. Shelby Lewis, "Africana Feminism: An Alternative Paradigm for Black Women in the Academy," in *Black Women in the Academy: Promises and Perils,* ed. Lois Benjamin (Gainesville: University Press of Florida, 1997), 48; Stanlie M. James, Frances Smith Foster, and Beverly Guy-Sheftall, eds., *Still Brave: The Evolution of Black Women's Studies* (New York: Feminist Press, 2009), 1–19.

12. See Umoren, *Race Women Internationalists;* Blain, *Set the World on Fire;* Blain and Gill, *To Turn the Whole World Over;* Judith Byfield, "From Ladies to Women: Funmilayo Ransome-Kuti and Women's Political Activism in Post-World War II Nigeria," in Bay, Griffin, Jones, and Savage, *Toward an Intellectual History of Black Women,* 197–213.

13. Cross-Cultural Black Women's Studies Summer Institute, "Applicant Information," 1989, box 14, n.p., Ayim Archive.

14. Jackson, "Cross-Cultural Black Women's Studies," 3.

15. Beginning in Harare, Zimbabwe in 1988, the journal then moved to Clark Atlanta University in 1989, with its last issue appearing in 1990. See Kathleen Sheldon, *Historical Dictionary of Women in Sub-Saharan Africa* (Lanham, Md.: Rowman & Littlefield, 2016); Challen Nicklen, "Rhetorics of Connection in the United Nations Conferences on Women, 1975–1995" (PhD diss., Penn State University, 2008), 121.

16. Jackson, "Cross-Cultural Black Women's Studies," 3.

17. Ibid., 3–4.

18. Ibid., 4; Cross-Cultural Black Women Studies, "1987 Women's Studies Summer Institute: Centre for Research and Education on Gender," University of London, Institute of Education, July 13–August 7, 1987, box 14, pp. 1–20, Ayim Archive. See also Cross-Cultural Black Women's Studies Summer Institute, "21st Anniversary Celebration Honorees, International Cross-cultural Black Women's Studies Institute: A Global Network" (New York, 2008), 6.

19. Jackson, "Cross-Cultural Black Women's Studies," 4.

20. Ibid., 4, 5; Cross-Cultural Black Women's Studies Summer Institute, "Women and the Politics of Food," August 7–26, 1989, box 14, n.p., Ayim Archive.

21. Andrée Nicola McLaughlin, "Third Annual Cross-Cultural Black Women's Studies Summer Institute: Harare, Zimbabwe," *Sage: A Scholarly Journal on Black Women* 6, no. 1 (1989): 80. See also Cross-Cultural Black Women's Studies Summer Institute, "21st Anniversary Celebration," 6; Jackson, "Cross-Cultural Black Women's Studies," 5.

22. Jackson, "Cross-Cultural Black Women's Studies," 5. See also Deborah K. King, "Multiple Jeopardy, Multiple Consciousness: The Context of a Black Feminist Ideology," *Signs* 14, no. 1 (1988): 42–72.

23. "International, Cross-Cultural Black Women's Studies Summer Institute: 1991 Resolutions," box 52, folder 791, p. 3, Lorde Papers. McLaughlin sent a letter dated January 16, 1992 to delegates with updated resolutions.

24. E. Patrick Johnson, "Introduction: 'Blackness' and Authenticity: What's Performance Got to Do With It?" in Johnson, *Appropriating Blackness: Performance and the Politics of Authenticity* (Durham, N.C.: Duke University Press, 2003), 2–3.

25. Anjuli Gupta, "Überlegungen zum 'Cross-Cultural Black Womans's Summer Institute,'" *Afrekete (schwarzer Feminismus)* 2, no. 3 (1988): 11. The misspelling is in the original.

26. Gupta, "Überlegungen zum 'Cross-Cultural,'" 11, 12.

27. Ibid.; Cross-Cultural Black Women's Studies Summer Institute, "Women and the Politics of Food." See also Helga Emde Letter to Jean Sindab, February 7, 1989, p. 2, 4223.7.18, Archive of the World Council of Churches, Geneva, Switzerland (cited hereafter as ArchWCC). I want to thank Pamela Ohene-Nyako for this source.

28. Jackson, "Cross-Cultural Black Women's Studies," 7.

29. Ibid., 8. Brawley falsely accused four white men of raping her.

30. Ibid. See also Andree Nicola McLaughlin, Cross-Cultural Black Women's Studies Summer Institute letter to members, June 27, 1989, box 14, n.p., Ayim Archive; Cross-Cultural Black Women's Studies Summer Institute, "Communications," July 11–30, 1988, New York City, box 14, n.p., Ayim Archive.

31. Jackson, "Cross-Cultural Black Women's Studies," 8.

32. Ibid., 11; Katharina [Oguntoye] (ISD Berlin), "Das Black Women Summer Institute in New York City," *afro look* no. 2 (1988): 6, the author's personal collection.

33. Interkulturelle Initiative Schwarzer Frauen für Minoritätenrechte und Studien in Deutschland and Nozizwe, *Fünftes Interkulturelles Sommer-Seminar,* 4; Cross-Cultural Black Women's Studies Summer Institute, 6; Cross-Cultural Black Women's Studies Summer Institute, "Women and the Politics of Food."

34. Cross-Cultural Black Women's Studies Summer Institute, "Update," January 26, 1989, box 14, p. 3, Ayim Archive.

35. McLaughlin, "Third Annual Cross-Cultural Black Women's Studies Summer Institute," 80.

36. Marion Kraft letter to Audre Lorde, September 21, 1989, box 3, folder 069, p. 2, Lorde Papers.

37. Kraft letter to Lorde, September 21, 1989, 2.

38. Jackson, "Cross-Cultural Black Women's Studies," 10.

39. Ibid., 11.

40. Appendix A: Preliminary Report on the Aotearoa Institute, 1991, box 14, p. 15, Ayim Archive.

41. Ibid.

42. Formed in 1994, the Pacific Women's Network sponsored the 1995 Institute in Hawaii. This conference predated the 1995 UN Fourth Conference on Women held in Beijing, China. See Robert Mast and Anne Mast, *Autobiography of Protest in Hawai'i*

(Honolulu: University of Hawai'i Press, 1996), 232; Cross-Cultural Black Women's Studies Summer Institute, 6.

43. In Germany, Women of Color activists and allies organized several conferences that tackled racism and anti-Semitism, including *Wege zu Bündnissen* on June 8–10, 1990 in Bremen; the second national congress for immigrants, Jewish, and Black German women on October 3–6, 1991 in Berlin; and *Feminism between Racism, Ignorance, and Marginalization* on October 5–8, 1990 in Frankfurt.

44. "Sommerseminar für Schwarze-Frauen-Studien," *Frankfurter Rundschau*, July 27, 1991, n.p.

45. Fifth Annual Cross-Cultural Black Women's Studies Summer Institute, Program, August 2–23, 1991, box 14, p. 3, Ayim Archive; McLaughlin, "Cross-Cultural Institute Letter and 1991 Resolutions," January 16, 1992, 1.

46. Interkulturelle Initiative Schwarzer Frauen für Minoritätenrechte und Studien in Deutschland and Nozizwe, *Fünftes Interkulturelles Sommer-Seminar Für Schwarze Frauen-Studien,* 2–3; Fifth Cross-Cultural Black Women's Studies Summer Institute, "Directory of Delegates," August 2–23, 1991, box 14, n.p., Ayim Archive; Helwerth, "Black Coming Out," *Die Tageszeitung,* August 25, 1991. More Black Germans were in attendance, and even Tina M. Campt participated.

47. Marion Kraft (IISF) letter, January 2, 1991, box 20, n.p., Ayim Archive; "Interkuturelle Initiative Schwarzer Frauen für die Entwicklung von Minoritätenrechten und Studien in Deutschland e.V.," December 1, 1990, box 14, pp. 1–10, Ayim Archive. An IISF membership list from March 1991 included Abigail van Rooyen, Angela Amankwaa, Barbara Walker, Bärbel Kampmann, Christiana Ampedu, Christina Jones, Dimitria Clayton, Gabriela Winbold, Hannah Aman, Helga Emde, Henny Tangande, Jasmin Eding, Judy Gummich, Katharina Williams, Magali Schmid, Maria Andres, Marie-Therese Aden, Marion Kraft, Mary Powell, Modupe Laja, Peggy Piesche, Ria Cheatom, and Shireen Aga. Clayton, Emde, Gummich, Tangande, Kraft, and Laja were a part of the executive board. See "IISF Adressenliste," March 1991, n.p., Cheatom Collection. The IISF ended in 1996.

48. Marion Kraft, "Cross-Cultural Sisterhood: Audre Lorde's Living Legacy in Germany," *The Feminist Wire,* February 20, 2014, http://thefeministwire.com/2014/02/cross-cultural-sisterhood-audre-lordes-living-legacy-in-germany-2/#_edn6.

49. McLaughlin, "Cross-Cultural Institute Letter and 1991 Resolutions," 2. Jean Sindab, an African American civil rights and environmental activist, was the executive secretary of the WCC's Programme to Combat Racism in Switzerland, where she worked from 1986 to 1991. She also supported and attended the 1991 institute. For more on Sindab, see Ohene-Nyako, "Black Women's Transnational Activism."

50. Ibid., 2, 4.

51. Ibid., 1.

52. Helga Emde quoted in Baureitbel, "Das Universum neu schaffen."

53. "Strategien gegen den Rassismus," *Frankfurter Allgemeine Zeitung.*

54. Heide Platen, "Schwarze Frauen analysieren Europa," *Die Tageszeitung,* August 5, 1991, n.p.

55. Interkulturelle Initiative Schwarzer Frauen für die Entwicklung von Minoritätenrechte und Studien in Deutschland, "5. Interkulturelles Sommer Seminar für Schwarze Frauen-Studien."

56. Fifth Annual Cross-Cultural Black Women's Studies Summer Institute, "Focus: Black People and the European Community," box 14, n.p., Ayim Archive.

57. Hartmann, "Neues Europa-neuer Feminismus?," 7.

58. Helwerth, "Black Coming Out."

59. Interkulturelle Initiative Schwarzer Frauen für Minoritätenrechte und Studien in Deutschland, "Black World," 2.

60. Ibid.

61. "Über die Identität der Schwarzen: Sommer-Seminar für Frauen mit internationalen Gästen," *Frankfurter Allgemeine Zeitung,* July 30, 1991, n.p., Cheatom Collection.

62. "Über die Identität der Schwarzen," *Frankfurter Allgemeine Zeitung.*

63. Ibid.

64. " 'Schwarze-Frauen-Studien' Sommerseminar am OS-Kolleg," *Neue Westfälische,* July 26, 1991, n.p., Cheatom Collection.

65. Ibid.; "Schwarze Frauen-Studien," *Bielefelder Stadtblatt,* August 1, 1991, n.p., Cheatom Collection.

66. MODEFEN was founded in 1981. Gilroy was prominent in her own right, but her son is the prominent scholar Paul Gilroy.

67. Baureitbel, "Das Universum neu schaffen."

68. Helga Emde quoted in "Schwarze Frauen stehen in Europa ganz am Rande," *Frankfurter Rundschau.*

69. Helwerth, "Black Coming Out."

70. Klimke, *The Other Alliance;* Davis, "A Whole World Opening Up"; Slobodian, *Foreign Front.* On foreign students in Eastern Europe, see Sara Pugach, "Agents of dissent: African student organizations in the German Democratic Republic," *Africa* 89, S1 (2019): 90–108; Eric Burton, "Navigating global socialism: Tanzanian students in and beyond East Germany," *Cold War History* 19, no. 1 (2019): 63–83; Maxim Matusevich, "Probing the Limits of Internationalism: African Students Confront Soviet Ritual," *Anthropology of East Europe Review* 27, no. 2 (2009): 19–39.

71. International, Cross-Cultural Black Women's Studies Summer Institute, "1991 Resolutions," p. 3, Lorde Papers.

72. See Steven Jensen, *The Making of International Human Rights: The 1960s, Decolonization, and the Reconstruction of Global Values* (New York: Cambridge University Press, 2016); Moyn, *The Last Utopia.* Other scholars believe the development of international human rights predates the 1960s and 1970s. See, for example, Katherine Marino, *Feminisms for the Americas: The Making of an International Human Rights Movement* (Chapel Hill: University of North Carolina, 2019).

73. See El-Tayeb, *European Others;* Stuart Hall, "The West and the Rest: Discourse and Power," in *Race and Racialization: Essential Readings*, eds. Tania Das Gupta, Carl E. James, Chris Anderson, Grace-Edward Galabuzi, and Roger C.A. Maaka (Toronto: Canadian Scholars, 2018), 85–93.

74. International, Cross-Cultural Institute, "1991 Resolutions," 3.

75. International, Cross-Cultural Institute, 3.

76. Ibid., 4.

77. Ibid., 5.

78. Ibid., 6.

79. Ibid., 7.

80. Ibid., 8. The treaty also granted them the rights of British subjects.

81. Ibid., 9.

82. Ibid., 10. The Council consisted of eight elders, including Lydie Dooh-Bunya and Beryl Gilroy.

83. Ibid., 12. See also Kwame Nimako, "About Them, But Without Them: Race and Ethnic Relations Studies in Dutch Universities," *Human Architecture: Journal of the Sociology of Self-Knowledge* 10, no. 1 (2012): 46.

84. Nimako, "About Them, But Without Them," 47. Essed had also worked at CRES. A year later, under new leadership, CRES reopened and was renamed the Institute for Migration and Ethnic Studies (IMES) with a slightly different focus.

85. International, Cross-Cultural Institute, 4.

86. Ibid. On racial violence and murder in Germany, see Panikos Panayi, "Racial Violence in the New Germany 1990–1993," *Contemporary European History* 3, no. 3 (1994): 265–88; Bruce-Jones, *Race in the Shadow of Law.*

87. International, Cross-Cultural Institute, 4.

88. Ahmed, *The Cultural Practice of Emotions*; Verta Taylor and Leila Rupp, *"Loving Internationalism: The Emotion Culture of Transnational Women's Organizations, 1888–1945,"* *Mobilization* 2, no. 2 (2002): 141–58.

89. International, Cross-Cultural Institute, 4.

90. Interkulturelle Initiative Schwarzer Frauen für Minoritätenrechte und Studien in Deutschland, 2.

91. International, Cross-Cultural Institute, 11.

92. Ibid., 4.

93. Kraft and Ashraf-Khan, "Einleitung," in Kraft and Ashraf-Kahn, *Schwarze Frauen der Welt*, 11. For a brief discussion of this volume, see also Ohene-Nyako, "Black Women's Transnational Activism."

94. Ibid., 11.

95. Ibid., 209.

96. Ibid., 211.

97. May Ayim, "Rassismus und Verdrängung im vereinten Deutschland," in Kraft and Ashraf-Khan, *Schwarze Frauen der Welt*, 29–34.

98. Marion Kraft, "Feminismus und Frauen afrikanischer Herkunft in Europa," in Kraft and Ashraf-Khan, *Schwarze Frauen der Welt,* 171–83.

99. Sheila Mysorekar, "Asiatisch-afrikanische Beziehungen-Probleme, Spaltung und Solidarität in der Diaspora," in Kraft and Ashraf-Khan, *Schwarze Frauen der Welt,* 191–99.

EPILOGUE

1. Kim Alecia Singletary, "Black Lives Matter Globally," *H-Black-Europe,* July 26, 2016, https://networks.h-net.org/node/113394/discussions/135619/ann-media-watch -black-lives-matter-globally.

2. European Network of People of African Descent (ENPAD), "#Ferguson is Everywhere #Black Lives Matter Photocampaign Berlin," https://www.enpad.net/EN/ teams/action-team/ferguson-is-everywhere-black-lives-matter-photocampaign -berlin/.

3. "#CampusRassismus," *Mädchenmannschaft,* December 15, 2015, https://maedchen mannschaft.net/campusrassismus/. In addition to this, ISD has also been involved with other forms of digital activism, including the 2015 hashtag campaign #CampusRassis-mus, which stressed the experiences of students of color with racism on white campuses across Germany. #Schauhin is another digital hashtag campaign that sought to bring awareness of the instances of everyday racism that People of Color face in Germany; Turkish-German Kübra Gümüsay began it in 2013.

4. See also Maisha Auma, "Black Lives Matter Berlin: Statement by Prof. Maisha Auma on Behalf of the Organization ADEFRA, Black Women in Germany," July 25, 2016, http://www.adefra.de/index.php/blog/73-black-lives-matter-berlin-statem.

5. See Muñoz, *Disidentifications.*

6. Josephine Apraku, Shaheen Wacker, Nela Biedermann, Kristin Lein, Jacqueline Mayen, and Mic Oala, "Wenn ich sage 'Black Lives Matter,' dann sage ich auch, dass mein eigenes Leben zählt," *Missy Magazine,* June 20, 2017, http://missy-magazine.de/blog/ 2017/06/20/wenn-ich-sage-black-lives-matter-dann-sage-ich-auch-dass-mein -eigenes-leben-zaehlt/.

7. See Jean Beaman, "From Ferguson to France," *Contexts* 14, no. 1 (2015): 65–67; Cooper, *Beyond Respectability,* 141–52.

8. George Steinmetz, "The First Genocide of the 20th Century and its Postcolonial Afterlives: Germany and the Namibian Ovaherero," *Journal of the International Institute* 12, no. 2 (2005), https://quod.lib.umich.edu/j/jii/4750978.0012.201/—first-genocide-of -the-20th-century-and-its-postcolonial?rgn=main;view=fulltext; Christopher Browning, *Ordinary Men: Reserve Police Battalion 101 and the Final Solution in Poland* (New York: Harper Collins, 2017); Marcel Fürstenau, "Neo-Nazi murder spree shocks Germany," *Deutsche Welle,* April 13, 2013, http://www.dw.com/en/neo-nazi-murder-spree -shocks-germany/a-16742061; Emran Feroz, "Living as a refugee in Germany under the shadow of violence," *TRT World,* January 16, 2019, https://www.trtworld.com/opinion/

living-as-a-refugee-in-germany-under-the-shadow-of-violence-23356. This is not to suggest that attacks against foreign nationals and Germans of color didn't previously occur, but there has been an uptick in attacks, especially with the presence of Syrian and other migrants in 2015 and 2016.

9. In the fall 2017 election, AfD claimed, for the first time, ninety-four seats in the national parliament (*Bundestag*), becoming the third-largest party in Germany. In October 2019, AfD surged to second place in the Thuringia state election; Thuringia is a state in east-central Germany. The AfD is similar to other European far-right groups such as France's National Front and the Dutch Freedom Party (PVV). The National Democratic Party of Germany (Nationaldemokratische Partei Deutschlands, NPD), founded in 1964, and the Patriotic European Against the Islamisation of the Occident (Patriotische Europäer gegen die Islamisierung des Abendlandes, Pegida), founded in 2014, are two additional examples of German far-right mobilization.

10. See El-Tayeb, *Undeutsch*; El-Tayeb, *European Others;* Kilomba, *Plantation Memories*.

11. Daniel Pelz, "Berlin's African quarter to change colonial-era street names," *Deutsche Welle*, April 20, 2018, http://www.dw.com/en/berlins-african-quarter-to-change -colonial-era-street-names/a-43474130. See also Berlin-Postkolonial http://www .berlin-postkolonial.de/.

12. See John A. Kantara, "Schwarz sein und deutsch dazu," *Die Zeit,* April 23, 1998, http://www.zeit.de/1998/18/schwarz.txt.19980423.xml. For the first time in 2013, Germans elected two politicians of African descent to the Bundestag: Karamba Diaby (SPD) and Charles Huber (CDU).

SELECTED BIBLIOGRAPHY

ARCHIVES

Audre Lorde Archiv, Universitätsarchiv, Freie Universität Berlin, Germany
The Collection of Audre Lorde, Spelman College, Atlanta, Georgia
May Ayim Archiv, Universitätsarchiv, Freie Universität Berlin, Germany
Frauenforschungs-, -bildungs-und Informationszentrum (FFBIZ), Berlin, Germany
Orlanda Frauenverlag, Berlin, Germany
Spinnboden Lesbenarchiv und Bibliothek, Berlin, Germany
Zentrale Bibliothek Frauenforschung, Gender & Queer Studies (ZBF&GQS), Hamburg, Germany

PRIVATE COLLECTIONS

The May Ayim Papers
The Private Collection of Ria Cheatom
The Private Collection of Ricky Reiser

PERIODICALS

Afrekete: Zeitung für afro-deutsche und schwarze Frauen
afro look: eine zeitschrift von schwarzen menschen in Deutschland / Onkel Toms Faust
AWA-FINNABA: An African Literary and Cultural Journal
BBC News
Bielefelder Stadtblatt

Der Spiegel
Deutsche Welle
Die Tagesspeigel
Die Tageszeitung (taz)
Die Zeit
Frankfurter Allgemeine Zeitung
Frankfurter Rundschau
Isivivane: Journal of Letters and Arts in Africa and the Diaspora
LesbenSitch: Das Lesbenmagazin für den Aufrechten Gang
Süddeutsche Zeitung
The European
The Guardian

FILMS

Binder, Maria. *Hoffnung im Herz: Mündliche Poesie*. 1997. DVD. New York: Third World Newsreel.
Griffin, Ada Gay, and Michelle Parkerson. *A Litany for Survival: The Life and Work of Audre Lorde*. 1995. DVD. New York: Third World Newsreel.
Kantara, John A. *Blues Schwarzweiss: Vier schwarze deutsche Leben*. 1998. Videocassette. Berlin.
Priemer, Christel. *Deustsche sind weiß, Neger können keine Deutschen sein!*. 1986. DVD. Germany: ARD.
———. *Ein bißchen schwarz ein bißchen, weiß oder was es heißt ein deutscher Neger zu sein*. 1984. DVD. Germany: ARD.
———. *Schwarze Frauen bekennen Farbe: Lebensgeschichten aus einem kalten Land*: 1992. DVD. Germany: ARD.
Rivera, Julia. *mEin Viertel 100—25 Jahre Bundestreffen*. 2011. DVD. Berlin.
Schultz, Dagmar, with Ika Hügel Marshall and Ria Cheatom. *Audre Lorde—The Berlin Years 1984-1992*. 2012. DVD. New York: Third World Newsreel.

AUDIO

Cheatom, Ria. Informal conversation. Sound recording. Berlin-Schöneberg, August 8, 2011. From the author's private collection, Real audio, MP3.

PRIMARY SOURCES

"A Eulogy for Audre Lorde: From Afro-German Women." *Aché* (1993), 7–9.
ADEFRA. "20 Jahre Schwarze Frauenbewegung in Deutschland,"/"20 Years of Black Women's Activism in Germany." Berlin: Museum Europäischer Kulturen, 2006.
Ani, Ekpenyong, Jasmin Eding, Maisha M. Eggers, Katja Kinder, and Peggy Piesche. "Schwarze Lesben im geteilten Feminismus." In *In Bewegung bleiben: 100 Jahre Politik*,

Kultur und Geschichte von Lesben, edited by Gabriele Dennert, Christiane Leidinger, and Franziska Rauchut, 297–99. Berlin: Querverlag, 2007.

Ani, Ekpenyong. "Die Frau, die Mut zeigt—der Verein ADEFRA Schwarze Deutsche Frauen/Schwarze Frauen in Deutschand." In *The BlackBook: Deutschlands Häutungen,* edited by AntiDiskriminierungsBüro Köln and cyberNomads. 145–49. Frankfurt am Main: IKO-Verlag für Interkulturelle Kommunikation, 2004.

AntiDiskriminierungsBüro Köln and cyberNomads, eds. *The BlackBook: Deutschlands Häutungen.* Frankfurt am Main: IKO-Verlag für Interkulturelle Kommunikation, 2004.

Ayim, May, and Nivedita Prasad, eds. *Dokumentation Wege zu Bündnissen.* Berlin: AStA Druckerei der FU, 1992.

Ayim (Opitz), May. "The Break." In *Showing Our Colors: Afro-German Women Speak Out,* edited by May Opitz, Katharina Oguntoye, and Dagmar Schultz, translated by Anne V. Adams, 207–9. Amherst: University of Massachusetts Press, 1992.

——. "Aufbruch." In *Farbe bekennen: Afro-deutsche Frauen auf den Spuren ihrer Geschichte,* edited by Katharina Oguntoye, May Opitz/Ayim, and Dagmar Schultz, 213–14. Berlin: Orlanda, 2006.

——, Katharina Oguntoye, and Dagmar Schultz, eds. *Showing Our Colours: Afro-German Women Speak Out,* translated by Anne V. Adams. Amherst: University of Massachusetts Press, 1992.

——, Katharina Oguntoye, and Dagmar Schultz, eds. *Showing Our Colours: Afro-German Women Speak Out.* London: Open Letters, 1992.

——, Katharina Oguntoye, and Dagmar Schultz, eds. *Farbe bekennen: Afro-deutsche Frauen auf den Spuren ihrer Geschichte.* Berlin: Orlanda, 2006.

——. *Blues in schwarz weiss.* Berlin: Orlando Verlag, 1995.

——. *Blues in Black and White: A Collection of Essays, Poetry, and Conversations,* translated by Anne V. Adams. Trenton, N.J.: Africa World Press, 2003.

——. "Afro-deutsch I." In *Blues in schwarz weiss,* 18. Berlin: Orlanda, 1995.

——. "Afro-German." In *Showing Our Colors: Afro-German Women Speak Out,* edited by May Opitz, Katharina Oguntoye, and Dagmar Schultz, translated by Anne Adams, 138–39. Amherst: University of Massachusetts Press, 1992.

——. "Afro-Deutsch." In *Farbe bekennen: Afro-deutsche Frauen auf den Spuren ihrer Geschichte,* edited by Katharina Oguntoye, May Opitz/Ayim, and Dagmar Schultz, 146. Berlin: Orlanda, 2006.

——. "Afro-German I." In *Blues in Black and White: A Collection of Essays, Poetry, and Conversations,* by May Ayim, translated by Anne V. Adams, 14–15. Trenton, N.J.: Africa World Press, 2003.

——. "Ein Brief aus Münster." In *Grenzenlos und unverschämt,* 9–12. Berlin: Orlanda, 1997.

——. "afro-deutsch II." In *Blues in schwarz weiss,* 25. Berlin: Orlanda, 1995.

——. "Afro-German II." In *Blues in Black and White: A Collection of Essays, Poetry, and Conversations,* by May Ayim, translated by Anne V. Adams, 16–17. Trenton, N.J.: Africa World Press, 2003.

——. "deutschland im herbst" and "gegen leberwurstgrau—für eine bunte republik talk-talk-show für den bla-bla-kampf." In *Blues in schwarz weiss,* 68–70 and 62–65. Berlin: Orlanda, 1995.

——. "Autumn in Germany" and "No more rotten gray—for a color republic: talk-talk-show for the blah-blah-struggle." In *Blues in Black and White: A Collection of Essays, Poetry, and Conversations,* by May Ayim, translated by Anne V. Adams, 109–11 and 60–63. Trenton, N.J.: Africa World Press, 2003.

——. "Die Afro-deutsche Minderheit." In *Ethnische Minderheiten in der Bundesrepublik Deutschland: Ein Lexikon,* edited by Cornelia Schmalz-Jacobesn and Georg Hansen, 39–51. Munich: Verlag C.H. Beck, 1995.

——. *Grenzenlos und unverschämt.* Berlin: Orlanda, 1997.

——. "Afro-Deutsche: Ihre Kultur-und Sozialgeschichte auf dem Hintergrund gesellschaftlicher Veränderungen." MA thesis, University of Regensburg, 1984.

——. "Eine Der Anderen-Rückkehr in mein Dorf." In *Schwarz Afrika der Frauen,* edited by Gabriela Mönnig, 267–79. München: Frauenoffensive, 1989.

——. "May Ayim, Curriculum Vitae." In *Blues in Black and White: A Collection of Essays, Poetry and Conversations,* by May Ayim, translated by Anne Adams, 171–72. Trenton, N.J.: Africa World Press, 2003.

——. *Nachtgesang.* Berlin: Orlanda, 1997.

——. "The Year 1990: Homeland and Unity from an Afro-German Perspective." In *Fringe Voices: An Anthology of minority Writing in the Federal Republic of Germany,* edited by Antje Harnisch, Anne-Marie Stokes, and Friedemann Weidauer, 105–19. Oxford, U.K.: Berg, 1998.

——. "Wir wollen aus der Isolation heraus." In *Grenzenlos und unverschämt,* by May Ayim, 45–48. Berlin: Orlanda, 1997.

——. "Das Jahr 1990: Heimat und Einheit aus afro-deutscher Perspektive." In *Entfernte Verbindungen: Rassismus, Antisemitismus, Klassenunterdrückung,* edited by Chris Lange, Ika Hügel, Ilona Bubeck, Gülsen Aktas, Dagmar Schultz, and May Ayim, 206–22. Berlin: Orlanda, 1993.

——. "Rassismus und Verdrängung im vereinten Deutschland." In *Schwarze Frauen der Welt: Europa and Migration,* edited by Marion Kraft and Rukhsana Shamim Ashraf-Khan, 29–34. Berlin: Orlanda, 1994.

Berger, Astrid. "Aren't you glad you can stay here?" In *Showing Our Colors: Afro-German Women Speak Out,* edited by May Opitz, Katharina Oguntoye, and Dagmar Schultz, translated by Anne Adams, 112–18. Amherst: University of Massachusetts Press, 1992.

——. "Sind sie nicht froh, daß sie immer hier bleiben dürfen?" In *Farbe bekennen: Afro-deutsche Frauen auf den Spuren ihrer Geschichte,* edited by Katharina Oguntoye, May Opitz/Ayim, and Dagmar Schultz, 122–28. Berlin: Orlanda, 2006.

Berger, Julia. "I do the same things as others do." In *Showing Our Colors: Afro-German Women Speak Out,* edited by May Opitz, Katharina Oguntoye, and Dagmar Schultz, translated by Anne Adams, 196–98. Amherst: University of Massachusetts Press, 1992.

———. "Ich mache dieselben Sachen wie die anderen." In *Farbe bekennen: Afro-deutsche Frauen auf den Spuren ihrer Geschichte,* edited by Katharina Oguntoye, May Opitz/ Ayim, and Dagmar Schultz, 202–4. Berlin: Orlanda, 2006.

Bergold-Caldwell, Denise, Laura Digoh, Hadija Haruna-Oelker, Christelle Nkwendja-Ngnoubamdjum, Camilla Ridha, and Eleonore Wiedenroth-Coulibaly, eds. *Spiegelblicke: Perspektiven Schwarzer Bewegung in Deutschland.* Berlin: Orlanda, 2015.

Byrd, Rudolph P., Johnnetta Betsch Cole, and Beverly Guy-Sheftall, eds. *I Am Your Sister: Collected and Unpublished Writings of Audre Lorde.* New York: Oxford University Press, 2009.

Cheatom, Ria, Jasmin Eding, Mary Powell, and Ulrike Gerhart. "Wage dein Leben Verlasse Dein Haus!: ADEFRA München über sich und das 5. Afro-deutsche Frauenbundestreffen." *Kofra: Zeitschrift für Feminismus und Arbeit (Rassismus von Frauen)* 10 (1991): 21–22.

Emde, Helga. "An 'Occupation Baby' in Postwar Germany." In *Showing Our Colors: Afro-German Women Speak Out,* edited by May Opitz, Katharina Oguntoye, and Dagmar Schultz, translated by Anne V. Adams, 101–9. Amherst: University of Massachusetts Press, 1992.

———. "Als 'Besatzungskind' im Nachkriegsdeutschland." In *Farbe bekennen: Afro-deutsche Frauen auf den Spuren ihrer Geschichte,* edited by Katharina Oguntoye, May Opitz/ Ayim, and Dagmar Schultz, 115–21. Berlin: Orlanda, 2006.

———. "The Cry." In *Showing Our Colors: Afro-German Women Speak Out,* edited by May Opitz, Katharina Oguntoye, and Dagmar Schultz, translated by Anne Adams, 111. Amherst: University of Massachusetts Press, 1992.

———. "Der Schrei." In *Farbe bekennen: Afro-deutsche Frauen auf den Spuren ihrer Geschichte,* edited by Katharina Oguntoye, May Opitz/Ayim, and Dagmar Schultz, 121. Berlin: Orlanda, 2006.

———. "I too am German—An Afro-German Perspective." In *Who is a German? Historical and Modern Perspectives of Africans in Germany,* edited by Leroy Hopkins, 33–42. Washington, D.C.: American Institute for Contemporary German Studies, 1999.

Eisenbrandt, Angelika. "All of a sudden I knew what I wanted." In *Showing Our Colors: Afro-German Women Speak Out,* edited by May Opitz, Katharina Oguntoye, and Dagmar Schultz, translated by Anne Adams, 191–95. Amherst: University of Massachusetts Press, 1992.

———. "Auf einmal wußte ich, was ich wollte." In *Farbe bekennen: Afro-deutsche Frauen auf den Spuren ihrer Geschichte,* edited by Katharina Oguntoye, May Opitz/Ayim, and Dagmar Schultz, 197–201. Berlin: Orlanda, 2006.

Fremgen, Gisela. ed. . . . *und wenn du dazu noch Schwarz bist: Berichte schwarzer Frauen in der Bundesrepublik.* Bremen: Edition Con., 1984.

Gummich, Judy. "Auffallen und verändern: Schwarze Deutsche." *Weibblick: Informationsblatt von Frauen für Frauen (Schwarze deutsche Frauen, Rassismus in der Sprache, weiße Frauen mit schwarzen Hindern)* 13 (1993): 5–8.

———. "Als schwarze diskriminiert—als Deutsche ignoriert: Schwarze Deutsche." *Perspektiven* (1993): 1–12.

Ha, Kien Nghi, Nicola Lauré al-Samarai, and Sheila Mysorekar, eds. *Re/visionen: Postkoloniale Perspektiven von People of Color auf Rassismus, Kulturpolitik und Widerstand in Deutschland.* Münster: Unrast, 2007.

Hall, Joan Wylie, ed. *Conversations with Audre Lorde.* Oxford: University Press of Mississippi, 2004.

Haus der Kulturen der Welt. *Adinkra: Symbolic language of the Ashanti/Adinkra: Symbolsprache der Ashanti.* Berlin: Movimento Drück, 1993.

Herrero-Villamor, Ana. "91," "Auf den Straßen unserer Stadt," "bin heimatlos," "Heaven," "wir Berliner," "Gold," "Blau/Indigo," "sie möchte deine lippen lesen," "Munsternde Blicke," and "I Am A Sister." In *Euer Schweigen schützt Euch nicht: Audre Lorde und die Schwarze Frauenbewegung in Deutschland,* edited by Peggy Piesche, 41, 52, 69–74, 156, 168–71, 186, 203–4, and 212–15. Berlin: Orlanda, 2012.

Hügel-Marshall, Ika. *Daheim Unterwegs: Ein deutsches Leben.* Berlin: Orlanda, 1998.

———. Invisible Woman: *Growing Up Black in Germany,* translated by Elizabeth Gaffney. New York: Continuum, 2001.

———. "Lesbischsein läßt sich verleugnen, schwarzsein nicht." In *Lesben, Liebe, Leidenschaft: Texte zur feministischen Psychologie und zu Liebesbeziehungen unter Frauen,* edited by JoAnn Loulan, 298–307. Berlin: Orlanda, 1992.

———. "Die Situation von Afrodeutschen nach dem Zweiten Weltkrieg (am Beispiel meiner Autobiographie: '*Daheim unterwegs. Ein deutsches Leben*') und heute." In *Früchte der Zeit: Afrika, Diaspora, Literatur und Migration,* edited by Helmuth Niederle, Ulrike Davis-Suilowski, and Thomas Fillitz, 75–84. Vienna: WUV Universitätsverlag, 2001.

ISD-Münich. ed. *Macht der Nacht: eine Schwarze Deutsche Anthologie.* München: ISD, 1991–1992.

Kantara, Jeannine. "Die Geschichte der Zeitschrift *afro look* und die Anfänge der ISD Berliner Frühlingserwachen." In *Black Berlin: Die deutsche Metropole und ihre afrikanische Diaspora in Geschichte und Gegenwart,* edited by Oumar Diallo and Joachim Zeller, 165–76. Berlin: Metropol, 2013.

———. "Die Geschichte der *afro look.*" In *The BlackBook: Deutschlands Häutungen,* edited by AntiDiskrimierungsBüro Köln and cyberNomads, 160–62. Frankfurt am Main: IKO-Verlag für Interkulturelle Kommunikation, 2004.

Kinder, Katja. "Rückblenden und Vorschauen: 20 Jahre Schwarze Frauenbewegung." In *Euer Schweigen schützt Euch nicht: Audre Lorde und die Schwarze Frauenbewegung in Deutschland,* edited by Peggy Piesche, 17–40. Berlin: Orlanda, 2012.

Kraft, Marion, and Rukhsana Shamim Ashraf-Khan, eds. *Schwarze Frauen der Welt: Europa und Migration.* Berlin: Orlanda, 1994.

———. ed. *Kinder der Befreiung: Transatlantische Erfahrungen und Perspektiven Schwarzer Deutscher der Nachkriegsgeneration.* Münster: Unrast, 2015.

———. ed. *Children of the Liberation: Transatlantic Experiences and Perspectives of Black Germans of the Post-War Generation.* Oxford, U.K.: Peter Lang, 2019.

Küppers, Michael. "professional kultur®evolution inna germany." In *The BlackBook: Deutschlands Häutungen,* edited by AntiDiskriminierungsBüro Köln and cyberNomads, 150–54. Frankfurt am Main: IKO-Verlag für Interkulturelle Kommunikation, 2004.

Lorde, Audre and James Baldwin. "Revolutionary Hope: A Conversation Between James Baldwin and Audre Lorde." *Essence* (1984): 72–74, 129–30, and 133.

——. "Audre Lorde: A New Spelling of Our Name." *Sojourner* 10, no. 5: (1985): 16–17.

——. *A Burst of Light: Essays.* Ithaca, N.Y.: Firebrand Books, 1988.

——. *Lichtflut: Neue Texte.* Berlin: Orlanda, 1988.

——. *The Cancer Journals.* San Francisco: Aunt Lute, 1997.

——. *Zami A New Spelling of My Name: A Biomythography.* Freedom, Calif.: Crossing Press, 1994.

——. *Die Quelle Unserer Macht: Gedichte,* translated by Marion Kraft and Sigrid Markmann. Berlin: Orlanda, 1994.

——. *Black Unicorn: Poems.* New York: W. W. Norton, 1995.

——. *The Collected Poems of Audre Lorde.* New York: Norton, 2000.

——. *Sister Outsider: Essays and Speeches.* Berkeley, Calif.: Crossing Press, 2007.

Lubinetzki/Birkenwald, Raja. "'I never wanted to write, I just couldn't help myself': Conversation with Raja Lubinetzki (age 23) GDR." In *Showing Our Colors: Afro-German Women Speak Out,* edited by May Opitz, Katharina Oguntoye, and Dagmar Schultz, translated by Anne Adams, 218–27. Amherst: University of Massachusetts Press, 1992.

——. "Gespräch mit Katherina Birkenwald (23 J.) DDR: 'Ich wollte nie schreiben, ich konnte nie anders.'" In *Farbe bekennen: Afro-deutsche Frauen auf den Spuren ihrer Geschichte,* edited by Katharina Oguntoye, May Opitz/Ayim, and Dagmar Schultz, 225–38. Berlin: Orlanda, 2006.

——. "ruf." In *Farbe bekennen: Afro-deutsche Frauen auf den Spuren ihrer Geschichte,* edited by Katharina Oguntoye, May Opitz/Ayim, and Dagmar Schultz, 232. Berlin: Orlanda, 2006.

——. "call." In *Showing Our Colors: Afro-German Women Speak Out,* edited by May Opitz, Katharina Oguntoye, and Dagmar Schultz, translated by Anne Adams, 224. Amherst: University of Massachusetts Press, 1992.

Oguntoye, Katharina. *Eine afro-deutsche Geschichte: Zur Lebenssituation von Afrikanern und Afro-Deutschen in Deutschland von 1884 bis 1950.* Berlin: Hoho Verlag Christine Hoffmann, 1997.

——. "Vorwort zur Neuauflage 2006." In *Farbe bekennen: Afro-deutsche Frauen auf den Spuren ihrer Geschichte,* edited by Katharina Oguntoye, May Opitz/Ayim, and Dagmar Schultz, 5–14. Berlin: Orlanda, 2006.

——. "Mein Coming-Out Schwarze Lesbe in Deutschland." In *In Bewegung bleiben: 100 Jahre Politik, Kultur und Geschichte von Lesben,* edited by Gabriele Dennert, Christiane Leidinger, and Franziska Rauchut, 160–63. Berlin: Querverlag, 2007.

——. "Ruckblenden und Vorschauen: 20 Jahre Schwarze Frauenbewegung." In *Euer Schweigen schützt Euch nicht: Audre Lorde und die Schwarze Frauenbewegung in Deutschland,* edited by Peggy Piesche, 17–40. Berlin: Orlanda, 2012.

———. "Reflection." In *Showing Our Colors: Afro-German Women Speak Out,* edited by May Opitz, Katharina Oguntoye, and Dagmar Schultz, translated by Anne Adams, 215. Amherst: University of Massachusetts Press, 1992.

———. "Spiegel." In *Farbe bekennen: Afro-deutsche Frauen auf den Spuren ihrer Geschichte,* edited by Katharina Oguntoye, May Opitz/Ayim, and Dagmar Schultz, 222. Berlin: Orlanda, 2006.

Piesche, Peggy. ed. *Euer Schweigen schützt Euch nicht: Audre Lorde und die Schwarze Frauenbewegung in Deutschland.* Berlin: Orlanda, 2012.

Schultz, Dagmar, ed. *Audre Lorde und Adrienne Rich Macht und Sinnlichkeit: Ausgewählte Texte,* translated by Renate Stendhal, Marion Kraft, Susanne Stern, and Erika Wisselinck. Berlin: Orlanda, 1993.

———. "Vorwort." In *Auf Leben und Tod: Krebstagebuch,* by Audre Lorde, translated by Renate Stendhal and Margarete Längsfeld. Frankfurt am Main: Fischer, 2000.

———. "Audre Lorde—Her Struggles and Her Visions." Berlin: Heinrich Böll Stiftung and Gunda Werde Institut: Feminismus und Geschlechterdemokratie, n.d, http://dagmarschultz.com/download/audre_lorde.pdf.

Wiedenroth-Coulibaly, Eleonore, and Sascha Zinflou. "20 Jahre Schwarze Organisierung in Deutschland—Ein Abriss." In *The BlackBook: Deutschlands Häutungen,* edited by AntiDiskriminierungsBüro Köln and cyberNomads, 133–44. Frankfurt am Main: IKO-Verlag für Interkulturelle Kommunikation, 2004.

Wiedenroth, Ellen. "What makes me so different in the eyes of others?" In *Showing Our Colors: Afro-German Women Speak Out,* edited by May Opitz, Katharina Oguntoye, and Dagmar Schultz, translated by Anne Adams, 165–77. Amherst: University of Massachusetts Press, 1992.

———. "Was macht mich so anders in den Augen der anderen?" In *Farbe bekennen: Afro-deutsche Frauen auf den Spuren ihrer Geschichte,* edited by Katharina Oguntoye, May Opitz/Ayim, and Dagmar Schultz, 172–83. Berlin: Orlanda, 2006.

SECONDARY SOURCES

Adams, Anne. "The Souls of Black *Volk*: Contradiction? Oxymoron?" In *Not So Plain as Black and White: Afro-German Culture and History, 1890–2000,* edited by Patricia Mazon and Reinheld Steingröver, 209–32. Rochester, N.Y.: University of Rochester Press, 2005.

———. "afro look: magazine of blacks in germany; An Africanist Analysis." In *Africa, Europe and (Post)Colonialism: Racism, Migration and Diaspora in African Literatures,* edited by Susan Arndt and Marek Spitezok von Brisinski, 257–78. Bayreuth: Bayreuth University, 2006.

Ahmed, Sara. *The Cultural Practice of Emotions.* Abingdon, UK: Routledge, 2004.

———. *Queer Phenomenology: Orientations, Objects, and Others.* Durham, N.C.: Duke University Press, 2006.

Aimes, Eric, Lora Wildenthal, and Marcia Klotz, eds. *Germany's Colonial Pasts.* Lincoln: University of Nebraska Press, 2005.

Aitken, Robbie. "Embracing Germany: Interwar German Society and Black Germans through the Eyes of African American Reporters." *Journal of American Studies* 52 (2018): 447–73.

Al-Samarai, Nicola. "Unwegsame Erinnerungen: Auto/biographische Zeugnisse von Schwarzen Deutschen aus der BRD und der DDR." In *Encounters/Begegnungen,* edited by Marianne Bechhaus-Gerst and Reinhard Klein-Arendt, 197–210. Münster: LIT, 2004.

Bach, Tina. "Schwarze Deutsche Literatur: Eine Einführung." *freitext* 18 (2011): 19–23.

Behrends, Jan, Thomas Lindenberger, and Patrice Poutrus, eds. *Fremde und Fremd-Sein in der DDR: Zu historischen Ursachen der Fremdenfeindlichkeit in Ostdeutschland.* Berlin: Metropol, 2003.

Blackshire-Belay, Carol Aisha. "The African Diaspora in Europe: African Germans Speak Out." *Journal of Black Studies* 31, no. 3 (2001): 264–87.

Blain, Keisha N. *Set the World on Fire: Black Nationalist Women and the Global Struggle for Freedom.* Philadelphia: University of Pennsylvania Press, 2018.

—— and Tiffany M. Gill, eds. *To Turn the Whole World Over: Black Women and Internationalism.* Urbana: University of Illinois Press, 2019.

Bowen, Angela. "Black Feminism." In *Lesbian Histories and Cultures: An Encyclopedia,* edited by Bonnie Zimmerman, 117–19. New York: Taylor & Francis, 2000.

Brown, Elsa Barkley. "Negotiating and Transforming the Public Sphere: African American Political Life in the Transition from Slavery to Freedom." *Public Culture* 7 (1994): 102–46.

Brown, Jacqueline Nassy. *Dropping Anchor, Setting Sail: Geographies of Race in Black Liverpool.* Princeton, N.J.: Princeton University Press, 2005.

Bruce-Jones, Eddie. *Race in the Shadow of the Law: State Violence in Contemporary Europe.* Abingdon, U.K.: Routledge, 2017.

Bryan, Beverly, Stella Dadzie, and Suzanne Scafe, eds. *The Heart of the Race: Black Women's Lives in Britain.* London: Virago, 2018.

Campt, M. Tina, and Paul Gilroy, eds. *Der Black Atlantic.* Berlin: Haus der Kulturen der Welt, 2004.

Campt, Tina M. *Other Germans: Black Germans and the Politics of Race, Gender, and Memory in the Third Reich.* Ann Arbor: University of Michigan Press, 2004.

——. *Image Matters: Archive, Photography, and the African Diaspora in Europe.* Durham, N.C.: Duke University Press, 2012.

——. "Afro-German Cultural Identity and the Politics of Positionality: Contests and Contexts in the Formation of a German Ethnic Identity." *New German Critique* 58 (1993): 109–26.

——. "The Crowded Space of Diaspora: Intercultural Address and the Tensions of Diasporic Relation." *Radical History Review* 83 (2002): 94–113.

Carby, Hazel. *Reconstructing Womanhood: The Emergence of the Afro-American Woman Novelist.* New York: Oxford University Press, 1987.

Chin, Rita, Heide Fehrenbach, Atina Grossmann, and Geoff Eley, eds. *After the Nazi Racial State: Difference and Democracy in Germany and Europe*. Ann Arbor: University of Michigan Press, 2009.

Chin, Rita. *The Guest Worker Question in Postwar Germany*. New York: Cambridge University Press, 2007.

Cohen, Cathy J. "Punks, Bulldaggers, and Welfare Queens: The Radical Potential of Queer Politics?" In *Black Queer Studies: A Critical Anthology*, edited by E. Patrick Johnson and Mae G. Henderson, 21–51. Durham, N.C.: Duke University Press, 2005.

Collins, Patricia Hill. *On Intellectual Activism*. Philadelphia: Temple University Press, 2013.

Cooper, Brittney. *Beyond Respectability: The Intellectual Thought of Race Women*. Urbana: University of Illinois Press, 2017.

Crawley, Erin Leigh. "Challenging Concepts of Cultural and National Homogeneity: Afro-German Women and the Articulation of Germanness." PhD diss., University of Wisconsin-Madison, 1996.

Crenshaw, Kimberlé. "Mapping the Margins: Intersectionality, Identity Politics, and Violence against Women of Color." *Stanford Law Review* 43, no. 6 (1991): 1241–99.

——. "Demarginalizing the Intersection of Race and Sex: A Black Feminist Critique of Antidiscrimination Doctrine, Feminist Theory and Antiracist Politics." *University of Chicago Legal Forum* 1 (1989): 139–67.

Cvetkovich, Ann. *An Archive of Feelings: Trauma, Sexuality, and Lesbian Public Cultures*. Durham, N.C.: Duke University Press, 2003.

Davies, Carole Boyce. *Black Women, Writing and Identity: Migrations of the Subject*. New York: Routledge, 1994.

——. *Left of Karl Marx: The Political Life of Black Communist Claudia Jones*. Durham, N.C.: Duke University Press, 2008.

De Veux, Alexis. *Warrior Poet: A Biography of Audre Lorde*. New York: W.W. Norton, 2004.

Diedrich, Maria I., and Jürgen Heinrichs, eds. *From Black to Schwarz: Cultural Crossovers between African America and Germany*. Münster: LIT, 2010.

Donaldson, Sonya. "(Ir)reconcilable Differences?: The Search for Identity in Afro-German Autobiography." PhD diss., University of Virginia, 2012.

Dubey, Madhu. "Gayl Jones and the Matrilineal Metaphor of Tradition." *Signs* 20, no. 2 (1995): 245–67.

Edwards, Brent Hayes. *The Practice of Diaspora: Literature, Translation, and the Rise of Black Internationalism*. Cambridge, Mass.: Harvard University Press, 2003.

Eggers, Maureen Maisha. "Knowledges of (Un-)Belonging: Epistemic Change as a Defining Mode for Black Women's Activism in Germany." In *Remapping Black Germany: New Perspectives on Afro-German History, Politics, and Culture*, edited by Sara Lennox, 33–45. Amherst: University of Massachusetts Press, 2016.

El-Tayeb, Fatima. *Undeutsch: Die Konstruktion des Anderen in der Postmigrantischen Gesellschaft*. Bielefeld: Transcript, 2016.

——. *European Others: Queering Ethnicity in Postnational Europe*. Minneapolis: University of Minnesota Press, 2011.

——. *Schwarze Deutsche: Der Diskurs um "Rasse" und nationale Identität, 1890–1933*. Frankfurt: Campus, 2001.

——. "'If You Can't Pronounce My Name, You Can Just Call Me Pride': Afro-German Activism, Gender and Hip Hop." *Gender and History* 15, no. 3 (2003): 459–85.

Essed, Philomena. *Understanding Everyday Racism: An Interdisciplinary Theory*. London: Sage Publications, 1991.

Faymonville, Carmen. "Black Germans and Transnational Identification." *Callaloo* 26, no. 2 (2003): 364–82.

Fehrenbach, Heide. *Race After Hitler: Black Occupation Children in Postwar Germany and America*. Princeton, N.J.: Princeton University Press, 2005.

Florvil, Tiffany N., and Vanessa D. Plumly, eds. *Rethinking Black German Studies: Approaches, Interventions and Histories*. London: Peter Lang, 2018.

Ford, Tanisha. "We Were the People of Soul." In Tanisha Ford, *Liberated Threads: Black Women, Style, and The Global Politics of Soul*, 123–57. Chapel Hill: University of North Carolina Press, 2015.

Franklin, V.P. *Living Our Stories, Telling Our Truths: Autobiography and the Making of the African American Intellectual Tradition*. New York: Oxford University Press, 1996.

Fuentes, Marisa. *Dispossessed Lives: Enslaved Women, Violence, and the Archive*. Philadelphia: University of Pennsylvania Press, 2016.

Germain, Felix. *Decolonizing the Republic: African and Caribbean Migrants in Postwar Paris*. East Lansing: Michigan State University Press, 2016.

Gerund, Katharina. "Visions of (Global) Sisterhood and Black Solidarity: Audre Lorde." In Katharina Gerund, *Transatlantic Cultural Exchange: African American Women's Art and Activism in West Germany*, 157–210. Bielefeld: Transcript, 2013.

Geyer, Michael, and Konrad Jarausch. *Shattered Past: Reconstructing German Histories*. Princeton, N.J.: Princeton University Press, 2003.

Geyer, Michael. ed. *The Power of Intellectuals in Contemporary Germany*. Chicago: University of Chicago Press, 2001.

Gilroy, Paul. *The Black Atlantic: Modernity and Double-Consciousness*. Cambridge, Mass.: Harvard University Press, 1993.

Glissant, Eduoard. *Caribbean Discourses: Selected Essays*, translated by Micheal J. Dash. Charlottesville: University of Virginia Press, 1989.

Goertz, Karein. "Borderless and Brazen: Ethnicity Redefined by Afro-German and Turkish German Poets." *Comparatist* 21 (1997): 68–91.

——. "Showing Her Colors: An Afro-German Writes the Blues in Black and White." *Callaloo* 26, no. 2 (2003): 306–19.

Gökturk, Deniz, David Gramling, and Anton Kaes, eds. *Germany in Transit: Nation and Migration, 1955–2005*. Berkeley: University of California Press, 2007.

Greene, Larry, and Anke Ortlepp, eds. *Germans and African Americans: Two Centuries of Exchange*. Oxford: University Press of Mississippi, 2011.

Grossmann, Atina. *Reforming Sex: The German Movement for Birth Control and Abortion Reform, 1920–1950*. New York: Oxford University Press, 1995.

———. *Jews, Germans, and Allies: Close Encounters in Occupied Germany*. Princeton, N.J.: Princeton University Press, 2007.

Guridy, Frank. *Forging Diaspora: Afro-Cubans and African Americans in a World of Empire and Jim Crow*. Chapel Hill: University of North Carolina Press, 2010.

Hackenesch, Silke. *Chocolate and Blackness: A Cultural History*. Frankfurt am Main: Campus, 2017.

Hall, Stuart. "Cultural Identity and Diaspora." In *Identity: Community, Culture, and Difference*, edited by Jonathan Rutherford, 222–37. London: Lawrence & Wishart, 1990.

———. "The Local and the Global: Globalization and Ethnicity." In *Dangerous Liaisons: Gender, Nation, and Postcolonial Perspectives*, edited by Anne McClintock, Aamir Mufti, and Ella Shohat, 173–87. Minneapolis: University of Minnesota Press, 1997.

Higashida, Cheryl. *Black Internationalist Feminism: Women Writers of the Black Left, 1945–1995*. Urbana: University of Illinois Press, 2011.

Higginbotham, Evelyn Brooks. "African-American Women's History and the Metalanguage of Race." *Signs* 17, no. 2 (1992): 251–74.

Hobsbawm, Eric. "Introduction: Inventing Traditions." In *The Invention of Tradition*, edited by Eric Hobsbawm and Terence Ranger, 1–14. Cambridge, U.K.: Cambridge University Press, 2012.

Hodges, Carolyn. "The Private/Plural Selves of Afro-German Women and the Search for a Public Voice." *Journal of Black Studies* 23, no. 2 (1992): 219–34.

Höhn, Maria, and Martin Klimke. *A Breath of Freedom: The Civil Rights Struggle, African American GIs, and Germany*. New York: Palgrave, 2010.

hooks, bell. *Outlaw Culture: Resisting Representations*. New York: Routledge, 2006.

Hopkins, Leroy. "Speak, so I might see you! Afro-German Literature." *World Literature Today* 69, no. 3 (1995): 533–38.

———. "Writing Diasporic Identity: Afro-German Literature Since 1985." In *Not So Plain as Black and White: Afro-German Culture and History, 1890–2000*, edited by Patricia Mazón and Reinhild Steingröver, 183–208. Rochester, N.Y.: University of Rochester Press, 2005.

———. "Race, Nationality and Culture: The African Diaspora in Germany." In *Who is a German? Historical and Modern Perspectives of Africans in Germany*, edited by Leroy Hopkins, 1–32. Washington, D.C.: American Institute for Contemporary German Studies, 1999.

Hull, Gloria T., Patricia Bell Scott, and Barbara Smith, eds. *But Some of US Are Brave: All the Women Are White, All the Blacks Are Men*. New York: CUNY, 1983.

Ifekwunigwe, Jayne O. "'Black Folk Here and There': Repositioning Other(ed) African Diaspora(s) in/and 'Europe.'" In *The African Diaspora and The Disciplines*, edited by Tejumola Olaniyan and James H. Sweet, 313–38. Bloomington: Indiana University Press, 2010.

Jobatey, Francine. "*Afro Look*: Die Geschichte einer Zeitschrift von Schwarzen Deut-schen." PhD diss., University of Massachusetts-Amherst, 2000.

Johnson, E. Patrick, and Mae G. Henderson, eds. *Black Queer Studies: A Critical Anthology*. Durham, N.C.: Duke University Press, 2005.

Kelley, Robin D.G. "But a Local Phase of a World Problem: Black History's Global Vision, 1883–1950." *Journal of American History* 86, no. 3 (1999): 1045–77.

———. *Freedom Dreams: The Black Radical Imagination*. Boston: Beacon Press, 2002.

King, Kevina. "Black, People of Color and Migrant Lives Should Matter: Racial Profiling, Police Brutality and Whiteness in Germany." In *Rethinking Black German Studies: Approaches, Interventions and Histories,* edited by Tiffany N. Florvil and Vanessa D. Plumly, 169–96. London: Peter Lang, 2018.

Klimke, Martin. *The Other Alliance: Student Protest in West Germany and the United States in the Global Sixties*. Princeton, N.J.: Princeton University Press, 2010.

Koepsell, Philipp Khabo, and Asoka Esuruoso, eds. *Arriving in the Future: Stories of Home and Exile: An Anthology of Poetry and Creative Writing by Black Writers in Germany*. Berlin: epubli, 2014.

Koepsell, Philipp Khabo. *The Afropean Contemporary: Literatur- und Gesellschaftsmagazin*. Berlin: epubli, 2015.

———. *Die Akte James Knopf*. Münster: Unrast, 2010.

Kosta, Barbara. *Recasting Autobiography: Women's Counterfictions in Contemporary German Literature and Film*. Ithaca, N.Y.: Cornell University Press, 1994.

Lemke Muñiz de Faria, Yara-Colette Lemke Muñiz. *Zwischen Fursorge und Ausgrenzung: Afrodeutsche "Besatzungskinder" im Nachkriegsdeutschland*. Berlin: Mertopol, 2002.

Lennox, Sara, Sara Friedrichsmeyer, and Susanne Zantop, eds. *The Imperialist Imagination: German Colonialism and Its Legacy*. Ann Arbor: University of Michigan Press, 1999.

Lennox, Sara. "Divided Feminism: Women, Racism, and German National Identity." *German Studies Review* 18, no. 3 (1995): 481–502.

———, ed. *Remapping Black Germany: New Perspectives on Afro-German History, Politics, and Culture*. Amherst: University of Masschusetts Press, 2016.

Lester, Rosemarie. *Trivialneger: Das Bild des Schwarzen im westdeutschen Illustriertenroman*. Stuttgart: Akademischer Verlag, 1982.

Lewis, Shelby F. "Africana Feminism: An Alternative Paradigm for Black Women in the Academy." In *Black Women in the Academy: Promises and Perils,* edited by Lois Benjamin, 41–52. Gainesville: University Press of Florida, 1997.

MacCarroll, Maggie. "May Ayim: A Woman in the Margin of German Society." MA thesis, Florida State University, 2005.

MacMaster, Neil. *Racism in Europe, 1870–2000*. New York: Palgrave, 2001.

Martin, Peter. *Schwarze Teufel, edle Mohren: Afrikaner in Geschichte und Bewusstsein der Deutschen*. Hamburg: Junius, 1993.

Matera, Marc. *Black London: The Imperial Metropolis and Decolonization in the Twentieth Century*. Oakland: University of California Press, 2015.

McDuffie, Erik S. *Sojourning for Freedom: Black Women, American Communism, and the Making of Black Left Feminism.* Durham, N.C.: Duke University Press, 2011.

McGill, Lisa G. *Constructing Black Selves: Caribbean American Narratives and the Second Generation.* New York: New York University Press, 2005.

McKittrick, Katherine. *Demonic Grounds: Black Women and the Cartographies of Struggle.* Minneapolis: University of Minnesota Press, 2006.

Mertins, Silke. "Blues in Black and White: A Biographical Essay." In *Blues in Black and White: A Collection of Essay, Poetry, and Conversations,* by May Ayim, translated by Anne Adams, 141–73. Trenton, N.J.: Africa World Press, 2003.

Muñoz, José Estaban. *Disidentifications: Queers of Color and the Performance of Politics.* Minneapolis: University of Minnesota Press, 1999.

Mysorekar, Sheila. "'Pass the Word and Break the Silence': The Significance of African-American and 'Third World' Literature for Black Germans." In *Moving Beyond Boundaries: International Dimensions of Black Women's Writing,* vol. 1, edited by Carole Boyce Davies and Molara Ogundipe-Leslie, 79–83. New York: New York University Press, 1995.

Nenno, Nancy. "Femininity, the Primitive, and Modern Urban Space: Josephine Baker in Berlin," in *Women in the Metropolis: Gender and Modernity in Weimar Culture,* edited by Katharina von Ankum, 141–67. Berkeley: University of California Press, 1997.

——. "*Here to Stay*: Black Austrian Studies." In *Rethinking Black German Studies: Approaches, Interventions and Histories,* edited by Tiffany N. Florvil and Vanessa D. Plumly, 71–104. London: Peter Lang, 2018.

Ohene-Nyako, Pamela. "Black Women's Transnational Activism and the World Council of Churches." *Open Cultural Studies* 3 (2019): 219–31.

Olaniyan, Tejumola, and James Sweet, eds. *The African Diaspora and the Disciplines.* Bloomington: Indiana University Press, 2010.

Otoo, Sharon Dodua. "But Some of Us Are Brave," migrazine.at online magazin von migrantinnen für alle no. 1 (2013), http://www.migrazine.at/artikel/some-us-are-brave-english.

Parés, Luis Nicolau. "Transformations of the Sea and Thunder Voduns in the Gbe-Speaking Area and in the Bahian Jeje Candomblé." In *Africa and the Americas: Interconnections during the Slave Trade,* edited by J. C. Curto and R. Soulodre-La France, 69–93. Trenton, N.J.: Africa World Press, 2005.

Patterson, Tiffany R., and Robin D.G. Kelley. "Unfinished Migrations: Reflections on the African Diaspora and the Making of the Modern World." *African Studies Review* 43 (2000): 11–45.

Perry, Kennetta Hammond. *London is the Place for Me: Black Britons, Citizenship, and the Politics of Race.* New York: Oxford University Press, 2015.

Piesche, Peggy. "Irgendwo ist immer Afrika. . . . Blackface' in DEFA-Filmen." In *The BlackBook: Deutschlands Häutungen,* edited by AntiDiskriminierungsBüro Köln and cyberNomads, 286–91. Frankfurt am Main: IKO-Verlag für Interkulturelle Kommunikation, 2004.

———. "Funktionalisierung und Repräsentation von multikuturellen Images in DDR-Comics." In *The BlackBook: Deutschlands Häutungen,* edited by AntiDiskriminierungs-Büro Köln and cyberNomads, 292–97. Frankfurt am Main: IKO-Verlag für Interkulturelle Kommunikation, 2004.

———. "Making African Diasporic Pasts Possible: A Retrospective View of the GDR and Its Black (Step-)Children." In *Remapping Black Germany: New Perspectives on Afro-German History, Politics, and Culture,* edited by Sara Lennox, 226–42. Amherst: University of Massachusetts Press, 2016.

Plumly, Vanessa. "'BLACK-Red-Gold in'der bunten Republik': Constructions and Performances of Heimat/en in Post-Wende Afro-/Black German Cultural Productions." PhD diss., University of Cincinnati, 2015.

———. "Refugee Assemblages, Cycles of Violence, and Body Politic(s) in Times of 'Celebratory Fear.'" *Women in German Yearbook* 32 (2016): 163–88.

Poikane-Daumke, Aija. *African Diasporas: Afro-German Literature in the Context of the African American Experience.* Münster: LIT, 2006.

Pommerin, Reiner. *Sterilisierung der Rheinlandbastarde: Das Schicksal einer farbigen deutschen Minderheit 1918–1937.* Düsseldorf: Droste Verlag, 1979.

Popoola, Olumide, and Annie Holmes. *Breach.* London: Peirene Press, 2016.

Popoola, Olumide, and Beldan Sezen, eds. *Talking Home: Heimat uns unserer eigenen Felder.* Amsterdam: Blue Moon, 1999.

Popoola, Olumide. *This is not about sadness.* Münster: Unrast, 2010.

———. *When we Speak of Nothing.* London: Cassava Republic Press, 2017.

———. *Also By Mail: A Play,* Witnessed ed. 2. Münster: Edition Assemblage, 2013.

Poutrus, Patrice. "Asylum in Postwar Germany: Refugee Admissions Policies and their Practical Implementation in the Federal Republic and the GDR between the late 1940s and the mid-1970s." *Journal of Contemporary History* 49, no. 1 (2014): 115–33.

Pugach, Sara. "Agents of dissent: African student organizations in the German Democratic Republic." *Africa* 89, S1 (2019): 90–108.

Ransby, Barbara. *Eslanda: The Large and Unconventional Life of Mrs. Paul Robeson.* New Haven, Conn.: Yale University Press, 2013.

Rasmussen, Natalia King. "Friends of Freedom, Allies of Peace: African Americans, The Civil Rights Movement, and East Germany, 1949–1989." PhD diss., Boston University, 2014.

Reed-Anderson, Paulette. *Rewriting the Footnotes: Berlin und die afrikanische Diaspora.* Berlin: Die Ausländerbeauftragte des Senats, 2000.

———. *Menschen, Orte, Themen: Zur Geschichte und Kultur der Afrikanischen Diaspora in Berlin.* Berlin: Senatsverwaltung für Arbeit, Integration und Frauen-Die Beauftragte für Integration und Migration, 2013.

Robinson, Victoria. "Schwarze Deutsche Kräfte: Über Die Absurdität der Integrationsdebatte." *360°: Das Studentische Journal Für Politik und Gesellschaft* (2007): 1–10.

Rosenhaft, Eve, and Robbie Aitken, eds. *Black Germany: The Making and Unmaking of a Diaspora Community, 1884–1960.* Cambridge, U.K.: Cambridge University Press, 2013.

Schwarzrund, *Biskaya: Afropolitaner Berlin-Roman*. Vienna: Zaglossus, 2016.

Sephocle, Marilyn. "Anton Wilhem Amo." *Journal of Black Studies* 23, no. 2 (1992): 182–87.

Sharpley-Whiting, Tracy Denean. *Negritude Women*. Minneapolis: University of Minnesota Press, 2002.

Sidbury, James. *Becoming African in America: Race and Nation in the Early Black Atlantic*. New York: Oxford University Press, 2007.

Singletary, Kimberly Alecia. "Everyday Matters: Haunting and the Black Diasporic Experience." In *Rethinking Black German Studies: Approaches, Interventions and Histories*, edited by Tiffany N. Florvil and Vanessa D. Plumly, 137–67. London: Peter Lang, 2018.

Slobodian, Quinn. *Foreign Front: Third World Politics in Sixties West Germany*. Durham, N.C.: Duke University Press, 2012.

Smith, Sidonie, and Julia Watson, eds. *De/Colonizing the Subject: The Politics of Gender in Women's Autobiography*. Minneapolis: University of Minnesota Press, 1992.

Sow, Noah. *Deutschland Schwarz Weiss: Der alltägliche Rassismus*. München: Goldmann, 2008.

Steingröver, Reinhild. "From *Farbe bekennen* to *Scholadenkind*: Generational Change in Afro-German Autobiographies." In *Generational Shifts in Contemporary German Culture*, edited by Laurel Cohen-Pfister and Susanne Vees-Gulani, 287–310. Rochester, N.Y.: Camden, 2010.

Swan, Quito. "Giving Berth: Fiji, Black Women's Internationalism, and the Pacific Women's Conference of 1975." *Journal of Civil and Human Rights* 4, no. 1 (2018): 37–63.

Taylor, Diana. "Acts of Transfer." In Diana Taylor, *The Archive and the Repertoire: Performing Cultural Memory in the Americas*, 1–53. Durham, N.C.: Duke University Press, 2003.

Taylor, Keeanga-Yamahtta, ed. *How We Get Free: Black Feminism and the Combahee River Collective*. Chicago: Haymarket Books, 2017.

Trouillot, Michel-Rolph. *Silencing the Past: Power and the Production of History*. Boston: Beacon Press, 1995.

Umoren, Imaobong. *Race Women Internationalists: Activist-Intellectuals and Global Freedom Struggles*. Oakland: University of California Press, 2018.

Von Dirke, Sabine. *"All Power to the Imagination!": The West German Counterculture from the Student Movement to the Greens*. Lincoln: University of Nebraska Press, 1997.

Waters, Kristin, and Carol B. Conaway, eds. *Black Women's Intellectual Traditions*. Burlington: University of Vermont Press, 2007.

Watkins, Jamele. "The Drama of Race: Contemporary Afro-German Theater." PhD diss., University of Massachusetts, 2017.

Wekker, Gloria. *White Innocence: Paradoxes of Colonialism and Race*. Durham, N.C.: Duke University Press, 2016.

Wright, Michelle M. *Becoming Black: Creating Identity in the African Diaspora*. Durham, N.C.: Duke University Press, 2004.

——. *Physics of Blackness: Beyond the Middle Passage Epistemology*. Minneapolis: University of Minnesota Press, 2015.

———. "Others-from-within from Without: Afro-German Subject Formation and the Challenge of a Counter-Discourse." *Callaloo* 26, no. 2 (2003): 296–305.

———. "In a Nation or a Diaspora?: Gender, Sexuality and Afro-German Subject Formation." In *From Black to Schwarz: Cultural Crossovers between African America and Germany,* edited by Maria I. Diedrich and Jürgen Heinrichs, 265–86. Münster: LIT, 2010.

Zeleza, Paul Tiyambe. "Rewriting the African Diaspora, Beyond the Black Atlantic." *African Affairs* 104, no. 414 (2005): 35–68.

INDEX

diaspora; diasporic activism; diasporic identity and community; diasporic resources; diasporic spatial politics; grassroots activism

Black Germans: diversity and, 36, 64, 65; documentaries on, 111; identity and culture, 104 (*see also Farbe bekennen*); isolation and marginalization of (*see* isolation; marginalization); organizations (*see* cultural-political organizations); population size, 4; use of term, 4, 35, 64. *See also* Black German men; Black German women

Black German studies (BGS), 6, 65, 139, 146

Black German women: affective community of (*see* affective communities); antiracist feminist activism, 1–7, 9–13 (*see also* antiracist activism; Black German feminism); Audre Lorde and (*see* Lorde, Audre); intellectualism, 11–12 (*see also* activist-intellectuals; intellectualism); internationalism, 10–12 (*see also* internationalism); ISD and, 54, 75 (*see also* ISD); queer identities, 9, 77–90, 216n46 (*see also* Black queer feminist organizations; queer politics)

Black global diaspora, 5–6, 23, 26, 47, 79, 103, 120, 182. *See also* diasporic identity and community; diasporic resources; diasporic spatial politics

BLACK Heidelberg, 59

Black Heritage Party, 149–50

Black history, 65, 82

Black History Month, 130–56; annual celebrations, 139–45, 232n37; antiracism and, 180; collaborative work and, 143–45; cultural, political, and intellectual aspects of, 24, 129, 131; diasporic spatial politics, 130, 133, 136, 138–39, 141, 146, 151, 155–56, 182; ISD-Berlin and, 61, 66–67, 70, 115; programs, 150; quotidian intellectuals and, 132, 134, 137, 139, 144, 146, 151; spacetimes of Blackness, 145–55; translocal and transnational networks in Berlin, 132–33; workshops, 130, 135–36

"The Black Horror on the Rhine" ("*Die Schwarze Schmach am Rhein*"), 14–15

Black intellectualism. *See* activist-intellectuals; intellectual activism; intellectualism; quotidian intellectuals

Black International Cinema, 138

Black internationalism. *See* internationalism

"Black is Beautiful" movement, 100, 109

BLACK Karlsruhe, 60

Black Liberation Sounds/Black Liberation Sound System (BLS), 67, 144

Black Lives Matter movement, 22, 178–82

Black Media Access (BMA), 66, 143

Black nationalism (in Harlem), 29

Blackness: appropriation of, 18; boundaries of, 3–4; celebrations of, 18, 129 (*see also* Black History Month); centering of, 54, 63–64, 70, 86; class and ethnic hierarchies and, 214n25; exoticization of, 18; gendered political, 177; intellectual cultural politics and, 129; negative connotations, 110–11; passing for white and, 48; as political identity, 135, 144, 153, 158–59, 162, 179, 185n11; racialized advertising and, 8; spacetimes of, 11–12, 37, 54, 92, 112, 132, 139, 145–55; visibility of, 180. *See also* Black German identity; Black global diaspora; skin color

Black Panther Party, 65, 80, 153; British, 66; Solidarity Committees, 17

"Black Pete" (Dutch Christmas tradition), 80

Black Power movement, 16–18

Black queer feminist organizations, 18, 77–79, 83–90. *See also* queer identities; queer politics

Black Student Organisation (BSO), 67

Black Unity Committee (BUC), 66–67

Black Women and Europe Network (BWEN), 10, 158, 227n91

Black Women of the World (1993), 159, 174–75

Black Women's European Alliance, 227n91

Black Women's Informal Information and Support Network, 116

Black women's studies, 160–61. *See also* Cross-Cultural Black Women's Studies Summer Institute

Blain, Keisha N., 11

Blyden, Edward, 138

Bochum, 60

minority populations, 121, 123; rights of, 20. *See also* marginalization

misogyny, 15, 80–81

mixed-race individuals, 4, 113–14, 184n10; biracial Afro-Germans, 43, 214n25. *See also* multiracial population

Mmanthatisi, 100

MODEFEN (Movement for the Defense of the Rights of Black Women), 169, 241n66

Moor *(Mohr)*, 111, 115, 188n28

Moore, Iris, 232n43

Moraga, Cherríe, 31, 225n63

Morel, Edmund D., 14

Morrison, Toni, 101, 108, 225n63

Mozambique, 152

Mpahlwa, Luyanda, 152

Ms. magazine, 122

Mukherjee, Bharati, 108

Mulak Nation, 169

multiculturalism, 3–4, 20, 22, 128, 182; integration and, 119

multiracial population, 3–4, 95, 125, 128, 182. *See also* mixed-race individuals

Munich, 134; ADEFRA-Munich, 85–86, 88–89, 103, 167; Black cultural events in, 141; intellectual communities in, 63; ISD-Munich, 60, 73, 135

Muñoz, José Esteban, 217n77

Muslim people, 20, 22

Mutasa, Chenzira J., 162

Mwangulu, Mahoma, 153

Mysorekar, Sheila, 45, 47, 54, 108, 149; Cross-Cultural Black Women's Studies Summer Institute and, 166; ISD and, 59; reading at literary events, 74

Mysorekar, Sheila (works): in *Black Women of the World*, 175; in *Contributions to Feminist Theory and Praxis*, 112

Nama descendants, 69

Nama genocide, 179

Namibia, 13, 138; German genocide in, 69, 179

naming, cultural politics of, 3–4

Nardal, Jane, 13

Nardal, Paulette, 13

Nassy Brown, Jacqueline, 19, 37

National Assembly, 14

National Democratic Party of Germany (NPD), 244n9

National Front (French organization), 144, 153, 244n9

nationalism, 145. *See also* ethno-nationalism

Nationality Law (1913), 19, 64

National Women's Studies Association (NWSA), 33–34

Nazi past (National Socialism): Black German lives in, 146; coming to terms with *(Vergangenheitsbewältigung)*, 7; fascism, 119; racial categories and, 4–5; racism and, 110; violence of, 179. *See also* neofascism; neo-Nazi violence

Ndebele, 165

Négritude movement, 185n11

Nejar, Marie, 127

neofascism, 11, 24

neo-Nazi violence, 20, 67, 139, 155, 179–80

Netherlands, 80, 87, 159, 163, 169

the Network (Berlin), 143–44

Newkirk, Love, 232n43

Newton, Huey P., 153

New York Institute (July 1988), 163

New Zealand, 163, 172. *See also* Aotearoa/New Zealand

Nigeria, 63, 152

Nkobi, Jacqueline, 59

Nogoma-Leipzig group, 60

Nomzamo (South African township), 100

North America, 161. *See also* Canada; United States

North Rhine-Westphalia, 59

Notting Hill Carnival, 142

Notting Hill Outdoor Carnival, 143

Nozizwe (migrant women's organization), 10, 143, 152, 154, 167

Nri, Monique Ngozi, 49–50

Nuremberg Laws, 5

Oala, Mic, 179

Obama, Auma, 116, 224n55

Obama, Barack, 224n55

Odum, Kwesi Anan, 59

TIFFANY N. FLORVIL is an associate professor in the Department of History at the University of New Mexico.

BLACK INTERNATIONALISM

The University of Illinois Press
is a founding member of the
Association of University Presses.

———————————————————————

University of Illinois Press
1325 South Oak Street
Champaign, IL 61820-6903
www.press.uillinois.edu